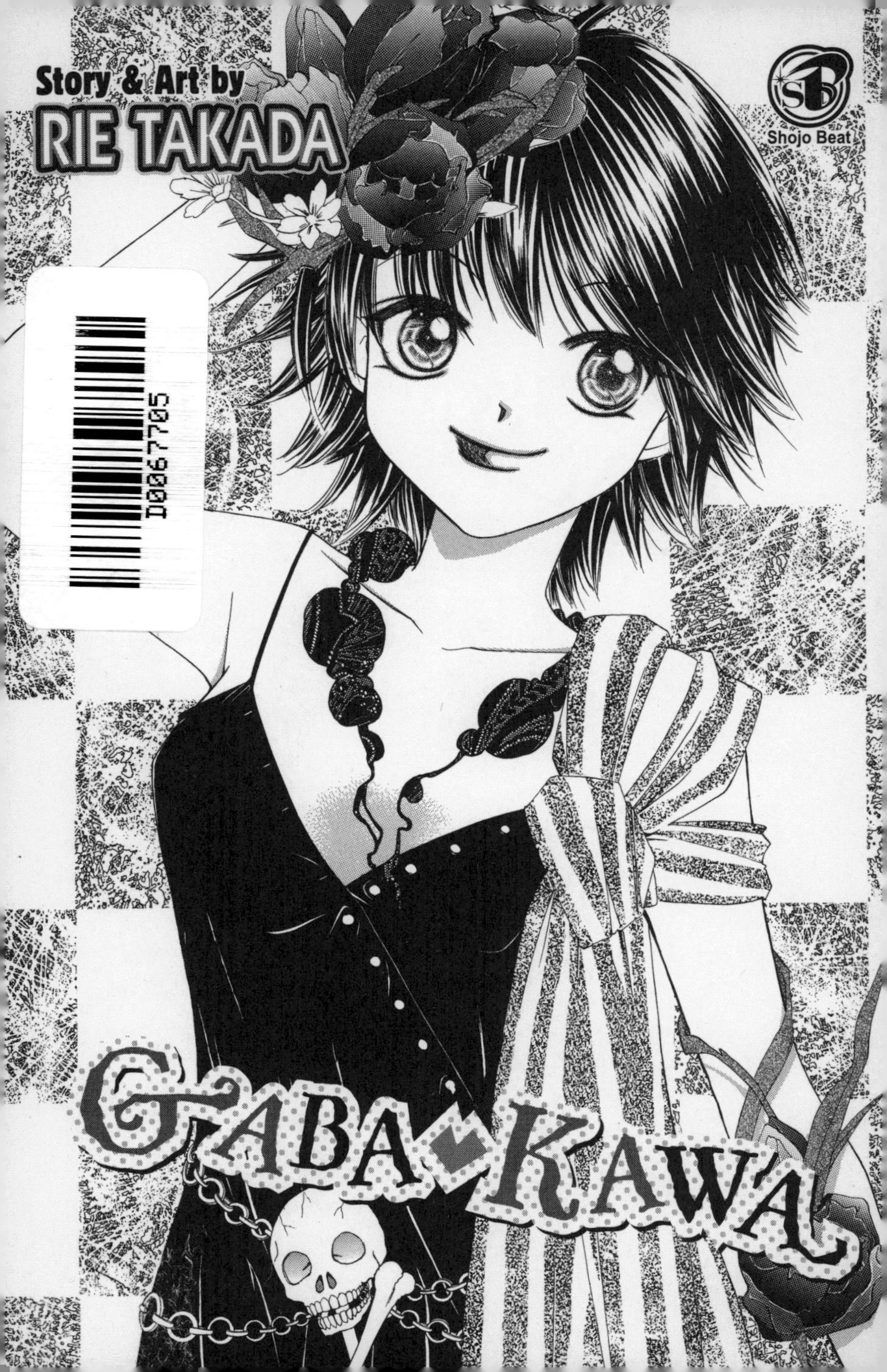
Story & Art by
RIE TAKADA
Shojo Beat
GABA-KAWA

GABA KAWA

Fioro

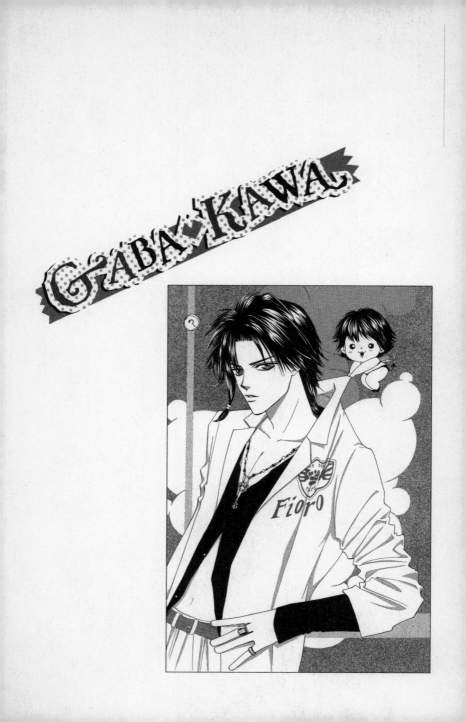

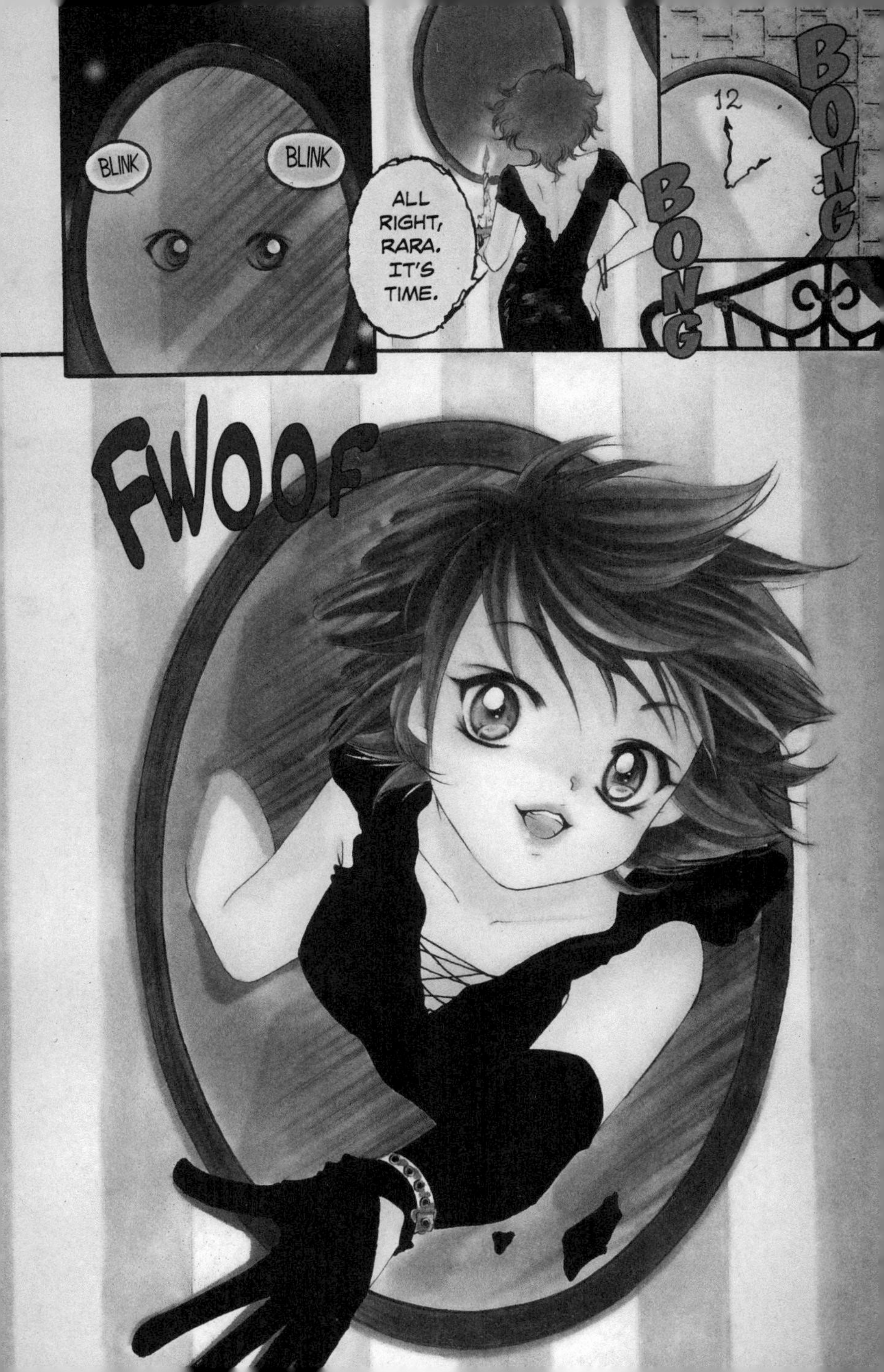
BONG
BONG
BONG
BONG
ALL RIGHT, RARA. IT'S TIME.
BLINK
BLINK
FWOOF

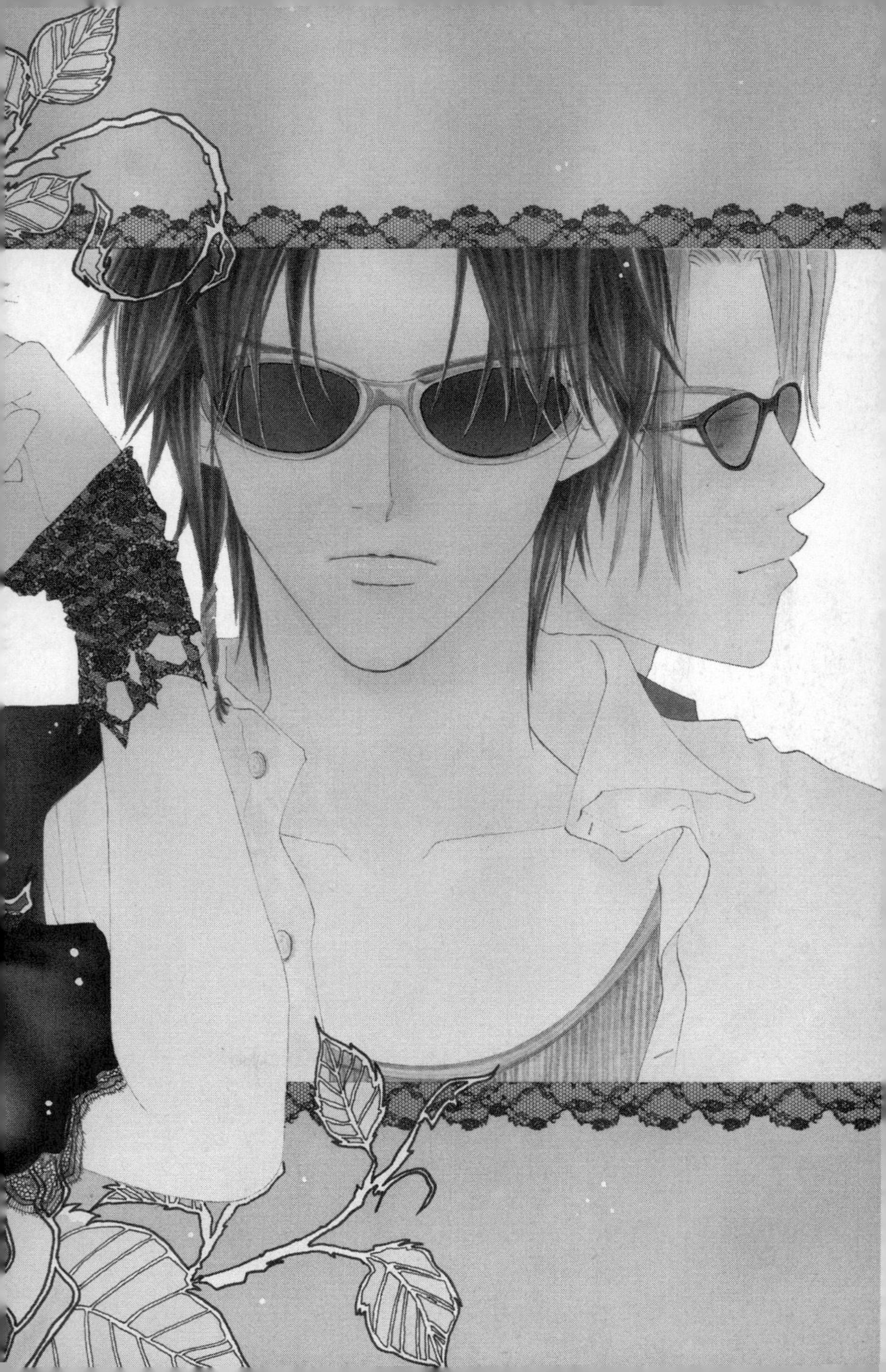

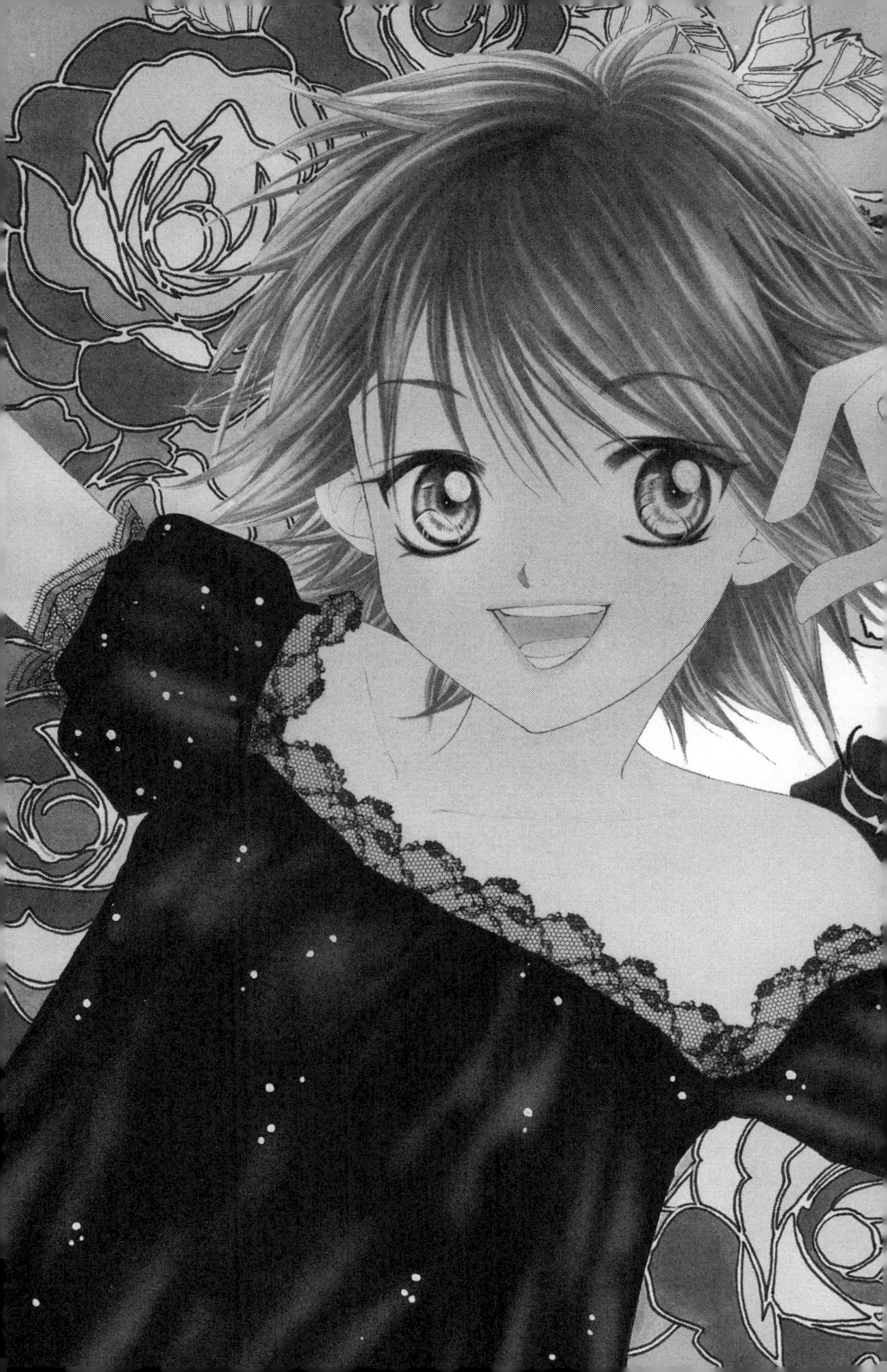

GABA KAWA

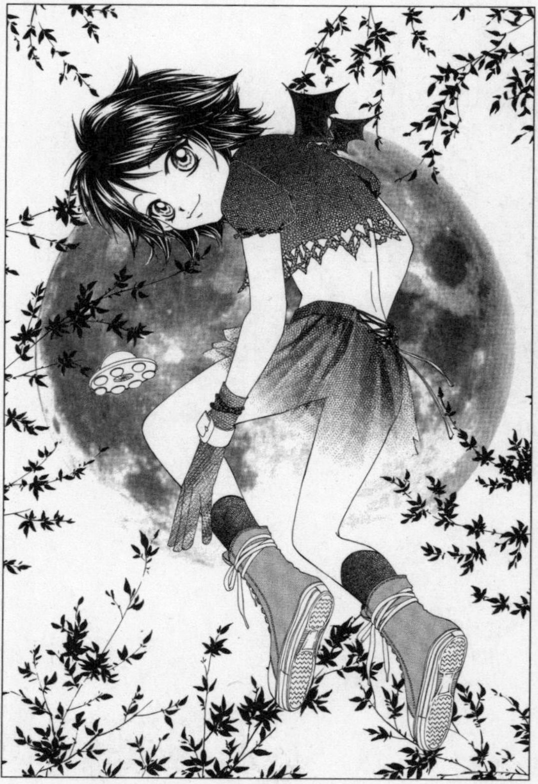

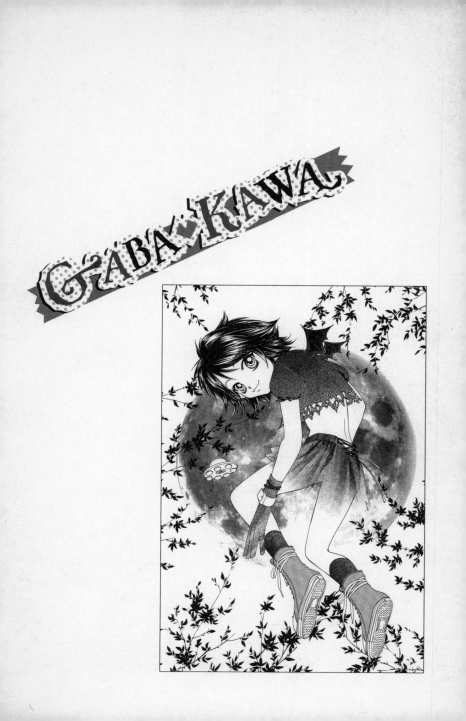

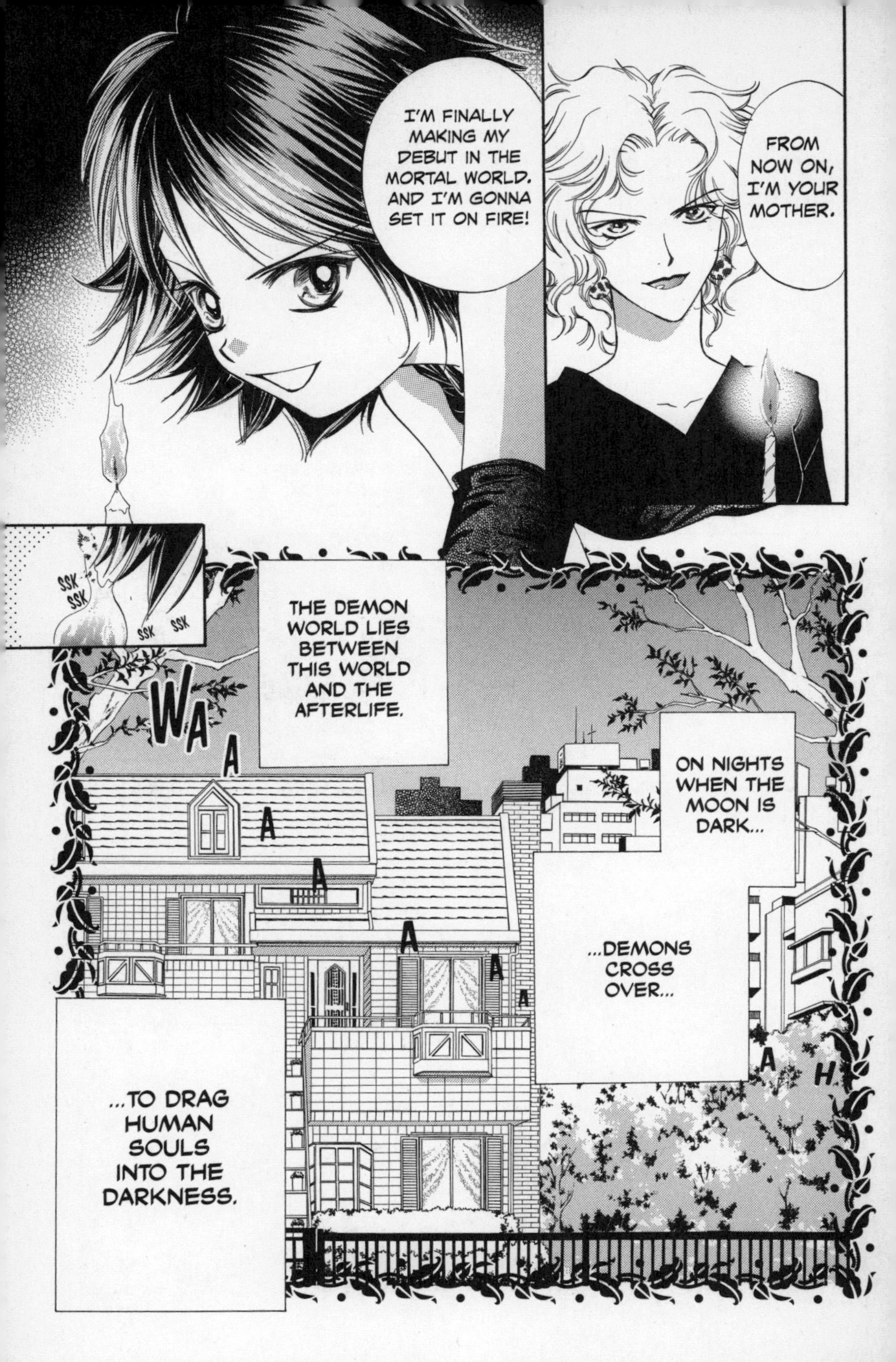
FROM NOW ON, I'M YOUR MOTHER.
I'M FINALLY MAKING MY DEBUT IN THE MORTAL WORLD. AND I'M GONNA SET IT ON FIRE!
SSK SSK
SSK SSK
THE DEMON WORLD LIES BETWEEN THIS WORLD AND THE AFTERLIFE.
ON NIGHTS WHEN THE MOON IS DARK...
...DEMONS CROSS OVER...
...TO DRAG HUMAN SOULS INTO THE DARKNESS.
WAAAAAAAAAH

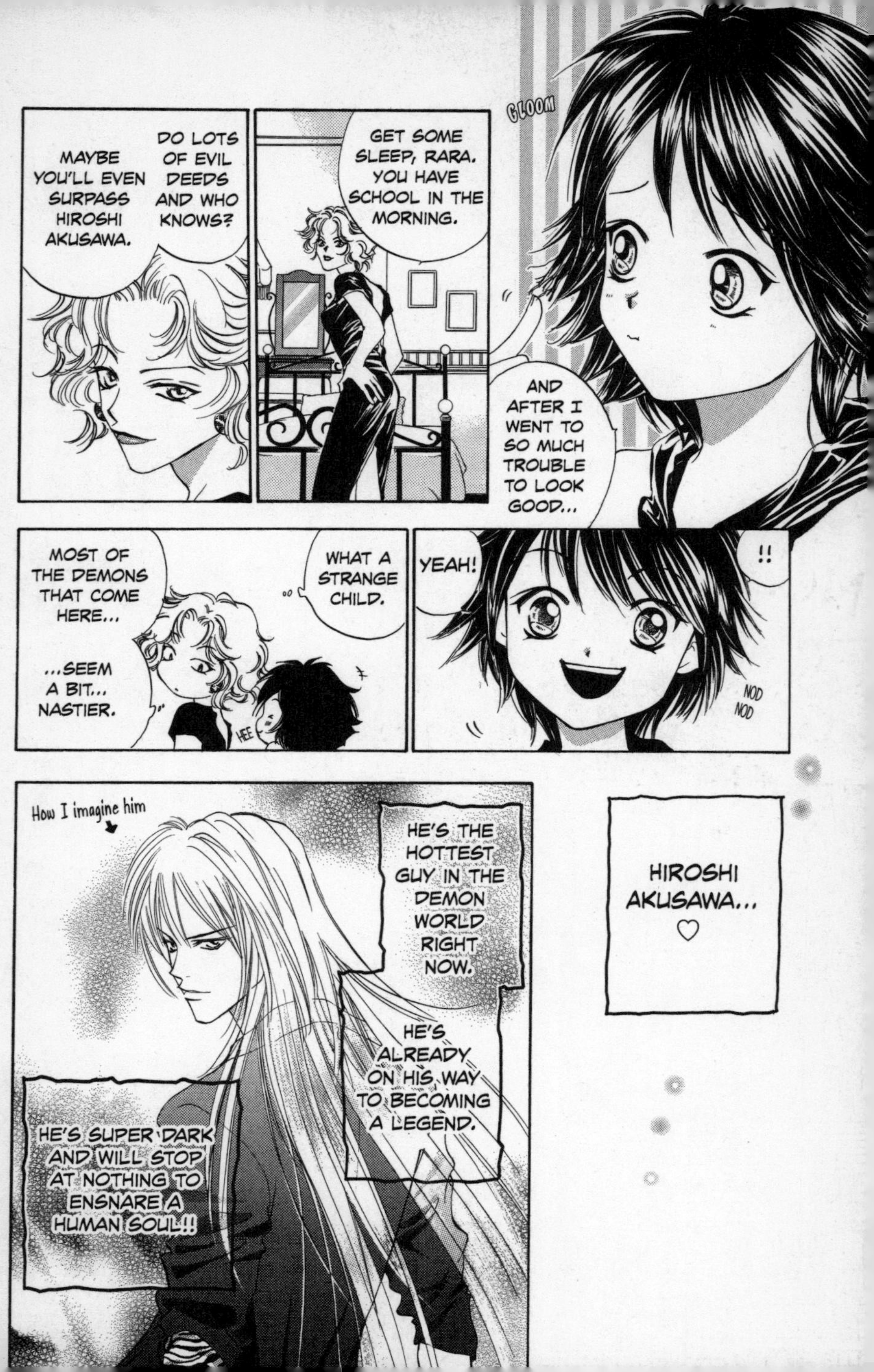
GLOOM
AND AFTER I WENT TO SO MUCH TROUBLE TO LOOK GOOD...
GET SOME SLEEP, RARA. YOU HAVE SCHOOL IN THE MORNING.
DO LOTS OF EVIL DEEDS AND WHO KNOWS?
MAYBE YOU'LL EVEN SURPASS HIROSHI AKUSAWA.
!!
YEAH!
NOD NOD
WHAT A STRANGE CHILD.
MOST OF THE DEMONS THAT COME HERE...
...SEEM A BIT... NASTIER.
HEE
HIROSHI AKUSAWA... ♡
How I imagine him
HE'S THE HOTTEST GUY IN THE DEMON WORLD RIGHT NOW.
HE'S ALREADY ON HIS WAY TO BECOMING A LEGEND.
HE'S SUPER DARK AND WILL STOP AT NOTHING TO ENSNARE A HUMAN SOUL!!

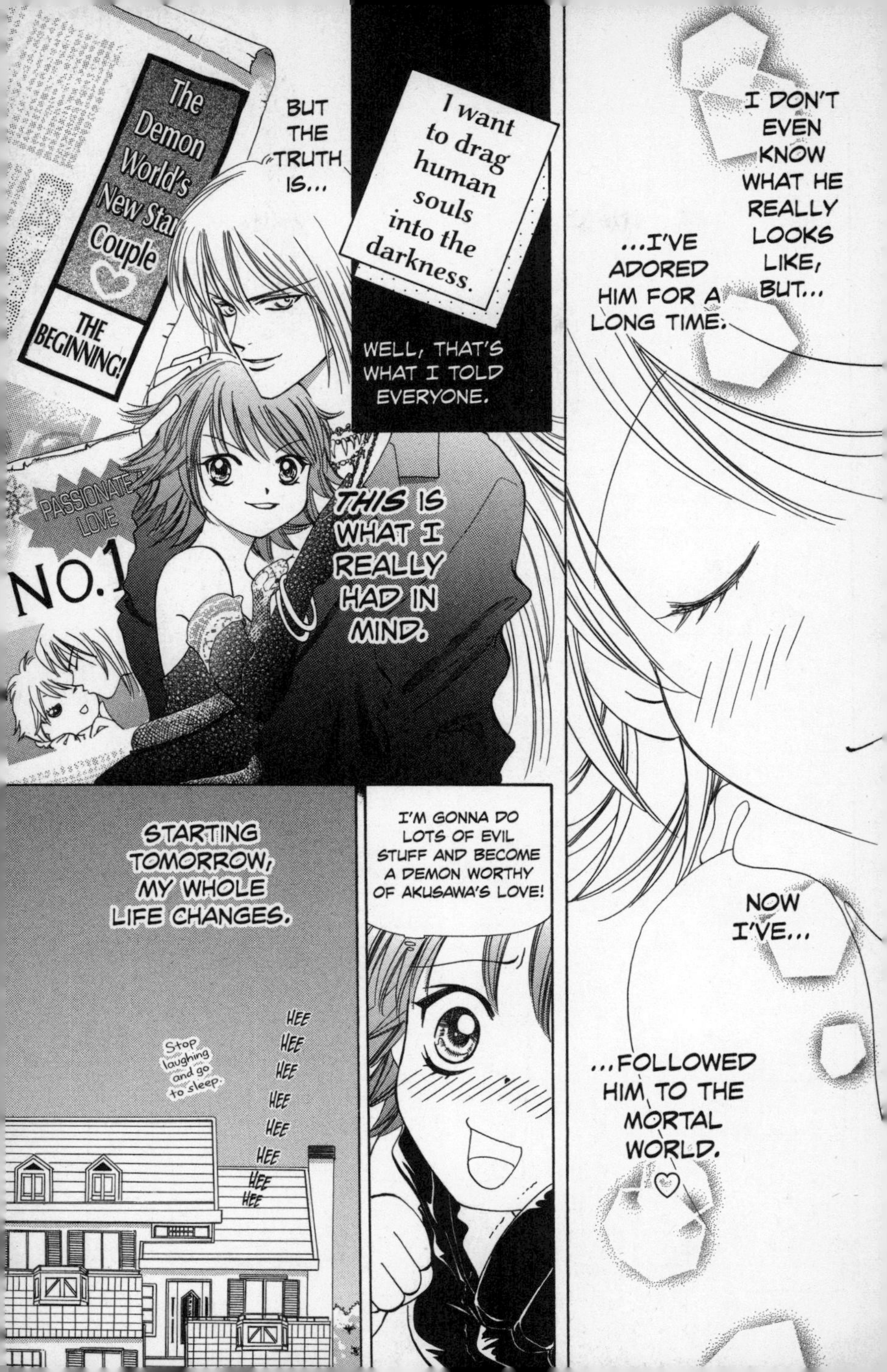
I DON'T EVEN KNOW WHAT HE REALLY LOOKS LIKE, BUT...
...I'VE ADORED HIM FOR A LONG TIME.
NOW I'VE...
...FOLLOWED HIM TO THE MORTAL WORLD.
I want to drag human souls into the darkness.
WELL, THAT'S WHAT I TOLD EVERYONE.
BUT THE TRUTH IS...
THIS IS WHAT I REALLY HAD IN MIND.
The Demon World's New Star Couple
THE BEGINNING!
PASSIONATE LOVE
NO.1
I'M GONNA DO LOTS OF EVIL STUFF AND BECOME A DEMON WORTHY OF AKUSAWA'S LOVE!
STARTING TOMORROW, MY WHOLE LIFE CHANGES.
HEE HEE HEE HEE HEE HEE HEE HEE
Stop laughing and go to sleep.

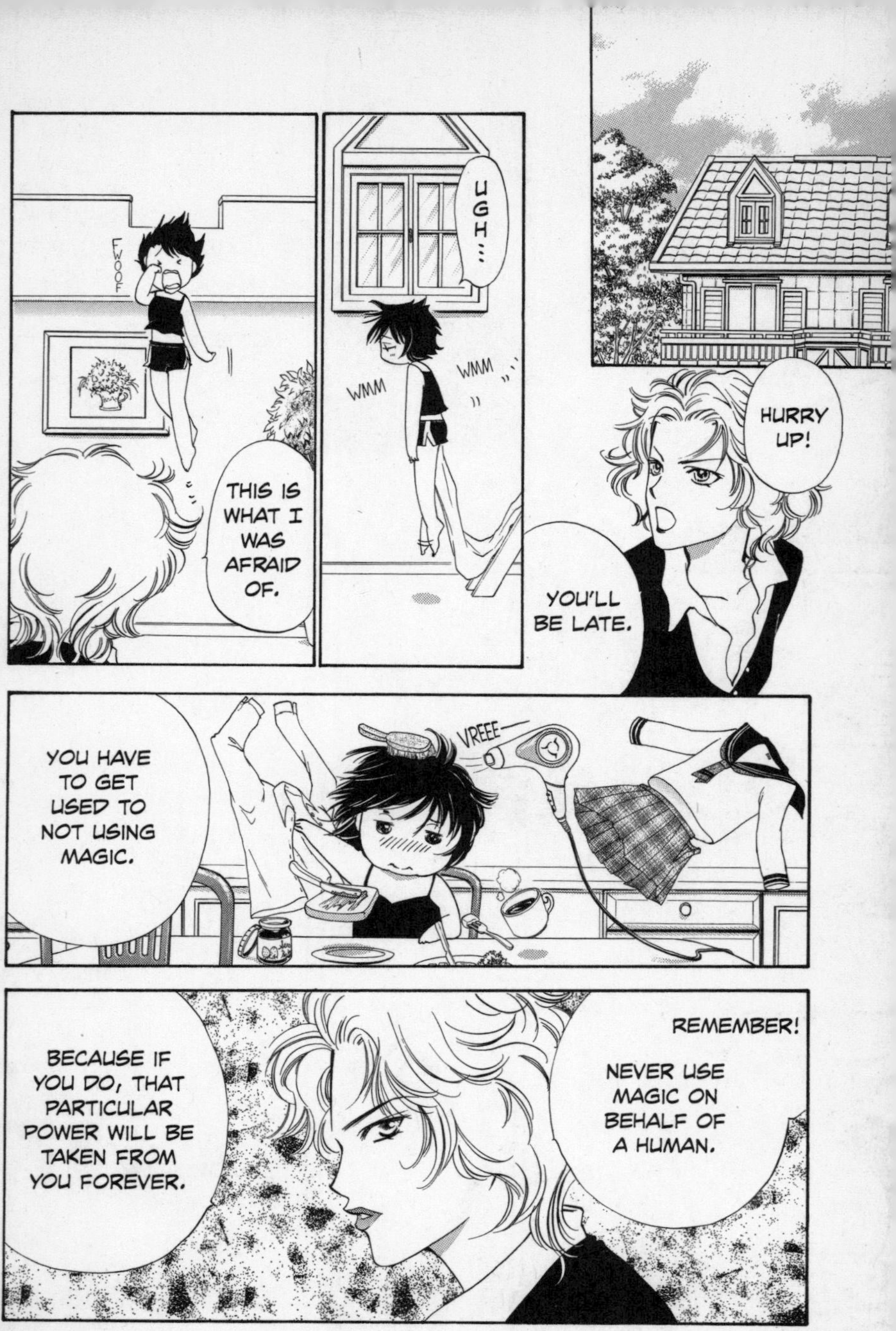
HURRY UP!
YOU'LL BE LATE.
UGH...
WMM
WMM
FWOOF
THIS IS WHAT I WAS AFRAID OF.
VREEE—
YOU HAVE TO GET USED TO NOT USING MAGIC.
REMEMBER!
NEVER USE MAGIC ON BEHALF OF A HUMAN.
BECAUSE IF YOU DO, THAT PARTICULAR POWER WILL BE TAKEN FROM YOU FOREVER.

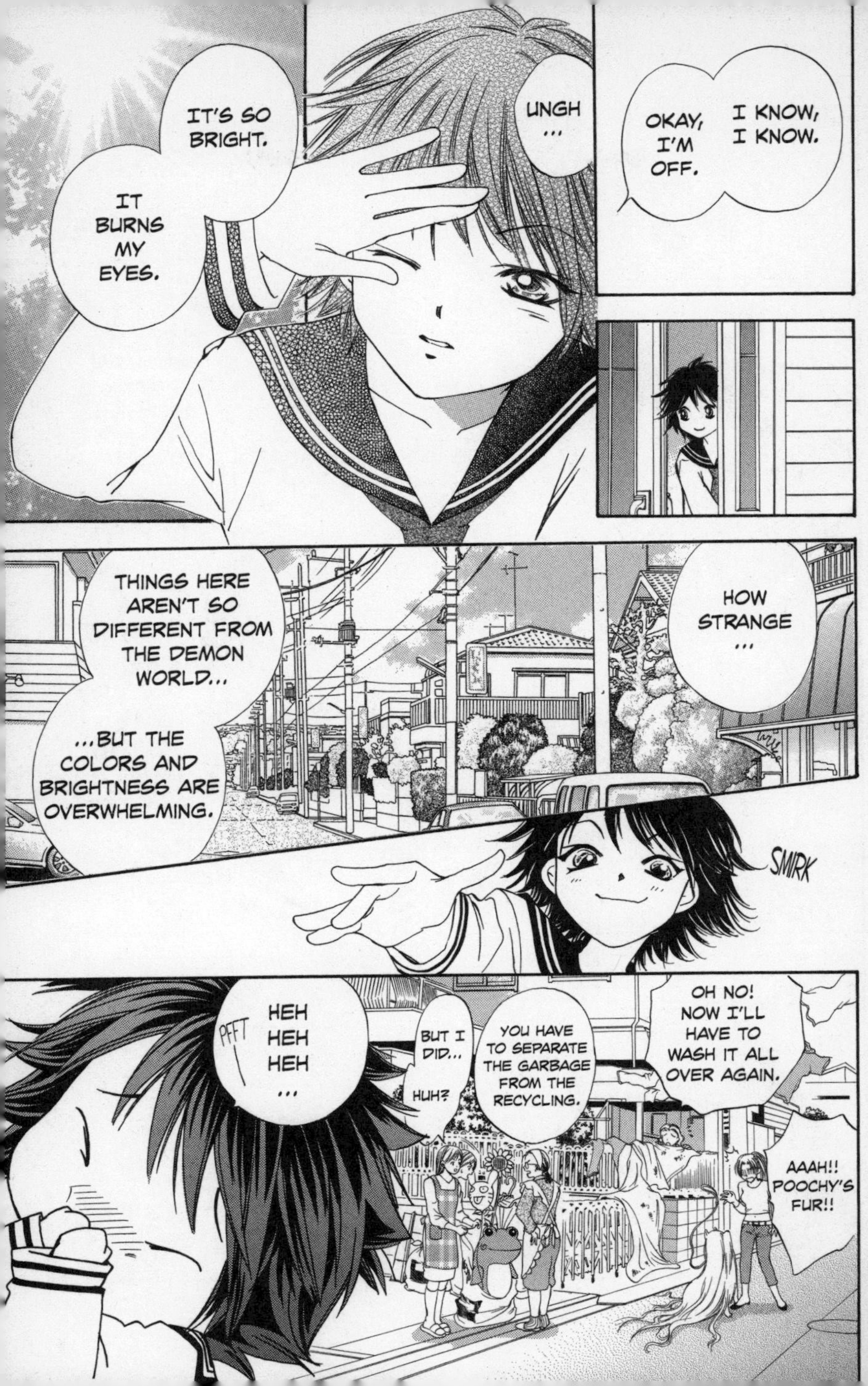
I KNOW, I KNOW.
OKAY, I'M OFF.
UNGH...
IT'S SO BRIGHT.
IT BURNS MY EYES.
HOW STRANGE...
THINGS HERE AREN'T SO DIFFERENT FROM THE DEMON WORLD...
...BUT THE COLORS AND BRIGHTNESS ARE OVERWHELMING.
SMIRK
OH NO! NOW I'LL HAVE TO WASH IT ALL OVER AGAIN.
AAAH!! POOCHY'S FUR!!
YOU HAVE TO SEPARATE THE GARBAGE FROM THE RECYCLING.
BUT I DID...
HUH?
HEH HEH HEH...
PFFT

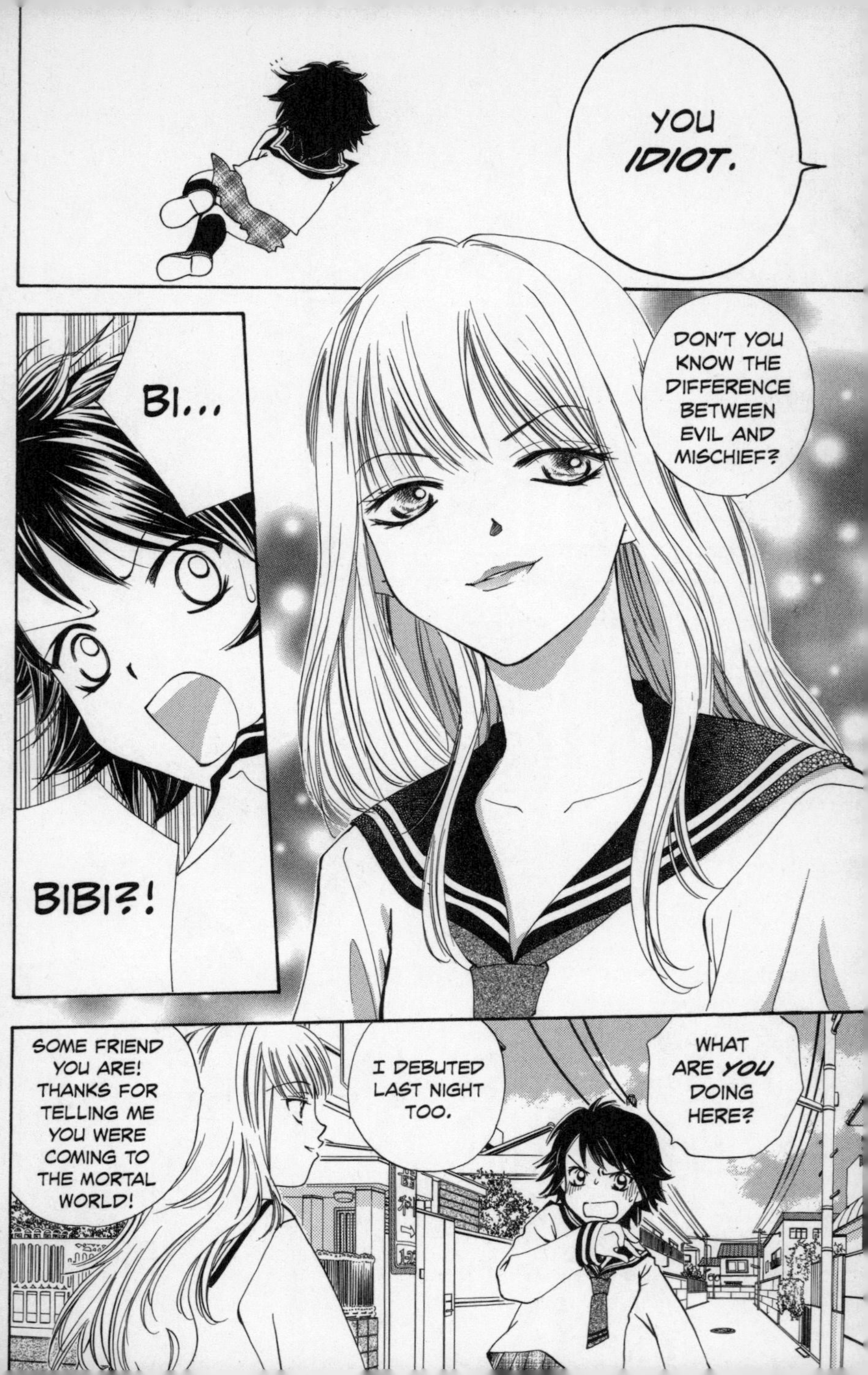
YOU IDIOT.
DON'T YOU KNOW THE DIFFERENCE BETWEEN EVIL AND MISCHIEF?
BI...
BIBI?!
WHAT ARE YOU DOING HERE?
I DEBUTED LAST NIGHT TOO.
SOME FRIEND YOU ARE! THANKS FOR TELLING ME YOU WERE COMING TO THE MORTAL WORLD!

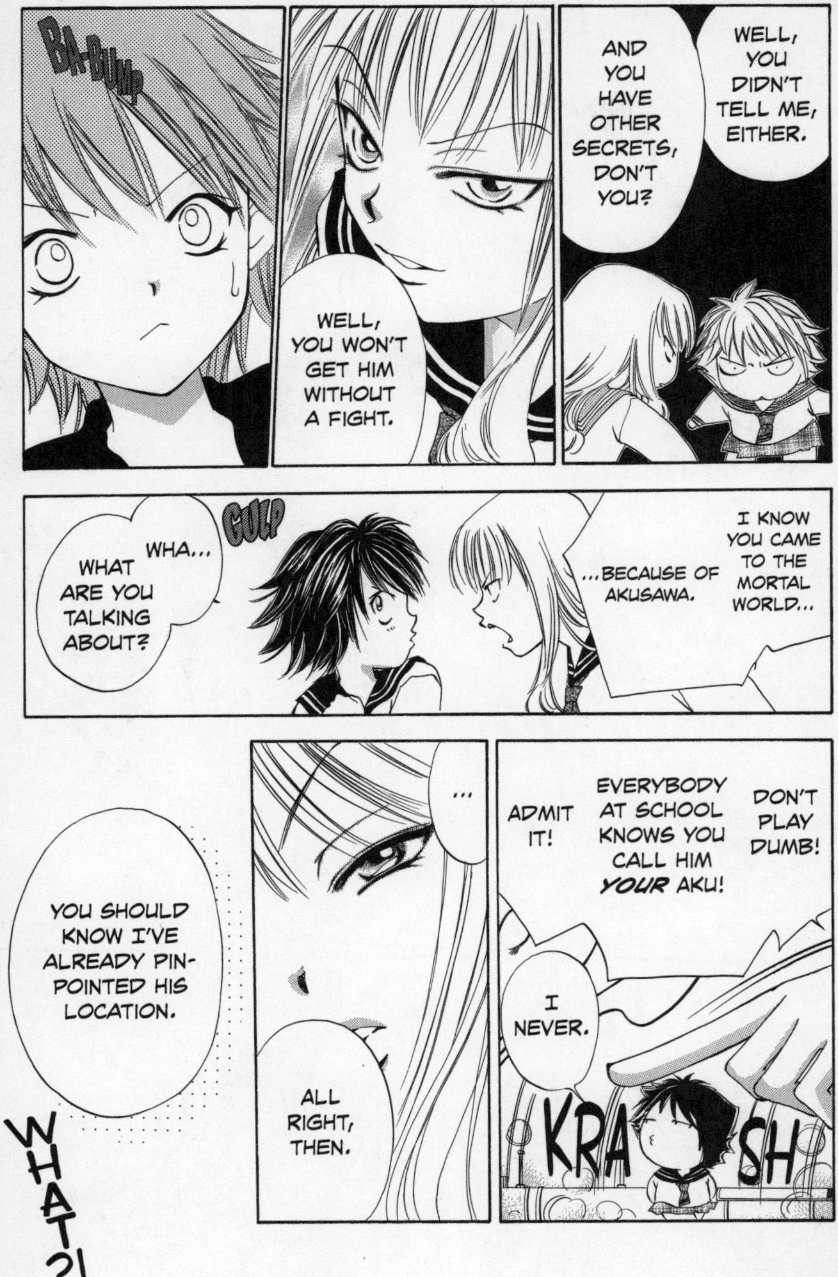
WELL, YOU DIDN'T TELL ME, EITHER.
AND YOU HAVE OTHER SECRETS, DON'T YOU?
WELL, YOU WON'T GET HIM WITHOUT A FIGHT.
BA-BUMP
I KNOW YOU CAME TO THE MORTAL WORLD...
...BECAUSE OF AKUSAWA.
GULP
WHA...
WHAT ARE YOU TALKING ABOUT?
DON'T PLAY DUMB!
EVERYBODY AT SCHOOL KNOWS YOU CALL HIM *YOUR* AKU!
ADMIT IT!
I NEVER.
KRASH
...
ALL RIGHT, THEN.
YOU SHOULD KNOW I'VE ALREADY PIN-POINTED HIS LOCATION.
WHAT?!

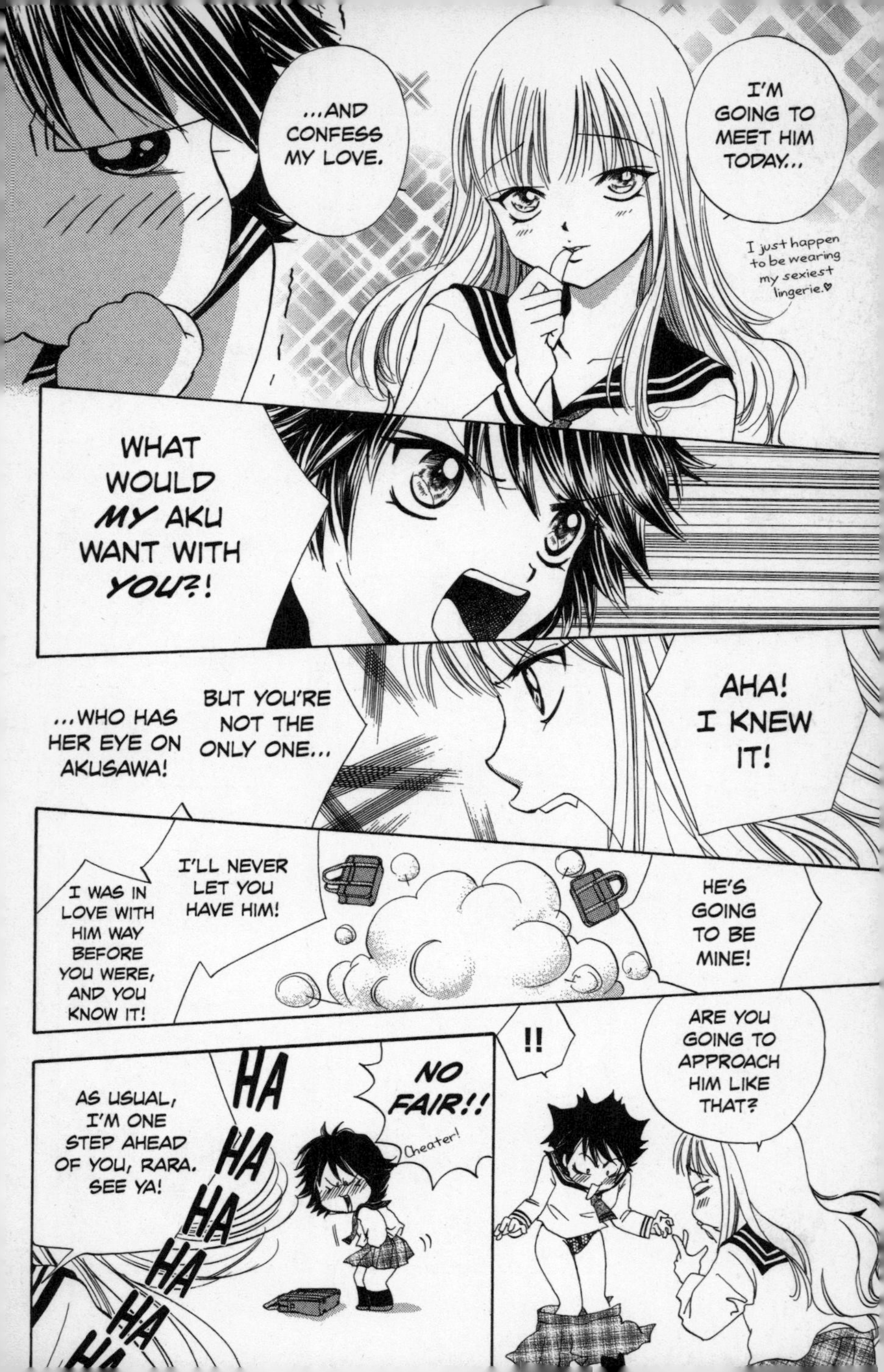
I'M GOING TO MEET HIM TODAY...
I just happen to be wearing my sexiest lingerie♥
...AND CONFESS MY LOVE.
WHAT WOULD *MY* AKU WANT WITH *YOU*?!
AHA! I KNEW IT!
BUT YOU'RE NOT THE ONLY ONE...
...WHO HAS HER EYE ON AKUSAWA!
HE'S GOING TO BE MINE!
I'LL NEVER LET YOU HAVE HIM!
I WAS IN LOVE WITH HIM WAY BEFORE YOU WERE, AND YOU KNOW IT!
ARE YOU GOING TO APPROACH HIM LIKE THAT?
!!
NO FAIR!!
Cheater!
HA HA HA HA HA HA HA
AS USUAL, I'M ONE STEP AHEAD OF YOU, RARA. SEE YA!

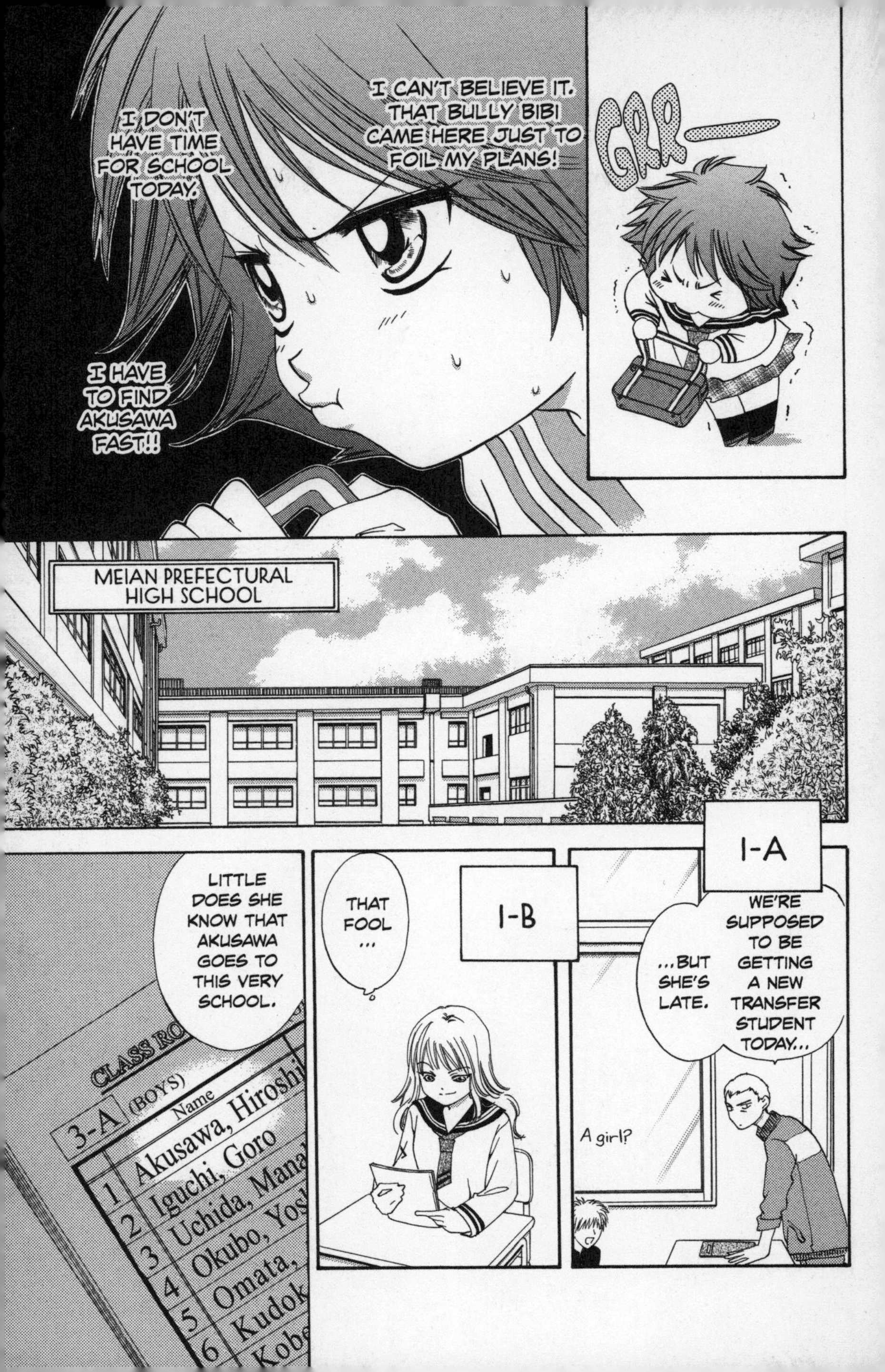
GRR—
I CAN'T BELIEVE IT. THAT BULLY BIBI CAME HERE JUST TO FOIL MY PLANS!
I DON'T HAVE TIME FOR SCHOOL TODAY.
I HAVE TO FIND AKUSAWA FAST!!
MEIAN PREFECTURAL HIGH SCHOOL
1-A
WE'RE SUPPOSED TO BE GETTING A NEW TRANSFER STUDENT TODAY...
...BUT SHE'S LATE.
A girl?
1-B
THAT FOOL ...
LITTLE DOES SHE KNOW THAT AKUSAWA GOES TO THIS VERY SCHOOL.
CLASS RO
3-A (BOYS)
Name
1 Akusawa, Hiroshi
2 Iguchi, Goro
3 Uchida, Mana
4 Okubo, Yos
5 Omata,
6 Kudok
Kobe

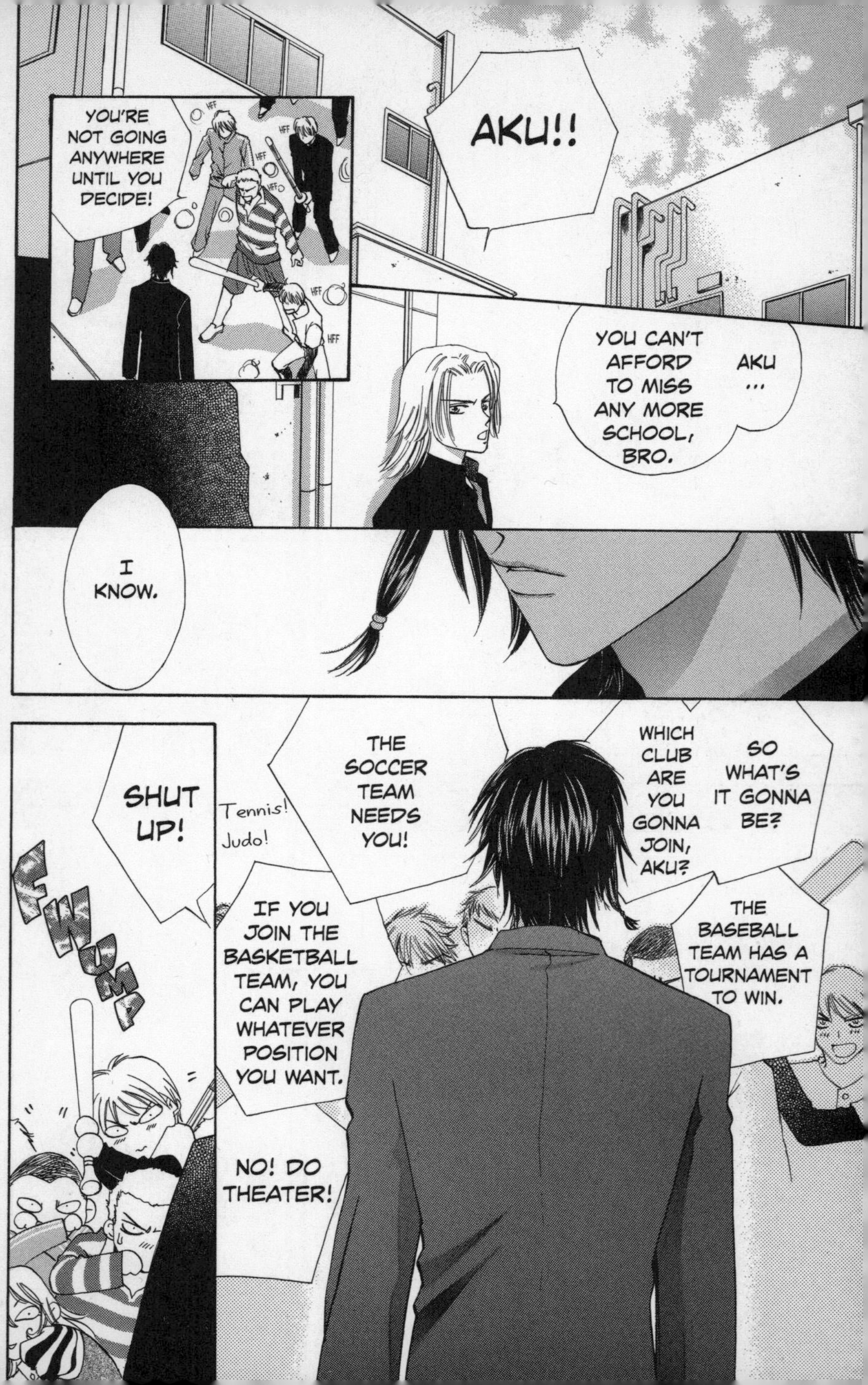
AKU!!
YOU'RE NOT GOING ANYWHERE UNTIL YOU DECIDE!
HFF
HFF
HFF
HFF
HFF
AKU ...
YOU CAN'T AFFORD TO MISS ANY MORE SCHOOL, BRO.
I KNOW.
SO WHAT'S IT GONNA BE?
WHICH CLUB ARE YOU GONNA JOIN, AKU?
THE SOCCER TEAM NEEDS YOU!
THE BASEBALL TEAM HAS A TOURNAMENT TO WIN.
IF YOU JOIN THE BASKETBALL TEAM, YOU CAN PLAY WHATEVER POSITION YOU WANT.
NO! DO THEATER!
Tennis!
Judo!
SHUT UP!
FWUMP

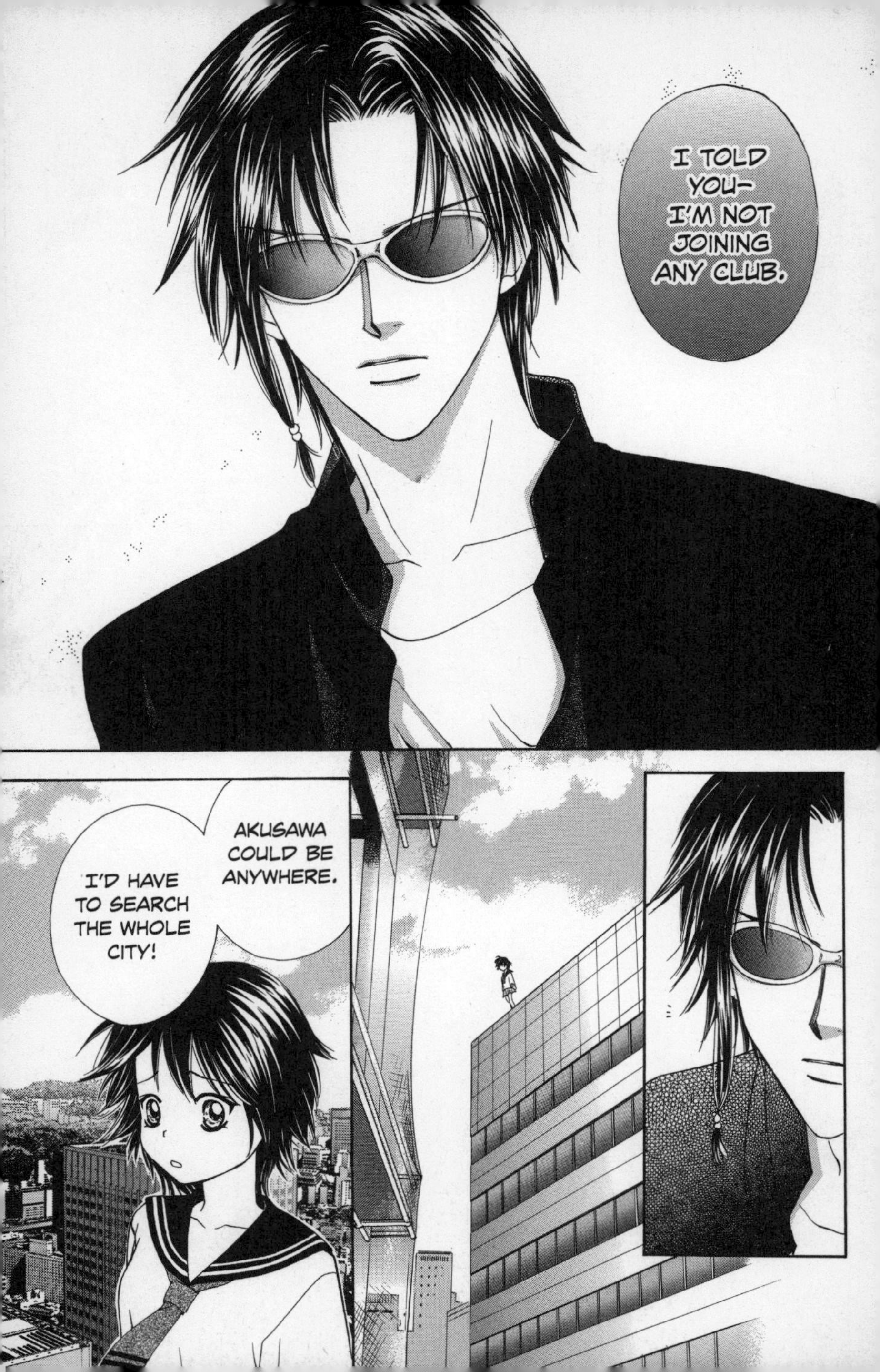
I TOLD YOU— I'M NOT JOINING ANY CLUB.
AKUSAWA COULD BE ANYWHERE. I'D HAVE TO SEARCH THE WHOLE CITY!

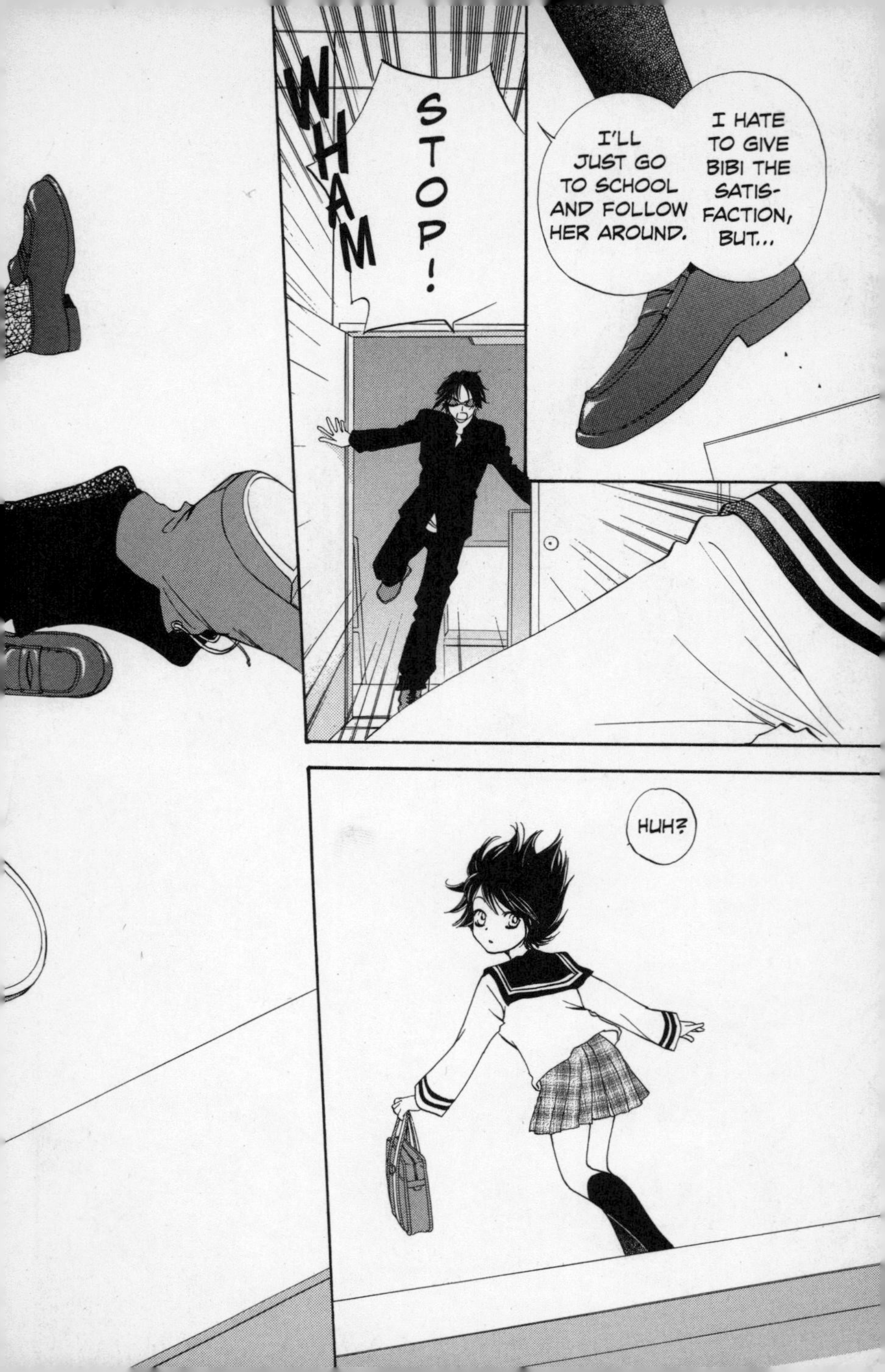
I HATE TO GIVE BIBI THE SATIS-FACTION, BUT...
I'LL JUST GO TO SCHOOL AND FOLLOW HER AROUND.
STOP!
WHAM
HUH?

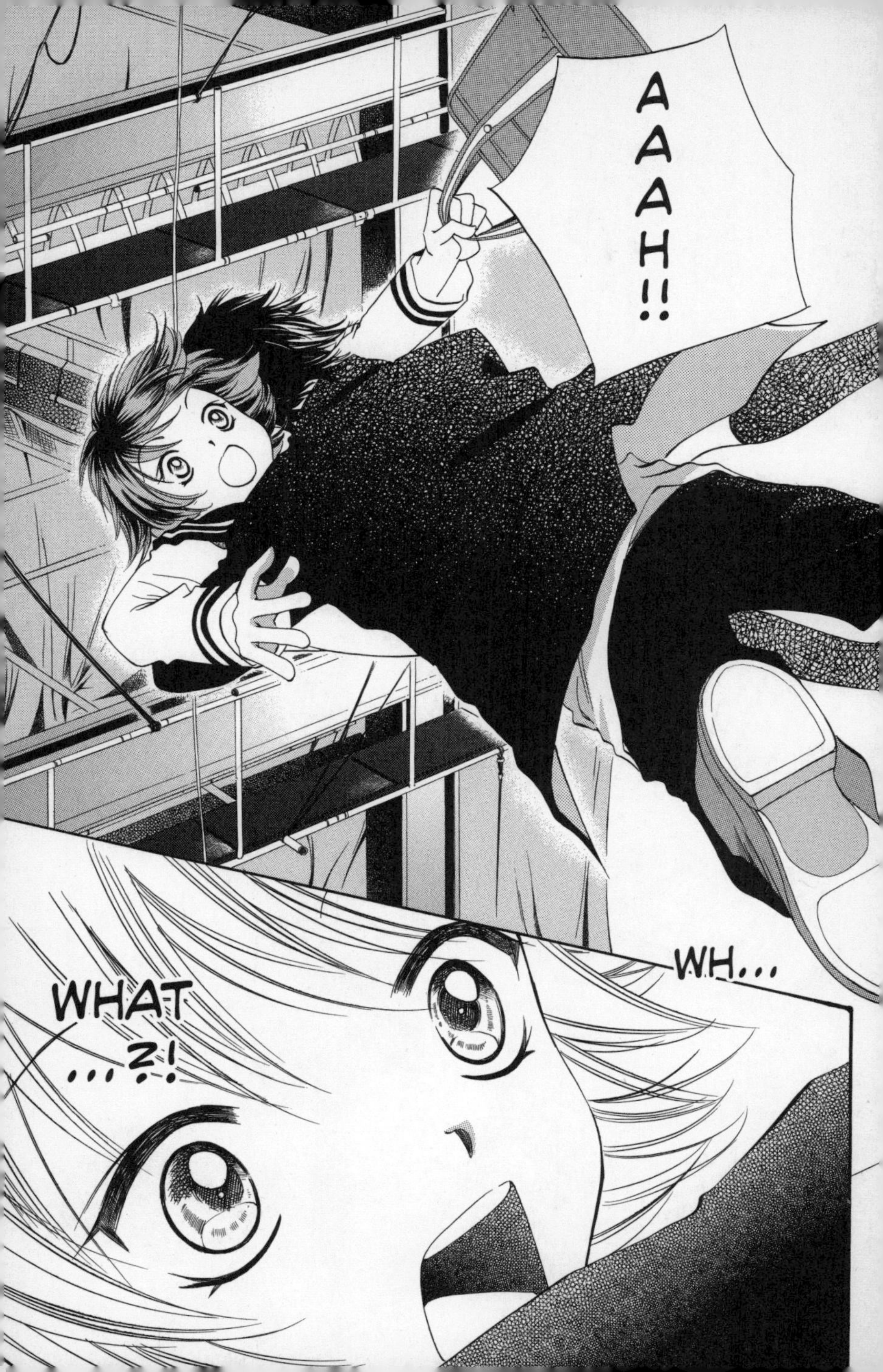
AAAH!!
WH...
WHAT...?!

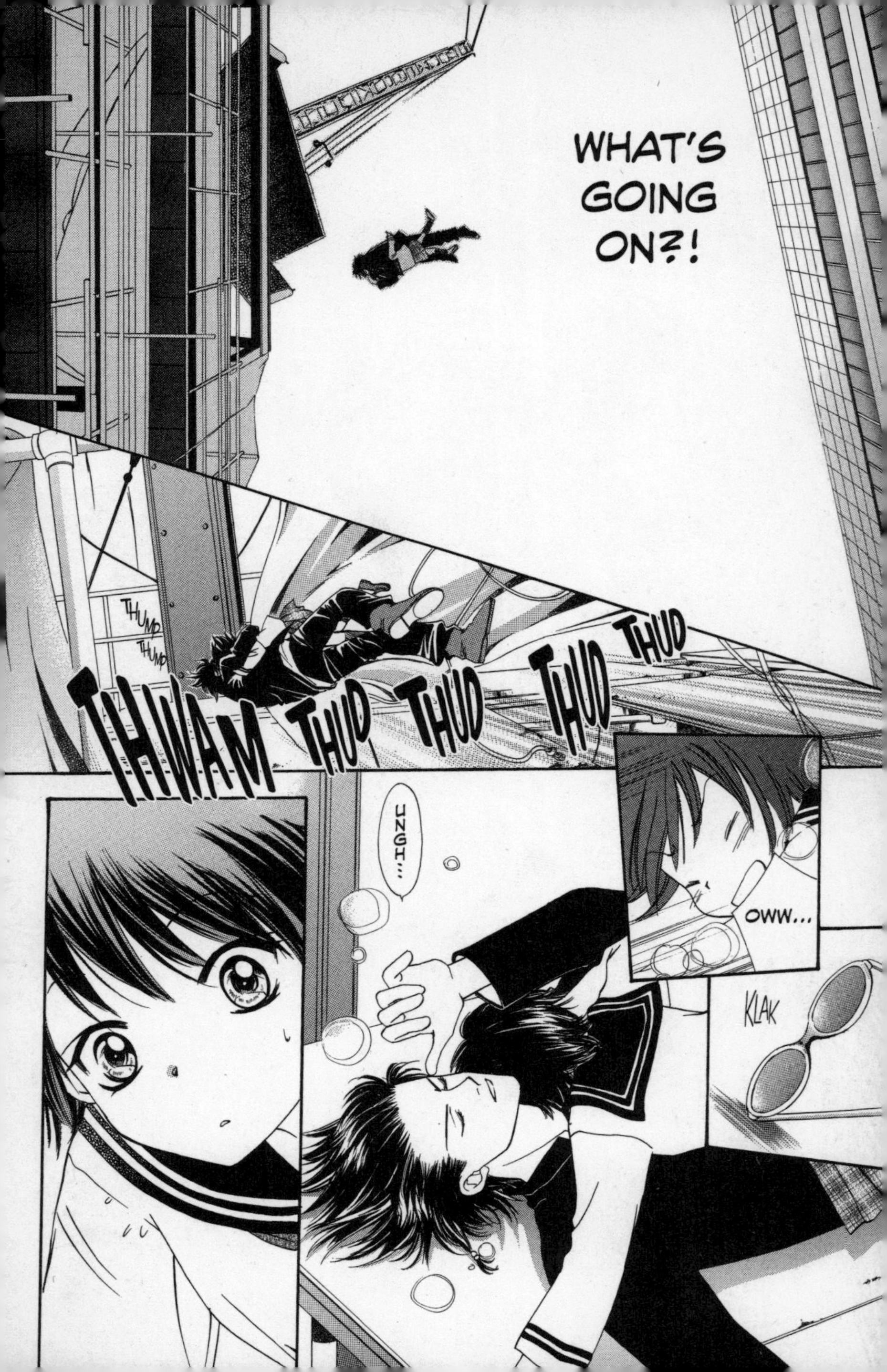
WHAT'S GOING ON?!
THUMP THUMP
THWAM THUD THUD THUD THUD
OWW...
KLAK
UNGH...

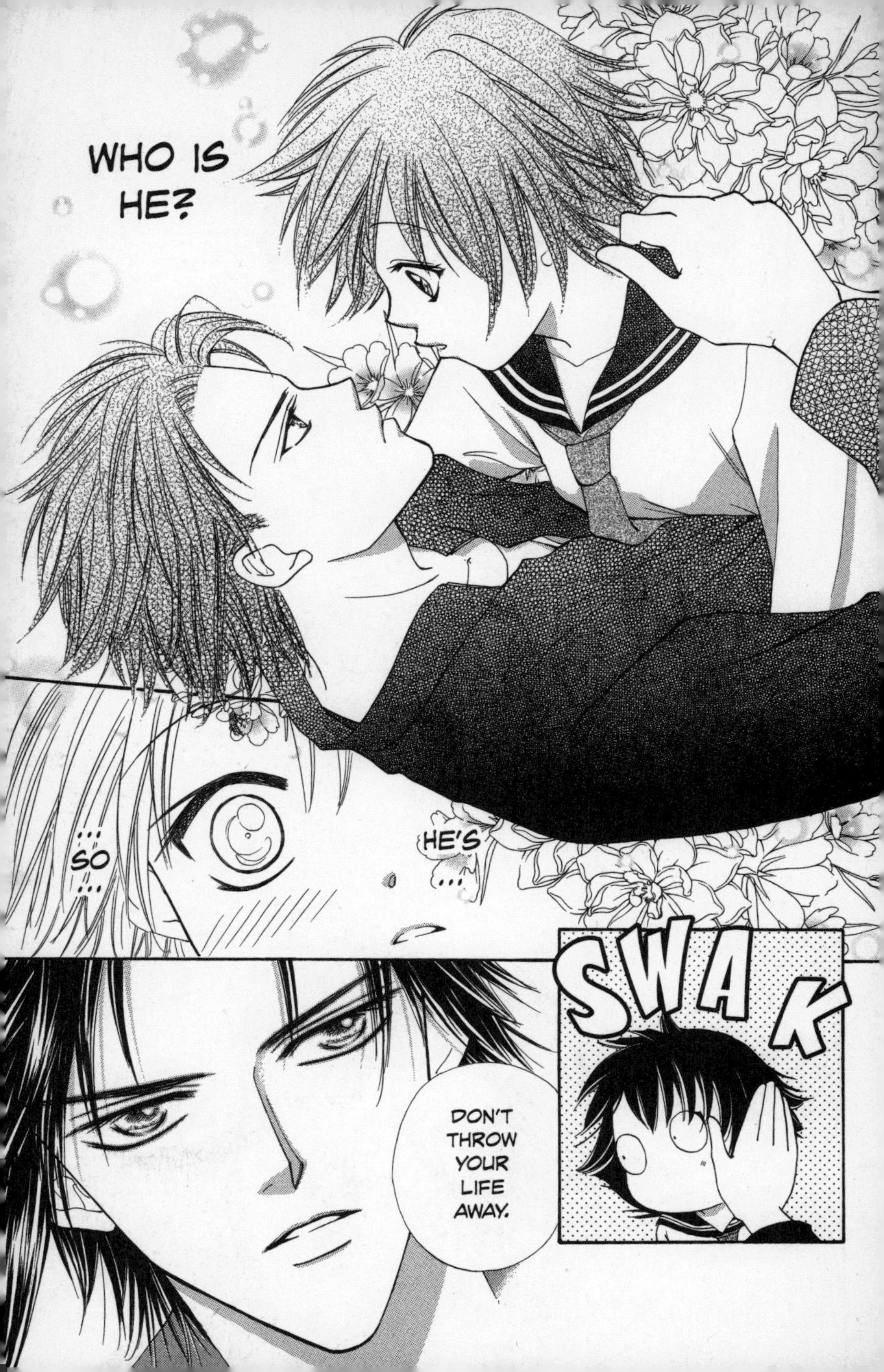
WHO IS HE?
HE'S ...
...SO...
SWAK
DON'T THROW YOUR LIFE AWAY.

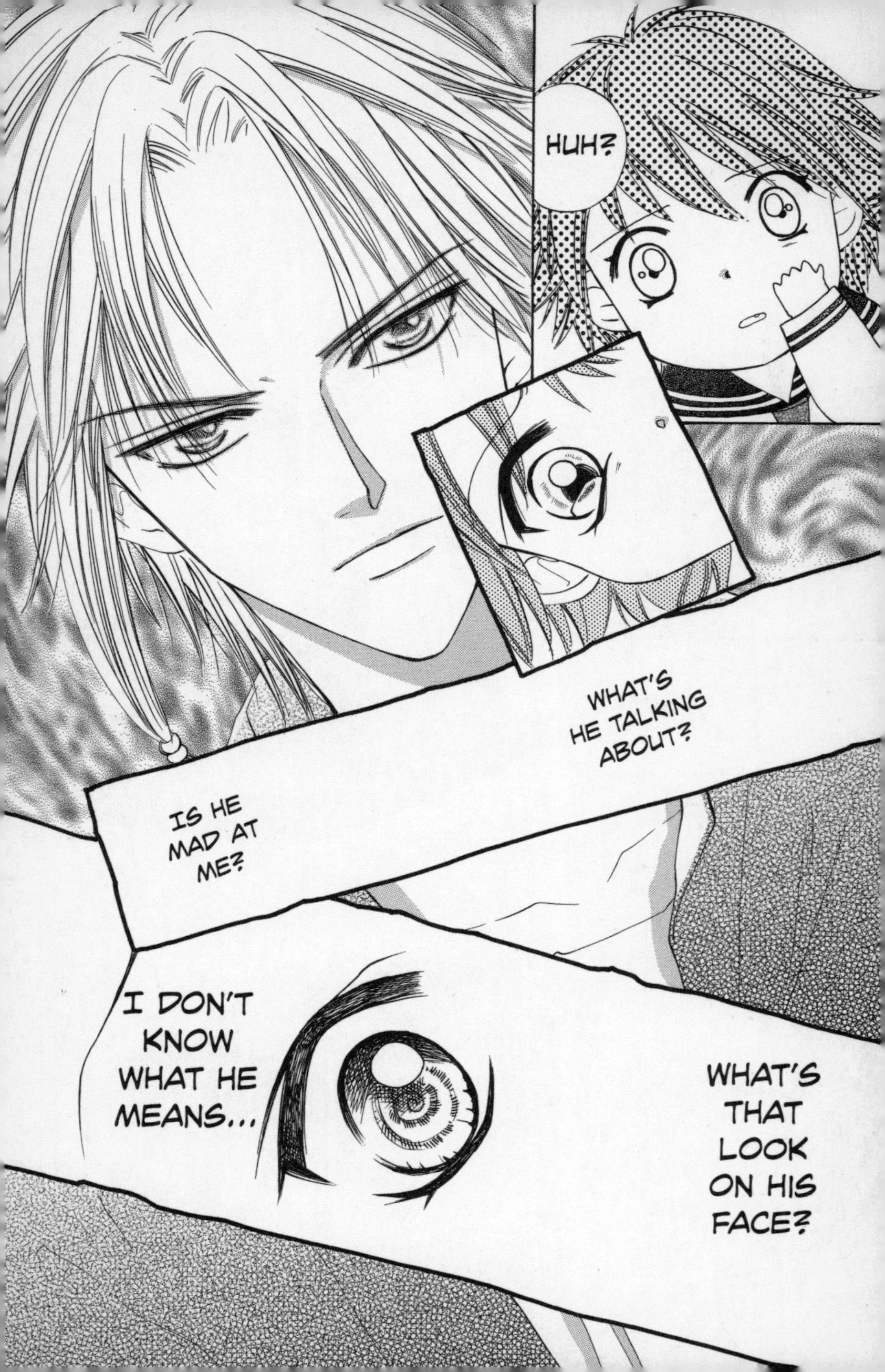
HUH?
WHAT'S HE TALKING ABOUT?
IS HE MAD AT ME?
WHAT'S THAT LOOK ON HIS FACE?
I DON'T KNOW WHAT HE MEANS...

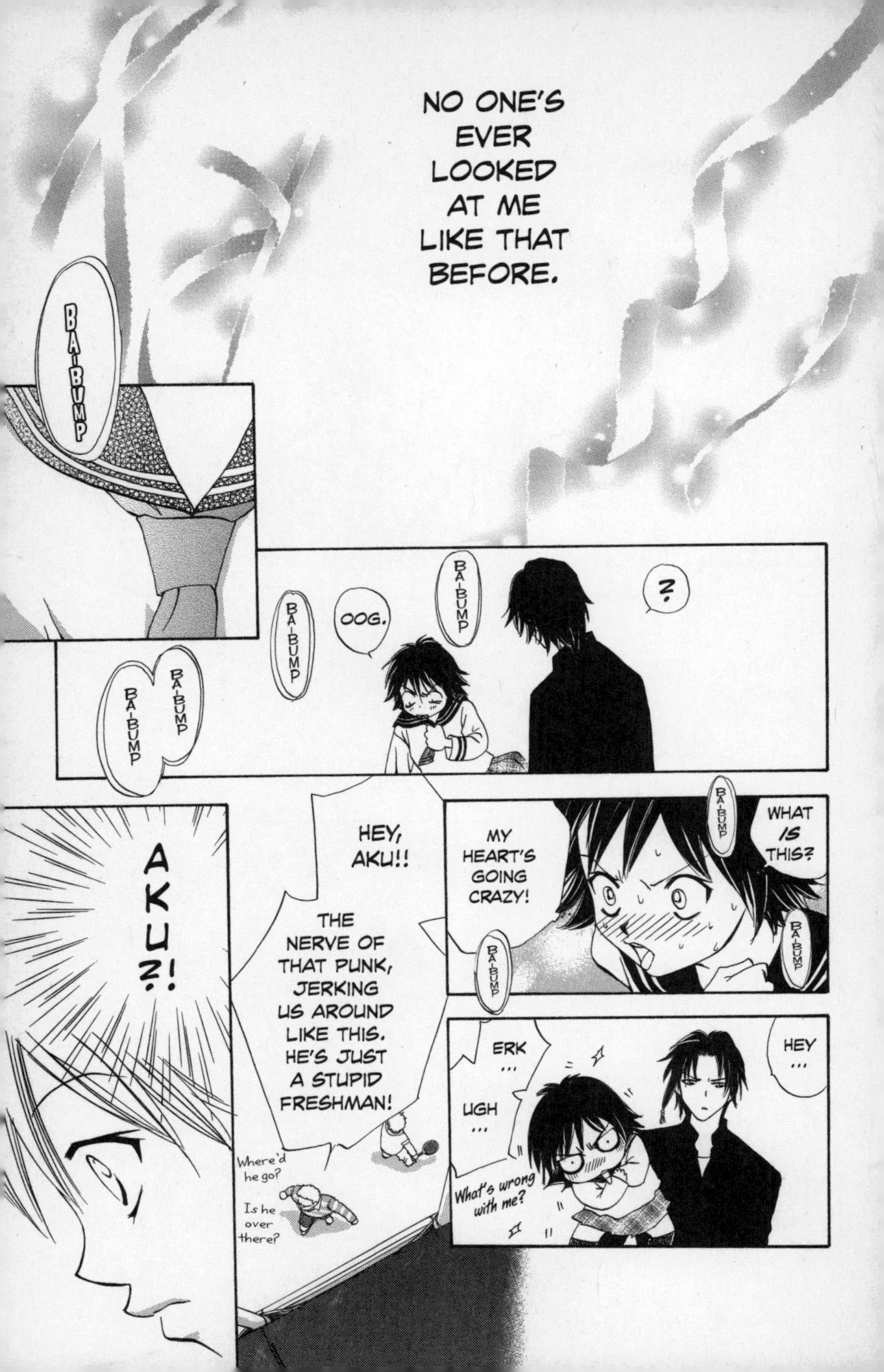
NO ONE'S EVER LOOKED AT ME LIKE THAT BEFORE.
BA-BUMP
?
BA-BUMP
OOG.
BA-BUMP
BA-BUMP BA-BUMP
WHAT IS THIS?
BA-BUMP
MY HEART'S GOING CRAZY!
BA-BUMP
BA-BUMP
HEY ...
ERK ...
UGH ...
What's wrong with me?
HEY, AKU!!
THE NERVE OF THAT PUNK, JERKING US AROUND LIKE THIS. HE'S JUST A STUPID FRESHMAN!
Where'd he go?
Is he over there?
AKU?!

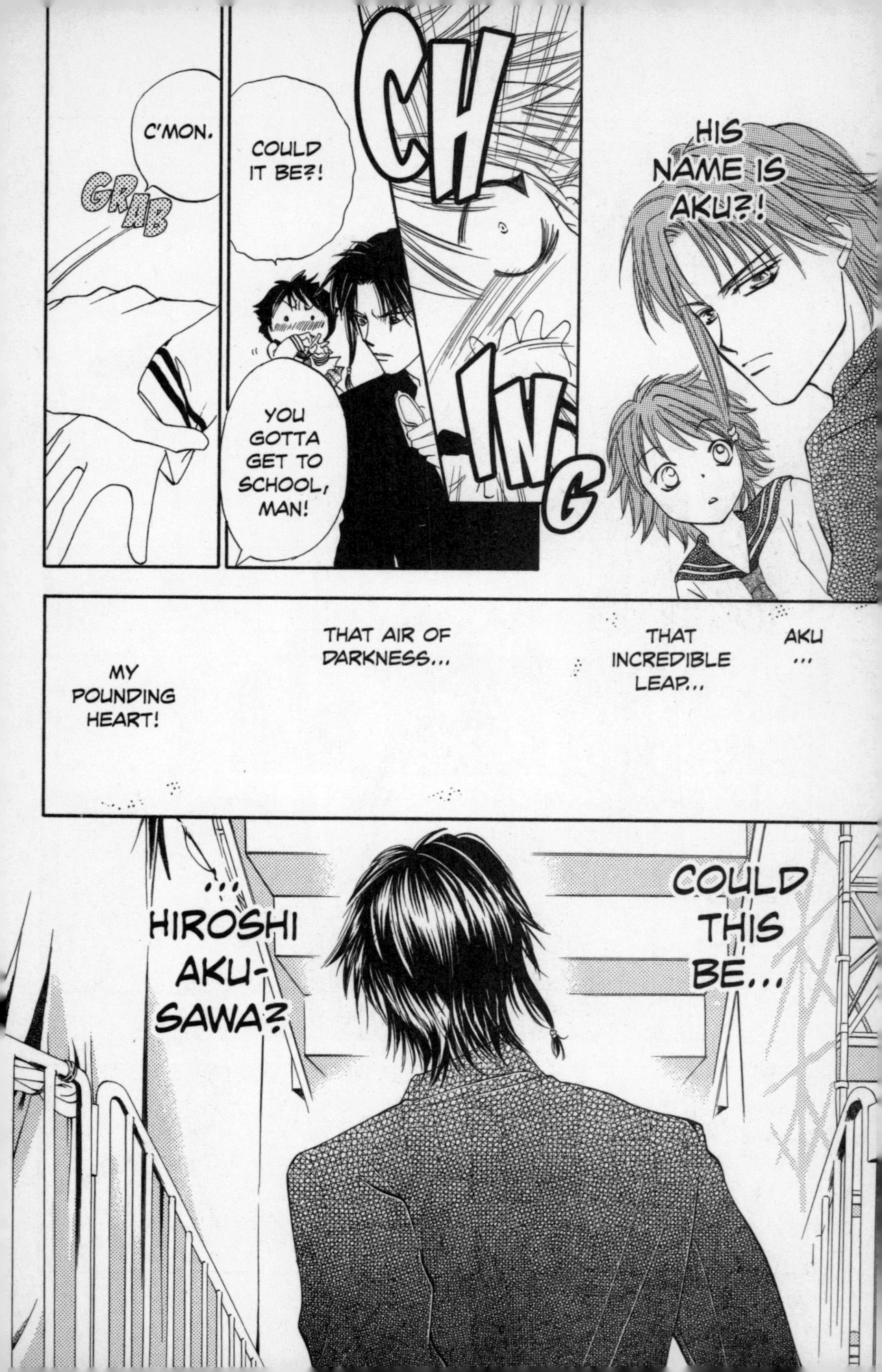
HIS NAME IS AKU?!
CHING
COULD IT BE?!
YOU GOTTA GET TO SCHOOL, MAN!
C'MON.
GRIB
AKU...
THAT INCREDIBLE LEAP...
THAT AIR OF DARKNESS...
MY POUNDING HEART!
COULD THIS BE...
...HIROSHI AKU-SAWA?

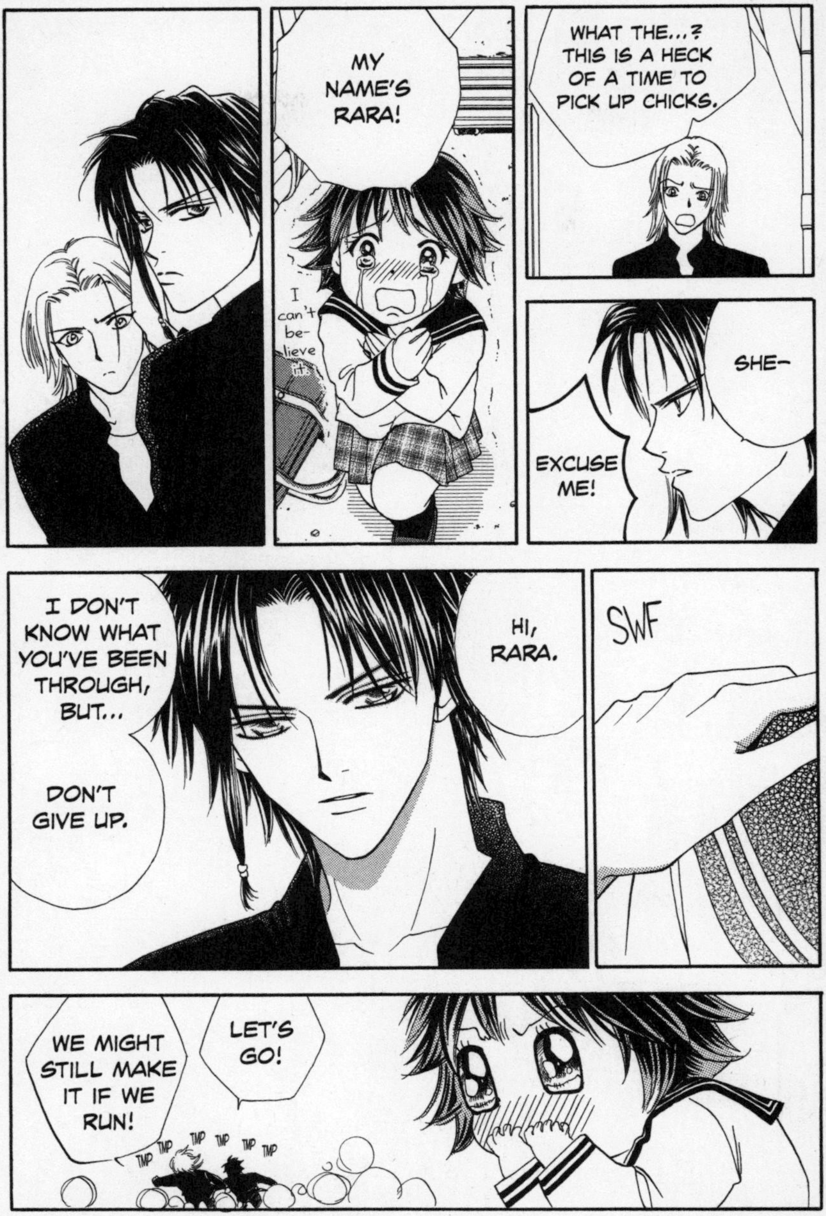
WHAT THE...? THIS IS A HECK OF A TIME TO PICK UP CHICKS.
SHE—
EXCUSE ME!
MY NAME'S RARA!
I can't be-lieve it.
SWF
HI, RARA.
I DON'T KNOW WHAT YOU'VE BEEN THROUGH, BUT...
DON'T GIVE UP.
LET'S GO!
WE MIGHT STILL MAKE IT IF WE RUN!
TMP TMP TMP TMP TMP TMP

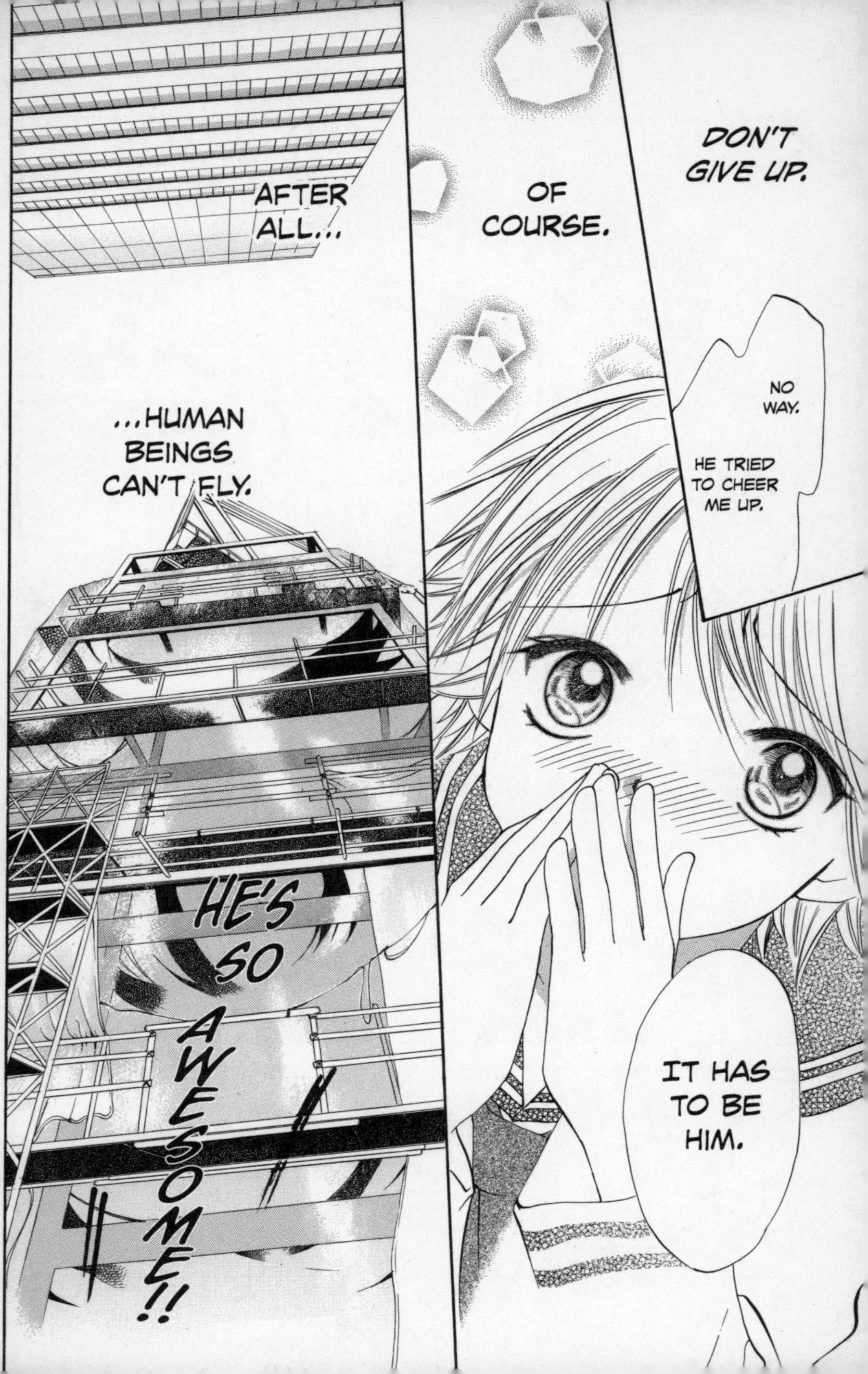
DON'T GIVE UP.
NO WAY.
HE TRIED TO CHEER ME UP.
IT HAS TO BE HIM.
OF COURSE.
AFTER ALL...
...HUMAN BEINGS CAN'T FLY.
HE'S SO AWESOME!!

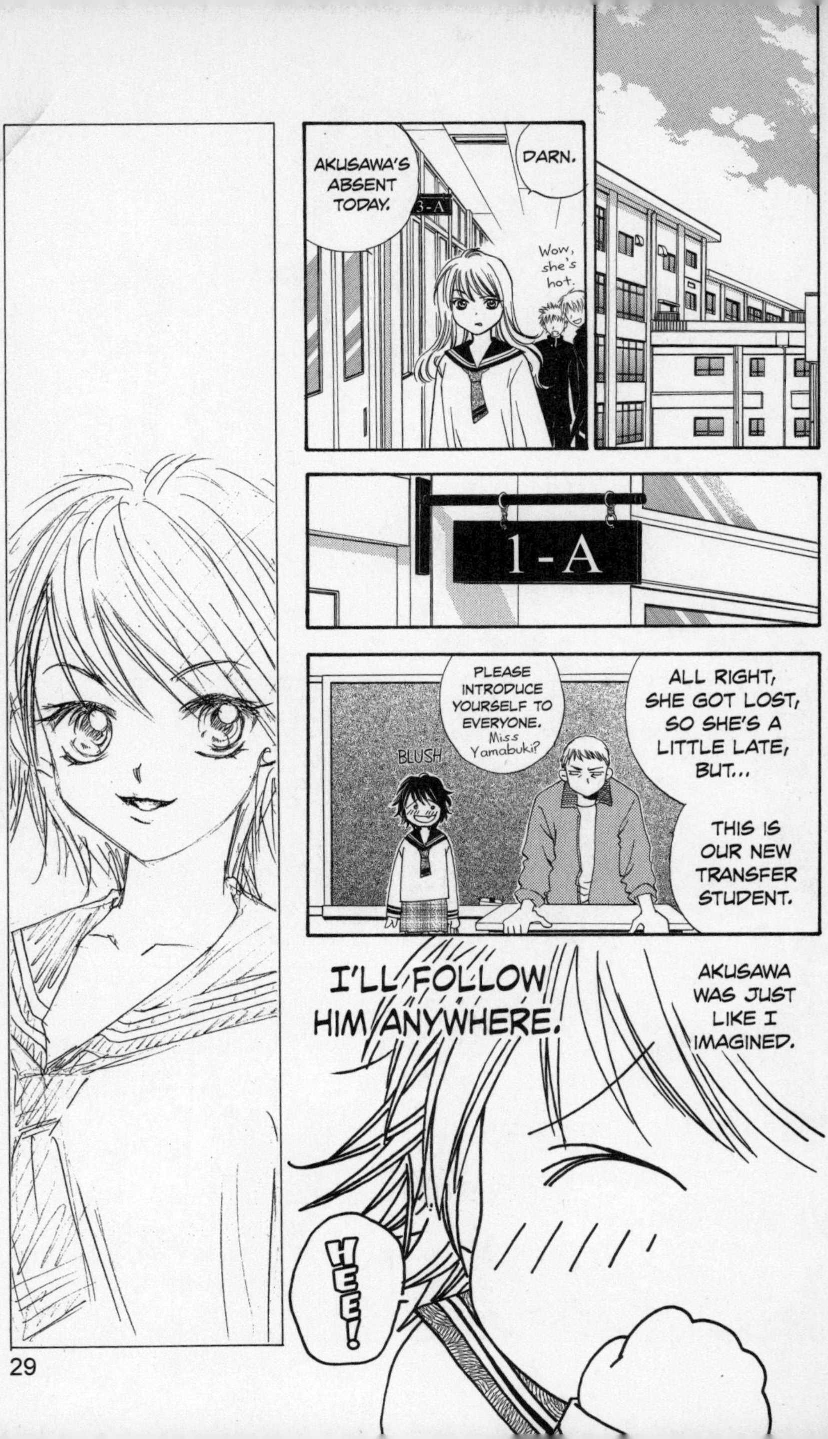
DARN.
AKUSAWA'S ABSENT TODAY.
Wow, she's hot.
1-A
ALL RIGHT, SHE GOT LOST, SO SHE'S A LITTLE LATE, BUT...
THIS IS OUR NEW TRANSFER STUDENT.
PLEASE INTRODUCE YOURSELF TO EVERYONE. Miss Yamabuki?
BLUSH
AKUSAWA WAS JUST LIKE I IMAGINED.
I'LL FOLLOW HIM ANYWHERE.
HEE!

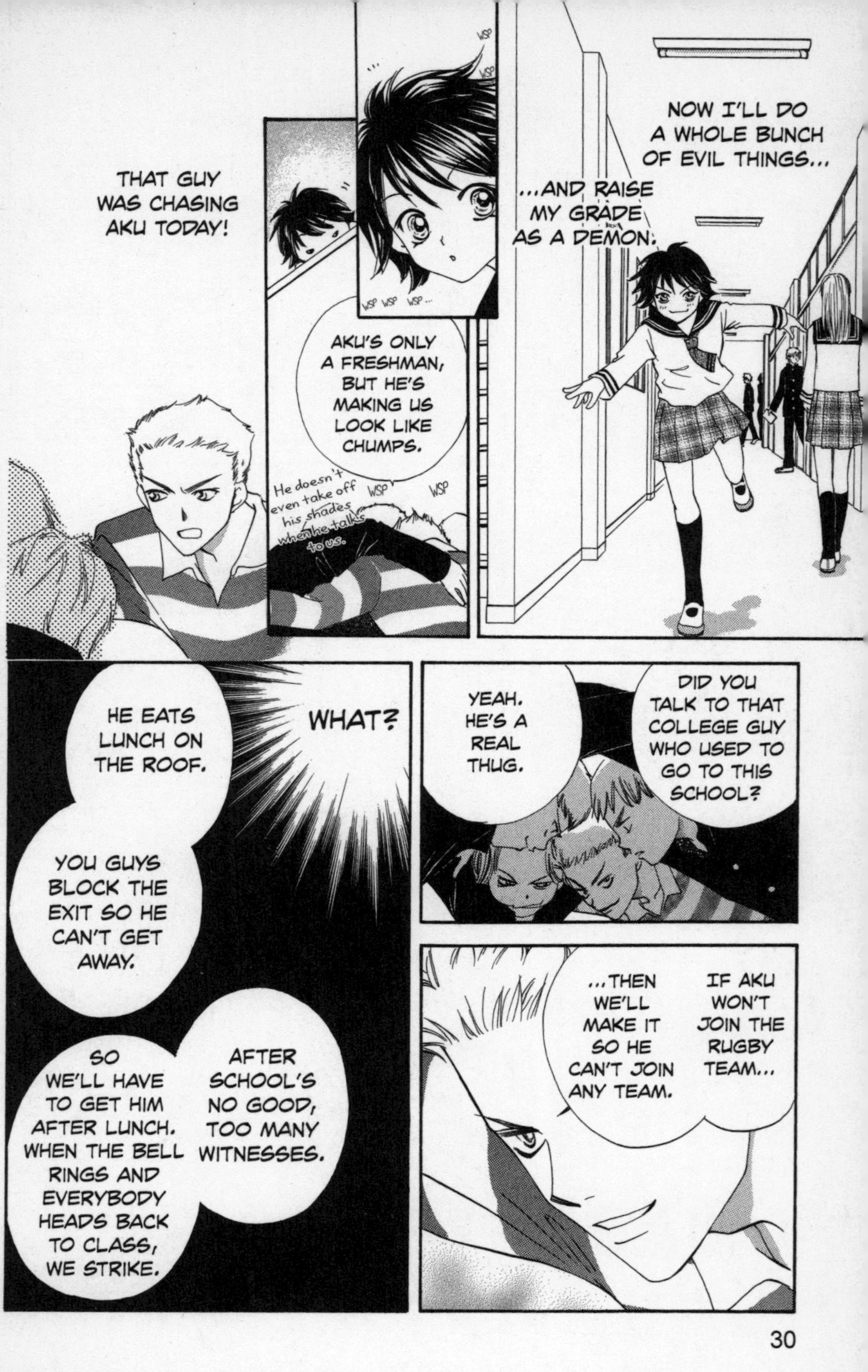
NOW I'LL DO A WHOLE BUNCH OF EVIL THINGS...
...AND RAISE MY GRADE AS A DEMON.
WSP
WSP
...
WSP WSP WSP...
THAT GUY WAS CHASING AKU TODAY!
AKU'S ONLY A FRESHMAN, BUT HE'S MAKING US LOOK LIKE CHUMPS.
He doesn't even take off his shades when he talks to us.
WSP
WSP
DID YOU TALK TO THAT COLLEGE GUY WHO USED TO GO TO THIS SCHOOL?
YEAH. HE'S A REAL THUG.
IF AKU WON'T JOIN THE RUGBY TEAM...
...THEN WE'LL MAKE IT SO HE CAN'T JOIN ANY TEAM.
WHAT?
HE EATS LUNCH ON THE ROOF.
YOU GUYS BLOCK THE EXIT SO HE CAN'T GET AWAY.
AFTER SCHOOL'S NO GOOD, TOO MANY WITNESSES.
SO WE'LL HAVE TO GET HIM AFTER LUNCH. WHEN THE BELL RINGS AND EVERYBODY HEADS BACK TO CLASS, WE STRIKE.

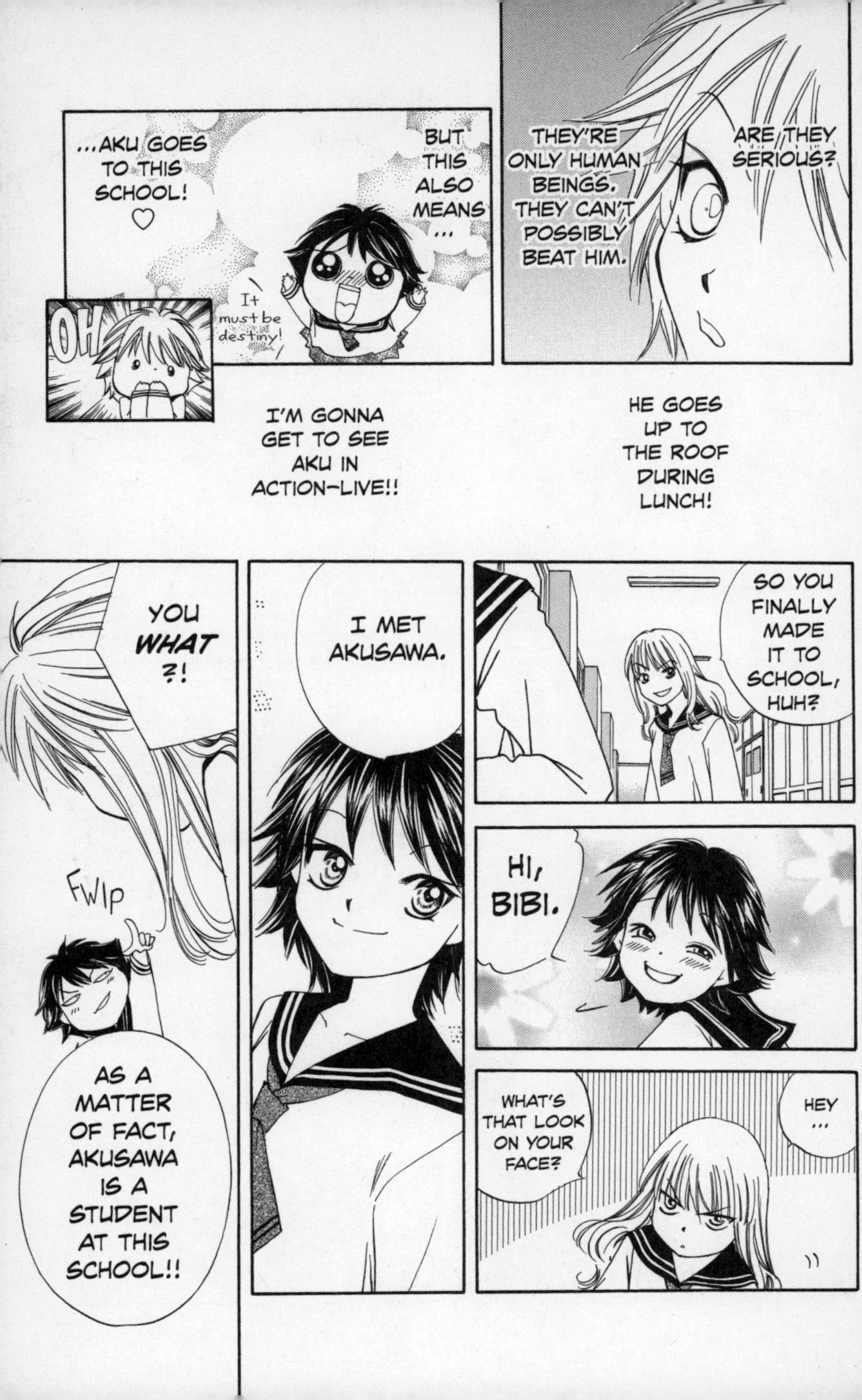
ARE THEY SERIOUS?
THEY'RE ONLY HUMAN BEINGS. THEY CAN'T POSSIBLY BEAT HIM.
BUT THIS ALSO MEANS...
...AKU GOES TO THIS SCHOOL! ♡
It must be destiny!
OH
HE GOES UP TO THE ROOF DURING LUNCH!
I'M GONNA GET TO SEE AKU IN ACTION—LIVE!!
SO YOU FINALLY MADE IT TO SCHOOL, HUH?
HI, BIBI.
HEY...
WHAT'S THAT LOOK ON YOUR FACE?
I MET AKUSAWA.
YOU WHAT?!
FWIP
AS A MATTER OF FACT, AKUSAWA IS A STUDENT AT THIS SCHOOL!!

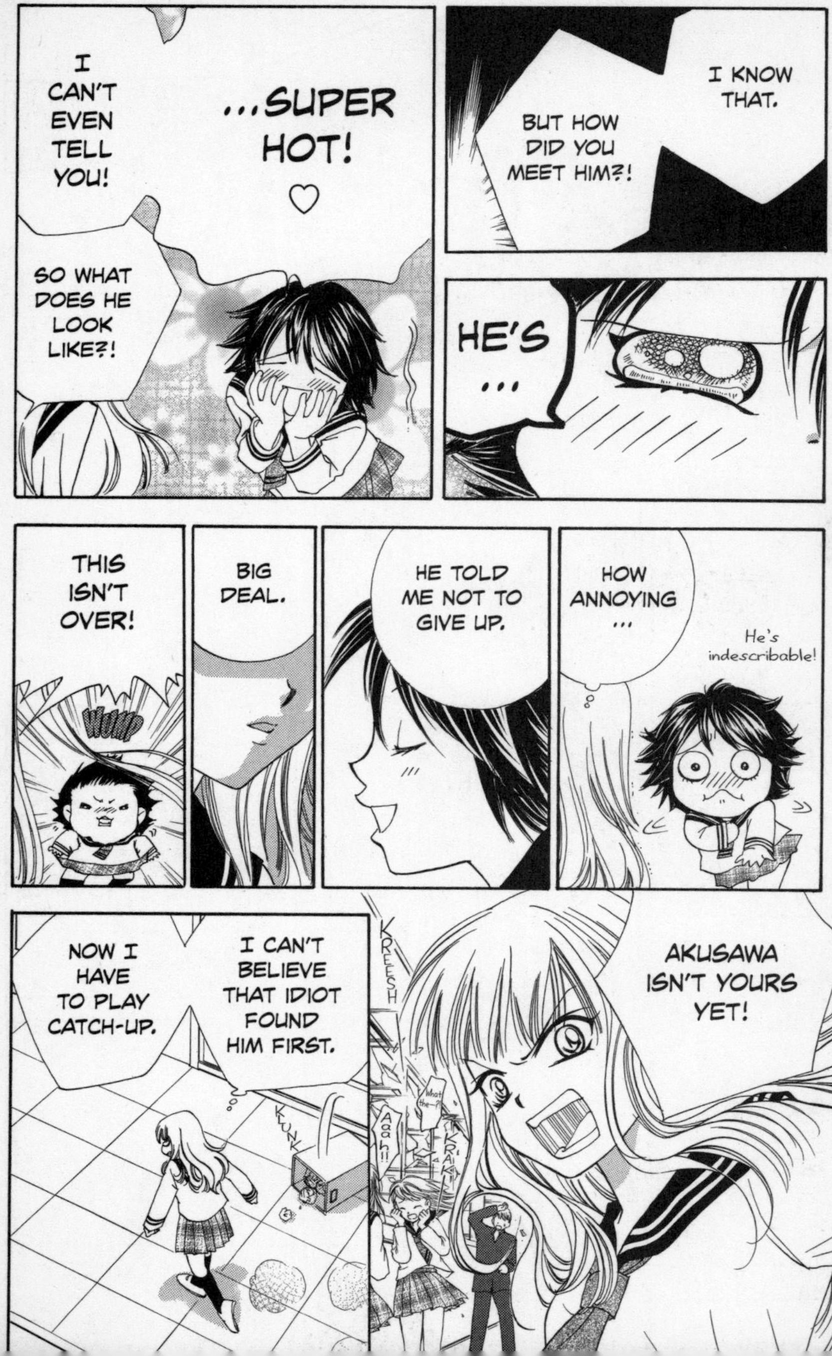
I KNOW THAT.
BUT HOW DID YOU MEET HIM?!
HE'S ...
I CAN'T EVEN TELL YOU!
...SUPER HOT! ♡
SO WHAT DOES HE LOOK LIKE?!
HOW ANNOYING ...
He's indescribable!
HE TOLD ME NOT TO GIVE UP.
BIG DEAL.
THIS ISN'T OVER!
WUMP
AKUSAWA ISN'T YOURS YET!
KREESH
What the–?!
Aaah!!
KRAK
I CAN'T BELIEVE THAT IDIOT FOUND HIM FIRST.
NOW I HAVE TO PLAY CATCH-UP.
KLUNK

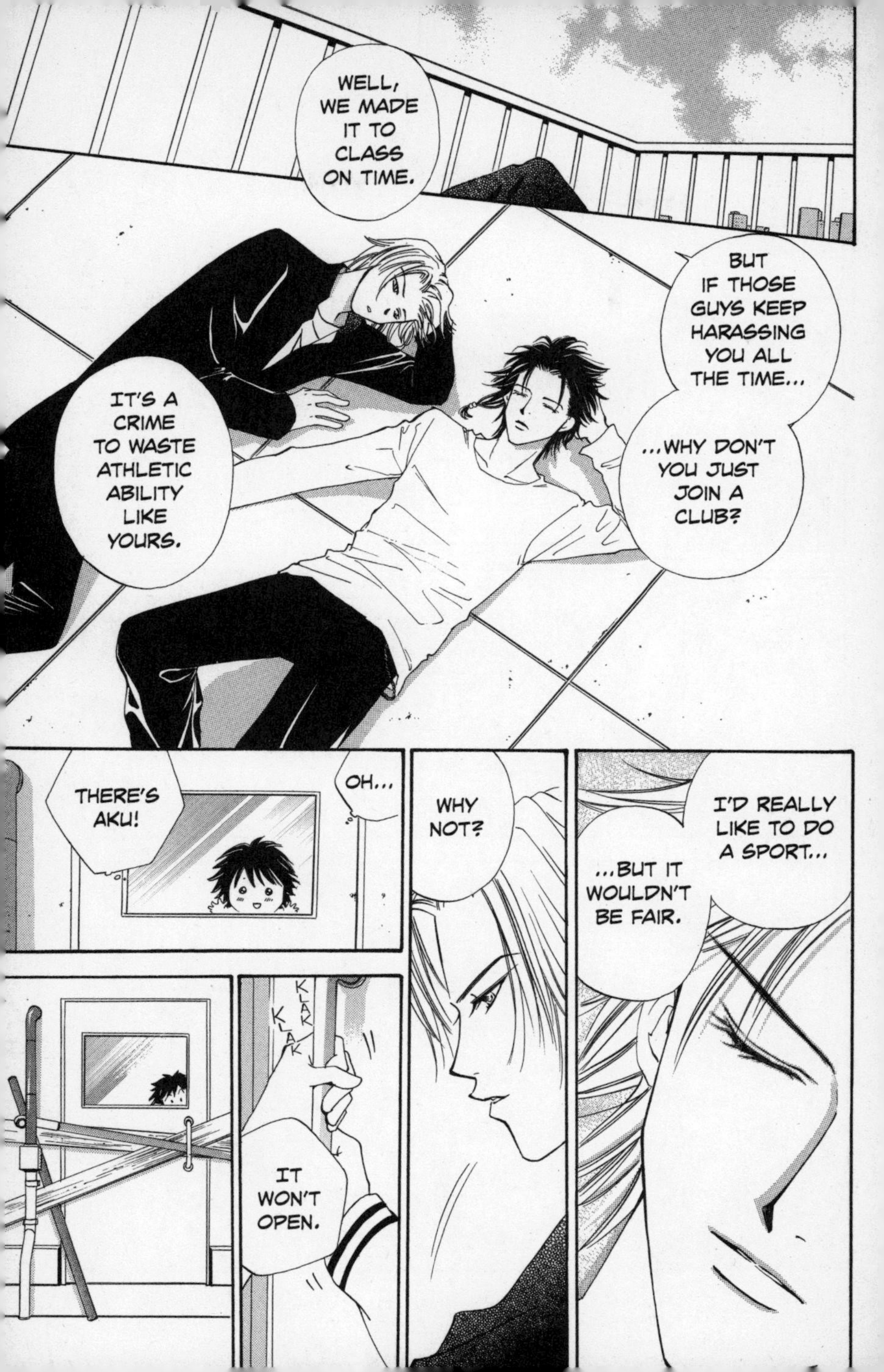
WELL, WE MADE IT TO CLASS ON TIME.
BUT IF THOSE GUYS KEEP HARASSING YOU ALL THE TIME...
...WHY DON'T YOU JUST JOIN A CLUB?
IT'S A CRIME TO WASTE ATHLETIC ABILITY LIKE YOURS.
I'D REALLY LIKE TO DO A SPORT...
...BUT IT WOULDN'T BE FAIR.
WHY NOT?
OH...
THERE'S AKU!
KLAK
KLAK
IT WON'T OPEN.

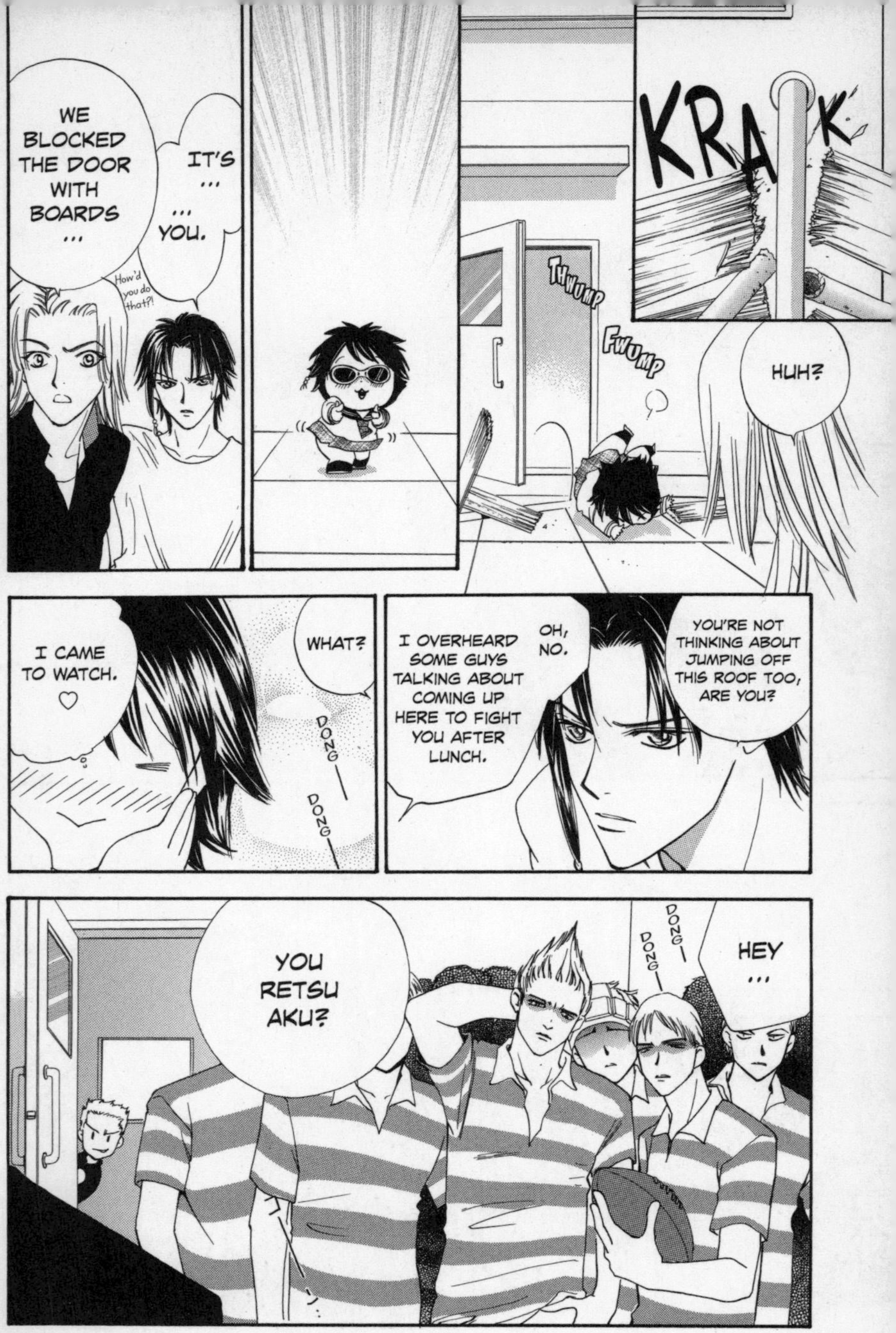
KRAK
THWUMP
FWUMP
HUH?
IT'S ... ... YOU.
WE BLOCKED THE DOOR WITH BOARDS ...
How'd you do that?!
YOU'RE NOT THINKING ABOUT JUMPING OFF THIS ROOF TOO, ARE YOU?
OH, NO.
I OVERHEARD SOME GUYS TALKING ABOUT COMING UP HERE TO FIGHT YOU AFTER LUNCH.
WHAT?
DONG DONG
I CAME TO WATCH. ♡
HEY ...
DONG DONG
YOU RETSU AKU?

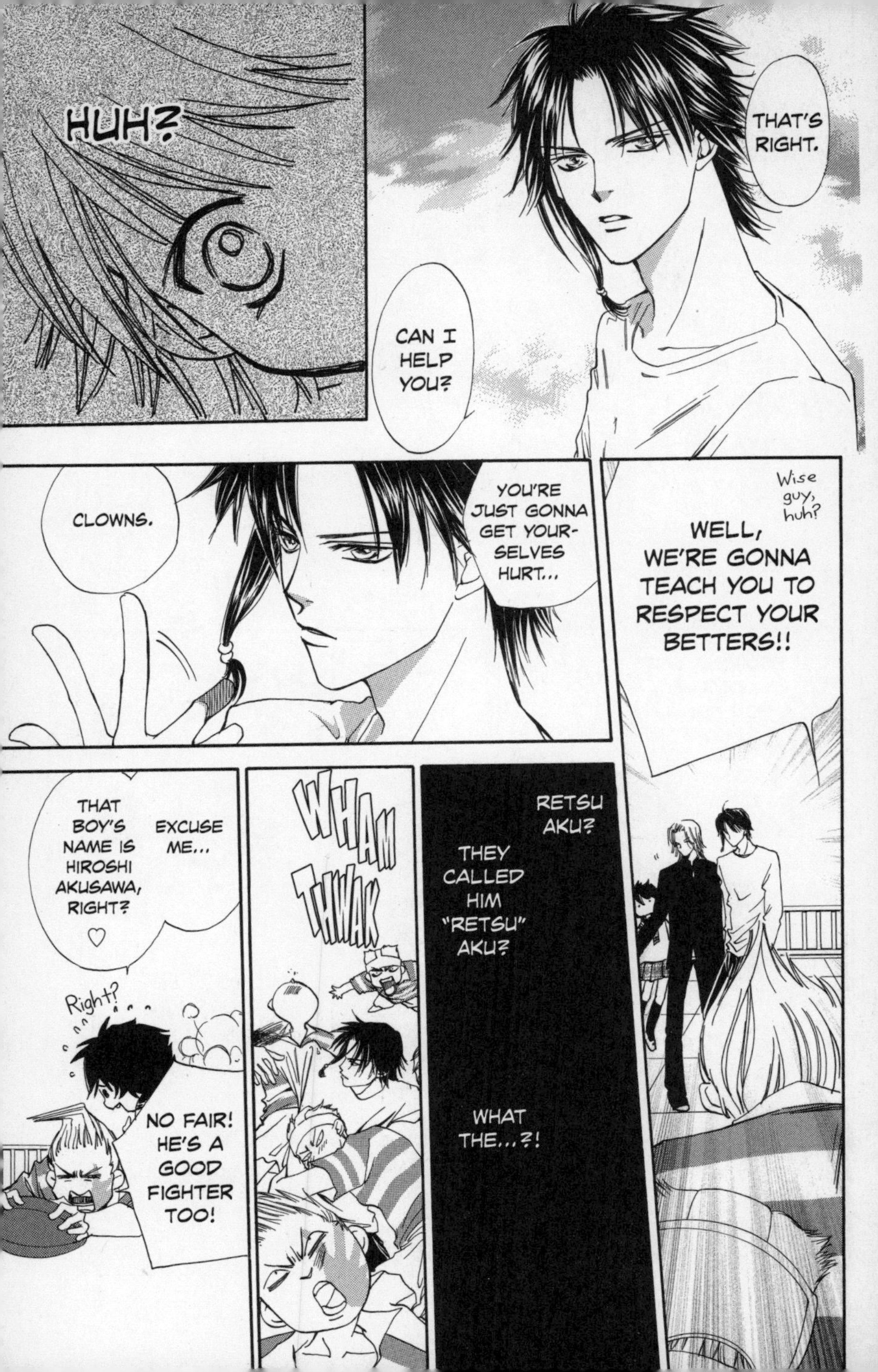
THAT'S RIGHT.
CAN I HELP YOU?
HUH?
Wise guy, huh?
WELL, WE'RE GONNA TEACH YOU TO RESPECT YOUR BETTERS!!
YOU'RE JUST GONNA GET YOUR-SELVES HURT...
CLOWNS.
RETSU AKU?
THEY CALLED HIM "RETSU" AKU?
WHAT THE...?!
WHAM
THWAK
EXCUSE ME...
THAT BOY'S NAME IS HIROSHI AKUSAWA, RIGHT? ♡
Right?
NO FAIR! HE'S A GOOD FIGHTER TOO!

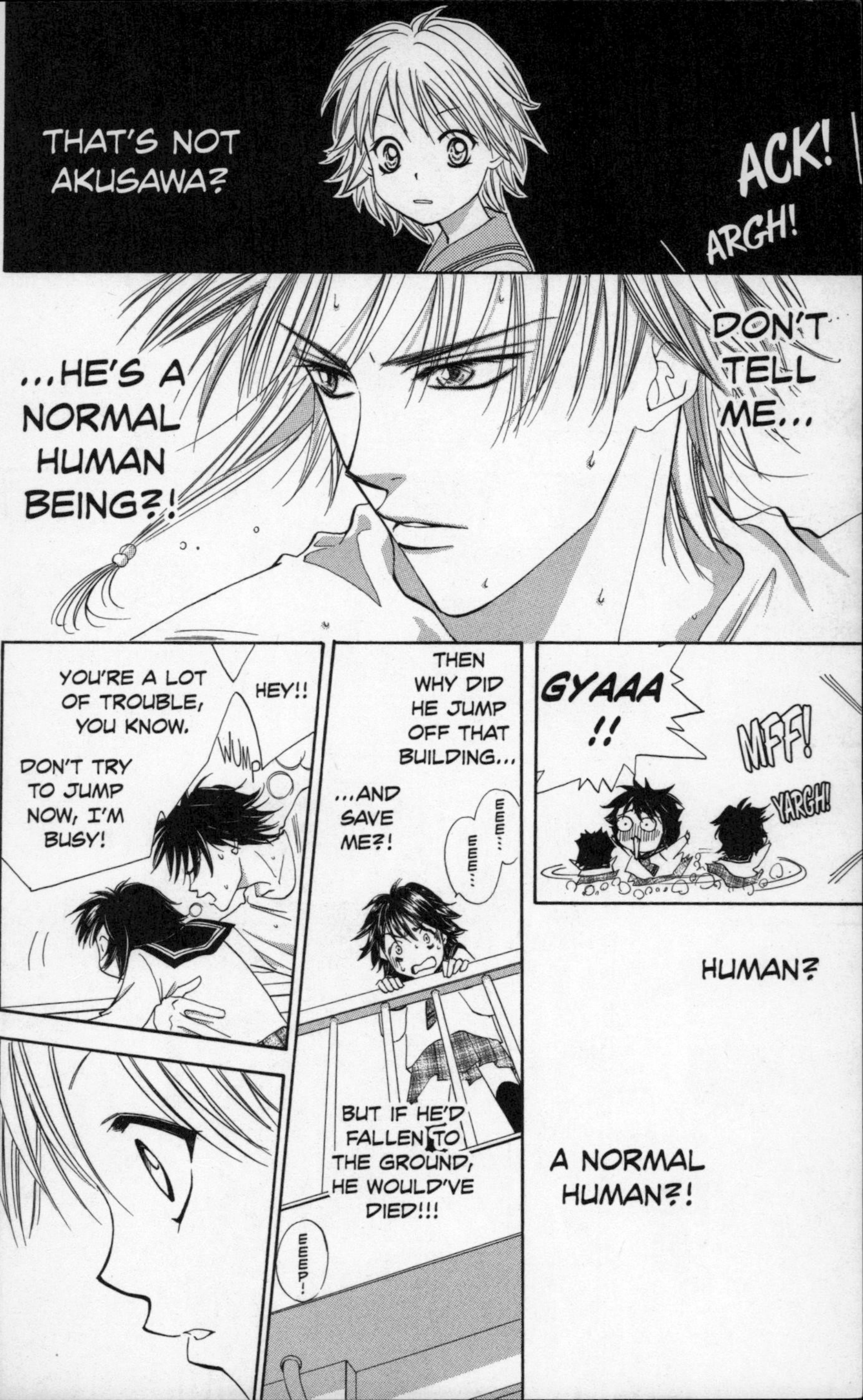
ACK!
ARGH!
THAT'S NOT AKUSAWA?
DON'T TELL ME...
...HE'S A NORMAL HUMAN BEING?!
GYAAA!!
MFF!
YARGH!
THEN WHY DID HE JUMP OFF THAT BUILDING...
...AND SAVE ME?!
EEEE...
EEE...
HEY!!
YOU'RE A LOT OF TROUBLE, YOU KNOW.
DON'T TRY TO JUMP NOW, I'M BUSY!
WUMP
HUMAN?
A NORMAL HUMAN?!
BUT IF HE'D FALLEN TO THE GROUND, HE WOULD'VE DIED!!!
EEEP!

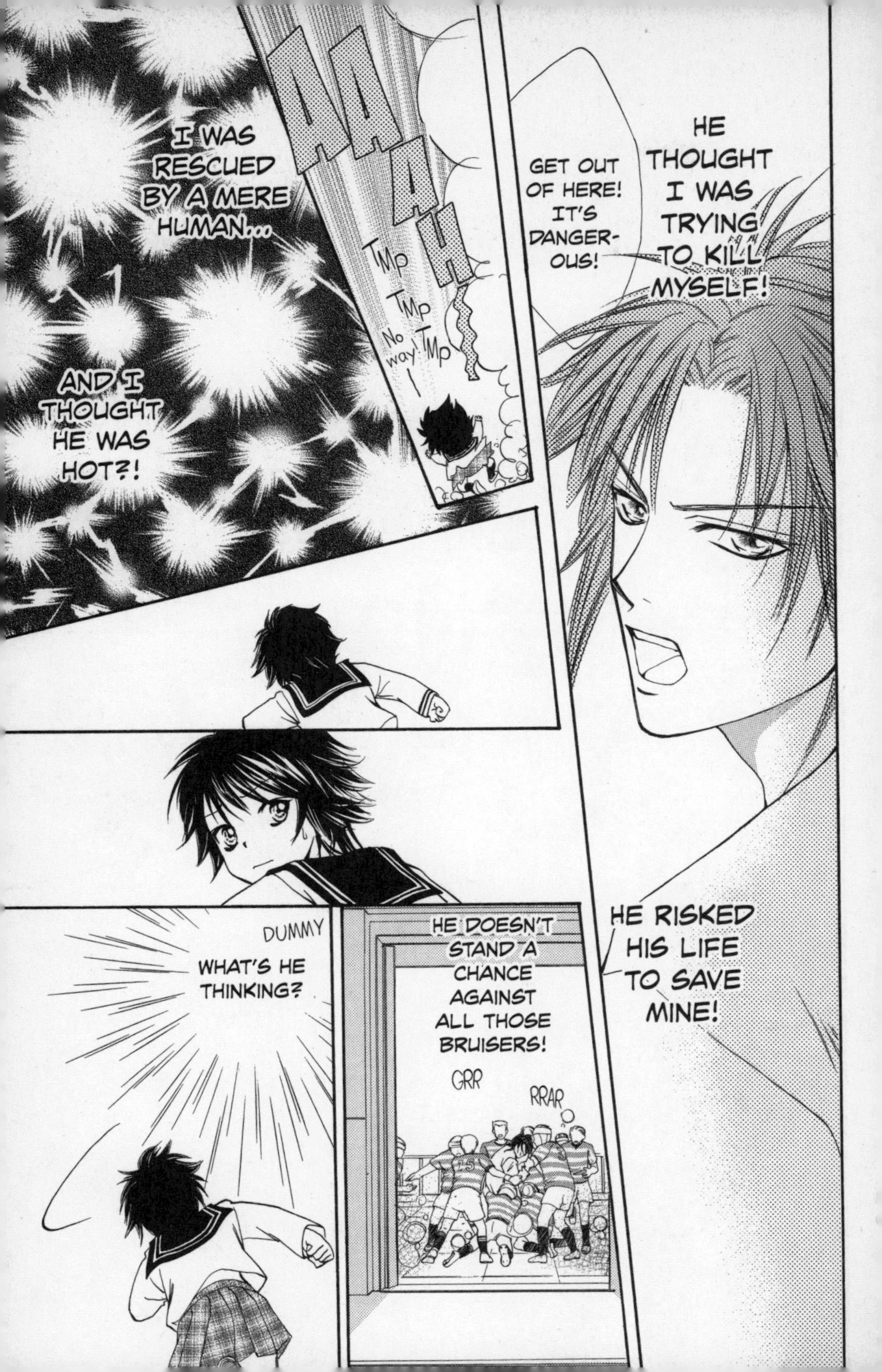
HE THOUGHT I WAS TRYING TO KILL MYSELF!
GET OUT OF HERE! IT'S DANGER-OUS!
HE RISKED HIS LIFE TO SAVE MINE!
AAAH
TMP TMP TMP
No way!
I WAS RESCUED BY A MERE HUMAN...
AND I THOUGHT HE WAS HOT?!
HE DOESN'T STAND A CHANCE AGAINST ALL THOSE BRUISERS!
GRR
RRAR
DUMMY
WHAT'S HE THINKING?

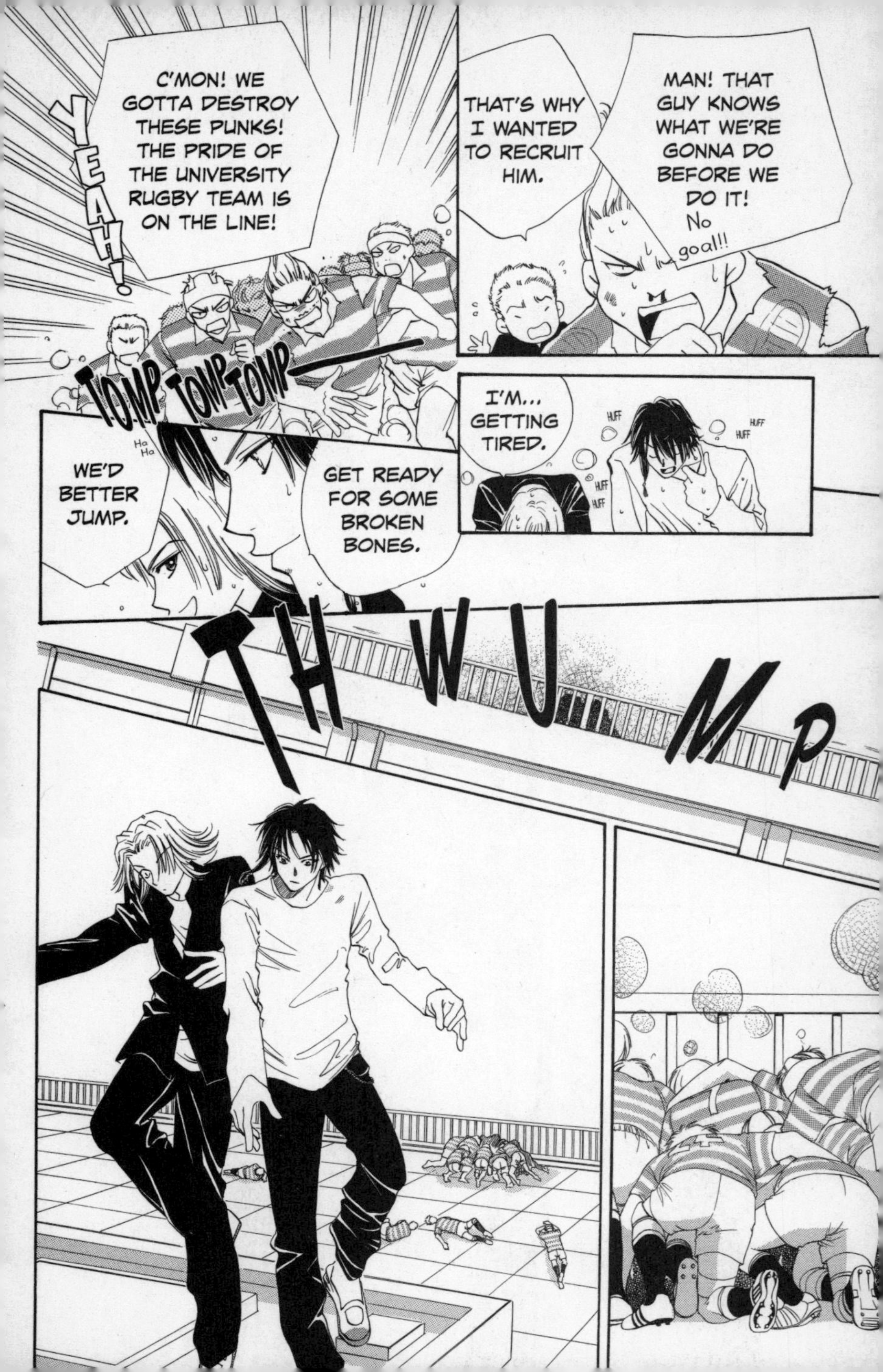
MAN! THAT GUY KNOWS WHAT WE'RE GONNA DO BEFORE WE DO IT!
THAT'S WHY I WANTED TO RECRUIT HIM.
No goal!!
C'MON! WE GOTTA DESTROY THESE PUNKS! THE PRIDE OF THE UNIVERSITY RUGBY TEAM IS ON THE LINE!
YEAH!
TOMP TOMP TOMP
I'M... GETTING TIRED.
HUFF HUFF
HUFF HUFF
GET READY FOR SOME BROKEN BONES.
Ha Ha
WE'D BETTER JUMP.
THWUMP

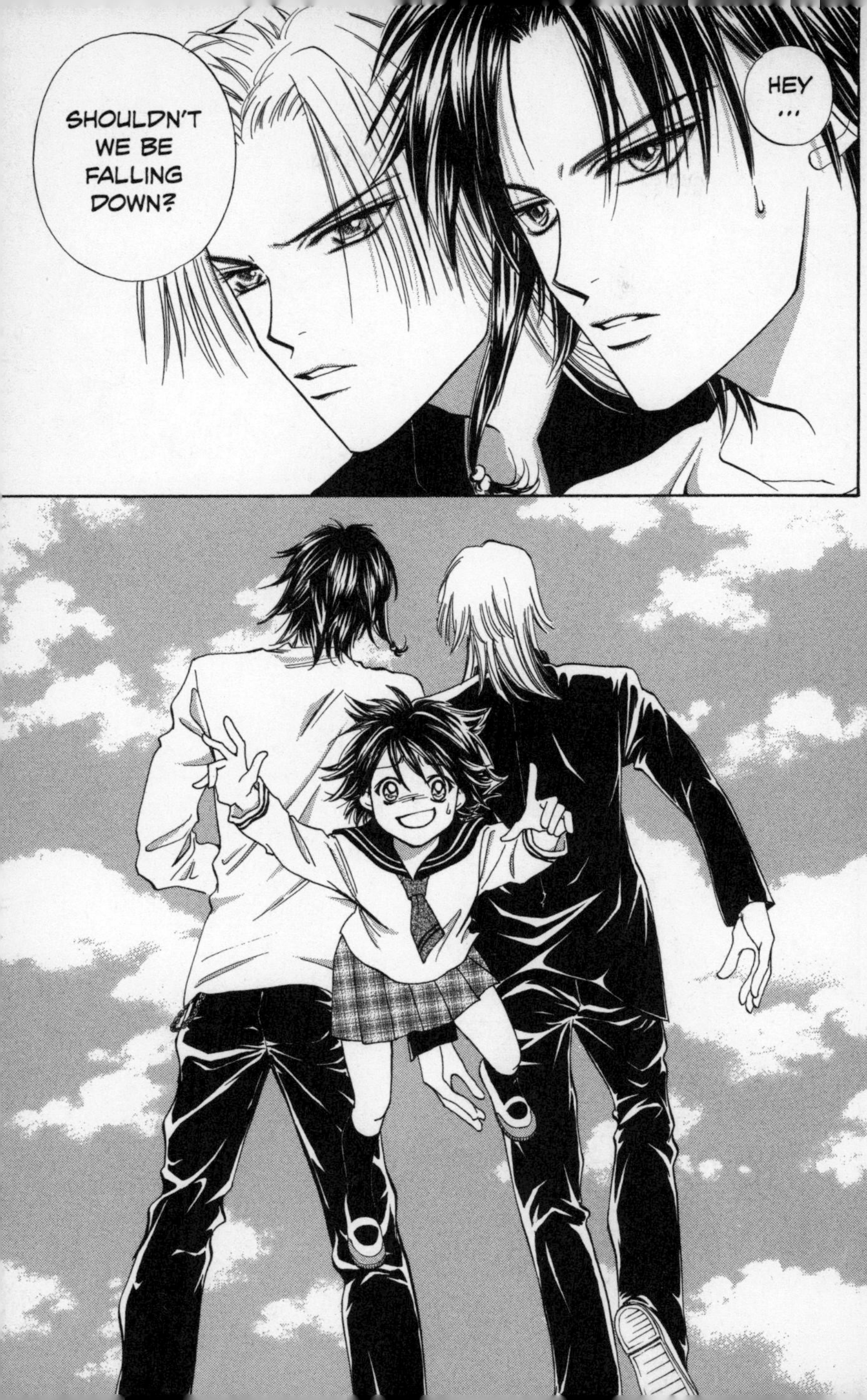
HEY ...
SHOULDN'T WE BE FALLING DOWN?

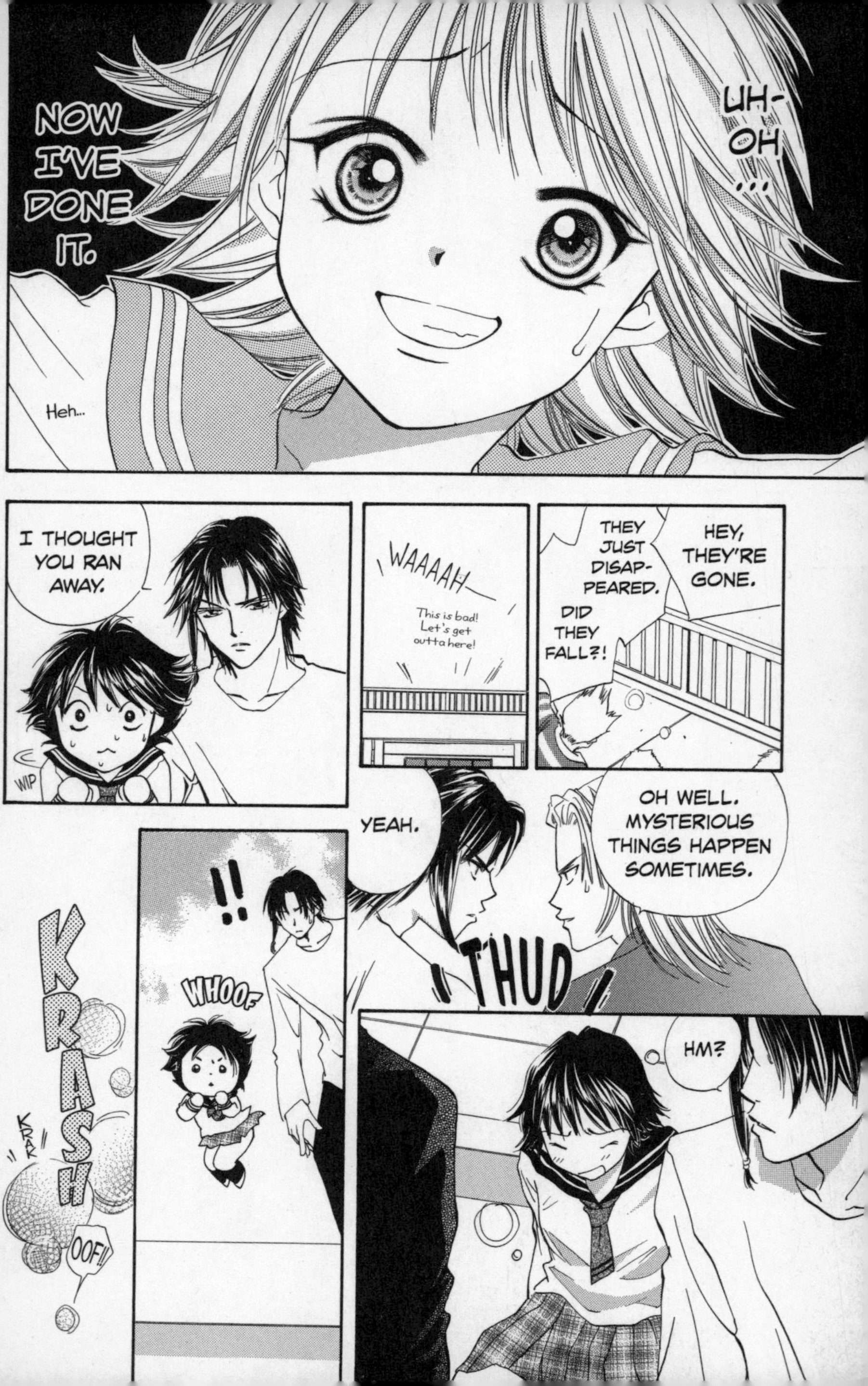
UH-OH...
NOW I'VE DONE IT.
Heh...
HEY, THEY'RE GONE.
THEY JUST DISAPPEARED.
DID THEY FALL?!
WAAAAH
This is bad! Let's get outta here!
I THOUGHT YOU RAN AWAY.
WIP
OH WELL. MYSTERIOUS THINGS HAPPEN SOMETIMES.
YEAH.
THUD
HM?
!!
WHOOF
KRASH
KRAK
OOF!!

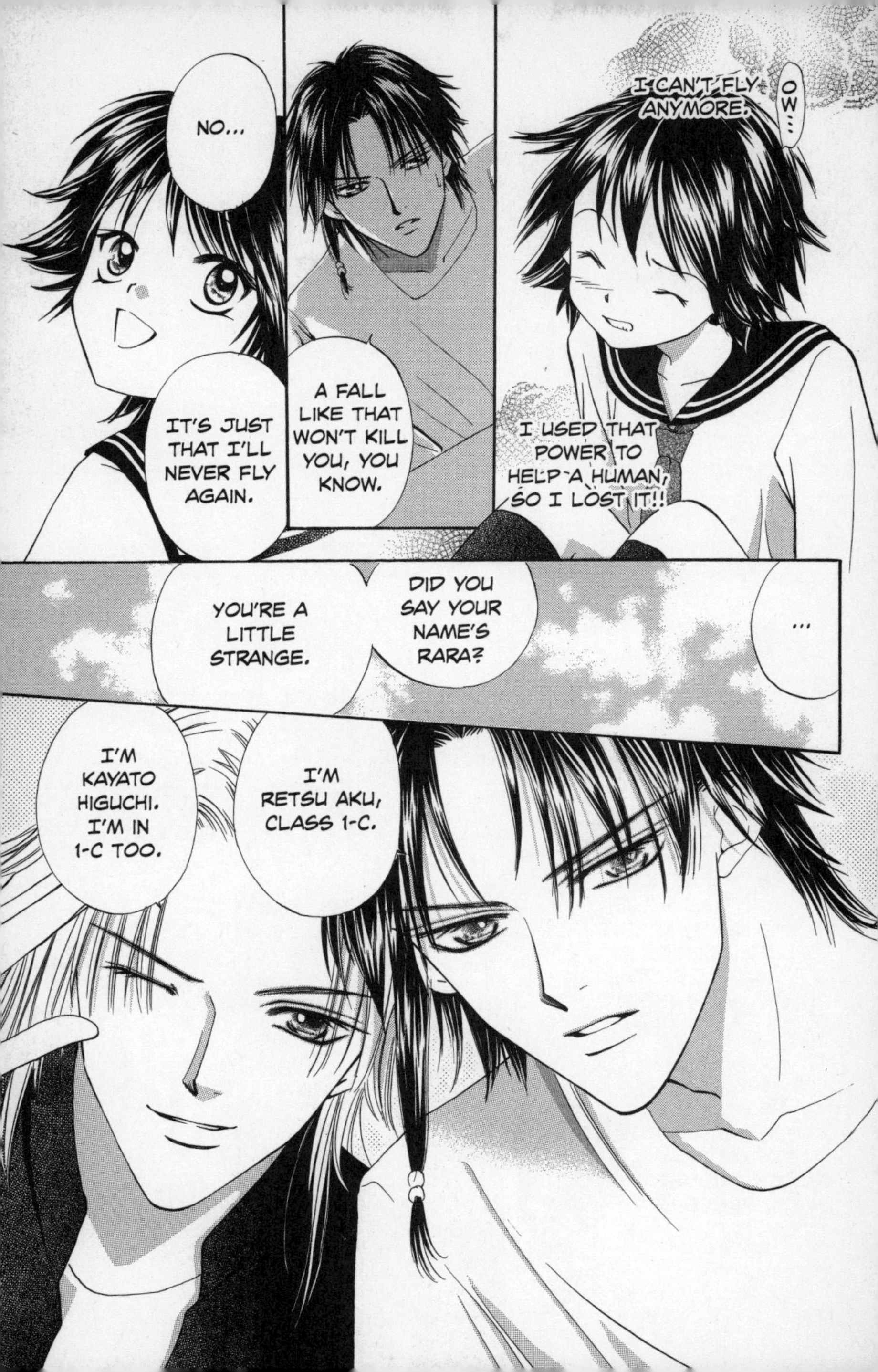
OW...
I CAN'T FLY ANYMORE.
I USED THAT POWER TO HELP A HUMAN, SO I LOST IT!!
A FALL LIKE THAT WON'T KILL YOU, YOU KNOW.
NO...
IT'S JUST THAT I'LL NEVER FLY AGAIN.
...
DID YOU SAY YOUR NAME'S RARA?
YOU'RE A LITTLE STRANGE.
I'M RETSU AKU, CLASS 1-C.
I'M KAYATO HIGUCHI. I'M IN 1-C TOO.

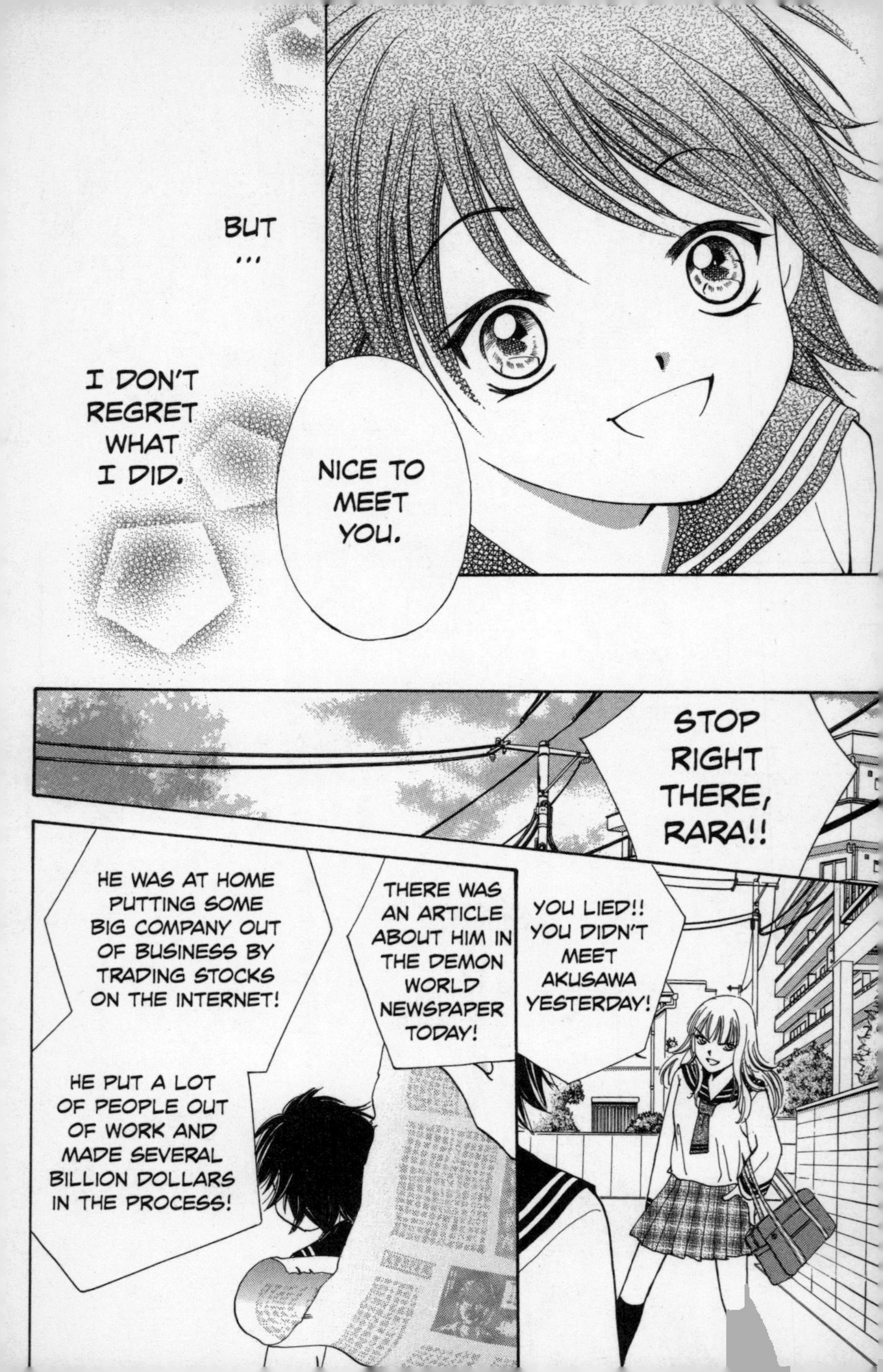
NICE TO MEET YOU.
BUT ...
I DON'T REGRET WHAT I DID.
STOP RIGHT THERE, RARA!!
YOU LIED!! YOU DIDN'T MEET AKUSAWA YESTERDAY!
THERE WAS AN ARTICLE ABOUT HIM IN THE DEMON WORLD NEWSPAPER TODAY!
HE WAS AT HOME PUTTING SOME BIG COMPANY OUT OF BUSINESS BY TRADING STOCKS ON THE INTERNET!
HE PUT A LOT OF PEOPLE OUT OF WORK AND MADE SEVERAL BILLION DOLLARS IN THE PROCESS!

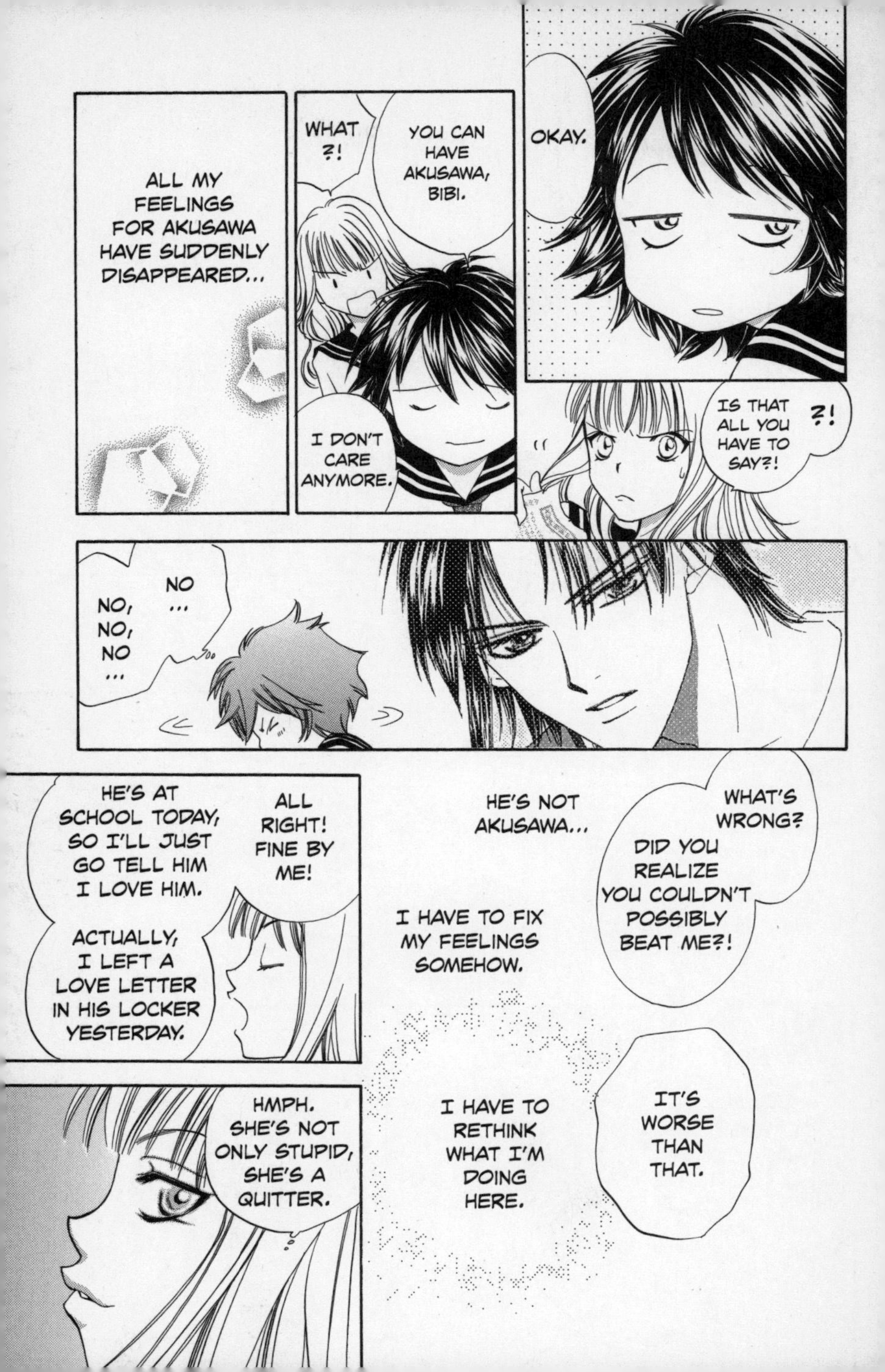
OKAY.
IS THAT ALL YOU HAVE TO SAY?!
?!
YOU CAN HAVE AKUSAWA, BIBI.
WHAT?!
I DON'T CARE ANYMORE.
ALL MY FEELINGS FOR AKUSAWA HAVE SUDDENLY DISAPPEARED...
NO...
NO, NO, NO...
WHAT'S WRONG?
DID YOU REALIZE YOU COULDN'T POSSIBLY BEAT ME?!
HE'S NOT AKUSAWA...
I HAVE TO FIX MY FEELINGS SOMEHOW.
ALL RIGHT! FINE BY ME!
HE'S AT SCHOOL TODAY, SO I'LL JUST GO TELL HIM I LOVE HIM.
ACTUALLY, I LEFT A LOVE LETTER IN HIS LOCKER YESTERDAY.
IT'S WORSE THAN THAT.
I HAVE TO RETHINK WHAT I'M DOING HERE.
HMPH. SHE'S NOT ONLY STUPID, SHE'S A QUITTER.

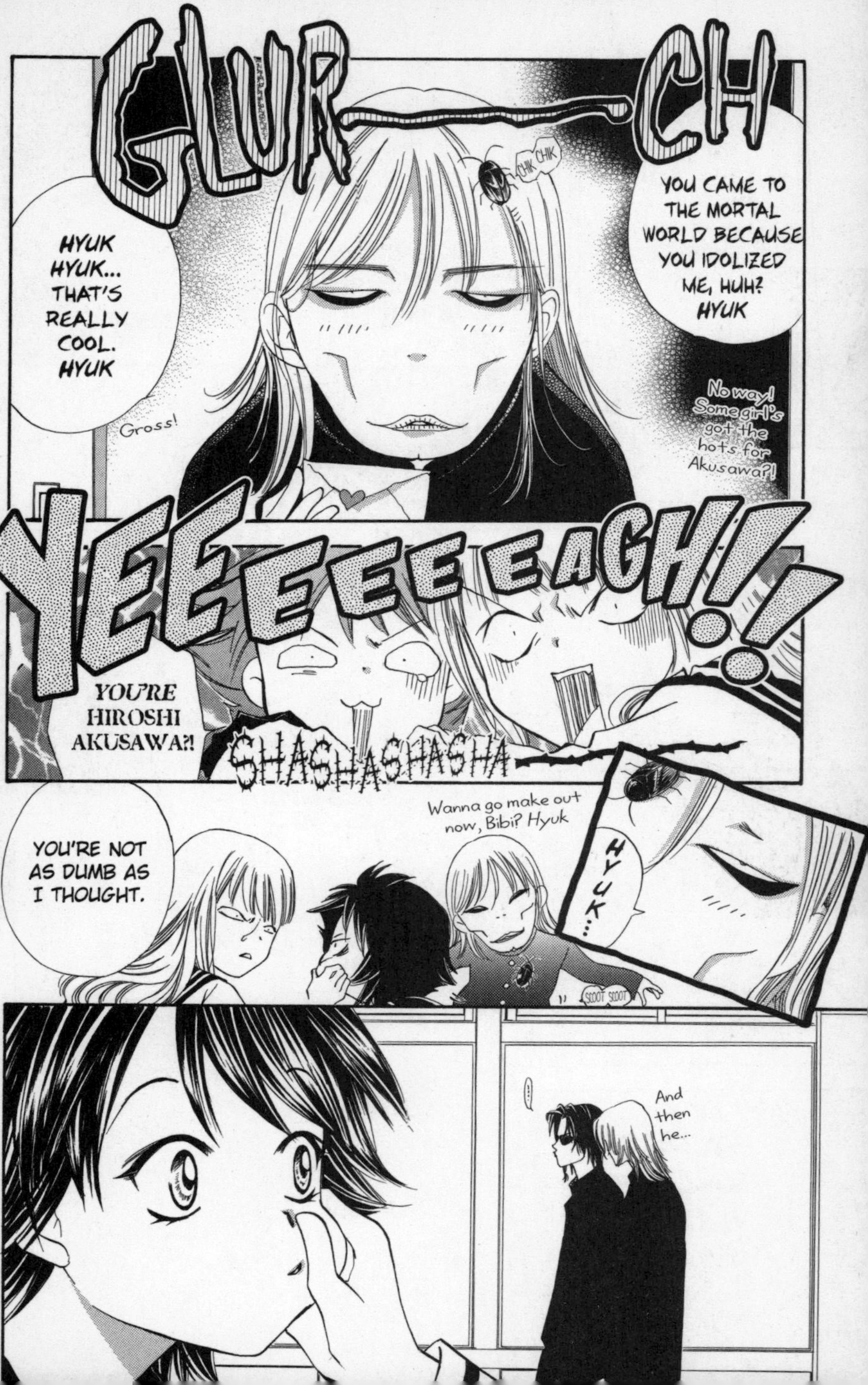
GLUR—CH
CHIK CHIK
YOU CAME TO THE MORTAL WORLD BECAUSE YOU IDOLIZED ME, HUH? HYUK
No way! Some girl's got the hots for Akusawa?!
HYUK HYUK... THAT'S REALLY COOL. HYUK
Gross!
YEEEEE EACH!!
YOU'RE HIROSHI AKUSAWA?!
SHASHASHASHA
HYUK...
Wanna go make out now, Bibi? Hyuk
YOU'RE NOT AS DUMB AS I THOUGHT.
SCOOT SCOOT
...!
And then he...

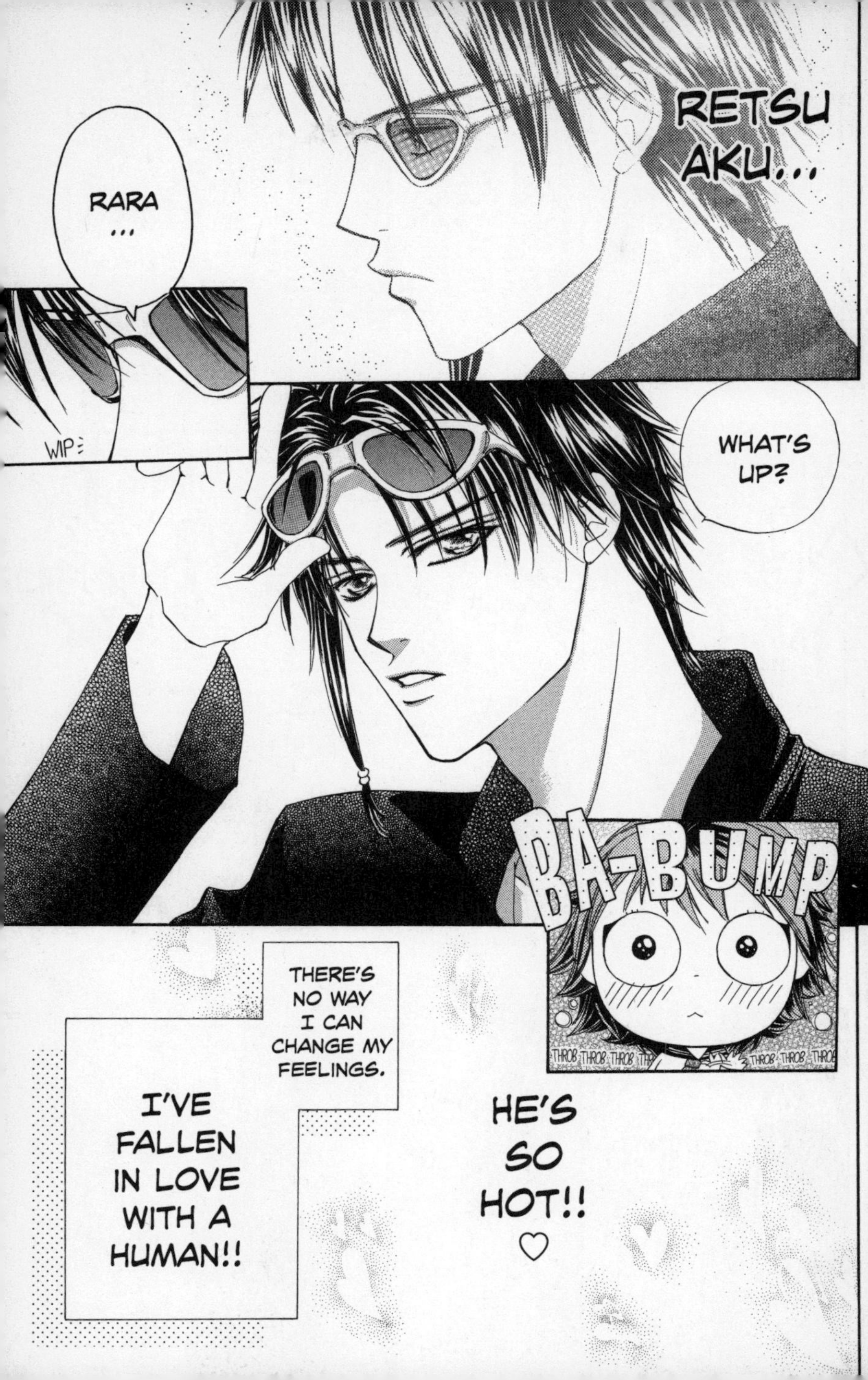
RETSU AKU...
RARA ...
WIP
WHAT'S UP?
BA-BUMP
THROB THROB THROB THROB THROB THROB THROB
HE'S SO HOT!! ♡
THERE'S NO WAY I CAN CHANGE MY FEELINGS.
I'VE FALLEN IN LOVE WITH A HUMAN!!

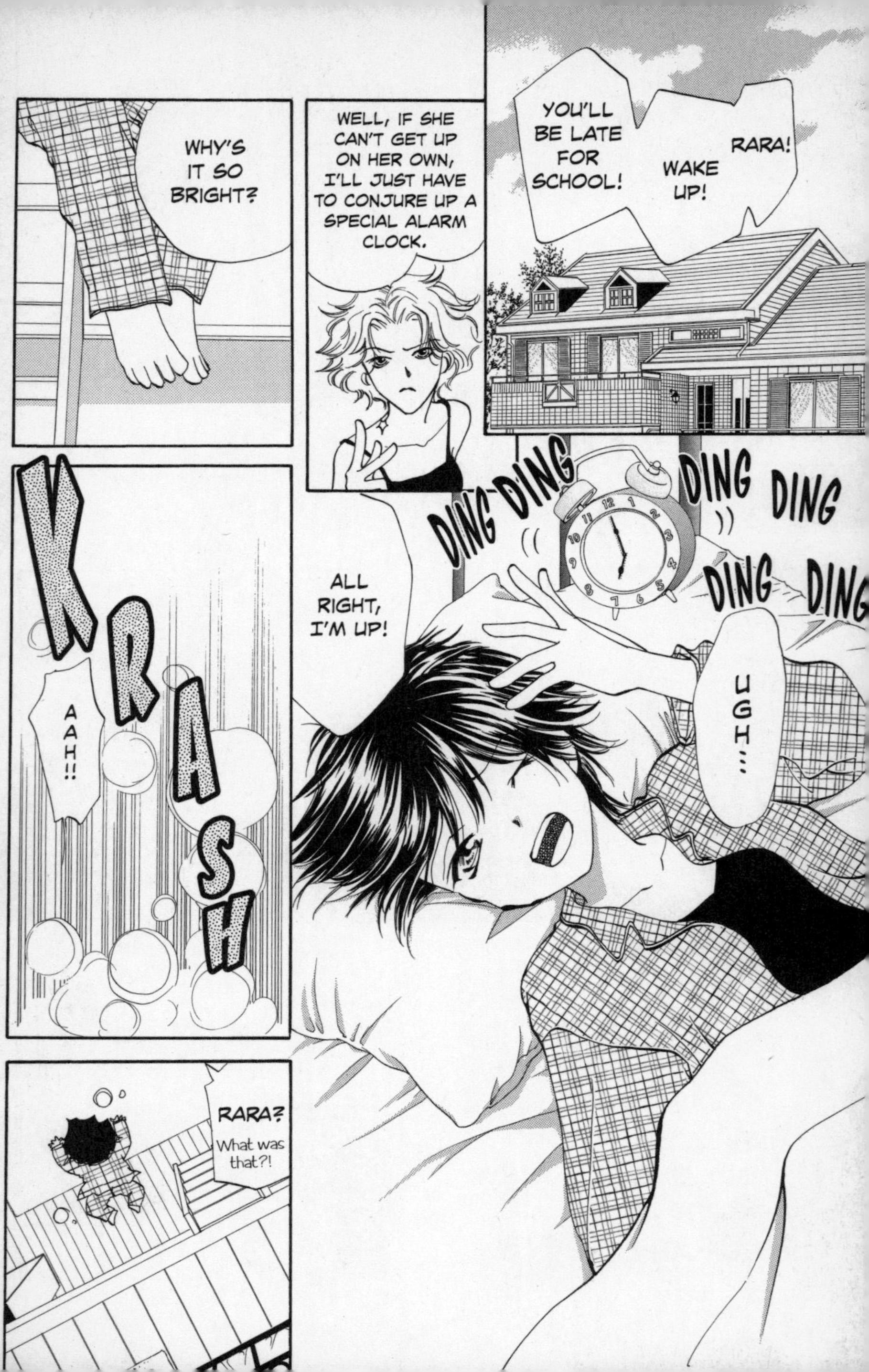
RARA!
WAKE UP!
YOU'LL BE LATE FOR SCHOOL!
WELL, IF SHE CAN'T GET UP ON HER OWN, I'LL JUST HAVE TO CONJURE UP A SPECIAL ALARM CLOCK.
WHY'S IT SO BRIGHT?
DING DING
DING DING
DING DING
UGH...
ALL RIGHT, I'M UP!
KRASH
AAH!!
RARA?
What was that?!

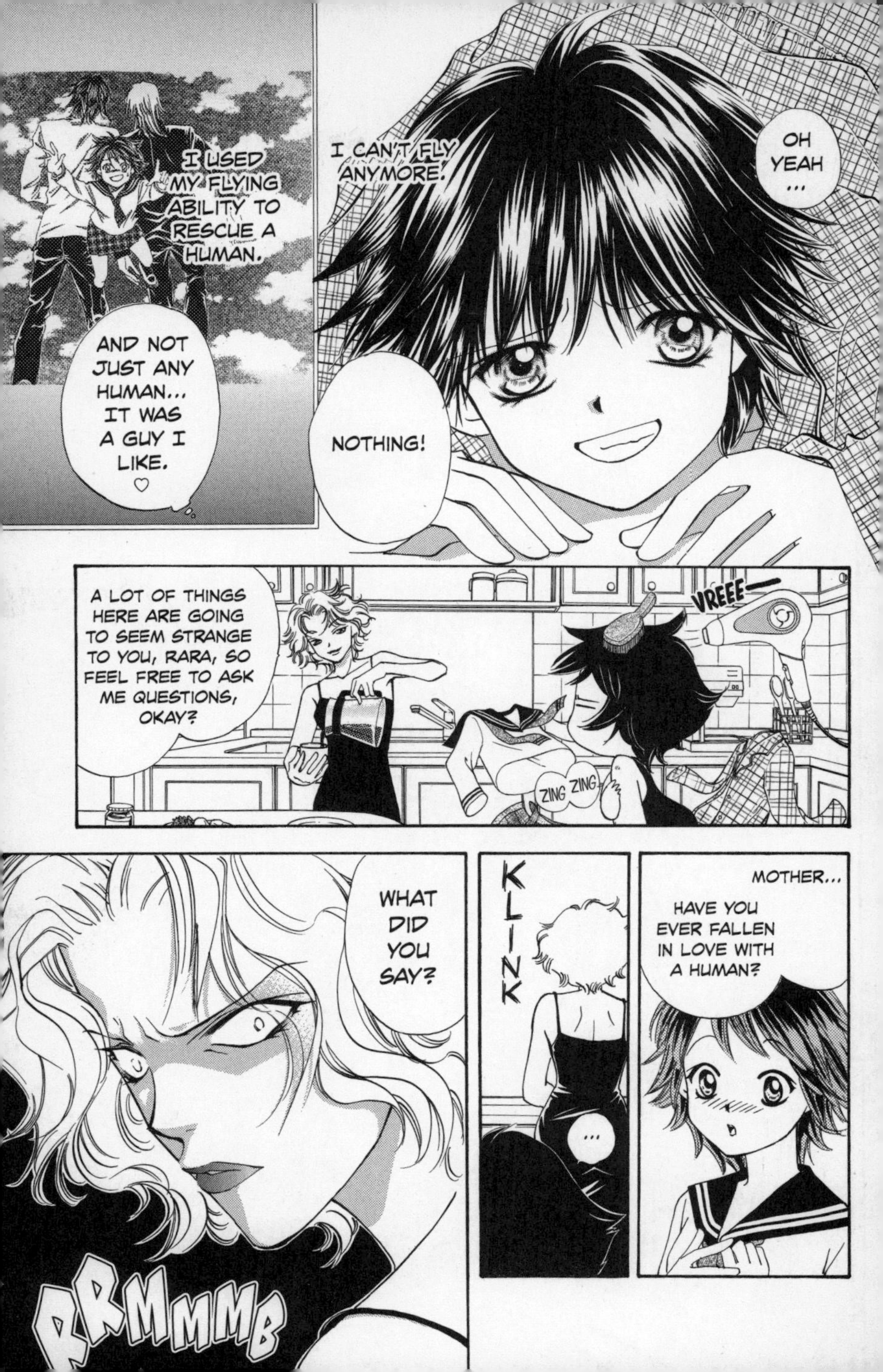
OH YEAH ...
I CAN'T FLY ANYMORE.
NOTHING!
I USED MY FLYING ABILITY TO RESCUE A HUMAN.
AND NOT JUST ANY HUMAN... IT WAS A GUY I LIKE. ♡
VREEE—
A LOT OF THINGS HERE ARE GOING TO SEEM STRANGE TO YOU, RARA, SO FEEL FREE TO ASK ME QUESTIONS, OKAY?
ZING ZING
MOTHER...
HAVE YOU EVER FALLEN IN LOVE WITH A HUMAN?
KLINK
...
WHAT DID YOU SAY?
RRMMMB

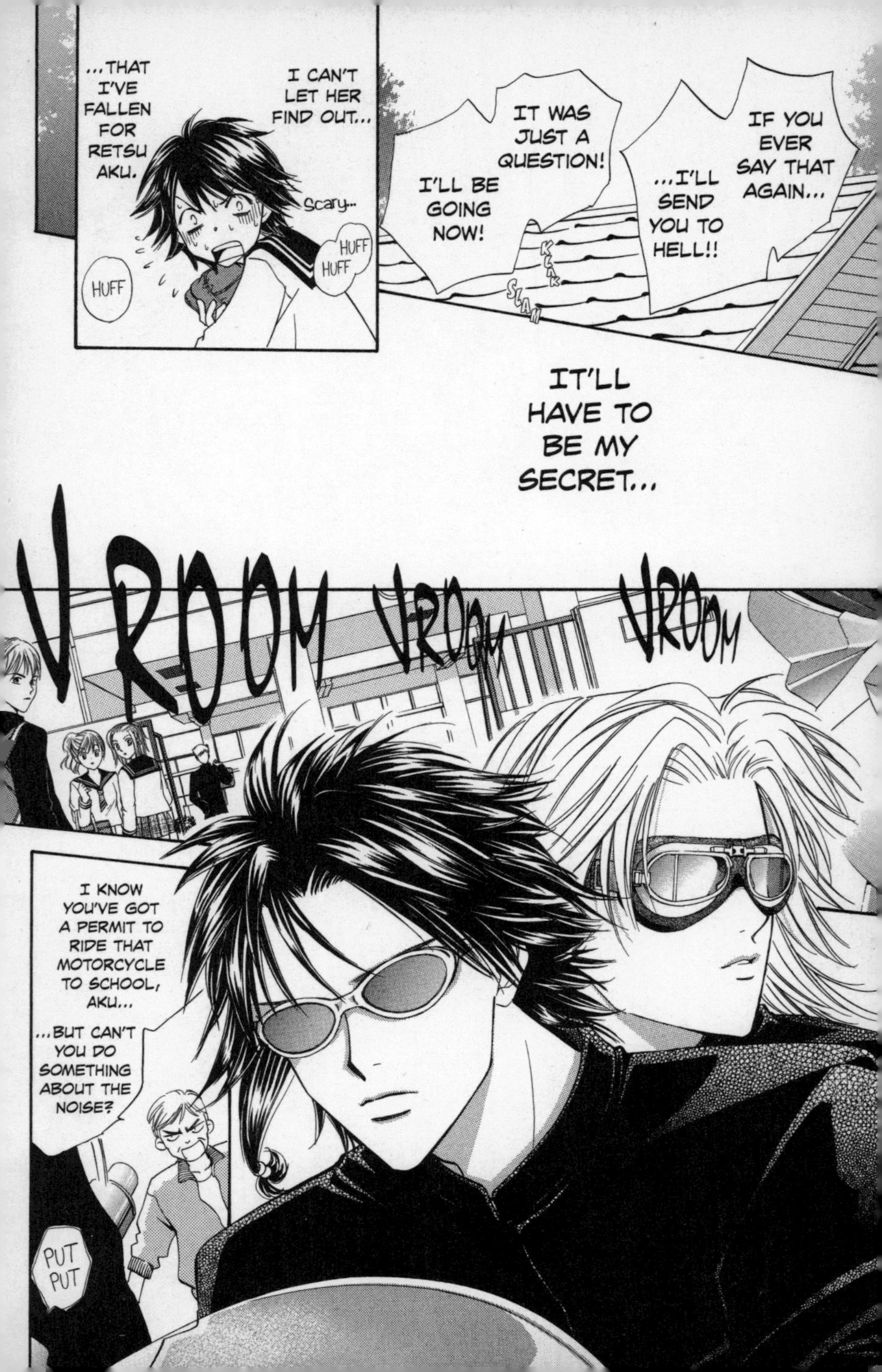
IF YOU EVER SAY THAT AGAIN...
...I'LL SEND YOU TO HELL!!
IT WAS JUST A QUESTION!
I'LL BE GOING NOW!
KLAK
SLAM
I CAN'T LET HER FIND OUT...
...THAT I'VE FALLEN FOR RETSU AKU.
Scary...
HUFF HUFF
HUFF
IT'LL HAVE TO BE MY SECRET...
VROOM VROOM VROOM
I KNOW YOU'VE GOT A PERMIT TO RIDE THAT MOTORCYCLE TO SCHOOL, AKU...
...BUT CAN'T YOU DO SOMETHING ABOUT THE NOISE?
PUT PUT

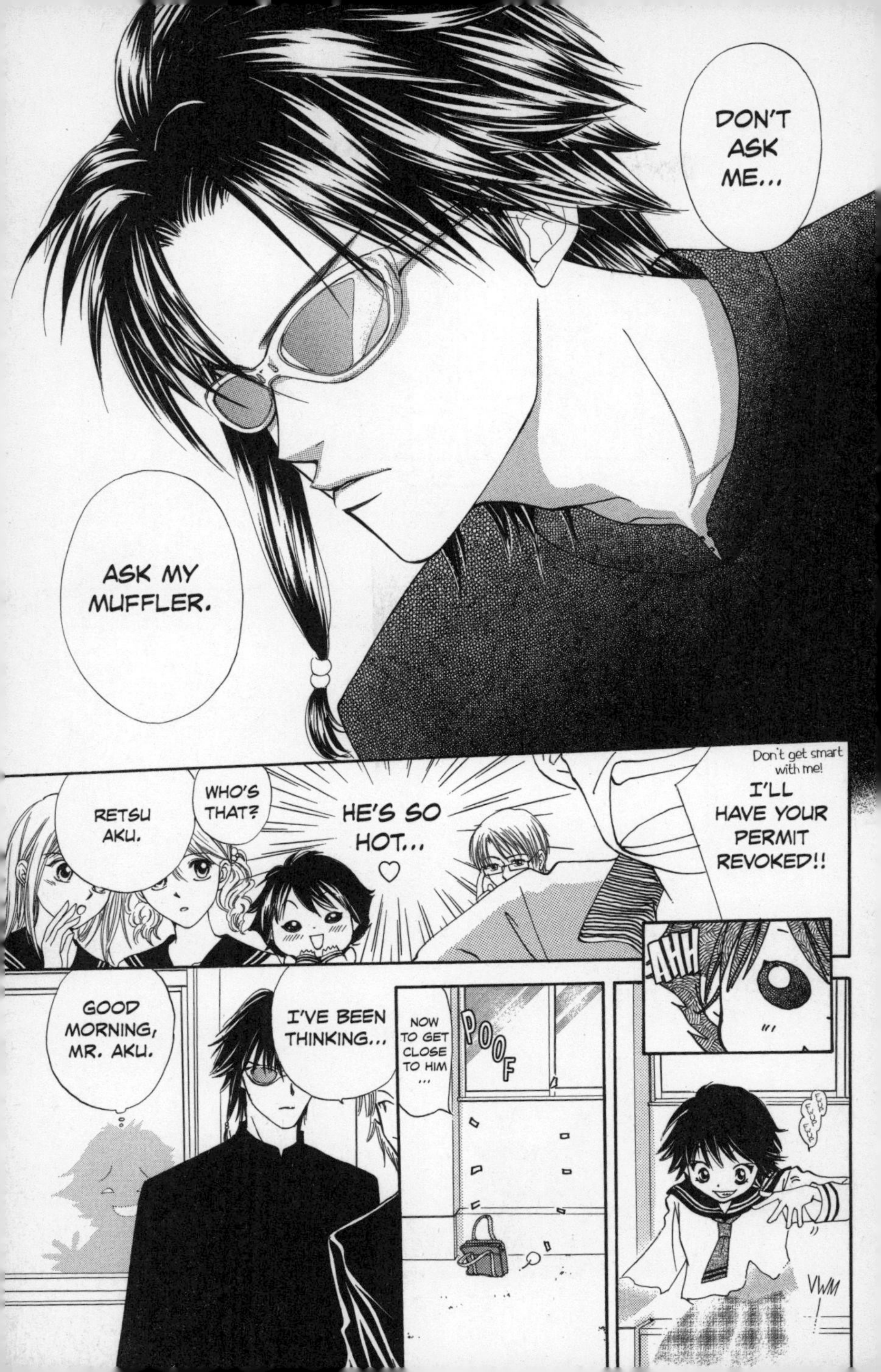
DON'T ASK ME...
ASK MY MUFFLER.
Don't get smart with me!
I'LL HAVE YOUR PERMIT REVOKED!!
HE'S SO HOT...
WHO'S THAT?
RETSU AKU.
AHH
VWM
POOF
NOW TO GET CLOSE TO HIM...
I'VE BEEN THINKING...
GOOD MORNING, MR. AKU.

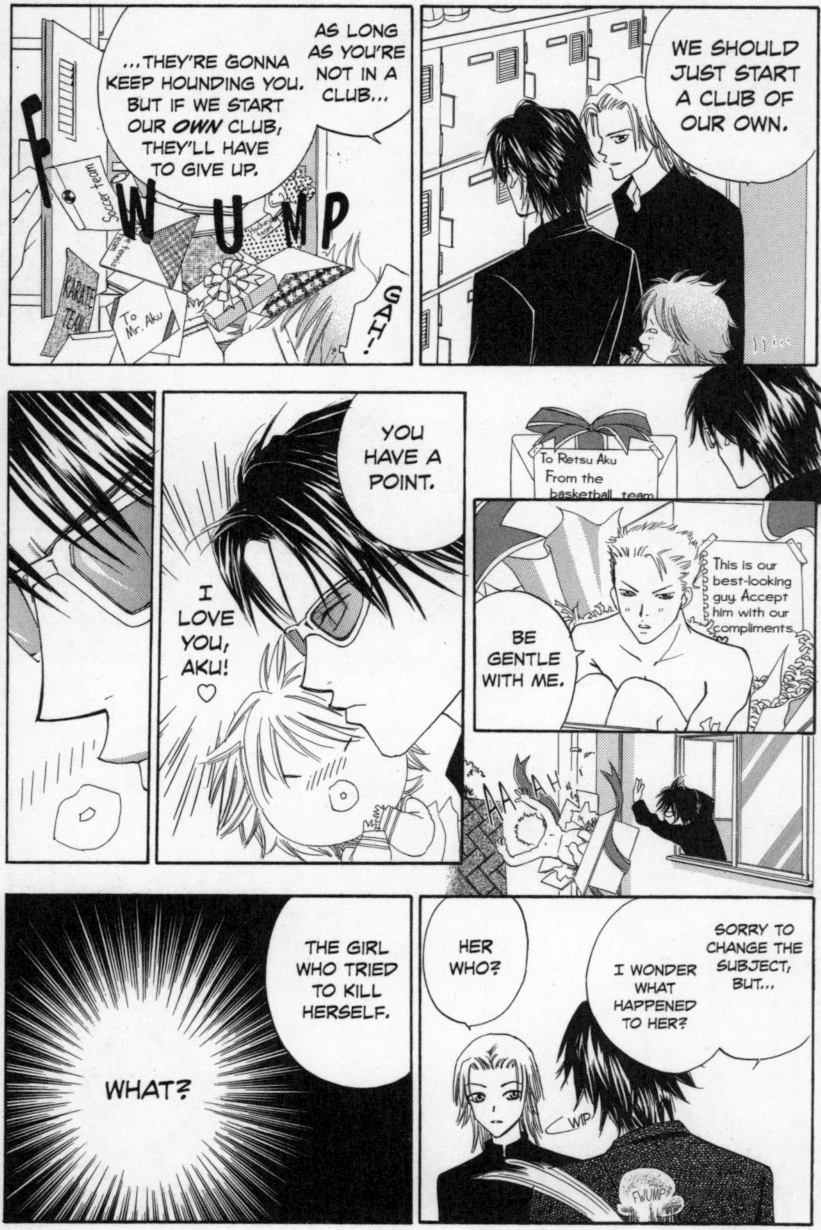
WE SHOULD JUST START A CLUB OF OUR OWN.
AS LONG AS YOU'RE NOT IN A CLUB...
...THEY'RE GONNA KEEP HOUNDING YOU. BUT IF WE START OUR *OWN* CLUB, THEY'LL HAVE TO GIVE UP.
FWUMP
Soccer team
Hockey team
tennis
KARATE TEAM
To Mr. Aku
GAH!
To Retsu Aku From the basketball team
This is our best-looking guy. Accept him with our compliments.
BE GENTLE WITH ME.
AAAAH
YOU HAVE A POINT.
I LOVE YOU, AKU! ♡
SORRY TO CHANGE THE SUBJECT, BUT...
I WONDER WHAT HAPPENED TO HER?
WIP
FWUMP
HER WHO?
THE GIRL WHO TRIED TO KILL HERSELF.
WHAT?

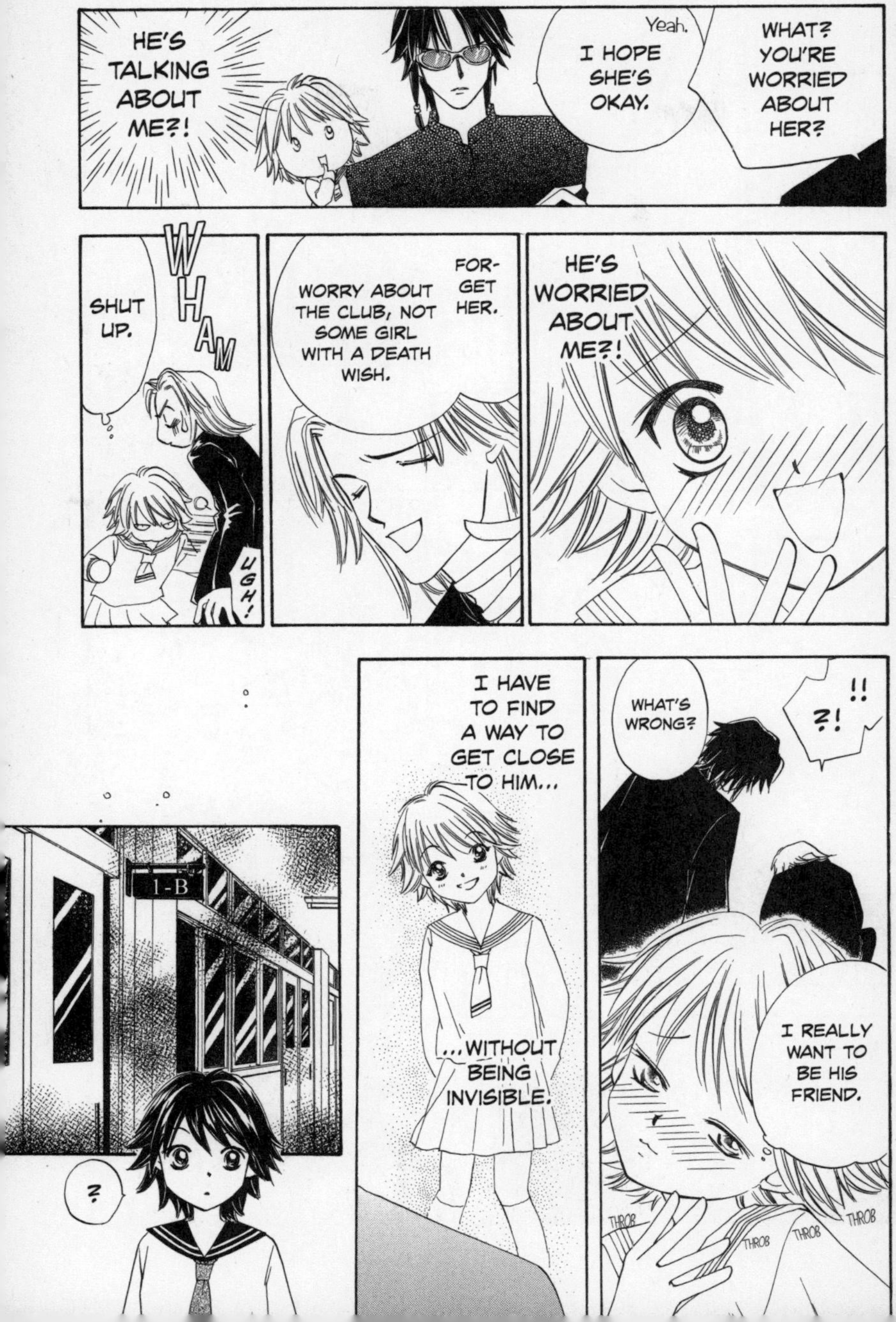
WHAT? YOU'RE WORRIED ABOUT HER?
Yeah. I HOPE SHE'S OKAY.
HE'S TALKING ABOUT ME?!
HE'S WORRIED ABOUT ME?!
FOR-GET HER.
WORRY ABOUT THE CLUB, NOT SOME GIRL WITH A DEATH WISH.
WHAM
SHUT UP.
UGH!
!!
?!
WHAT'S WRONG?
I REALLY WANT TO BE HIS FRIEND.
THROB THROB THROB THROB
I HAVE TO FIND A WAY TO GET CLOSE TO HIM...
...WITHOUT BEING INVISIBLE.
1-B
?

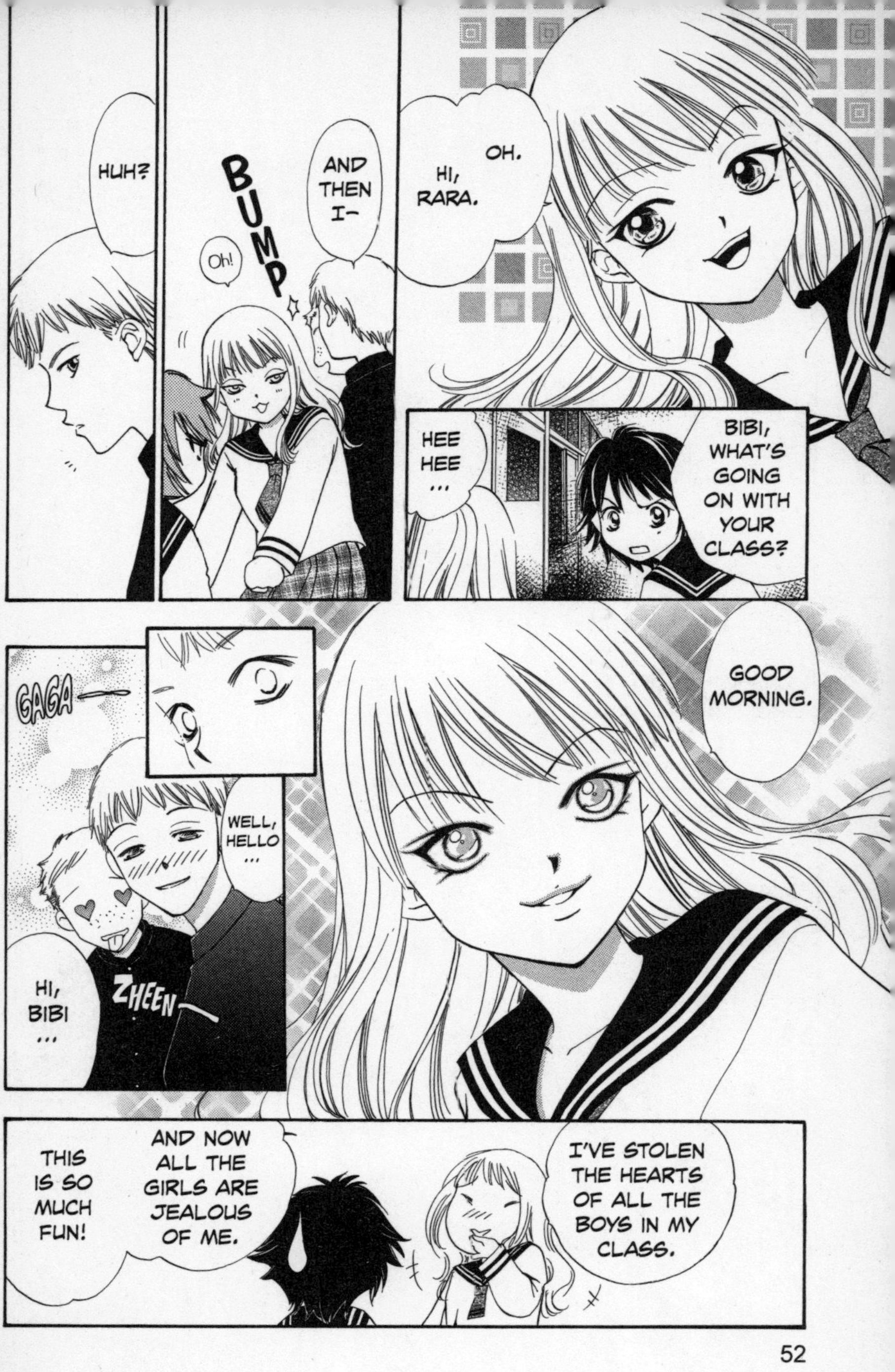
OH.
HI, RARA.
BIBI, WHAT'S GOING ON WITH YOUR CLASS?
HEE HEE ...
AND THEN I-
BUMP
Oh!
HUH?
GOOD MORNING.
GAGA
WELL, HELLO ...
HI, BIBI ...
ZHEEN
I'VE STOLEN THE HEARTS OF ALL THE BOYS IN MY CLASS.
AND NOW ALL THE GIRLS ARE JEALOUS OF ME.
THIS IS SO MUCH FUN!

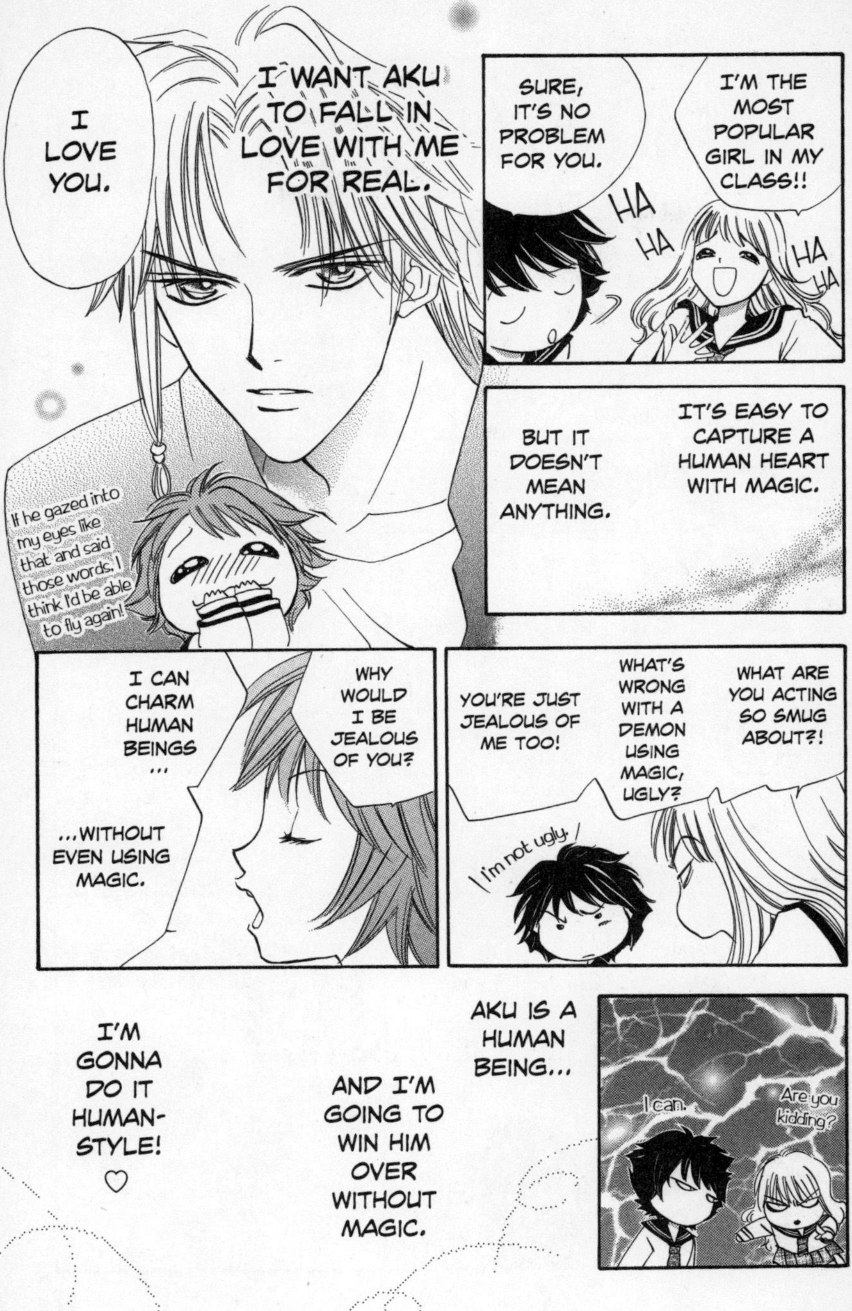
I'M THE MOST POPULAR GIRL IN MY CLASS!!
HA HA HA HA
SURE, IT'S NO PROBLEM FOR YOU.
IT'S EASY TO CAPTURE A HUMAN HEART WITH MAGIC.
BUT IT DOESN'T MEAN ANYTHING.
I WANT AKU TO FALL IN LOVE WITH ME FOR REAL.
I LOVE YOU.
If he gazed into my eyes like that and said those words, I think I'd be able to fly again!
WHAT ARE YOU ACTING SO SMUG ABOUT?!
WHAT'S WRONG WITH A DEMON USING MAGIC, UGLY?
YOU'RE JUST JEALOUS OF ME TOO!
I'm not ugly.
WHY WOULD I BE JEALOUS OF YOU?
I CAN CHARM HUMAN BEINGS...
...WITHOUT EVEN USING MAGIC.
AKU IS A HUMAN BEING...
Are you kidding?
I can.
AND I'M GOING TO WIN HIM OVER WITHOUT MAGIC.
I'M GONNA DO IT HUMAN-STYLE! ♡

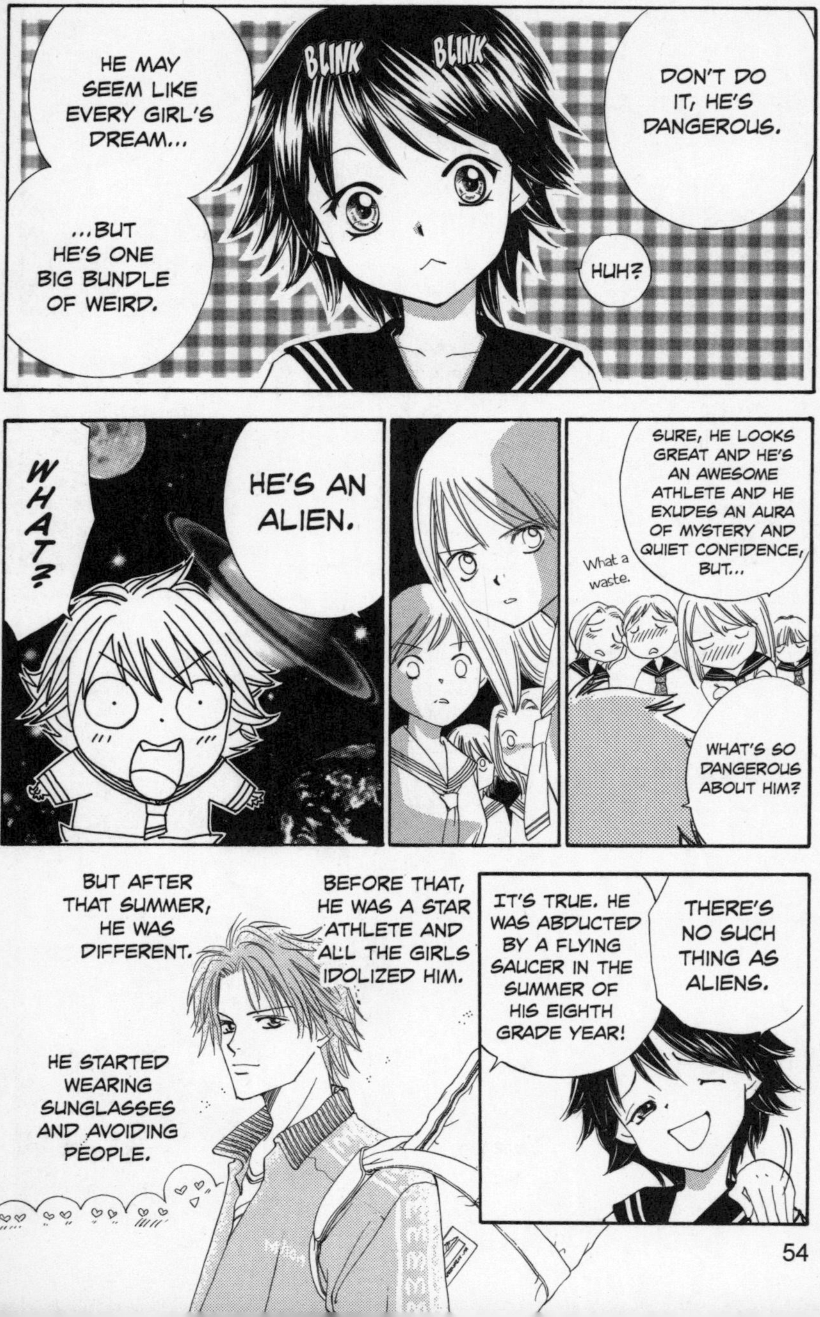
DON'T DO IT, HE'S DANGEROUS.
BLINK
BLINK
HUH?
HE MAY SEEM LIKE EVERY GIRL'S DREAM...
...BUT HE'S ONE BIG BUNDLE OF WEIRD.
SURE, HE LOOKS GREAT AND HE'S AN AWESOME ATHLETE AND HE EXUDES AN AURA OF MYSTERY AND QUIET CONFIDENCE, BUT...
What a waste.
WHAT'S SO DANGEROUS ABOUT HIM?
HE'S AN ALIEN.
WHAT?
THERE'S NO SUCH THING AS ALIENS.
IT'S TRUE. HE WAS ABDUCTED BY A FLYING SAUCER IN THE SUMMER OF HIS EIGHTH GRADE YEAR!
BEFORE THAT, HE WAS A STAR ATHLETE AND ALL THE GIRLS IDOLIZED HIM.
BUT AFTER THAT SUMMER, HE WAS DIFFERENT.
HE STARTED WEARING SUNGLASSES AND AVOIDING PEOPLE.

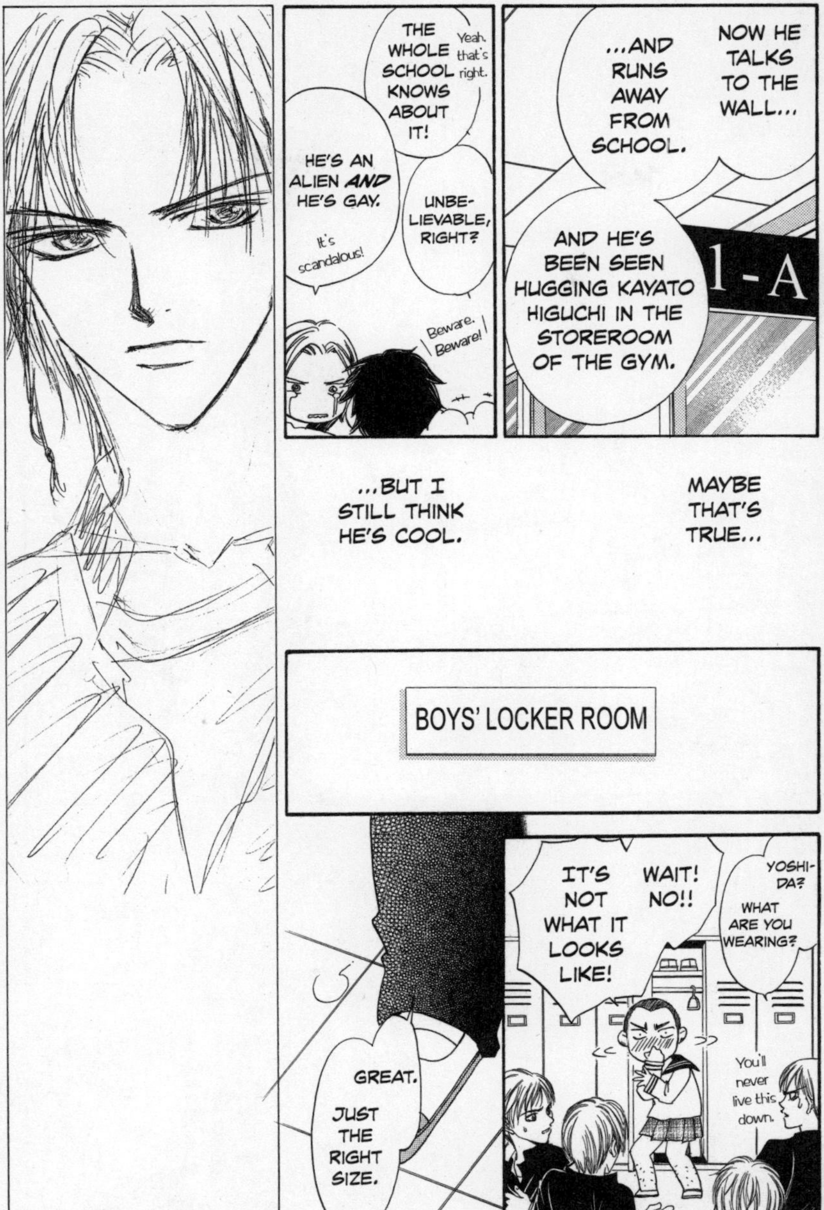
NOW HE TALKS TO THE WALL...
...AND RUNS AWAY FROM SCHOOL.
AND HE'S BEEN SEEN HUGGING KAYATO HIGUCHI IN THE STOREROOM OF THE GYM.
1-A
THE WHOLE SCHOOL KNOWS ABOUT IT!
Yeah, that's right.
HE'S AN ALIEN AND HE'S GAY.
UNBE-LIEVABLE, RIGHT?
It's scandalous!
Beware. Beware!
MAYBE THAT'S TRUE...
...BUT I STILL THINK HE'S COOL.
BOYS' LOCKER ROOM
YOSHI-DA? WHAT ARE YOU WEARING?
WAIT! NO!!
IT'S NOT WHAT IT LOOKS LIKE!
You'll never live this down.
GREAT.
JUST THE RIGHT SIZE.

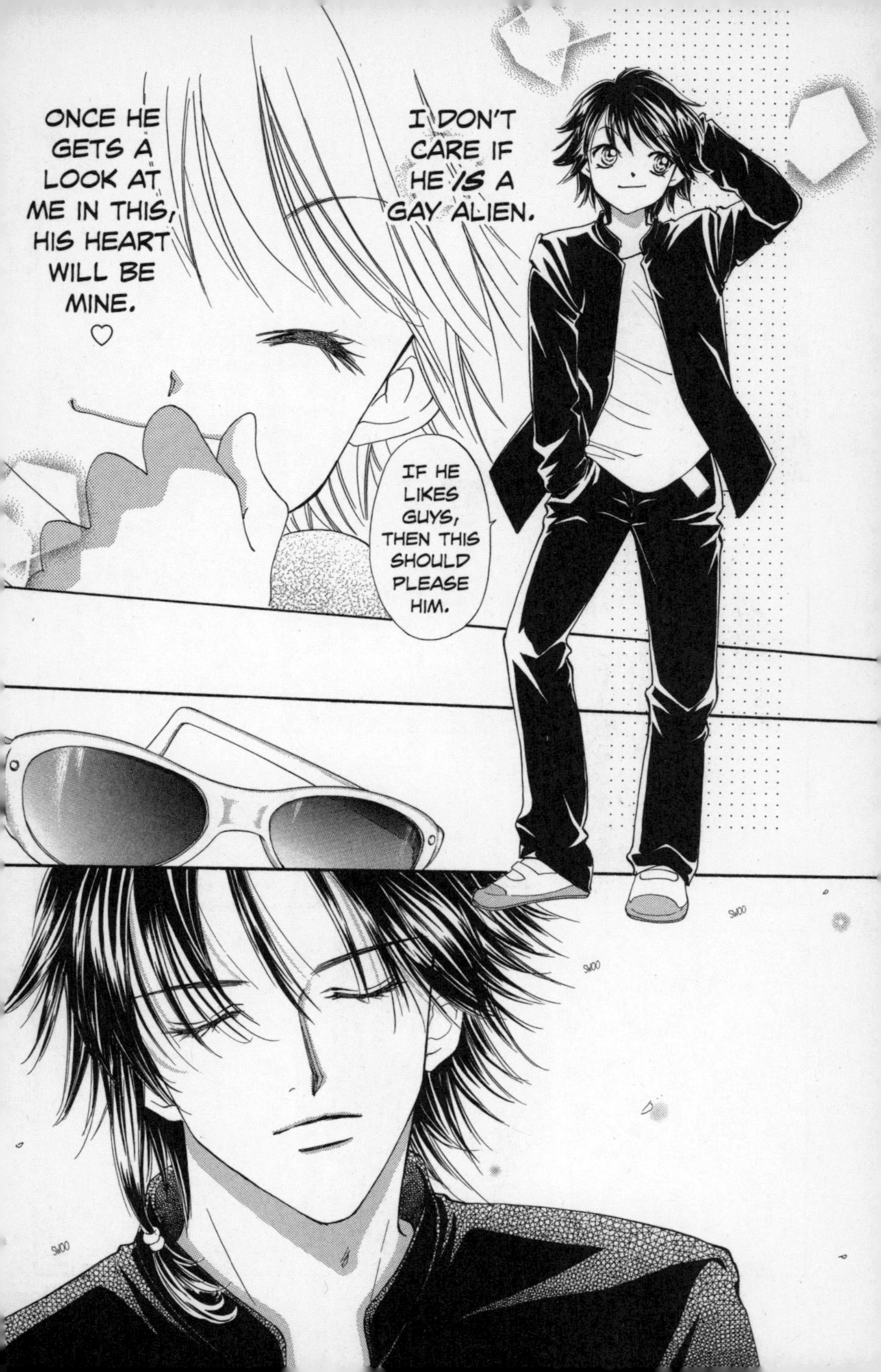
I DON'T CARE IF HE *IS* A GAY ALIEN.
ONCE HE GETS A LOOK AT ME IN THIS, HIS HEART WILL BE MINE. ♡
IF HE LIKES GUYS, THEN THIS SHOULD PLEASE HIM.
SWOO
SWOO
SWOO

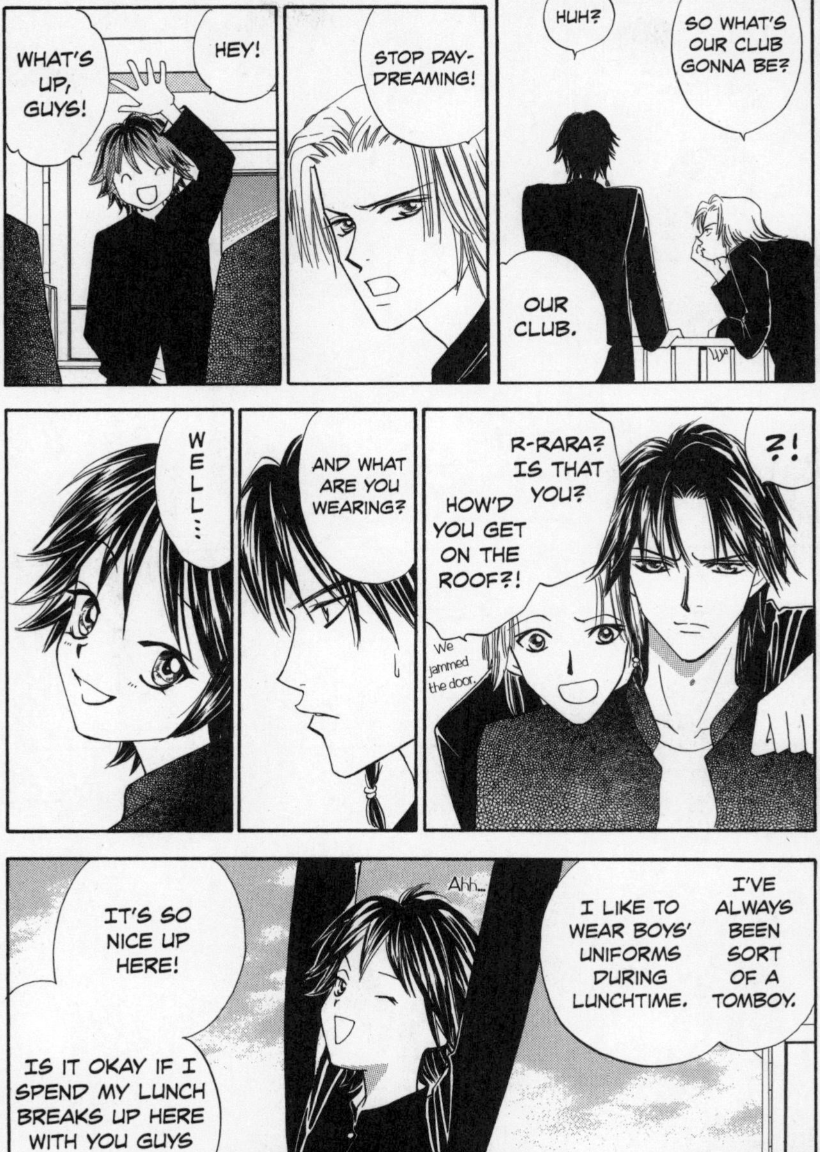
SO WHAT'S OUR CLUB GONNA BE?
HUH?
OUR CLUB.
STOP DAY-DREAMING!
HEY!
WHAT'S UP, GUYS!
?!
R-RARA? IS THAT YOU?
HOW'D YOU GET ON THE ROOF?!
We jammed the door.
AND WHAT ARE YOU WEARING?
WELL...
I'VE ALWAYS BEEN SORT OF A TOMBOY.
I LIKE TO WEAR BOYS' UNIFORMS DURING LUNCHTIME.
Ahh...
IT'S SO NICE UP HERE!
IS IT OKAY IF I SPEND MY LUNCH BREAKS UP HERE WITH YOU GUYS FROM NOW ON?

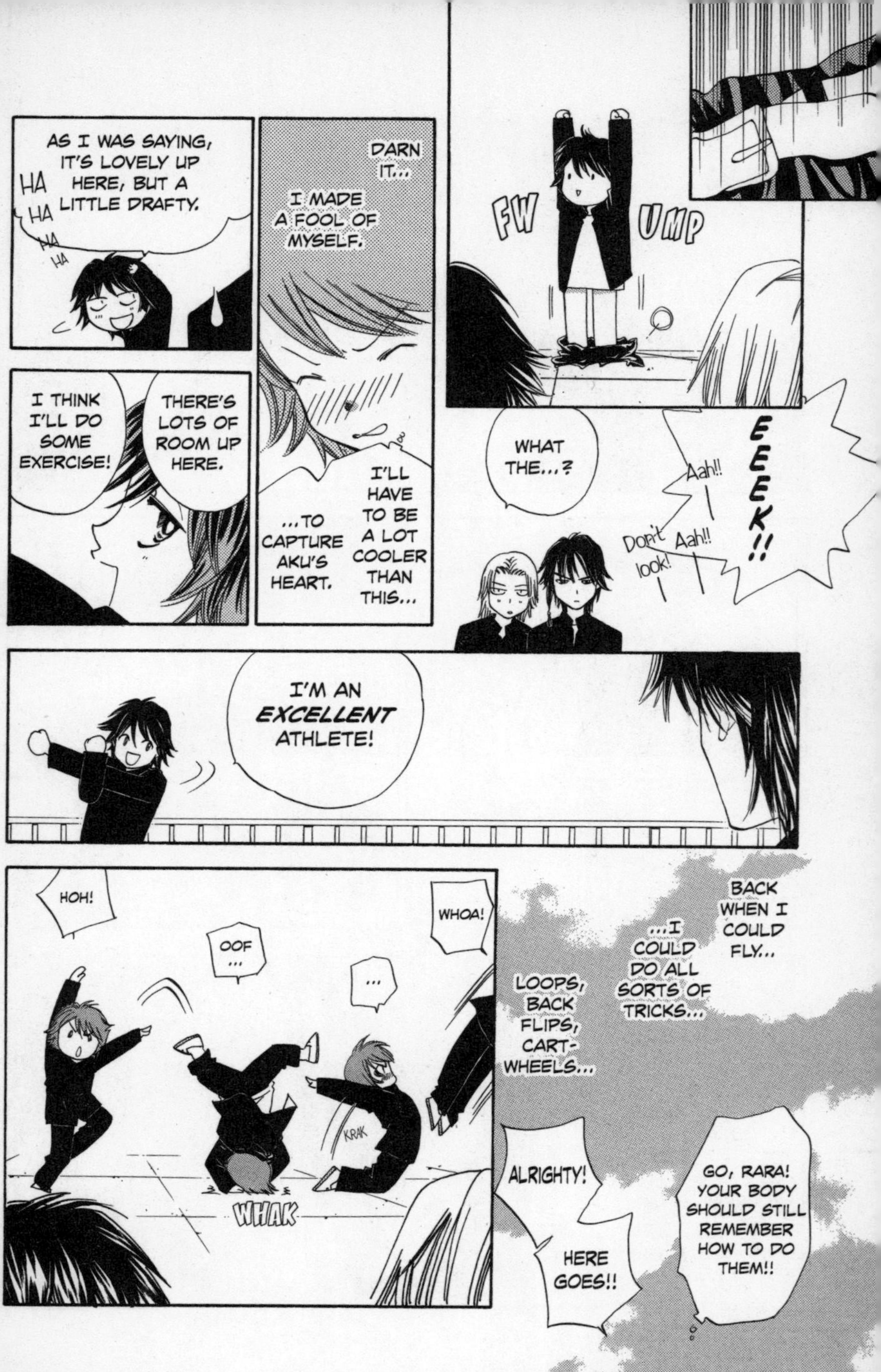
FW
UMP
WHAT THE...?
EEEK!!
Aah!!
Aah!!
Don't look!
DARN IT...
I MADE A FOOL OF MYSELF.
I'LL HAVE TO BE A LOT COOLER THAN THIS...
...TO CAPTURE AKU'S HEART.
AS I WAS SAYING, IT'S LOVELY UP HERE, BUT A LITTLE DRAFTY.
HA HA HA HA
THERE'S LOTS OF ROOM UP HERE.
I THINK I'LL DO SOME EXERCISE!
I'M AN EXCELLENT ATHLETE!
BACK WHEN I COULD FLY...
...I COULD DO ALL SORTS OF TRICKS...
LOOPS, BACK FLIPS, CART-WHEELS...
GO, RARA! YOUR BODY SHOULD STILL REMEMBER HOW TO DO THEM!!
ALRIGHTY!
HERE GOES!!
WHOA!
...
OOF...
HOH!
KRAK
WHAK

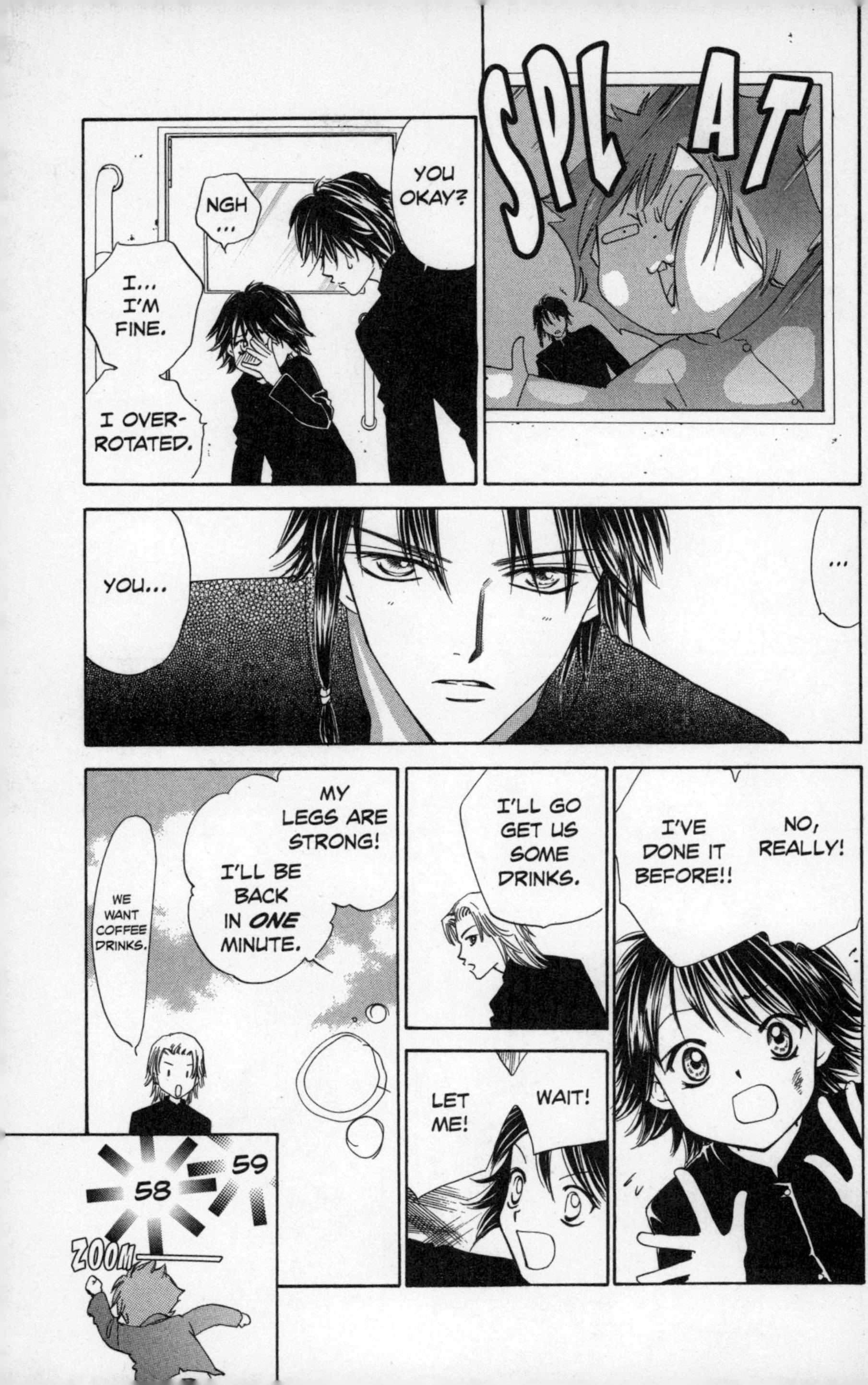
SPLAT
YOU OKAY?
NGH ...
I... I'M FINE.
I OVER-ROTATED.
...
YOU...
NO, REALLY!
I'VE DONE IT BEFORE!!
I'LL GO GET US SOME DRINKS.
WAIT!
LET ME!
MY LEGS ARE STRONG!
I'LL BE BACK IN ONE MINUTE.
WE WANT COFFEE DRINKS.
59
58
ZOOM

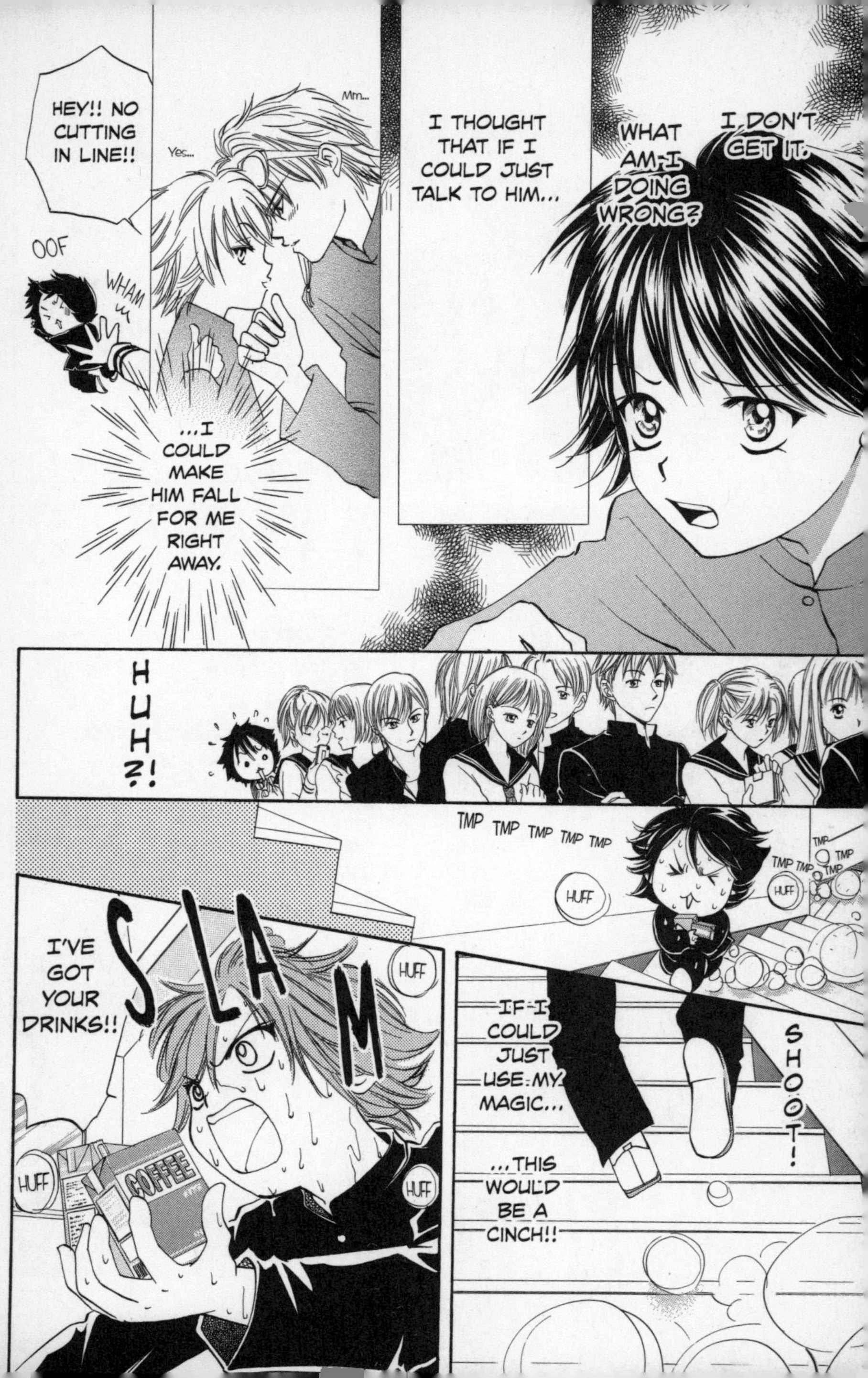
I DON'T GET IT.
WHAT AM I DOING WRONG?
I THOUGHT THAT IF I COULD JUST TALK TO HIM...
Mm...
Yes...
...I COULD MAKE HIM FALL FOR ME RIGHT AWAY.
HEY!! NO CUTTING IN LINE!!
OOF
WHAM
HUH?!
TMP TMP TMP TMP TMP
TMP TMP TMP TMP TMP
HUFF
HUFF
SHOOT!
IF I COULD JUST USE MY MAGIC...
...THIS WOULD BE A CINCH!!
SLAM
HUFF
I'VE GOT YOUR DRINKS!!
HUFF
HUFF
COFFEE

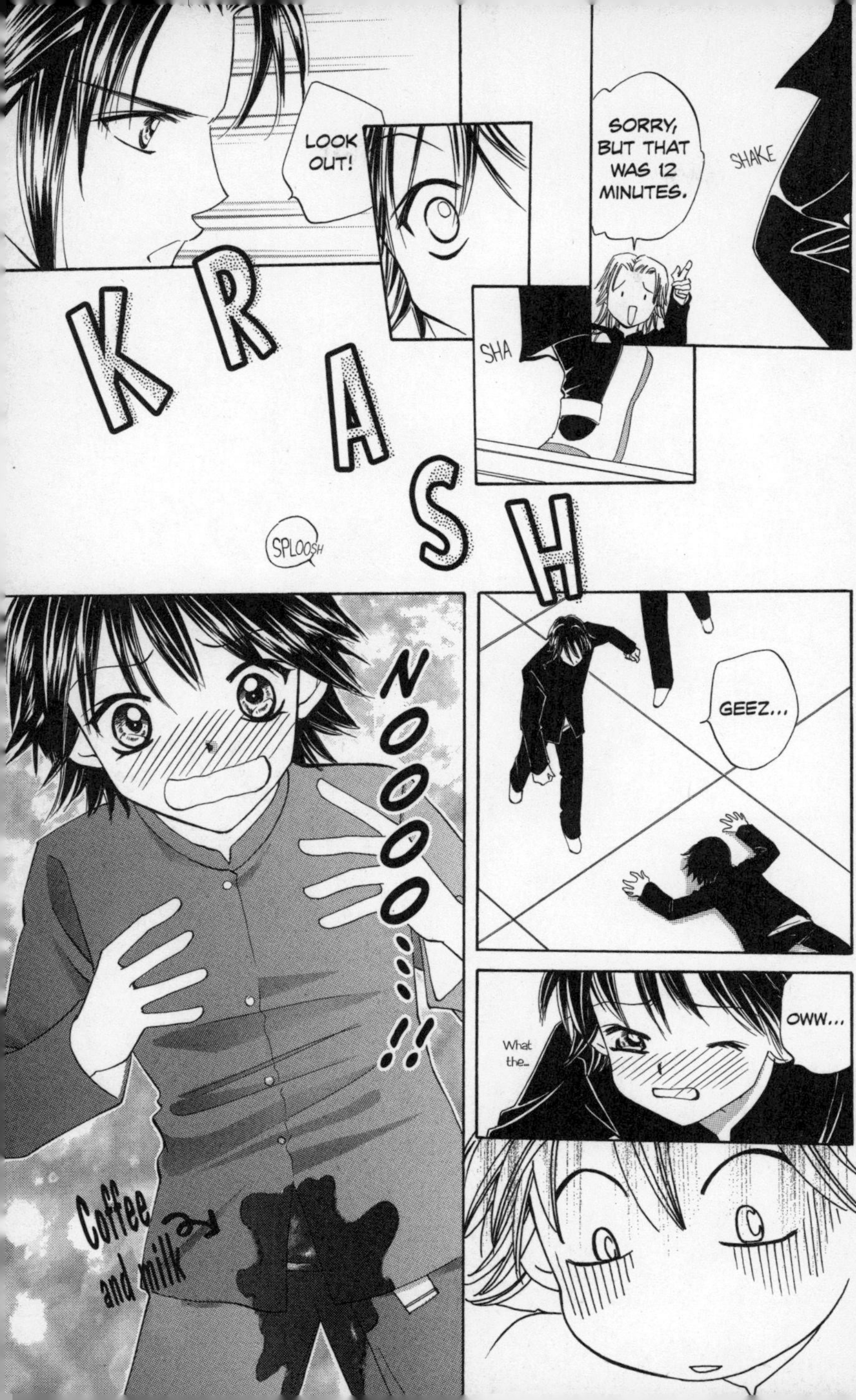
SHAKE
SORRY, BUT THAT WAS 12 MINUTES.
SHA
LOOK OUT!
KRASH
SPLOOSH
GEEZ...
OWW...
What the...
NOOOO...!!
Coffee and milk

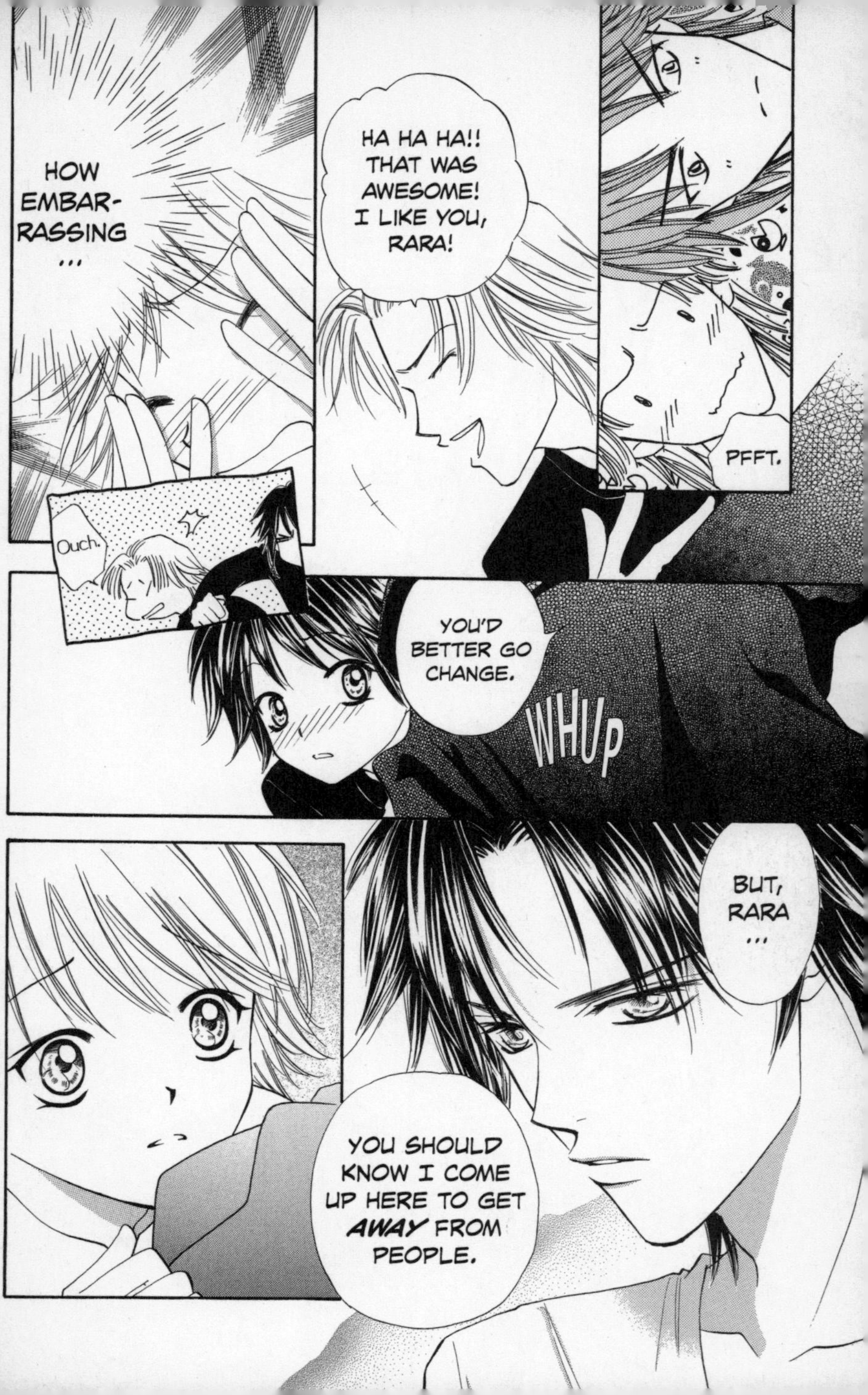
PFFT.
HA HA HA!! THAT WAS AWESOME! I LIKE YOU, RARA!
HOW EMBAR-RASSING ...
Ouch.
YOU'D BETTER GO CHANGE.
WHUP
BUT, RARA ...
YOU SHOULD KNOW I COME UP HERE TO GET *AWAY* FROM PEOPLE.

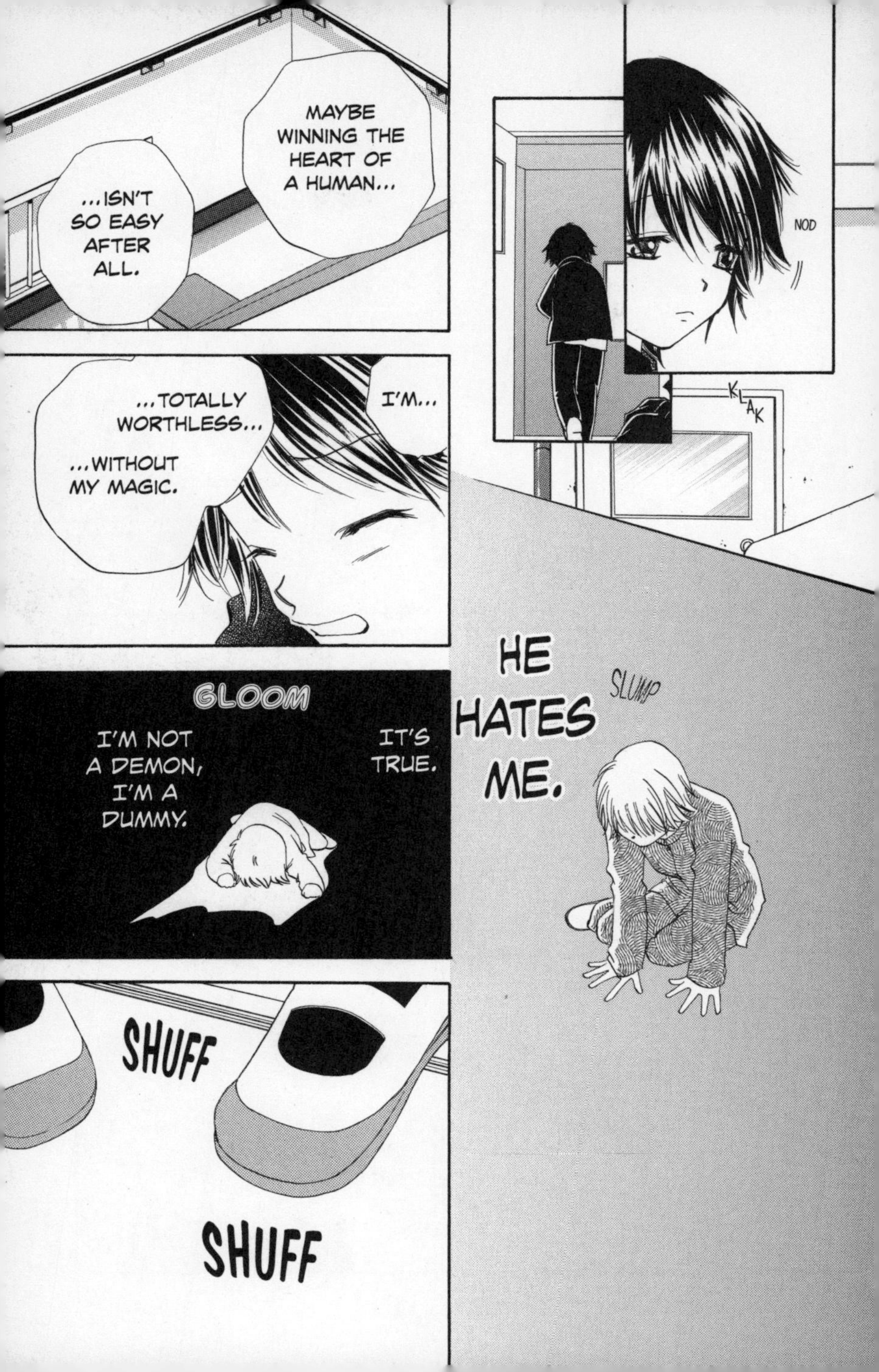
NOD
KLAK
MAYBE WINNING THE HEART OF A HUMAN...
...ISN'T SO EASY AFTER ALL.
HE HATES ME.
SLUMP
I'M...
...TOTALLY WORTHLESS...
...WITHOUT MY MAGIC.
GLOOM
IT'S TRUE.
I'M NOT A DEMON, I'M A DUMMY.
SHUFF
SHUFF

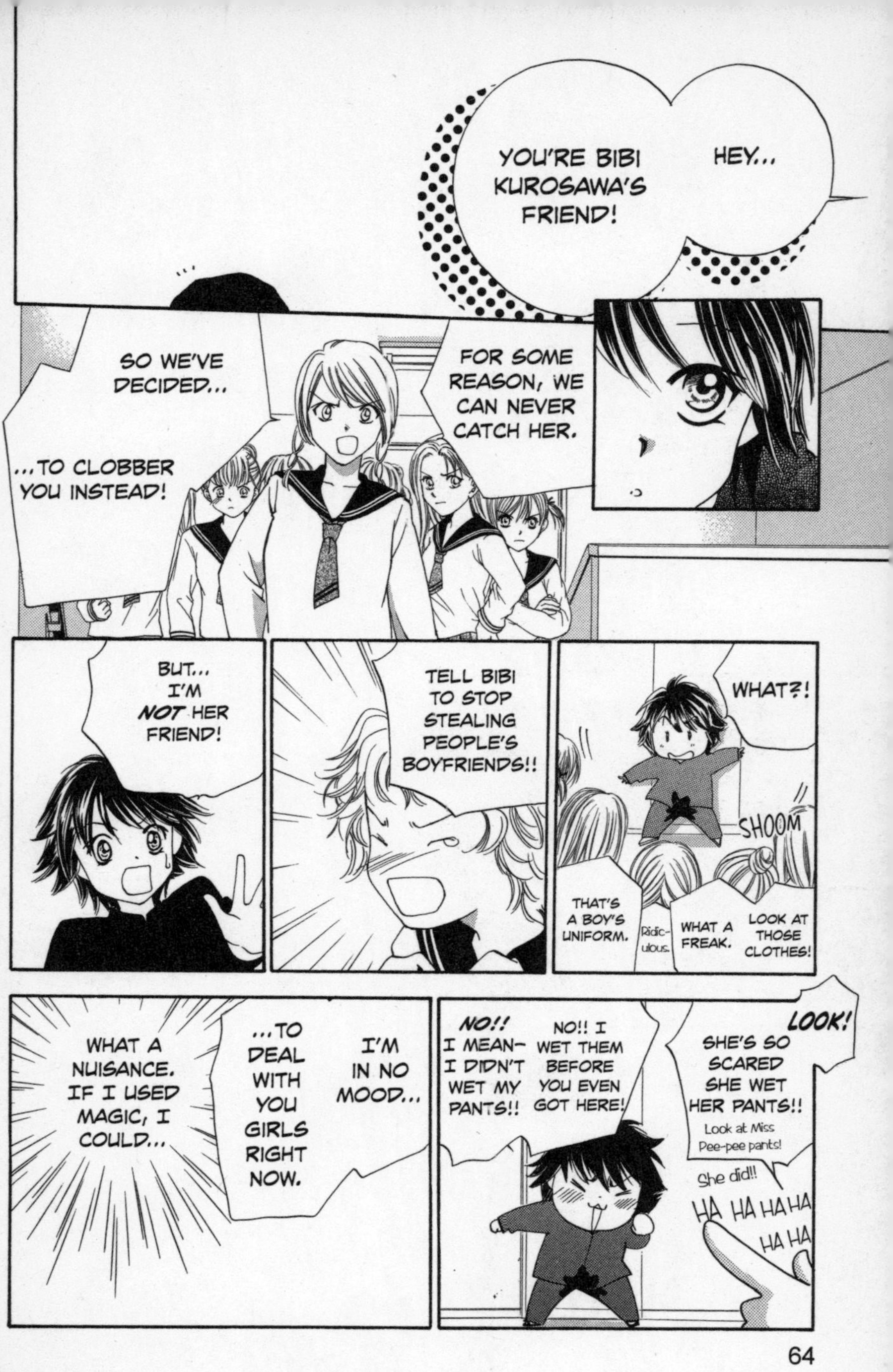
HEY...
YOU'RE BIBI KUROSAWA'S FRIEND!
FOR SOME REASON, WE CAN NEVER CATCH HER.
SO WE'VE DECIDED...
...TO CLOBBER YOU INSTEAD!
WHAT?!
SHOOM
LOOK AT THOSE CLOTHES!
WHAT A FREAK.
Ridic-ulous.
THAT'S A BOY'S UNIFORM.
TELL BIBI TO STOP STEALING PEOPLE'S BOYFRIENDS!!
BUT... I'M *NOT* HER FRIEND!
LOOK!
SHE'S SO SCARED SHE WET HER PANTS!!
Look at Miss Pee-pee pants!
She did!!
HA HA HA HA HA HA
NO!! I WET THEM BEFORE YOU EVEN GOT HERE!
NO!! I MEAN— I DIDN'T WET MY PANTS!!
I'M IN NO MOOD...
...TO DEAL WITH YOU GIRLS RIGHT NOW.
WHAT A NUISANCE. IF I USED MAGIC, I COULD...

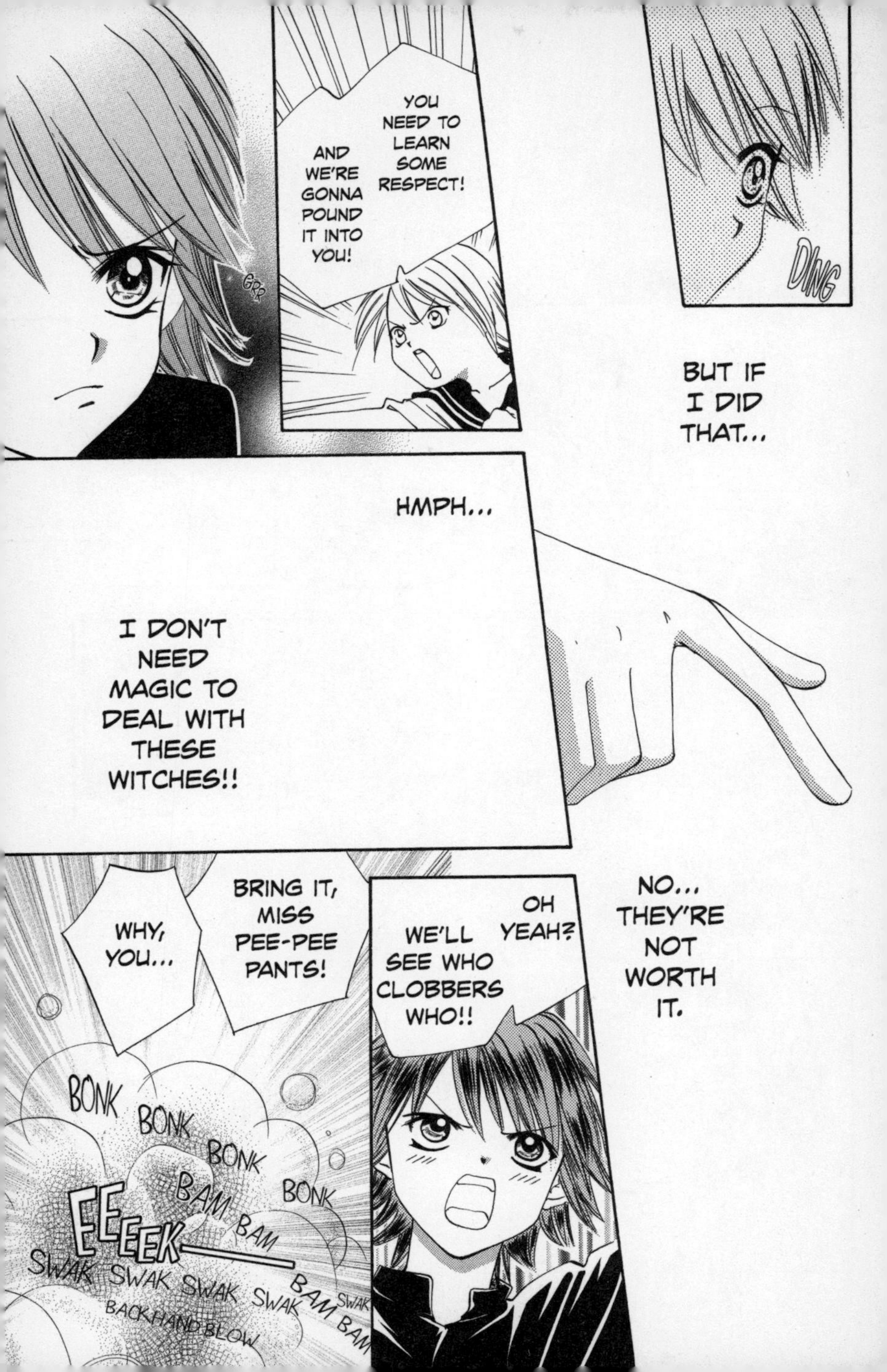
DING
YOU NEED TO LEARN SOME RESPECT!
AND WE'RE GONNA POUND IT INTO YOU!
GRR
BUT IF I DID THAT...
HMPH...
I DON'T NEED MAGIC TO DEAL WITH THESE WITCHES!!
NO... THEY'RE NOT WORTH IT.
OH YEAH?
WE'LL SEE WHO CLOBBERS WHO!!
BRING IT, MISS PEE-PEE PANTS!
WHY, YOU...
BONK BONK BONK BONK
BAM BAM BAM BAM
EEEEEK
SWAK SWAK SWAK SWAK SWAK
BACKHAND BLOW

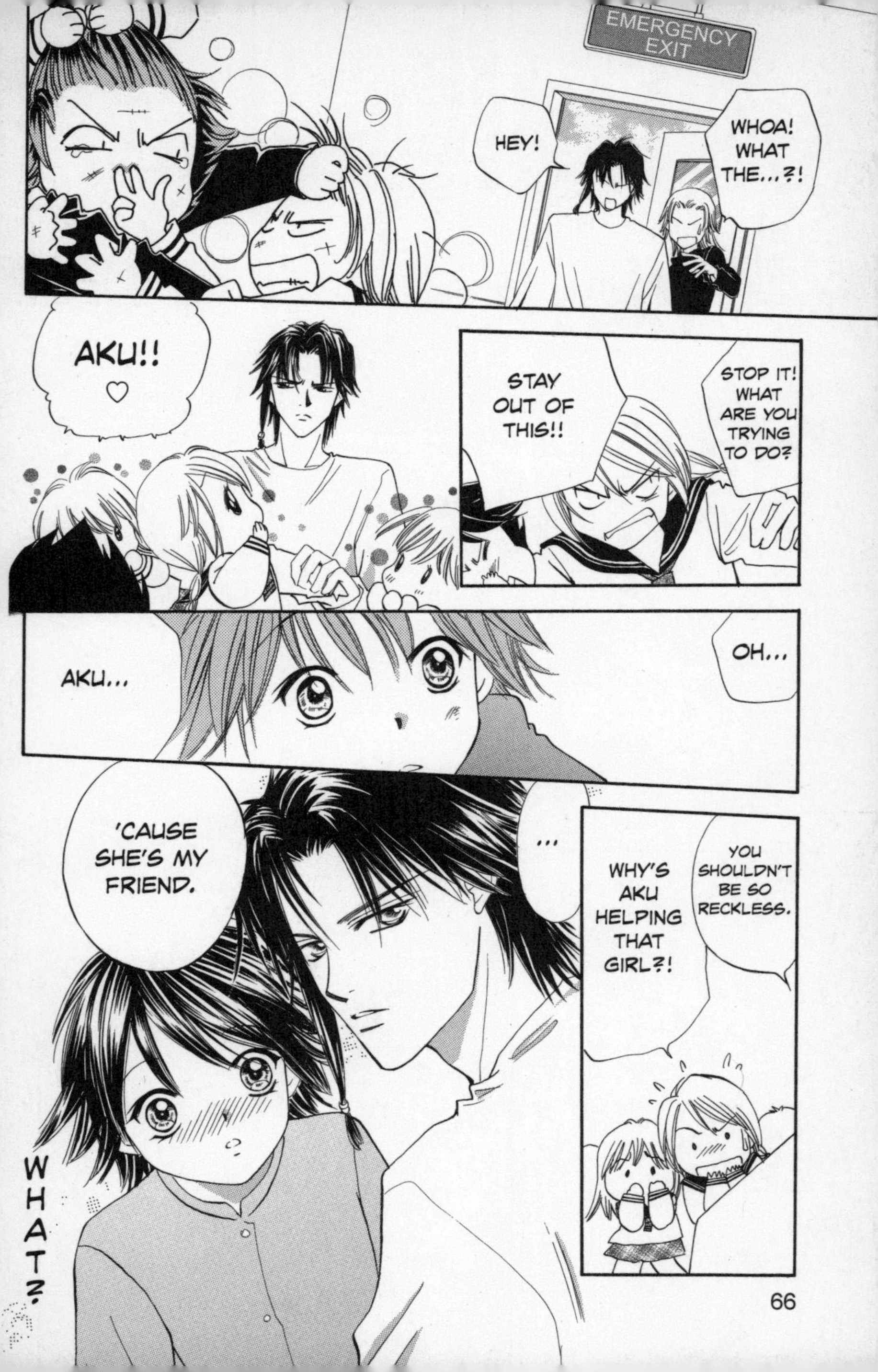
EMERGENCY EXIT
WHOA! WHAT THE...?!
HEY!
STOP IT! WHAT ARE YOU TRYING TO DO?
STAY OUT OF THIS!!
AKU!! ♡
OH...
AKU...
YOU SHOULDN'T BE SO RECKLESS.
WHY'S AKU HELPING THAT GIRL?!
...
'CAUSE SHE'S MY FRIEND.
WHAT?

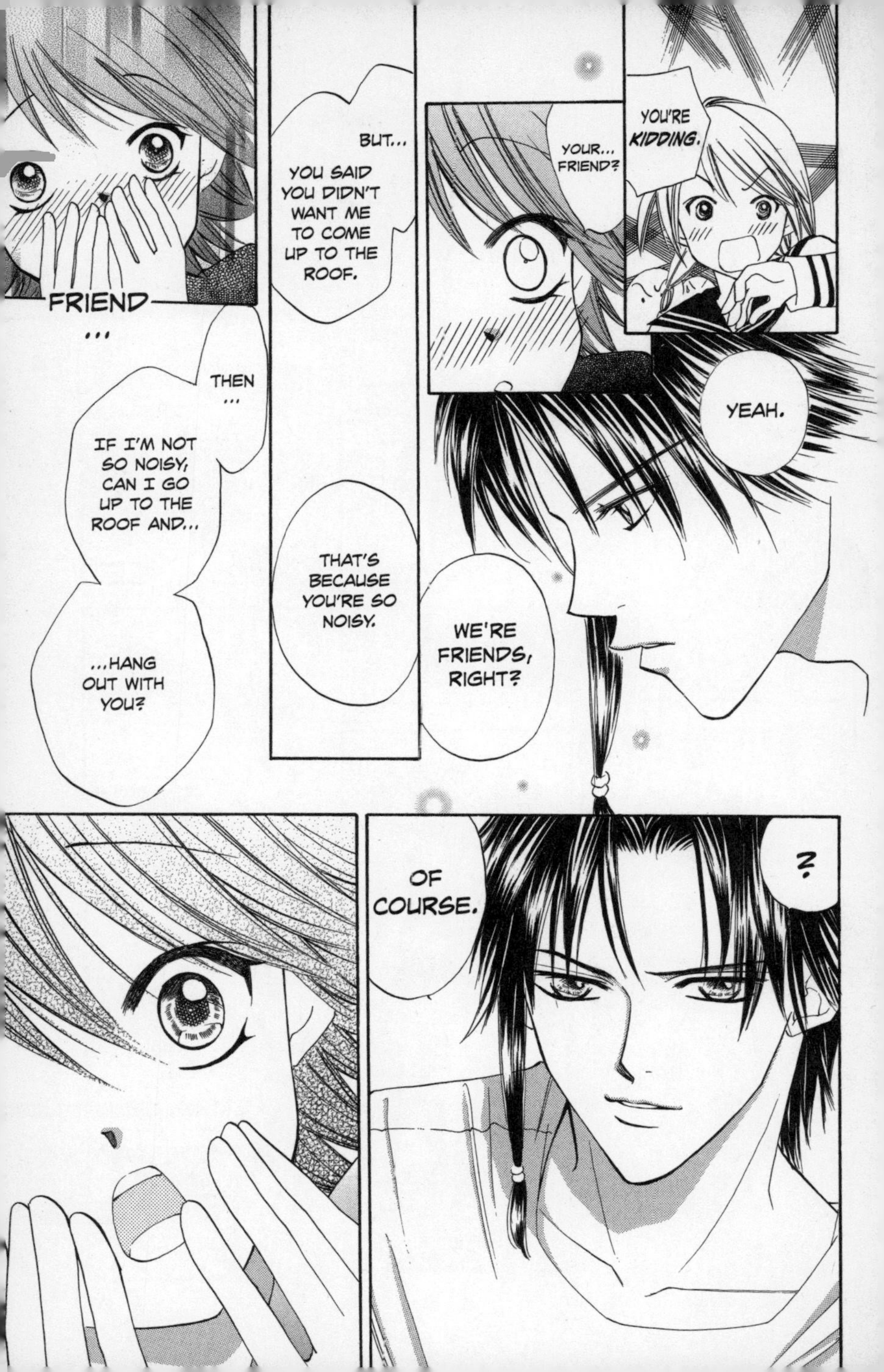
YOU'RE KIDDING.
YOUR... FRIEND?
YEAH.
WE'RE FRIENDS, RIGHT?
BUT... YOU SAID YOU DIDN'T WANT ME TO COME UP TO THE ROOF.
THAT'S BECAUSE YOU'RE SO NOISY.
FRIEND...
THEN... IF I'M NOT SO NOISY, CAN I GO UP TO THE ROOF AND...
...HANG OUT WITH YOU?
?
OF COURSE.

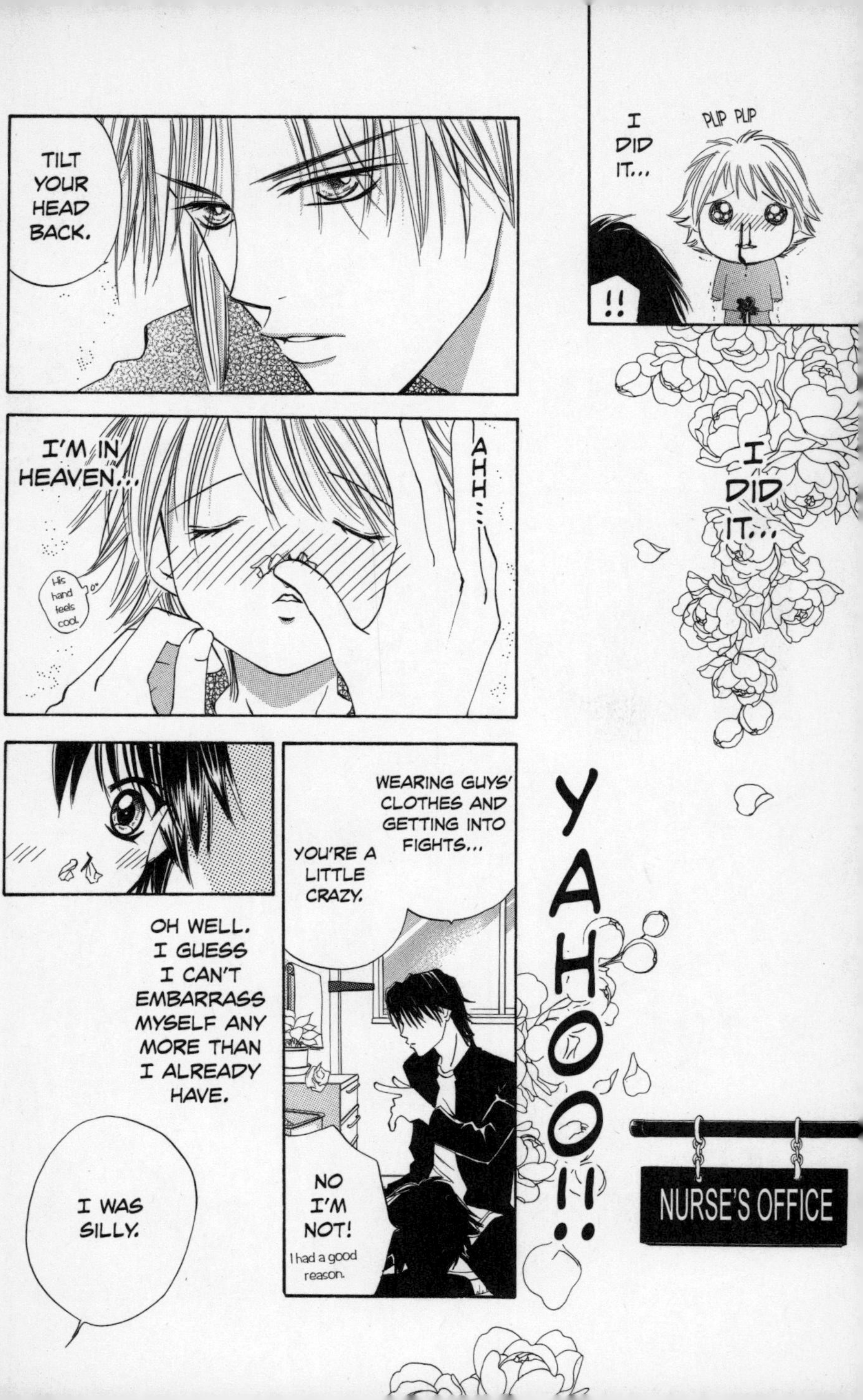
I DID IT...
PLIP PLIP
!!
I DID IT...
YAHOO!!
NURSE'S OFFICE
TILT YOUR HEAD BACK.
I'M IN HEAVEN...
AHH...
His hand feels cool.
WEARING GUYS' CLOTHES AND GETTING INTO FIGHTS...
YOU'RE A LITTLE CRAZY.
NO I'M NOT!
I had a good reason.
OH WELL. I GUESS I CAN'T EMBARRASS MYSELF ANY MORE THAN I ALREADY HAVE.
I WAS SILLY.

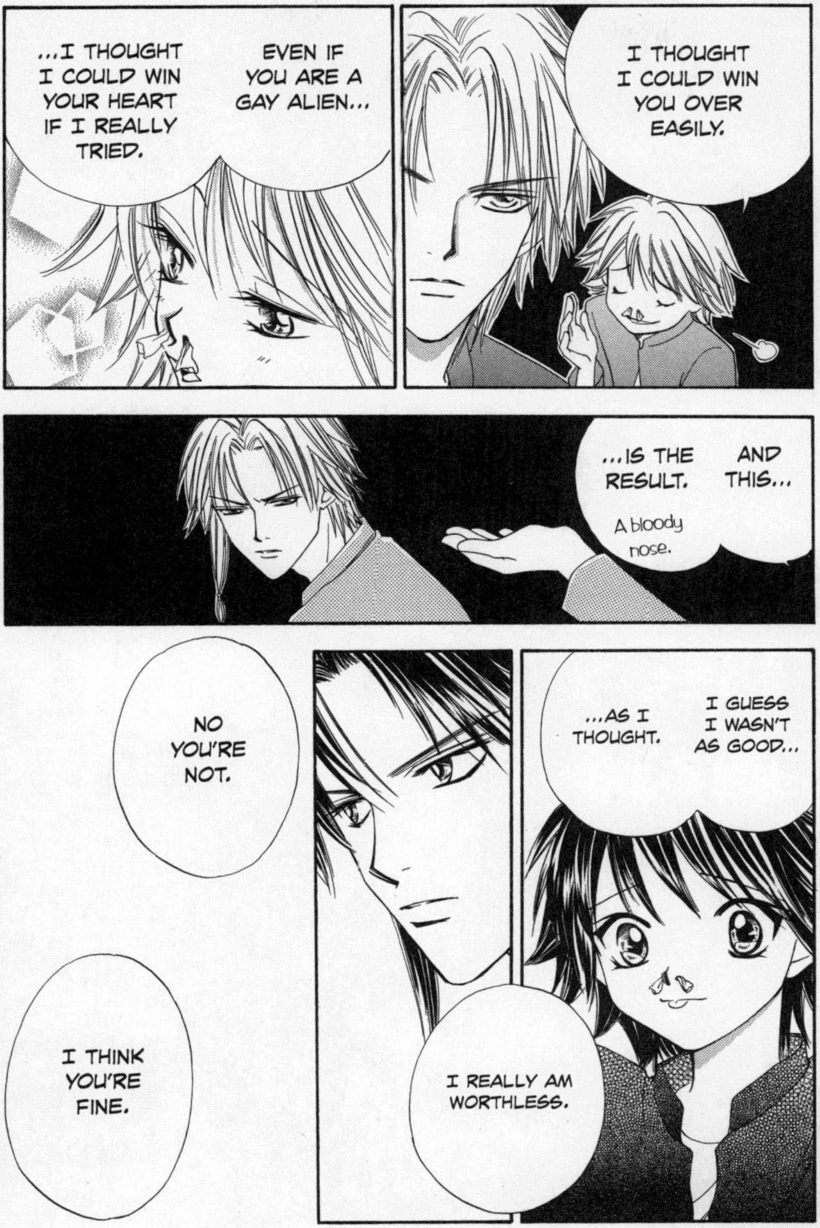
I THOUGHT I COULD WIN YOU OVER EASILY.
EVEN IF YOU ARE A GAY ALIEN...
...I THOUGHT I COULD WIN YOUR HEART IF I REALLY TRIED.
AND THIS...
...IS THE RESULT.
A bloody nose.
I GUESS I WASN'T AS GOOD...
...AS I THOUGHT.
I REALLY AM WORTHLESS.
NO YOU'RE NOT.
I THINK YOU'RE FINE.

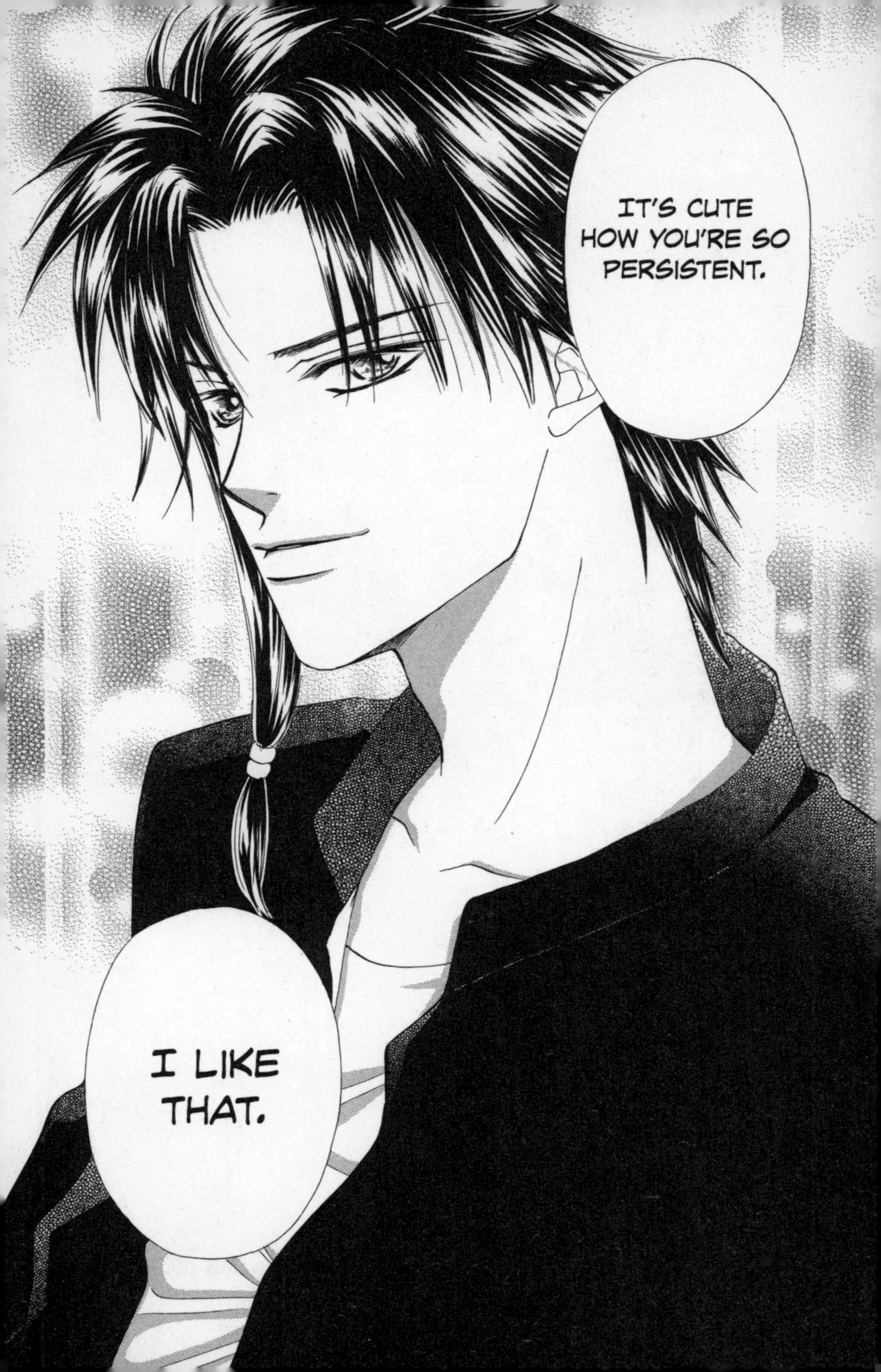
IT'S CUTE HOW YOU'RE SO PERSISTENT.
I LIKE THAT.

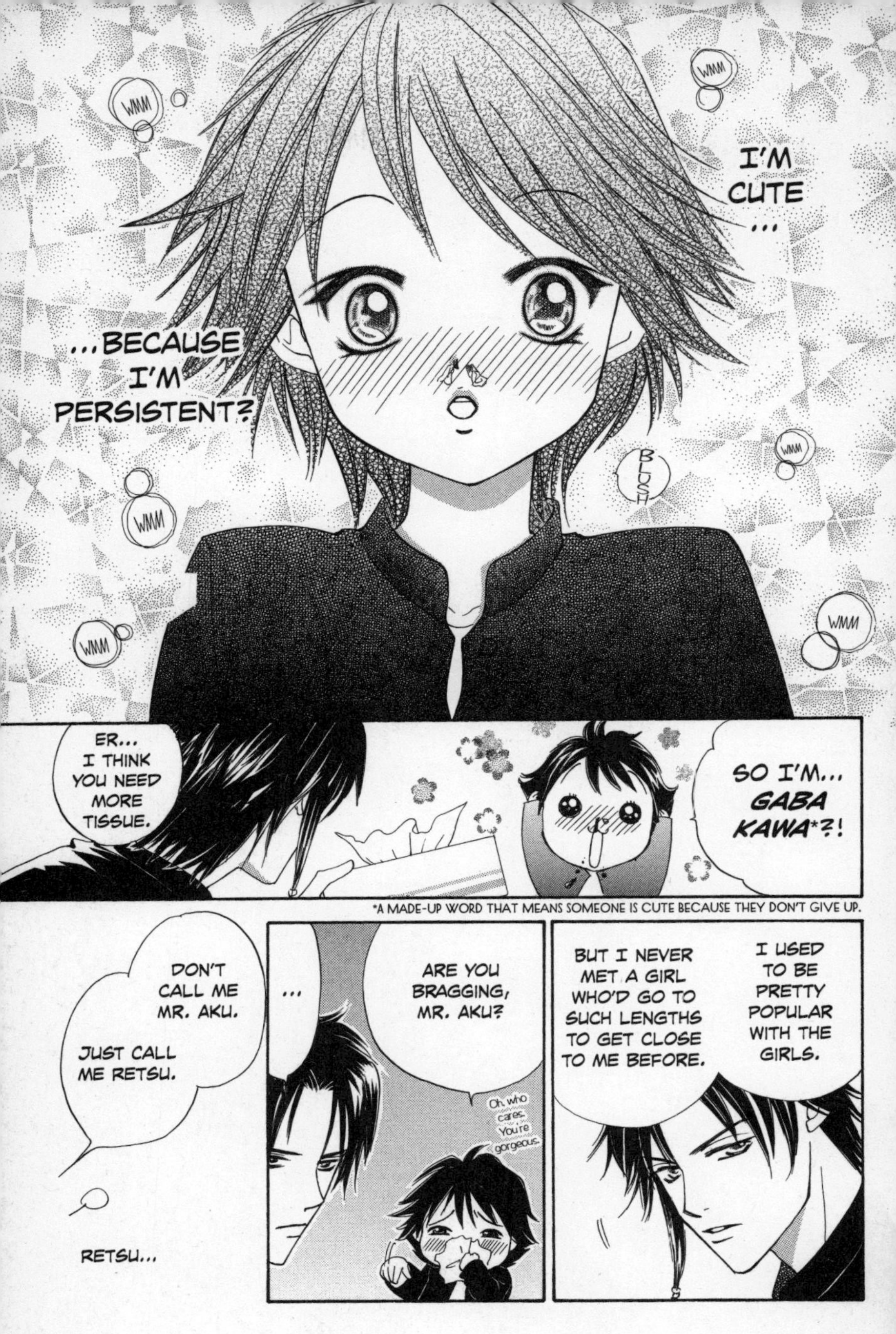
I'M CUTE ...
WMM
WMM
...BECAUSE I'M PERSISTENT?
BLUSH
WMM
WMM
WMM
WMM
SO I'M... *GABA KAWA**?!
ER... I THINK YOU NEED MORE TISSUE.
*A MADE-UP WORD THAT MEANS SOMEONE IS CUTE BECAUSE THEY DON'T GIVE UP.
I USED TO BE PRETTY POPULAR WITH THE GIRLS.
BUT I NEVER MET A GIRL WHO'D GO TO SUCH LENGTHS TO GET CLOSE TO ME BEFORE.
ARE YOU BRAGGING, MR. AKU?
...
Oh, who cares. You're gorgeous.
DON'T CALL ME MR. AKU.
JUST CALL ME RETSU.
RETSU...

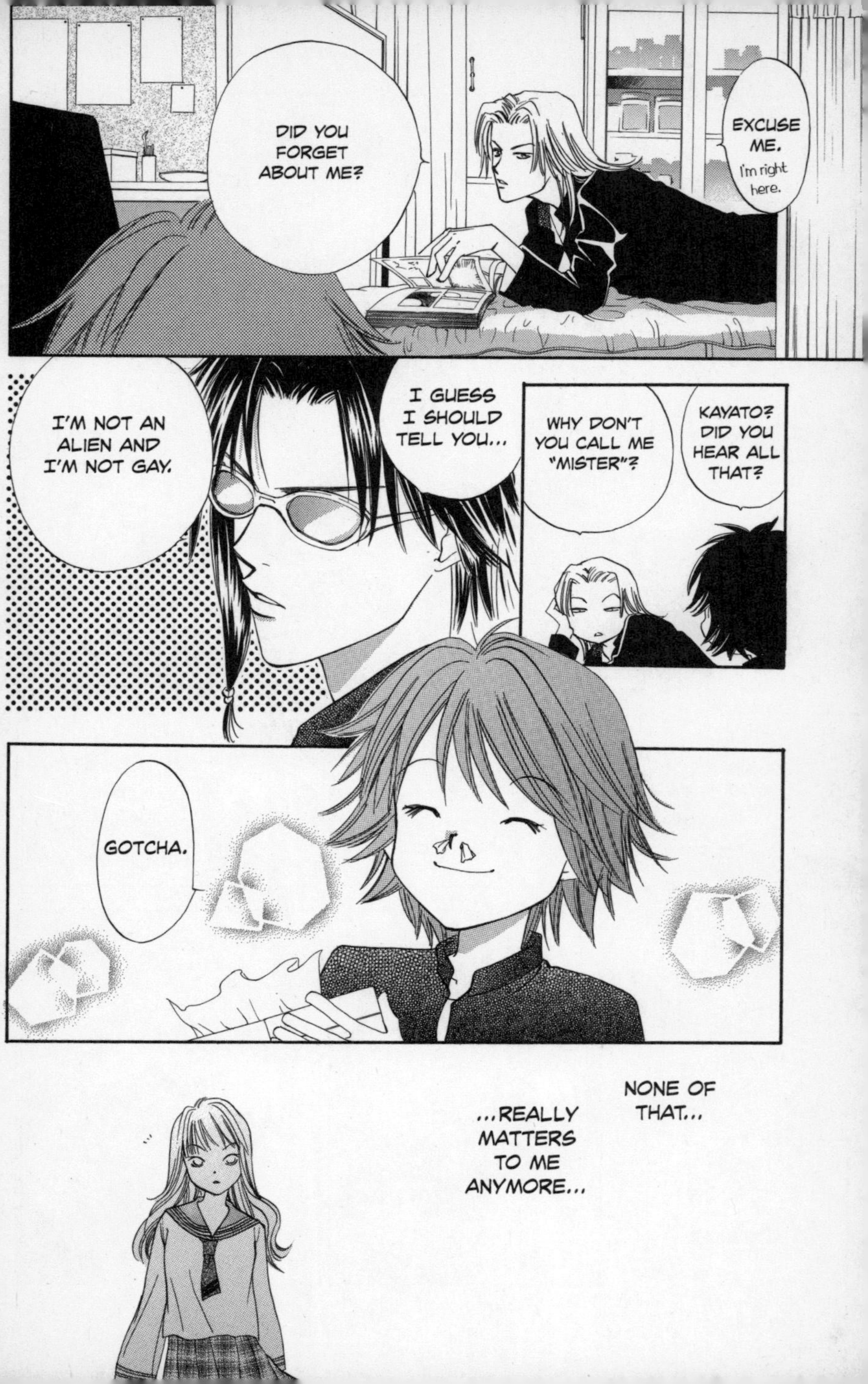
EXCUSE ME.
I'm right here.
DID YOU FORGET ABOUT ME?
KAYATO? DID YOU HEAR ALL THAT?
WHY DON'T YOU CALL ME "MISTER"?
I GUESS I SHOULD TELL YOU...
I'M NOT AN ALIEN AND I'M NOT GAY.
GOTCHA.
NONE OF THAT...
...REALLY MATTERS TO ME ANYMORE...

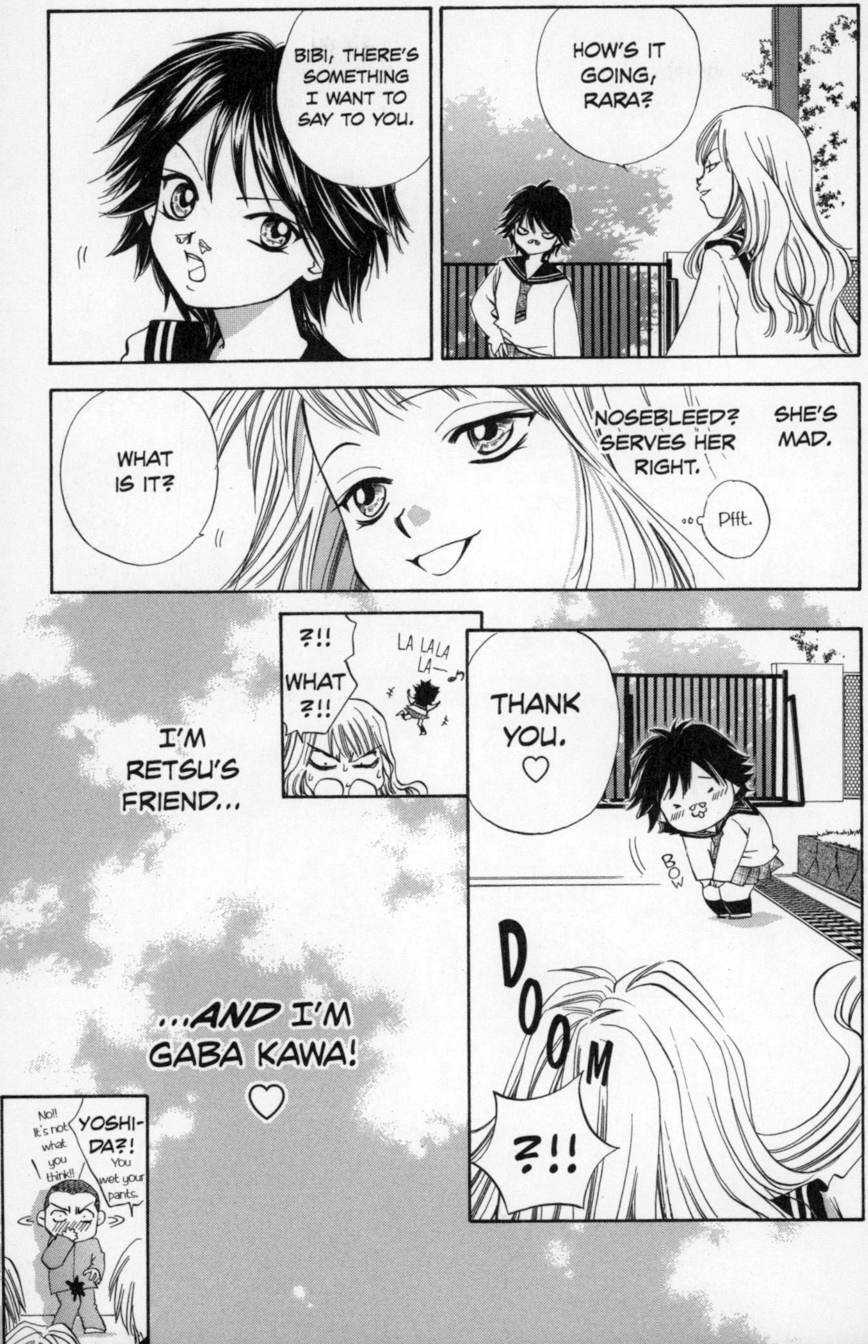
HOW'S IT GOING, RARA?
BIBI, THERE'S SOMETHING I WANT TO SAY TO YOU.
SHE'S MAD.
NOSEBLEED? SERVES HER RIGHT.
Pfft.
WHAT IS IT?
THANK YOU. ♡
BOW
DOOOM
?!!
LA LA LA LA—
?!! WHAT?!!
I'M RETSU'S FRIEND...
...AND I'M GABA KAWA! ♡
YOSHI-DA?! You wet your pants.
No!! It's not what you think!!

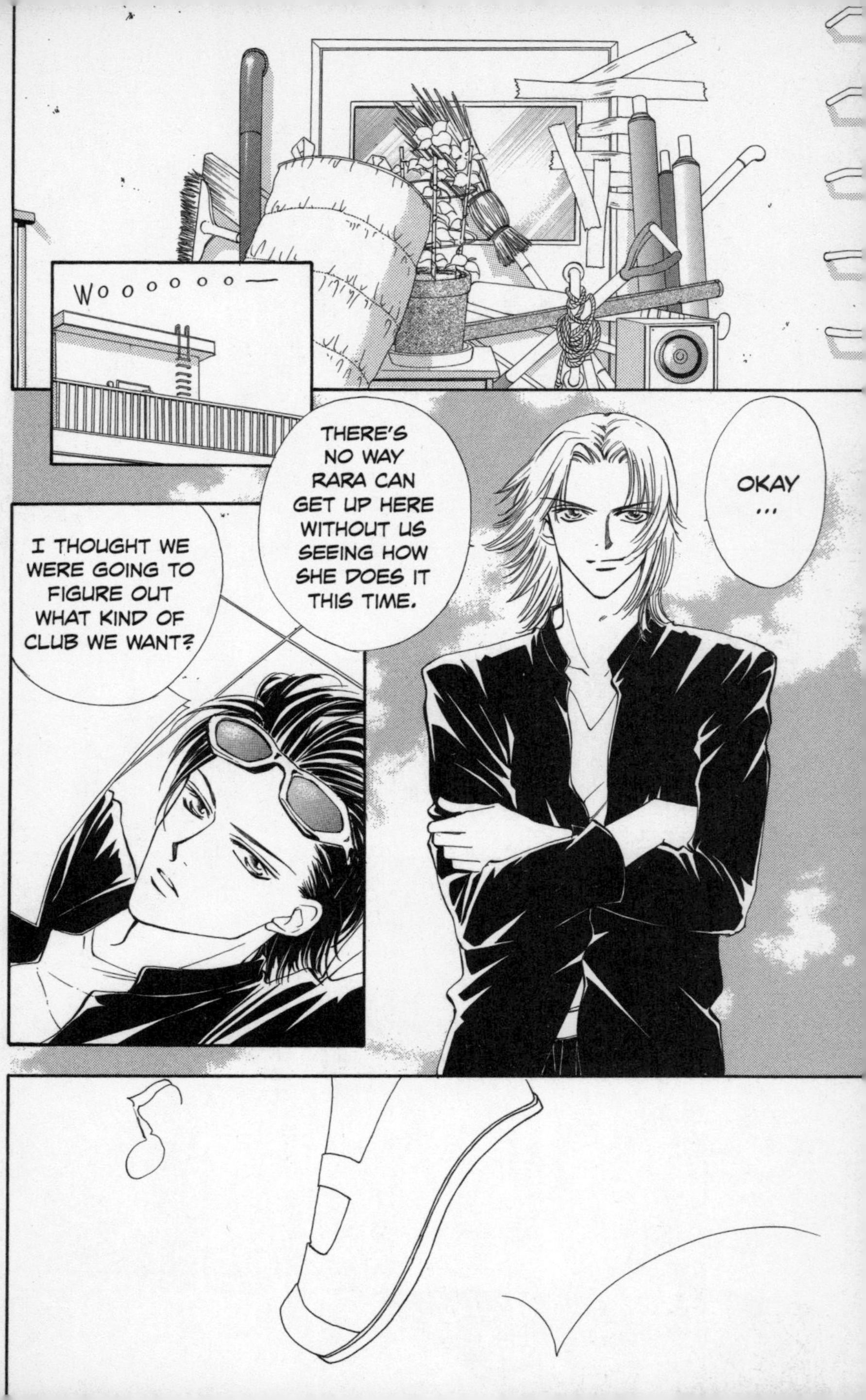
Wooooooo—
OKAY ...
THERE'S NO WAY RARA CAN GET UP HERE WITHOUT US SEEING HOW SHE DOES IT THIS TIME.
I THOUGHT WE WERE GOING TO FIGURE OUT WHAT KIND OF CLUB WE WANT?

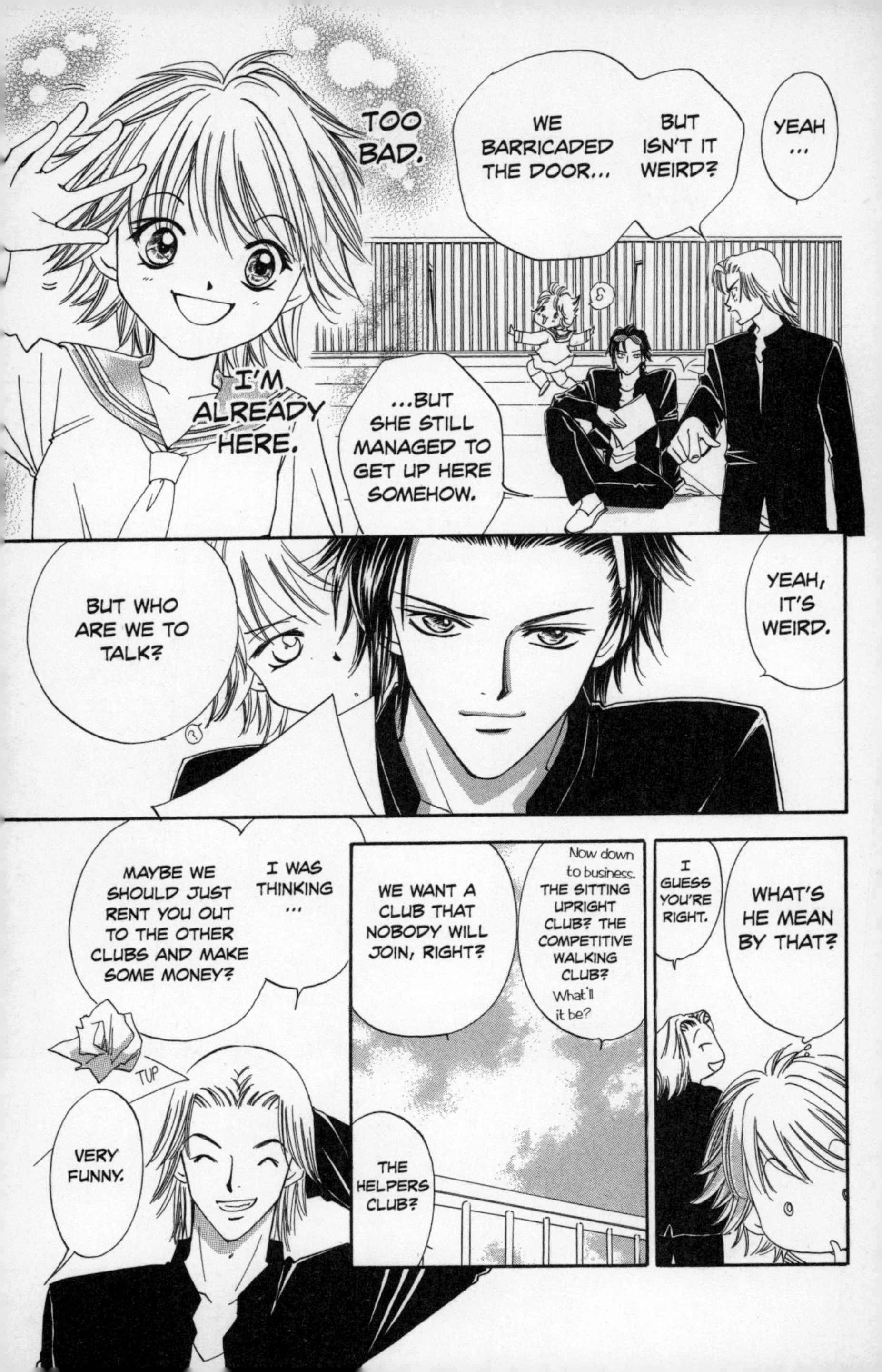
YEAH ...
BUT ISN'T IT WEIRD?
WE BARRICADED THE DOOR...
...BUT SHE STILL MANAGED TO GET UP HERE SOMEHOW.
TOO BAD.
I'M ALREADY HERE.
YEAH, IT'S WEIRD.
BUT WHO ARE WE TO TALK?
WHAT'S HE MEAN BY THAT?
I GUESS YOU'RE RIGHT.
Now down to business. THE SITTING UPRIGHT CLUB? THE COMPETITIVE WALKING CLUB? What'll it be?
WE WANT A CLUB THAT NOBODY WILL JOIN, RIGHT?
THE HELPERS CLUB?
I WAS THINKING ...
MAYBE WE SHOULD JUST RENT YOU OUT TO THE OTHER CLUBS AND MAKE SOME MONEY?
TUP
VERY FUNNY.

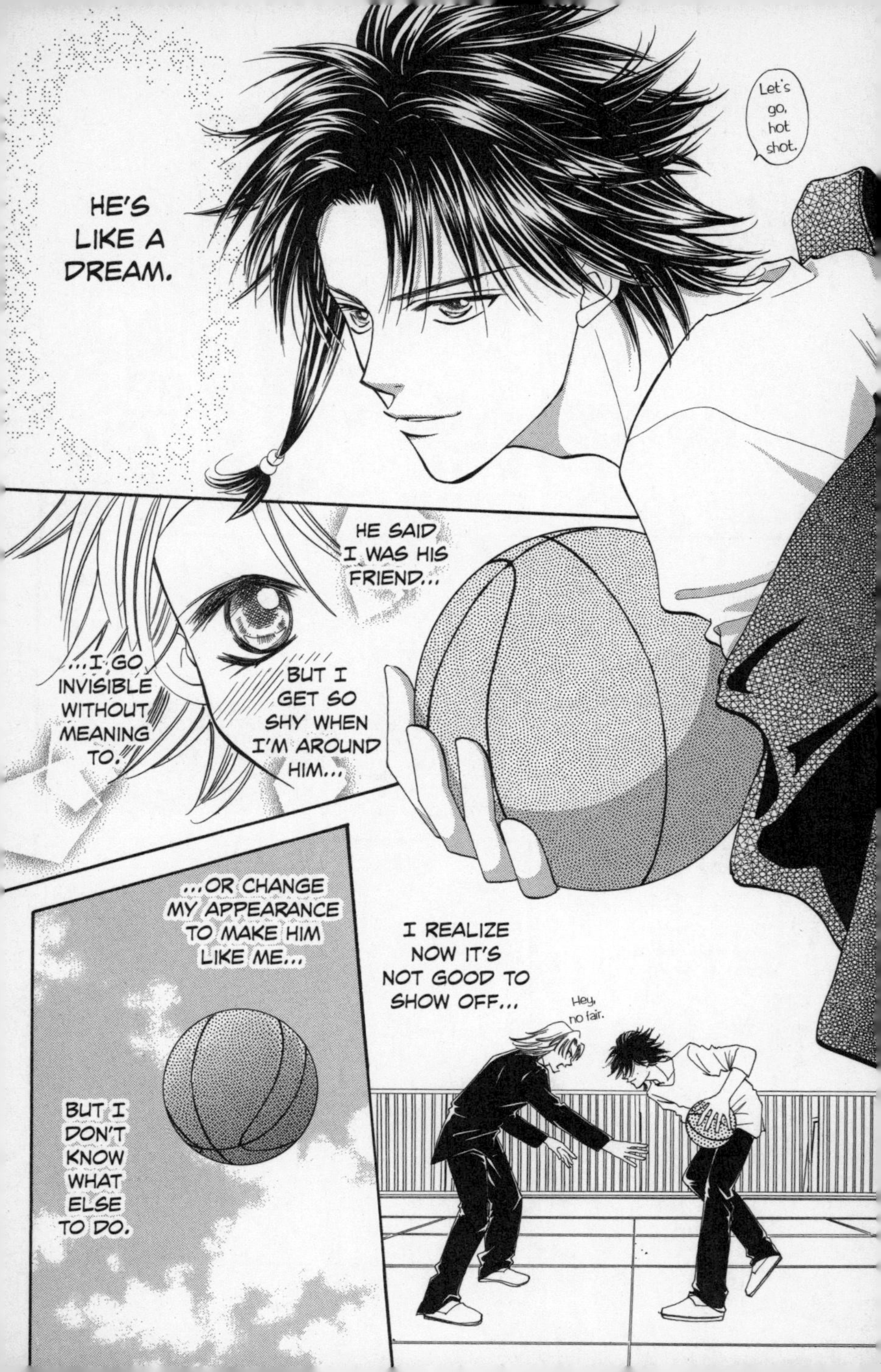
Let's go, hot shot.
HE'S LIKE A DREAM.
HE SAID I WAS HIS FRIEND...
BUT I GET SO SHY WHEN I'M AROUND HIM...
...I GO INVISIBLE WITHOUT MEANING TO.
I REALIZE NOW IT'S NOT GOOD TO SHOW OFF...
Hey, no fair.
...OR CHANGE MY APPEARANCE TO MAKE HIM LIKE ME...
BUT I DON'T KNOW WHAT ELSE TO DO.

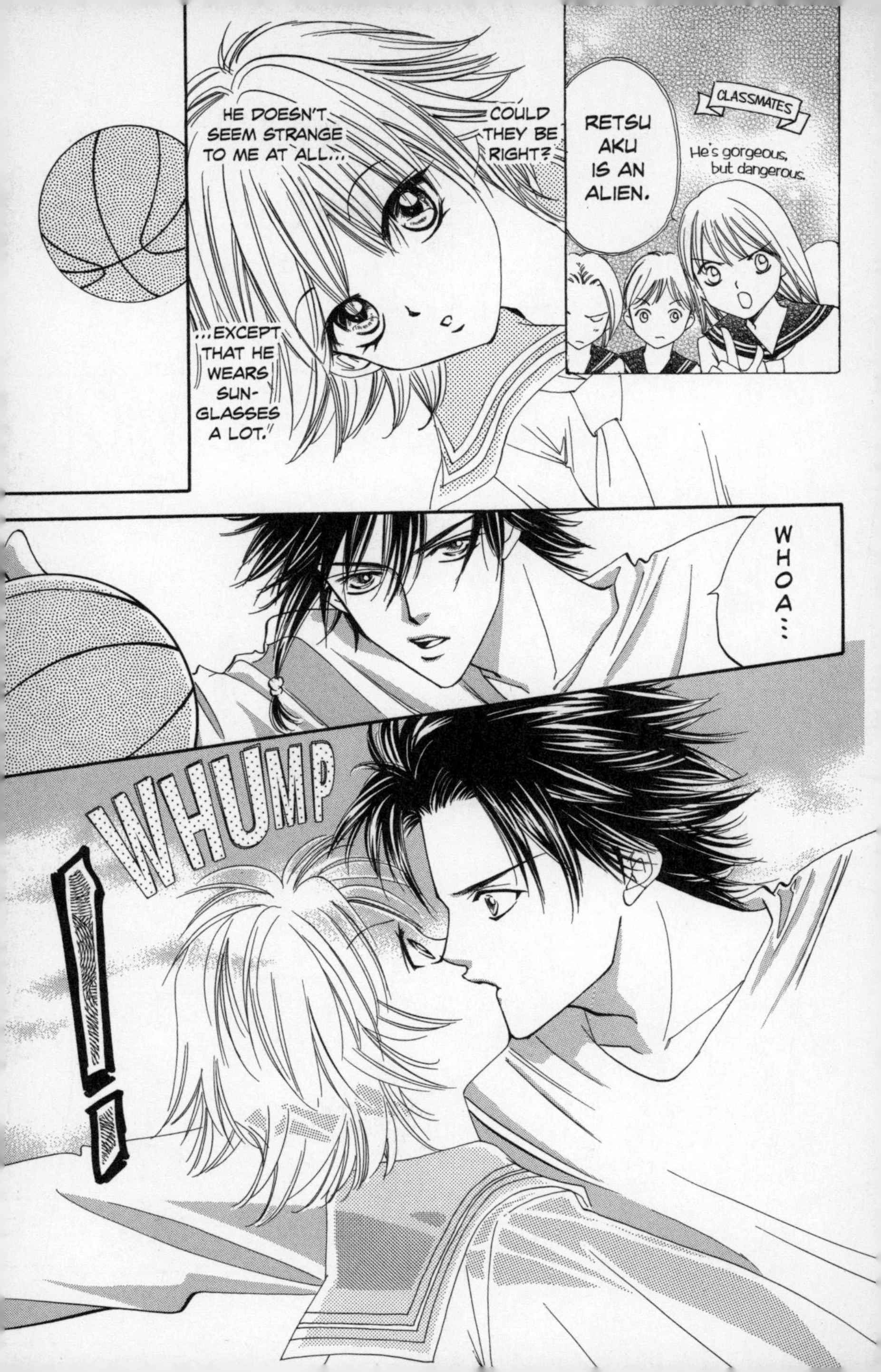
CLASSMATES
RETSU AKU IS AN ALIEN.
He's gorgeous, but dangerous.
COULD THEY BE RIGHT?
HE DOESN'T SEEM STRANGE TO ME AT ALL...
...EXCEPT THAT HE WEARS SUN-GLASSES A LOT.
WHOA...
WHUMP
!

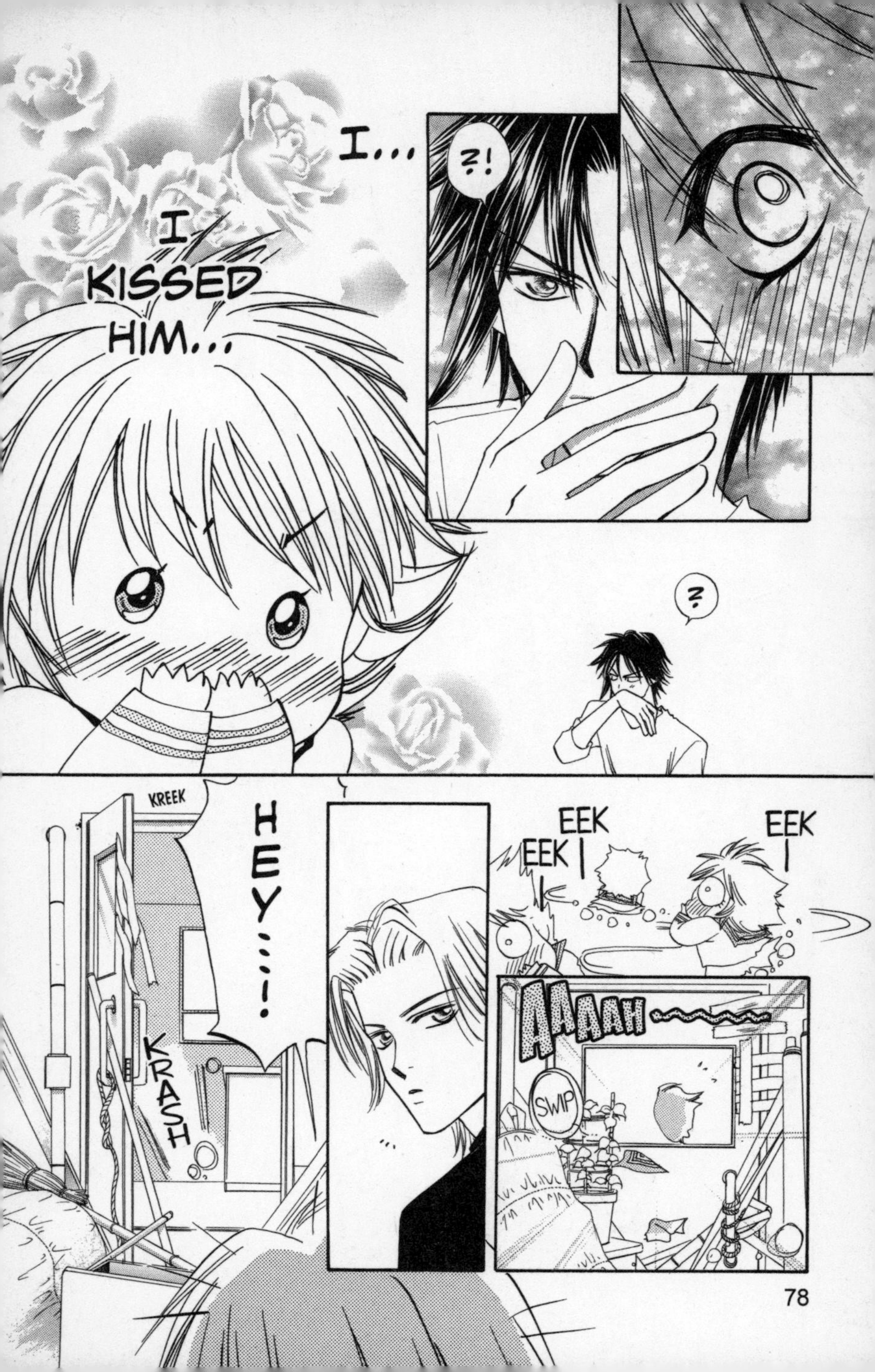
?!
I...
I KISSED HIM...
?
EEK
EEK
EEK
AAAAH
SWIP
...
KREEK
HEY...!
KRASH

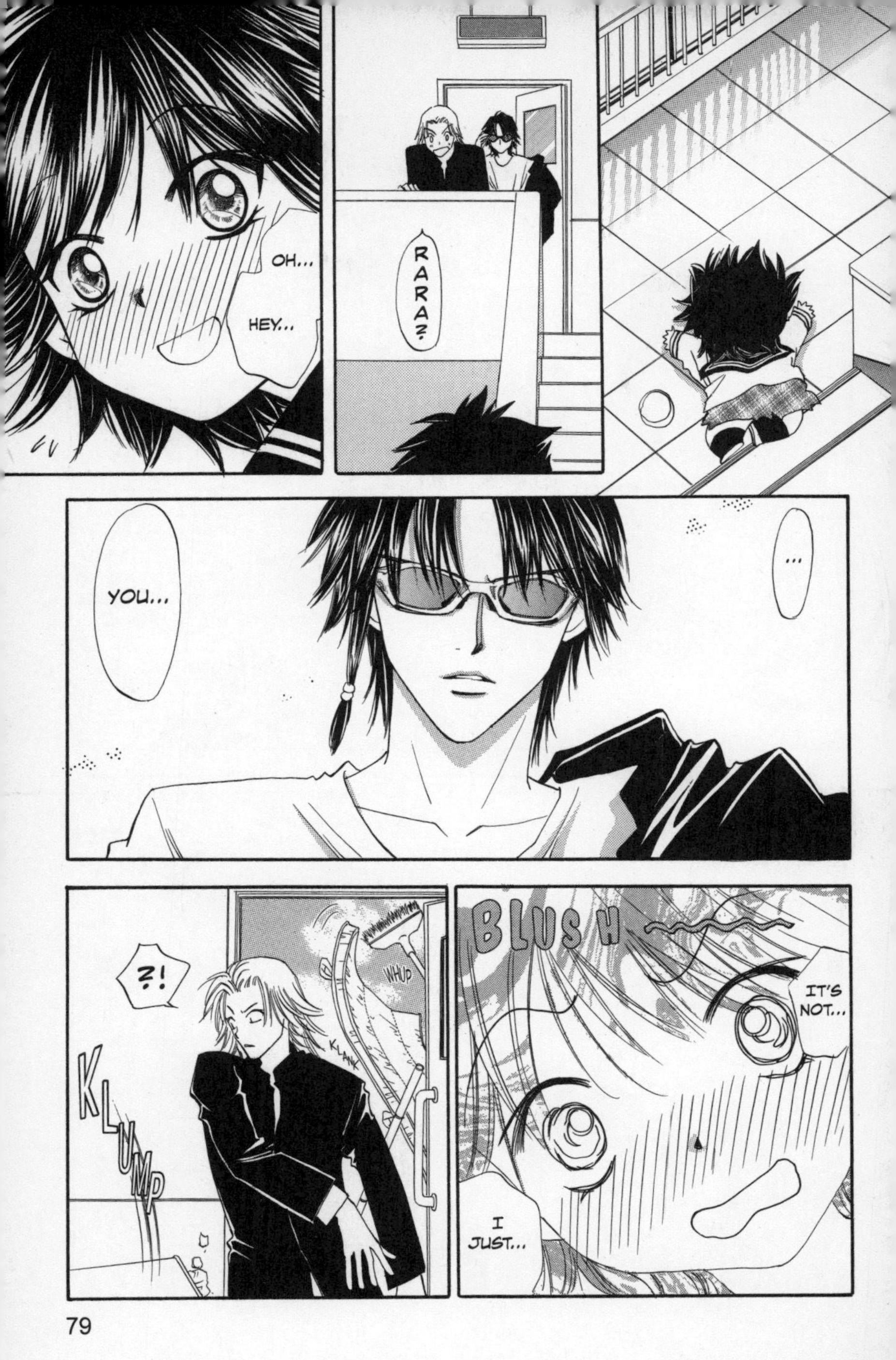
RARA?
OH...
HEY...
...
YOU...
BLUSH
IT'S NOT...
I JUST...
?!
WHUP
KLANK
KLUMP

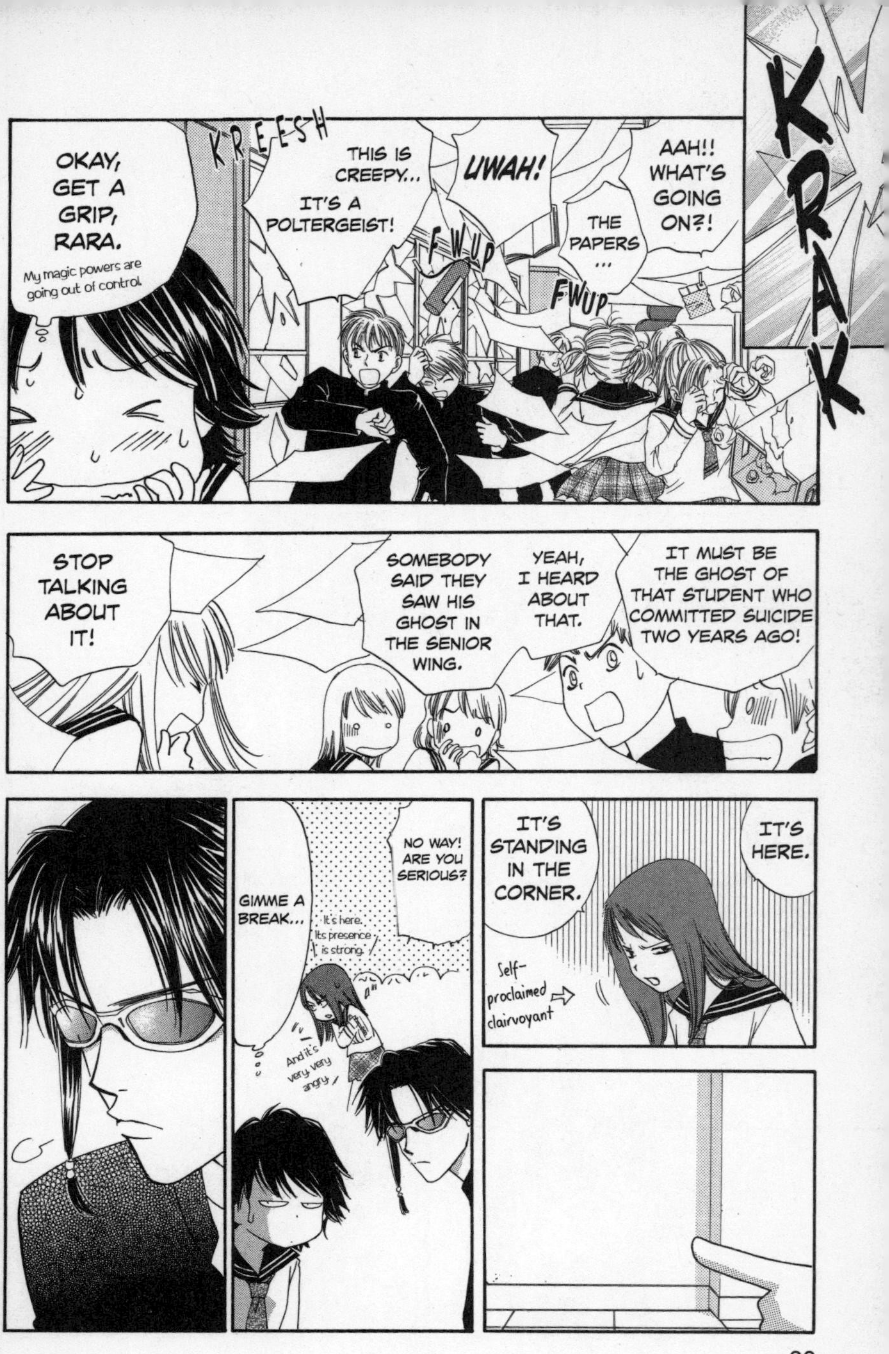
KRAK
AAH!! WHAT'S GOING ON?!
THE PAPERS...
UWAH!
FWUP
FWUP
THIS IS CREEPY...
IT'S A POLTERGEIST!
KREESH
OKAY, GET A GRIP, RARA.
My magic powers are going out of control.
IT MUST BE THE GHOST OF THAT STUDENT WHO COMMITTED SUICIDE TWO YEARS AGO!
YEAH, I HEARD ABOUT THAT.
SOMEBODY SAID THEY SAW HIS GHOST IN THE SENIOR WING.
STOP TALKING ABOUT IT!
IT'S HERE.
IT'S STANDING IN THE CORNER.
Self-proclaimed clairvoyant
NO WAY! ARE YOU SERIOUS?
GIMME A BREAK...
It's here. Its presence is strong.
And it's very, very angry.

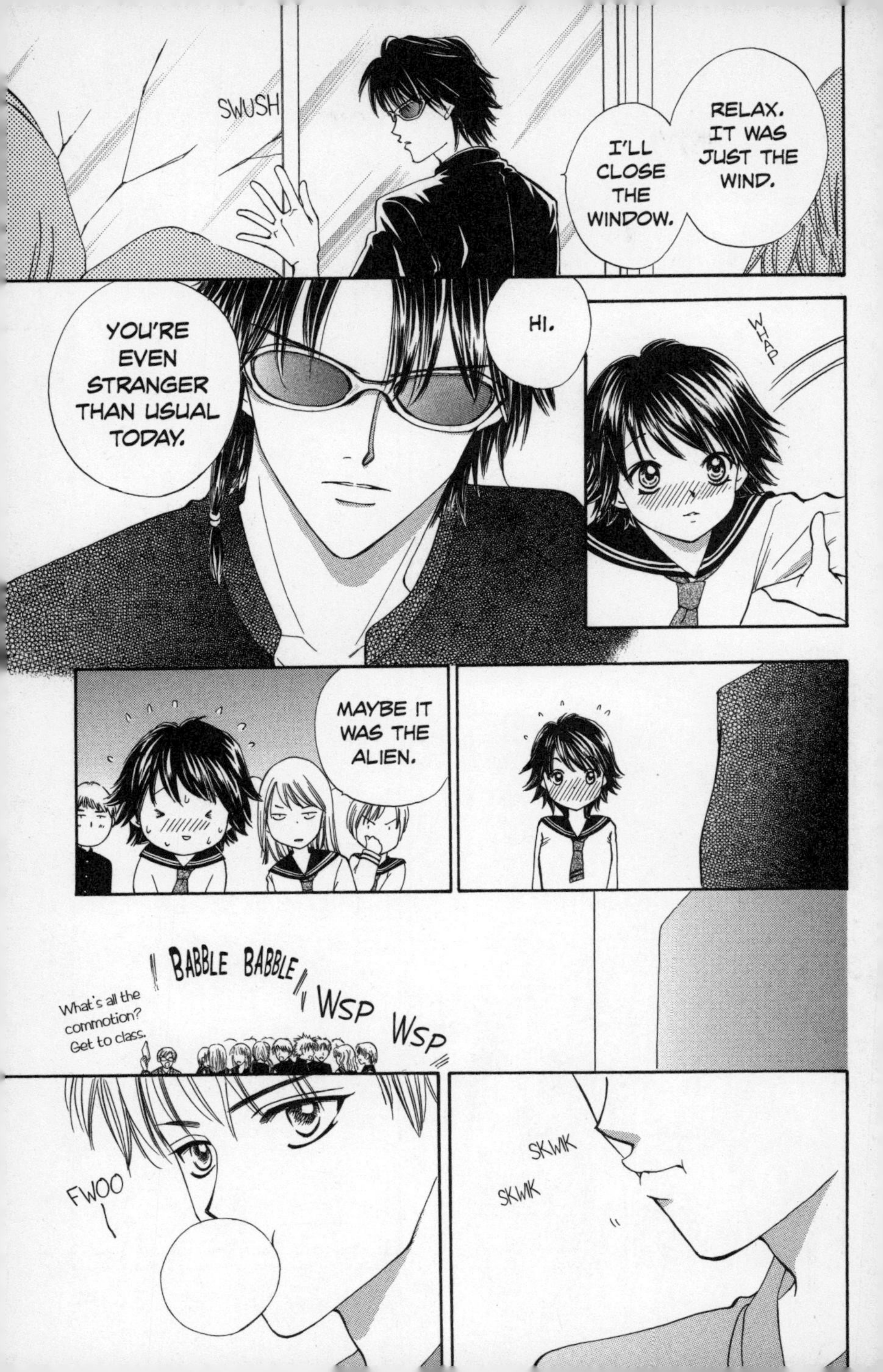
RELAX. IT WAS JUST THE WIND.
I'LL CLOSE THE WINDOW.
SWUSH
WHAP
HI.
YOU'RE EVEN STRANGER THAN USUAL TODAY.
MAYBE IT WAS THE ALIEN.
BABBLE BABBLE
WSP WSP
What's all the commotion? Get to class.
SKWIK
SKWIK
FWOO

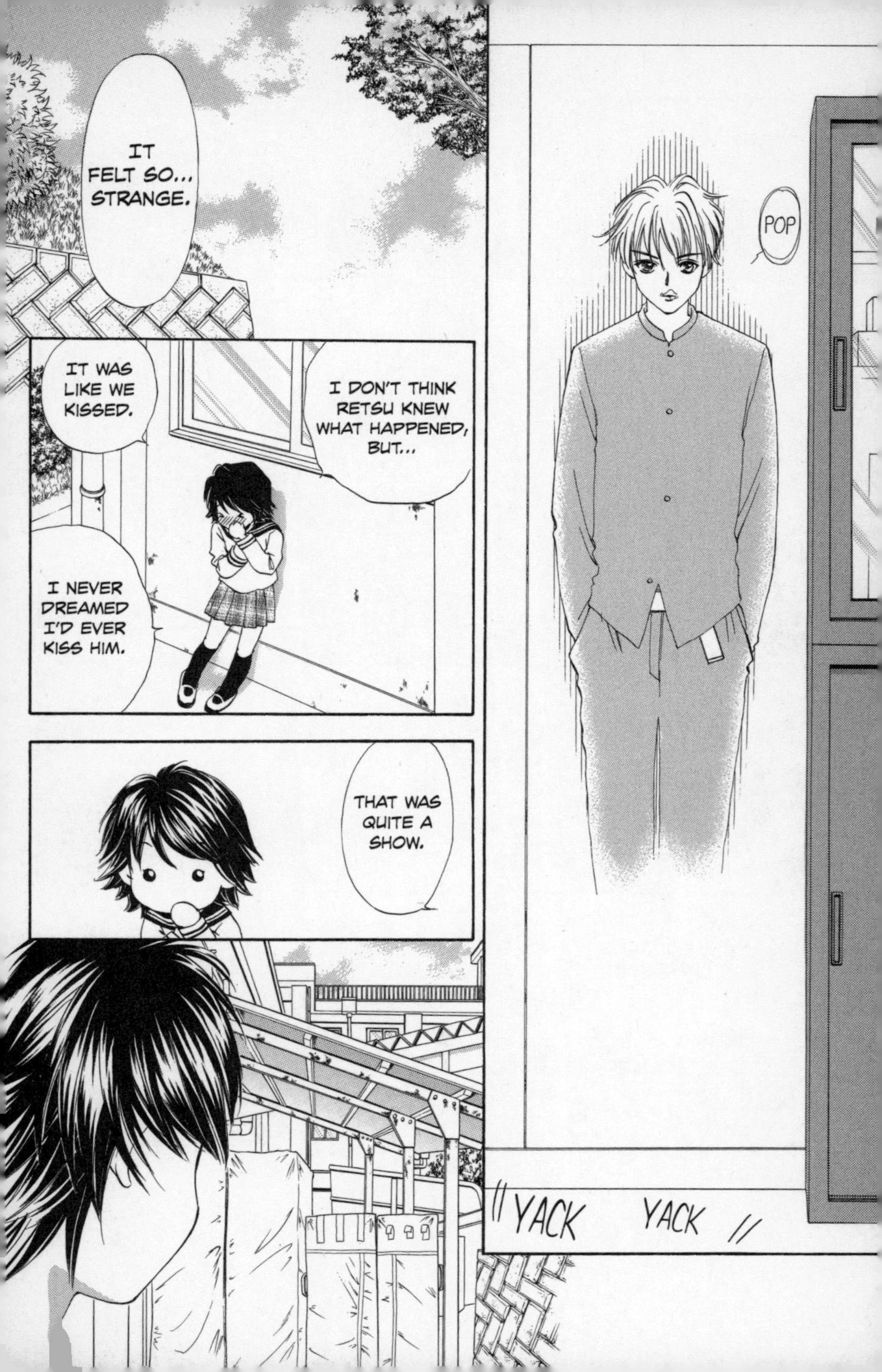
POP
YACK YACK
IT FELT SO... STRANGE.
I DON'T THINK RETSU KNEW WHAT HAPPENED, BUT...
IT WAS LIKE WE KISSED.
I NEVER DREAMED I'D EVER KISS HIM.
THAT WAS QUITE A SHOW.

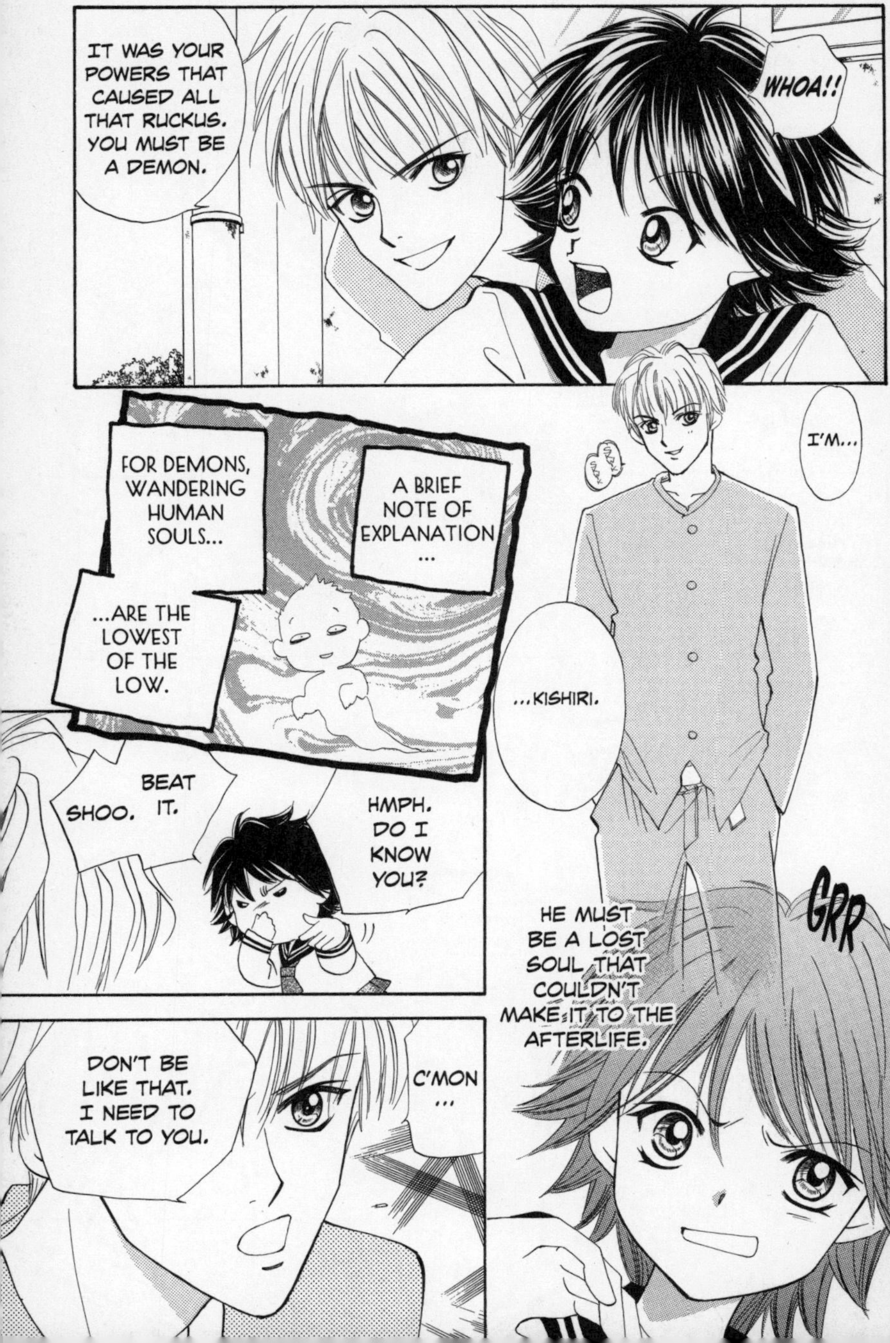
WHOA!!
IT WAS YOUR POWERS THAT CAUSED ALL THAT RUCKUS. YOU MUST BE A DEMON.
I'M...
...KISHIRI.
GRR
HE MUST BE A LOST SOUL THAT COULDN'T MAKE IT TO THE AFTERLIFE.
A BRIEF NOTE OF EXPLANATION...
FOR DEMONS, WANDERING HUMAN SOULS...
...ARE THE LOWEST OF THE LOW.
HMPH. DO I KNOW YOU?
BEAT IT.
SHOO.
C'MON...
DON'T BE LIKE THAT. I NEED TO TALK TO YOU.

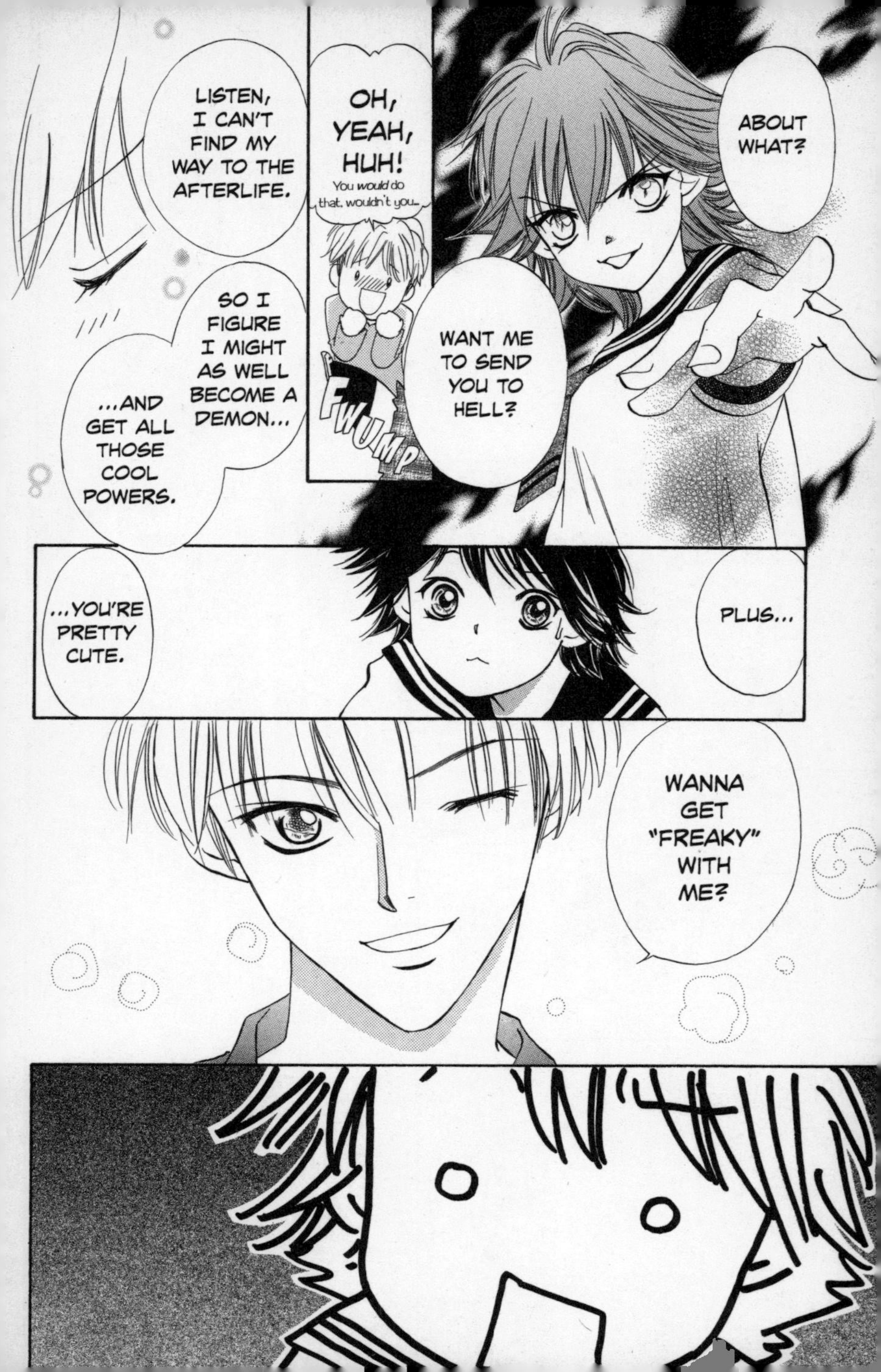
ABOUT WHAT?
WANT ME TO SEND YOU TO HELL?
OH, YEAH, HUH!
You *would* do that, wouldn't you...
FWUMP
LISTEN, I CAN'T FIND MY WAY TO THE AFTERLIFE.
SO I FIGURE I MIGHT AS WELL BECOME A DEMON...
...AND GET ALL THOSE COOL POWERS.
PLUS...
...YOU'RE PRETTY CUTE.
WANNA GET "FREAKY" WITH ME?

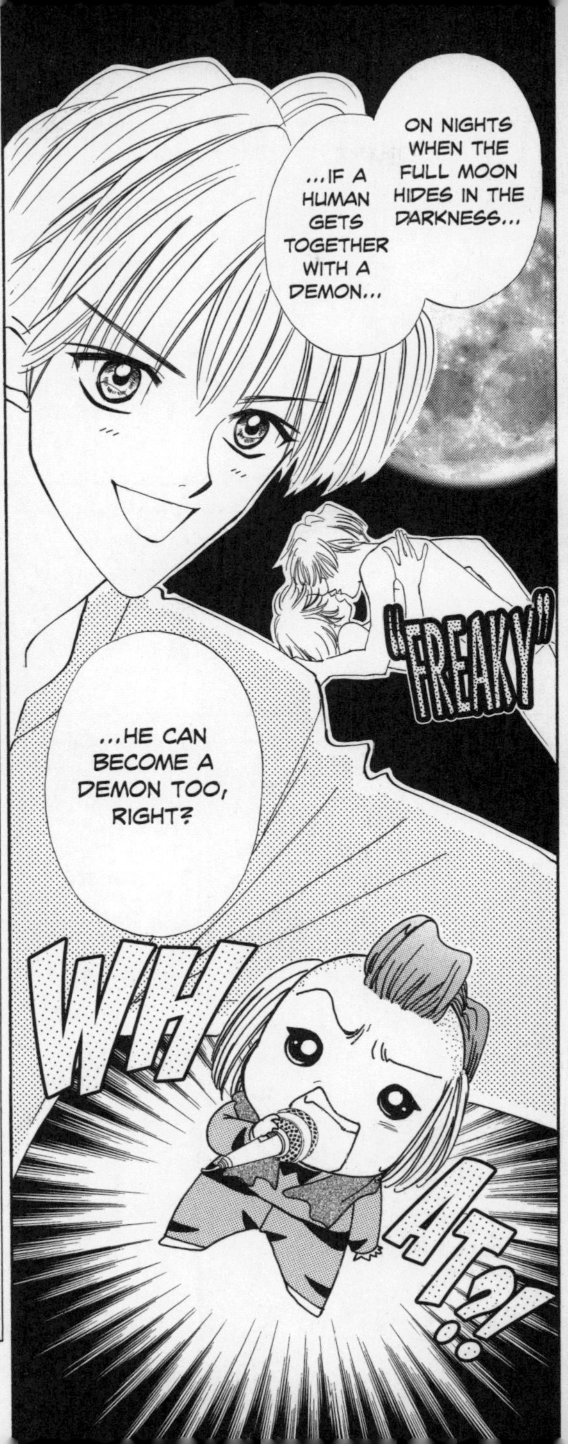
ON NIGHTS WHEN THE FULL MOON HIDES IN THE DARKNESS...
...IF A HUMAN GETS TOGETHER WITH A DEMON...
"FREAKY"
...HE CAN BECOME A DEMON TOO, RIGHT?
WHAT?!

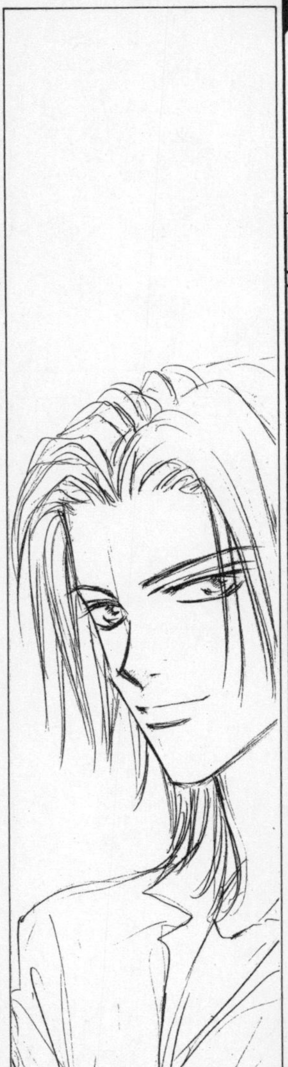

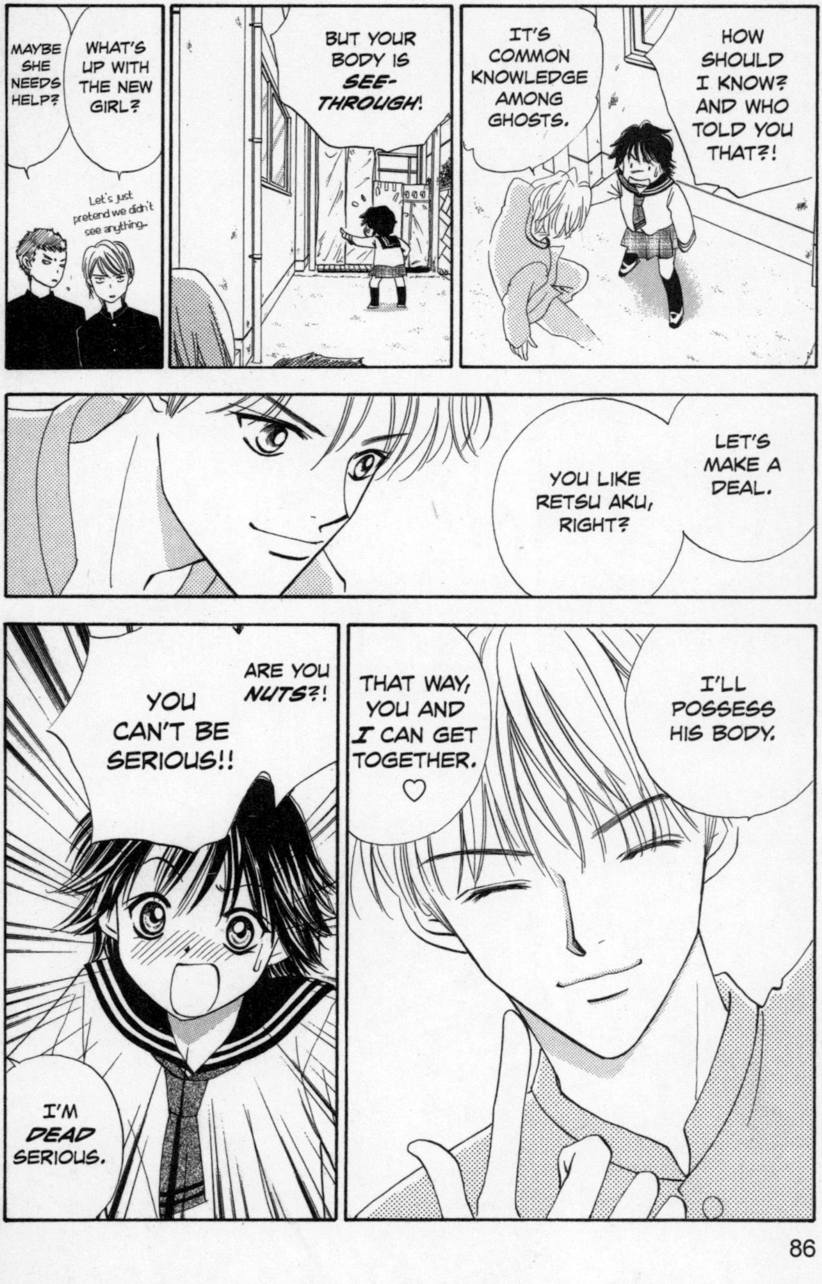
HOW SHOULD I KNOW? AND WHO TOLD YOU THAT?!
IT'S COMMON KNOWLEDGE AMONG GHOSTS.
BUT YOUR BODY IS *SEE-THROUGH*!
WHAT'S UP WITH THE NEW GIRL?
MAYBE SHE NEEDS HELP?
Let's just pretend we didn't see anything...
LET'S MAKE A DEAL.
YOU LIKE RETSU AKU, RIGHT?
I'LL POSSESS HIS BODY.
THAT WAY, YOU AND *I* CAN GET TOGETHER. ♡
ARE YOU *NUTS*?!
YOU CAN'T BE SERIOUS!!
I'M *DEAD* SERIOUS.

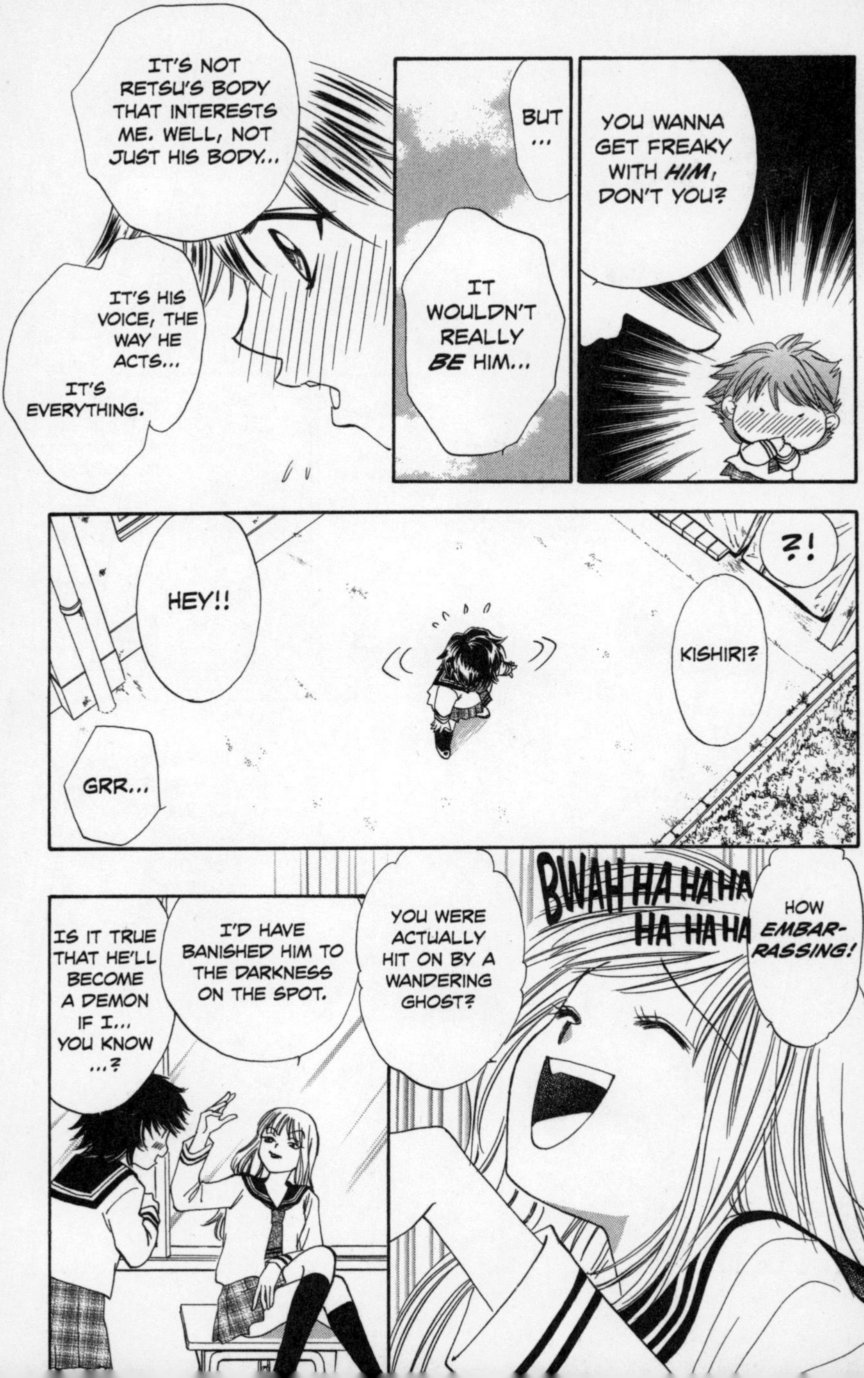
YOU WANNA GET FREAKY WITH *HIM*, DON'T YOU?
BUT...
IT WOULDN'T REALLY *BE* HIM...
IT'S NOT RETSU'S BODY THAT INTERESTS ME. WELL, NOT JUST HIS BODY...
IT'S HIS VOICE, THE WAY HE ACTS...
IT'S EVERYTHING.
?!
KISHIRI?
HEY!!
GRR...
HOW *EMBARRASSING!*
BWAH HA HA HA
HA HA HA
YOU WERE ACTUALLY HIT ON BY A WANDERING GHOST?
I'D HAVE BANISHED HIM TO THE DARKNESS ON THE SPOT.
IS IT TRUE THAT HE'LL BECOME A DEMON IF I... YOU KNOW...?

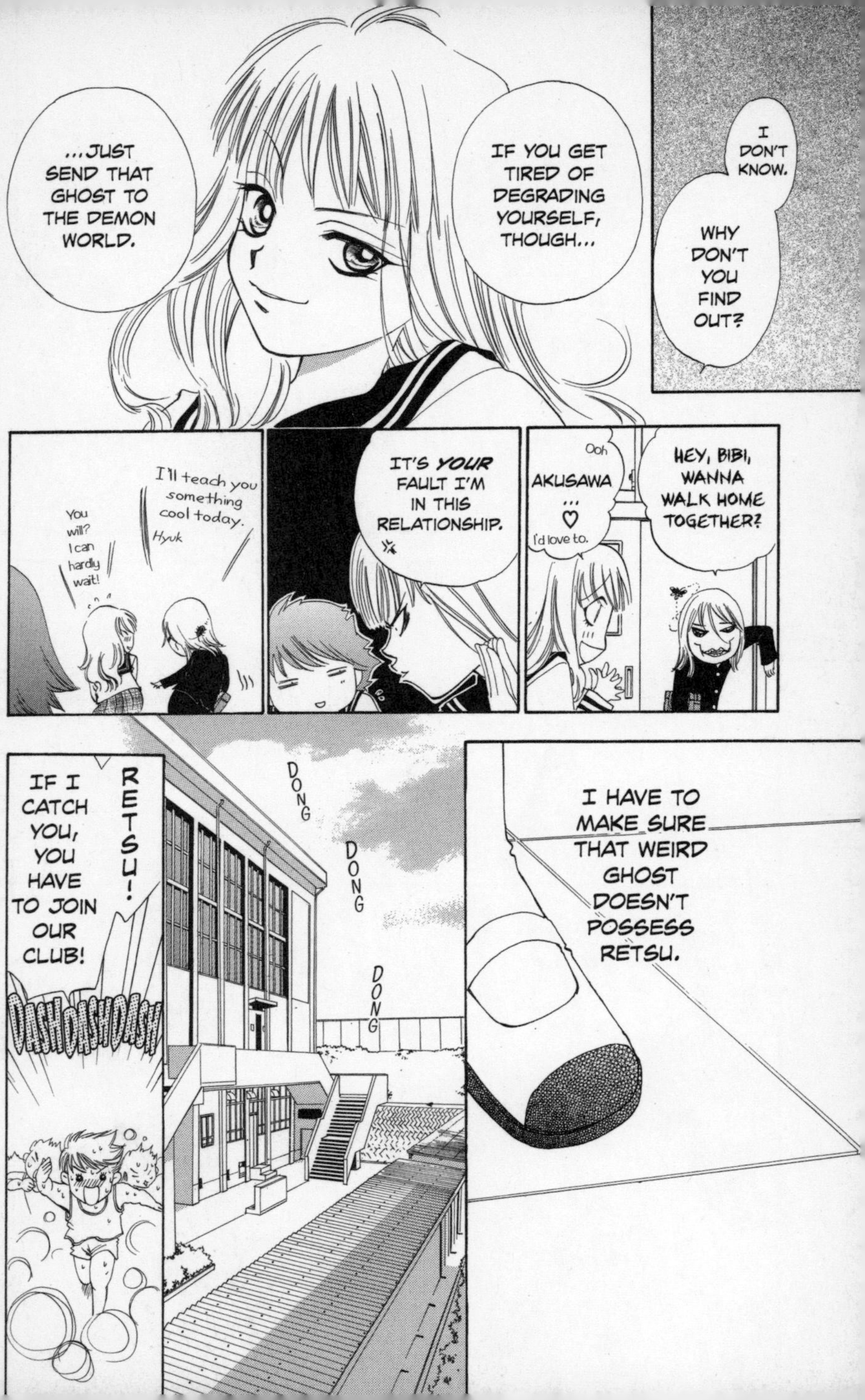
I DON'T KNOW.
WHY DON'T YOU FIND OUT?
IF YOU GET TIRED OF DEGRADING YOURSELF, THOUGH...
...JUST SEND THAT GHOST TO THE DEMON WORLD.
HEY, BIBI, WANNA WALK HOME TOGETHER?
Ooh
AKUSAWA ... ♡
I'd love to.
IT'S *YOUR* FAULT I'M IN THIS RELATIONSHIP.
I'll teach you something cool today.
Hyuk
You will? I can hardly wait!
I HAVE TO MAKE SURE THAT WEIRD GHOST DOESN'T POSSESS RETSU.
DONG
DONG
DONG
RETSU!
IF I CATCH YOU, YOU HAVE TO JOIN OUR CLUB!
DASHDASHDASH

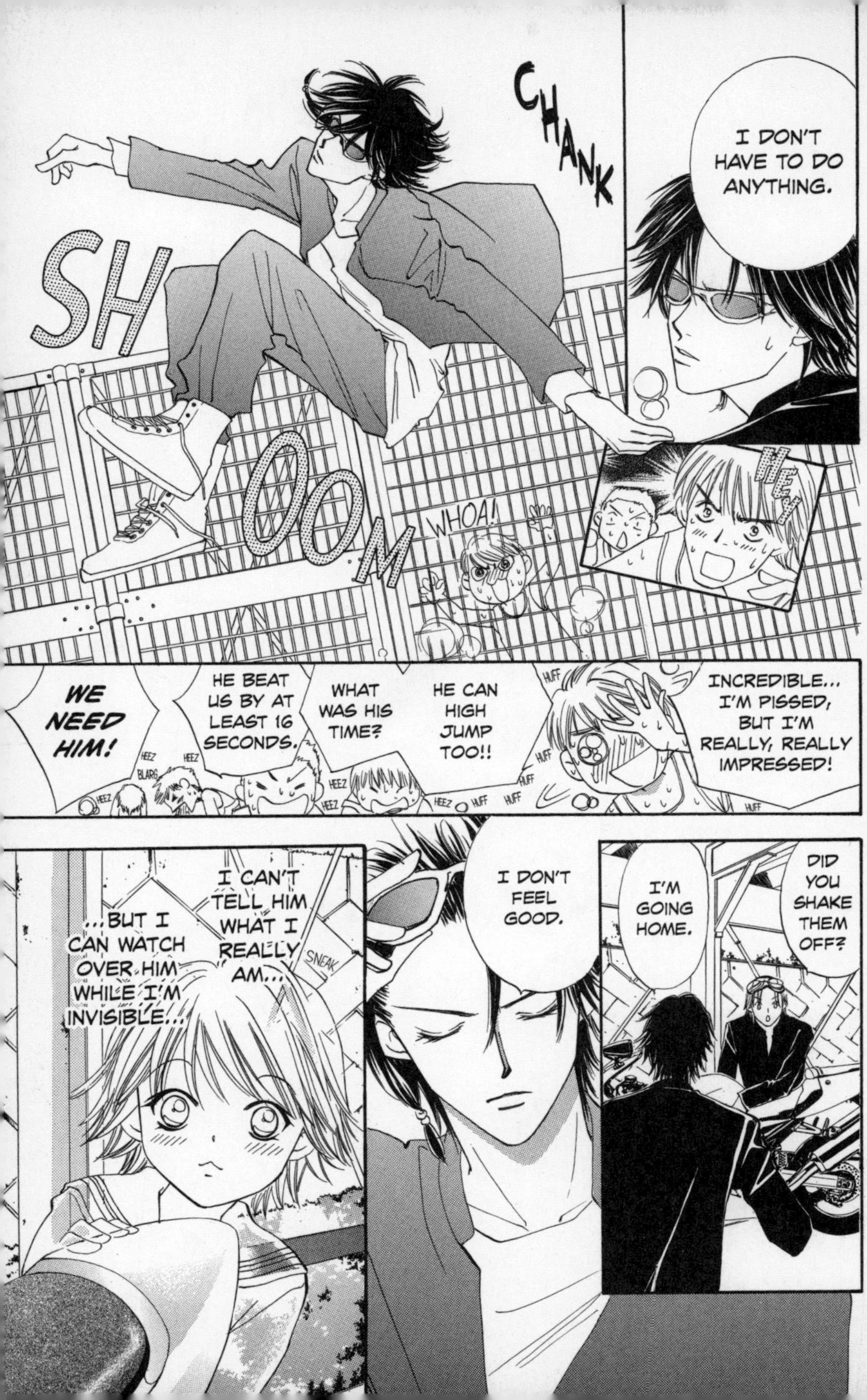
I DON'T HAVE TO DO ANYTHING.
HEY
CHANK
SHOOOM
WHOA!
INCREDIBLE... I'M PISSED, BUT I'M REALLY, REALLY IMPRESSED!
HUFF HUFF HUFF
HE CAN HIGH JUMP TOO!!
WHAT WAS HIS TIME?
HE BEAT US BY AT LEAST 16 SECONDS.
WE NEED HIM!
HEEZ HEEZ BLARG HEEZ
DID YOU SHAKE THEM OFF?
I'M GOING HOME.
I DON'T FEEL GOOD.
I CAN'T TELL HIM WHAT I REALLY AM...
...BUT I CAN WATCH OVER HIM WHILE I'M INVISIBLE...
SNEAK

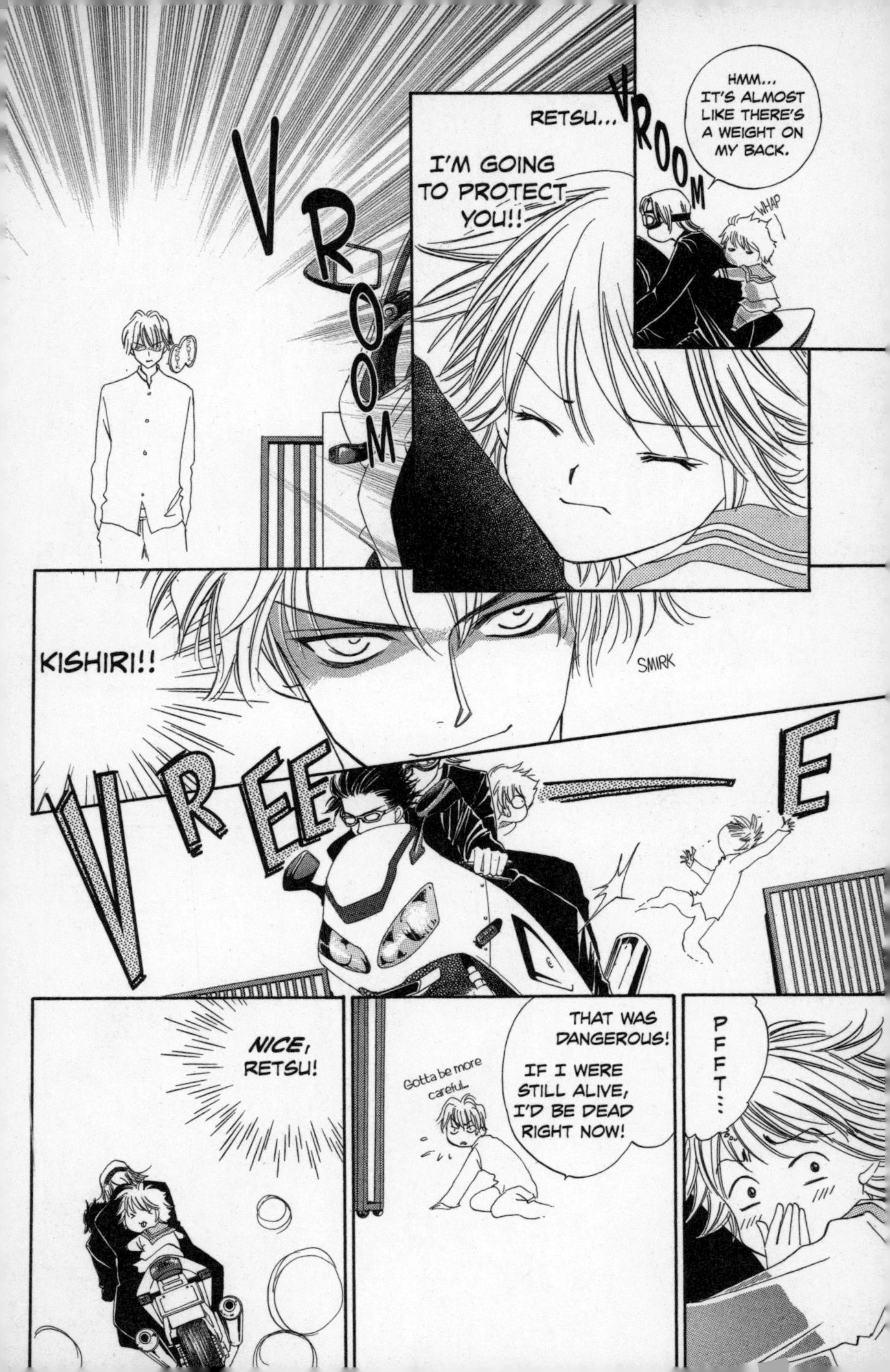
HMM... IT'S ALMOST LIKE THERE'S A WEIGHT ON MY BACK.
WHAP
VROOM
RETSU...
I'M GOING TO PROTECT YOU!!
VROOM
KISHIRI!!
SMIRK
VREEE—E
PFFT...
THAT WAS DANGEROUS!
IF I WERE STILL ALIVE, I'D BE DEAD RIGHT NOW!
Gotta be more careful...
NICE, RETSU!

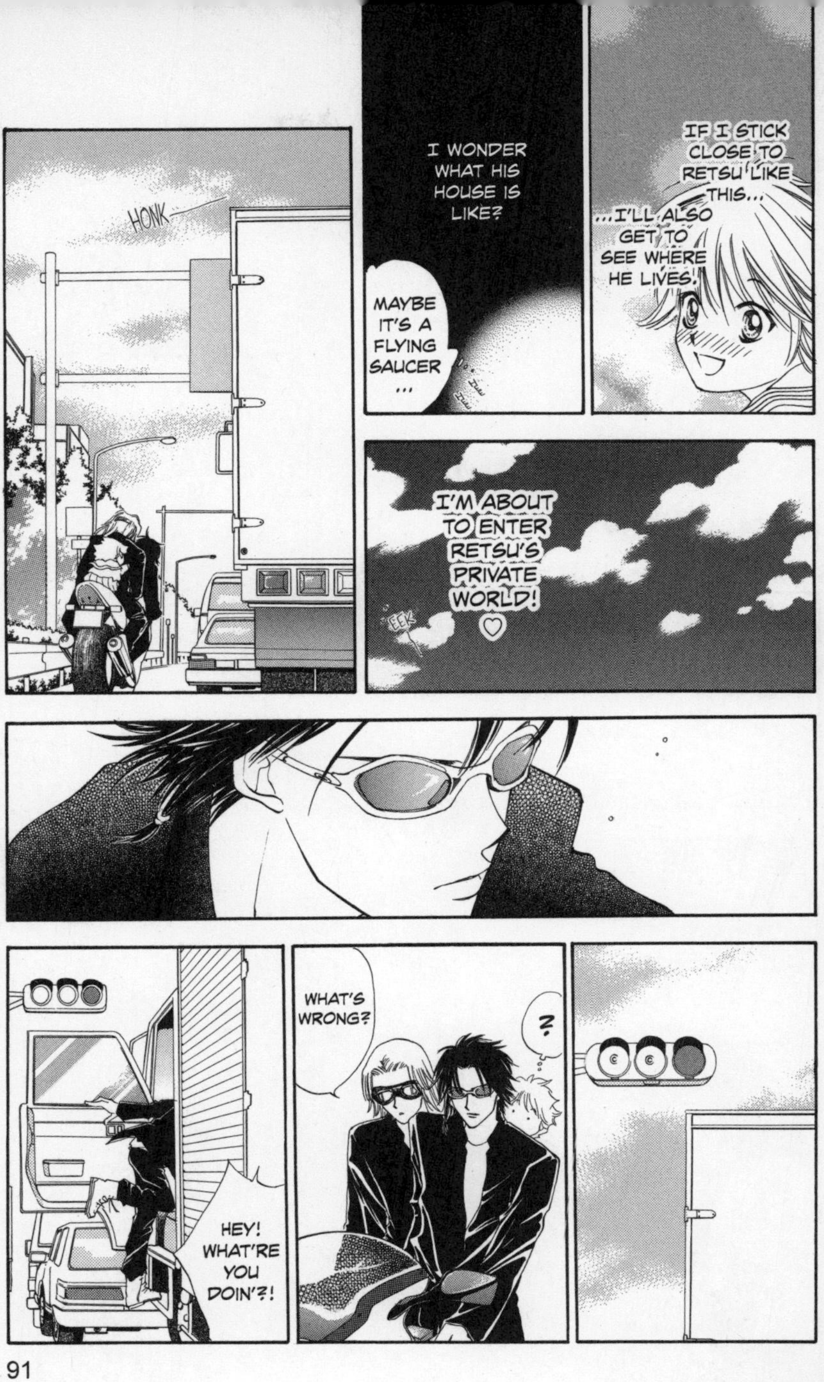
IF I STICK CLOSE TO RETSU LIKE THIS...
...I'LL ALSO GET TO SEE WHERE HE LIVES.
I WONDER WHAT HIS HOUSE IS LIKE?
MAYBE IT'S A FLYING SAUCER...
I'M ABOUT TO ENTER RETSU'S PRIVATE WORLD! ♡
EEK
HONK
?
WHAT'S WRONG?
HEY! WHAT'RE YOU DOIN'?!

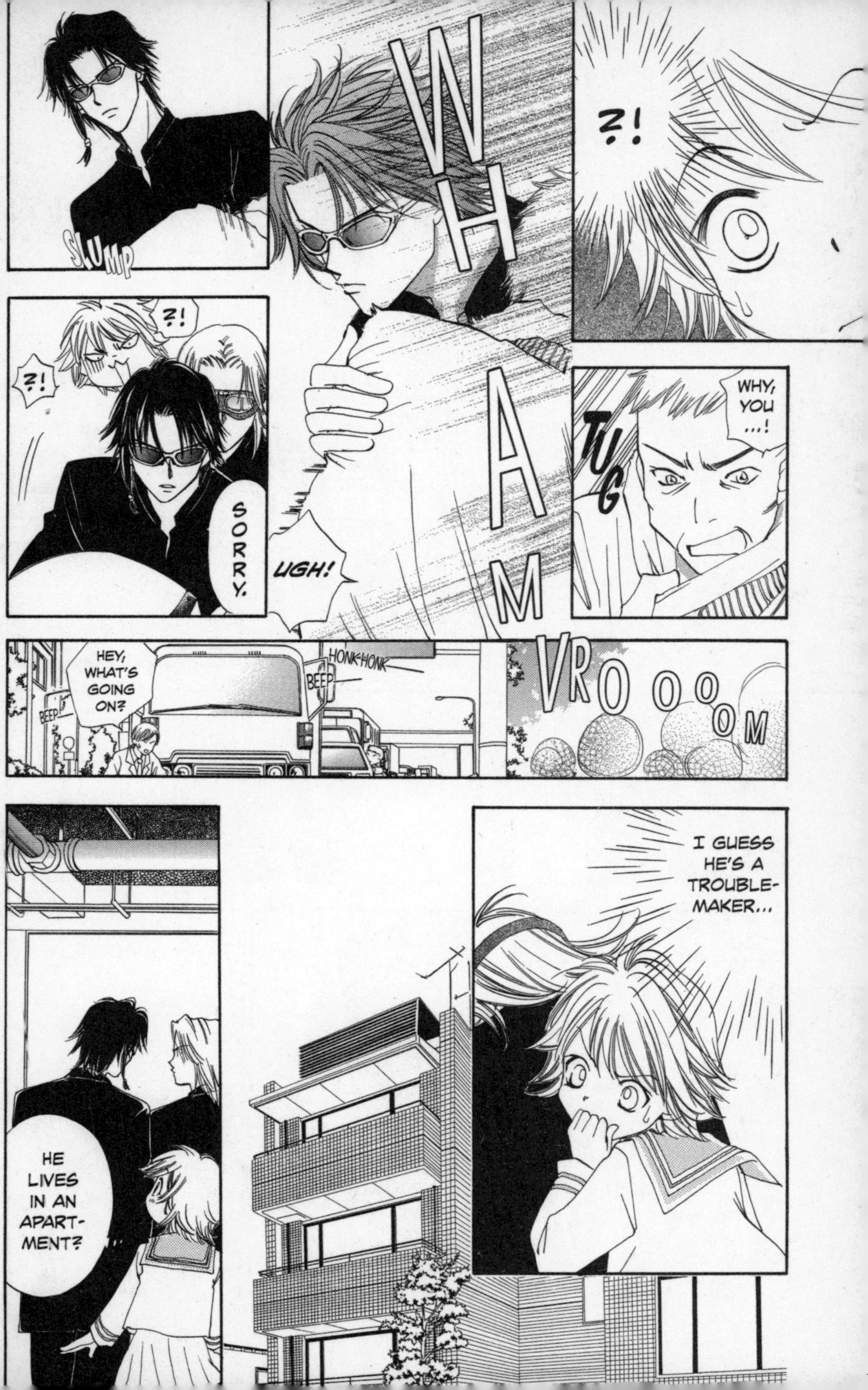
?!
TUG
WHY, YOU ...!
WHAM
UGH!
SLUMP
?!
?!
SORRY.
VROOOOOM
HONK-HONK
BEEP
HEY, WHAT'S GOING ON?
BEEP
I GUESS HE'S A TROUBLE-MAKER...
HE LIVES IN AN APART-MENT?

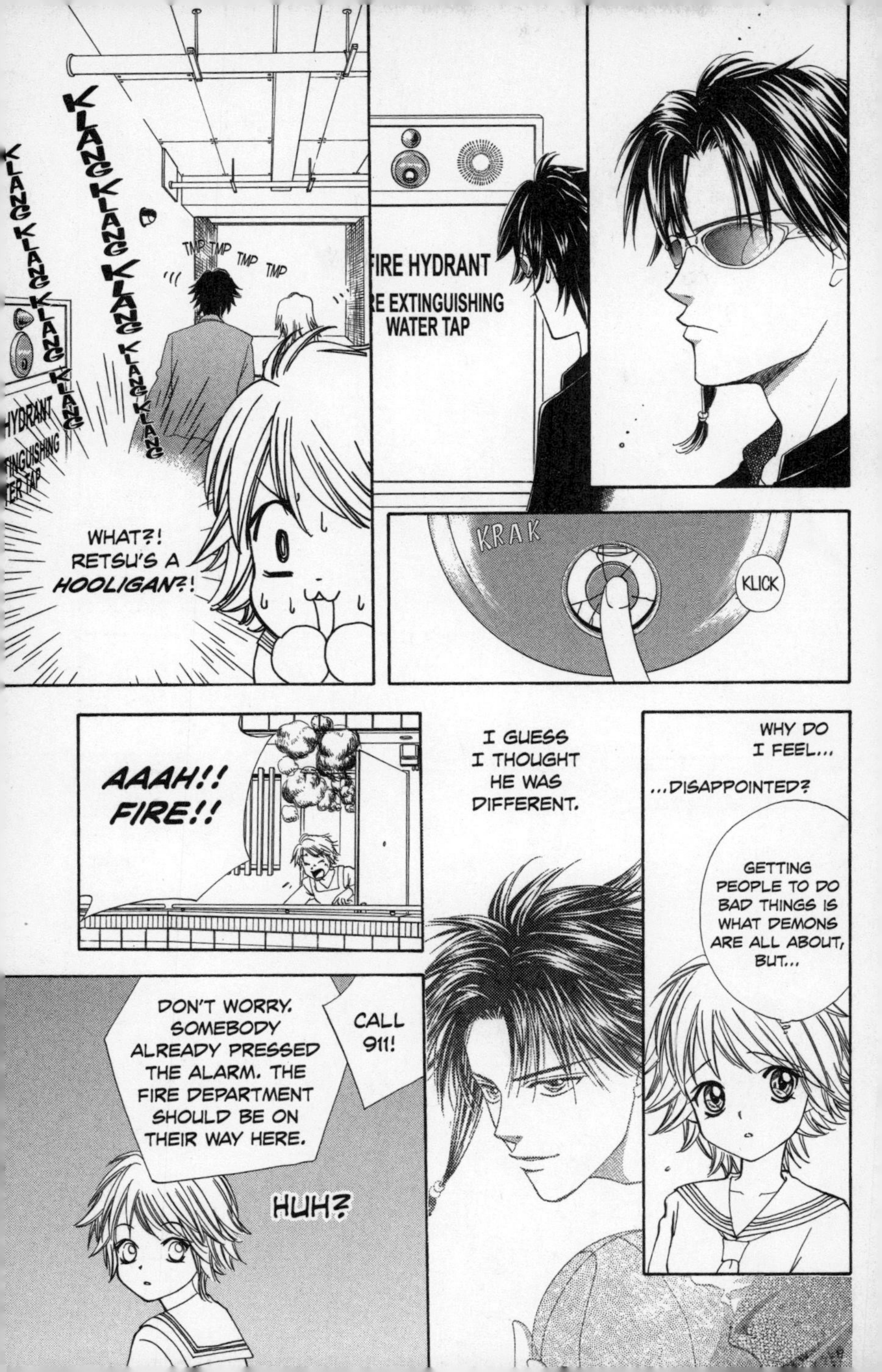
FIRE HYDRANT
RE EXTINGUISHING
WATER TAP
KRAK
KLICK
KLANG KLANG KLANG KLANG KLANG KLANG
KLANG KLANG KLANG KLANG KLANG KLANG
TMP TMP TMP TMP
WHAT?! RETSU'S A *HOOLIGAN*?!
WHY DO I FEEL...
...DISAPPOINTED?
GETTING PEOPLE TO DO BAD THINGS IS WHAT DEMONS ARE ALL ABOUT, BUT...
I GUESS I THOUGHT HE WAS DIFFERENT.
AAAH!! FIRE!!
CALL 911!
DON'T WORRY. SOMEBODY ALREADY PRESSED THE ALARM. THE FIRE DEPARTMENT SHOULD BE ON THEIR WAY HERE.
HUH?

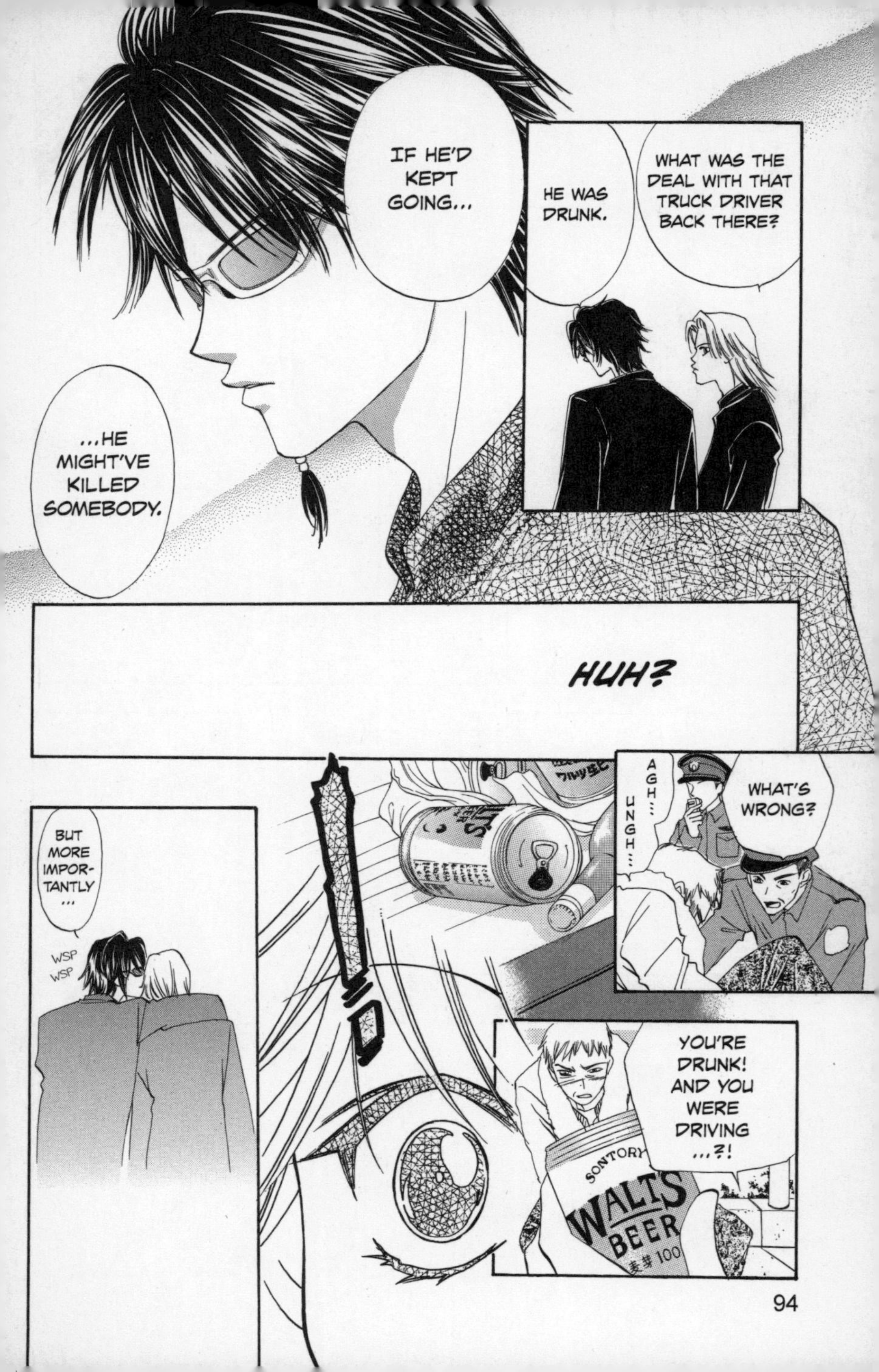
WHAT WAS THE DEAL WITH THAT TRUCK DRIVER BACK THERE?
HE WAS DRUNK.
IF HE'D KEPT GOING...
...HE MIGHT'VE KILLED SOMEBODY.
HUH?
WHAT'S WRONG?
AGH... UNGH...
YOU'RE DRUNK! AND YOU WERE DRIVING ...?!
SONTORY
WALTS BEER
100
!
BUT MORE IMPORTANTLY...
WSP WSP

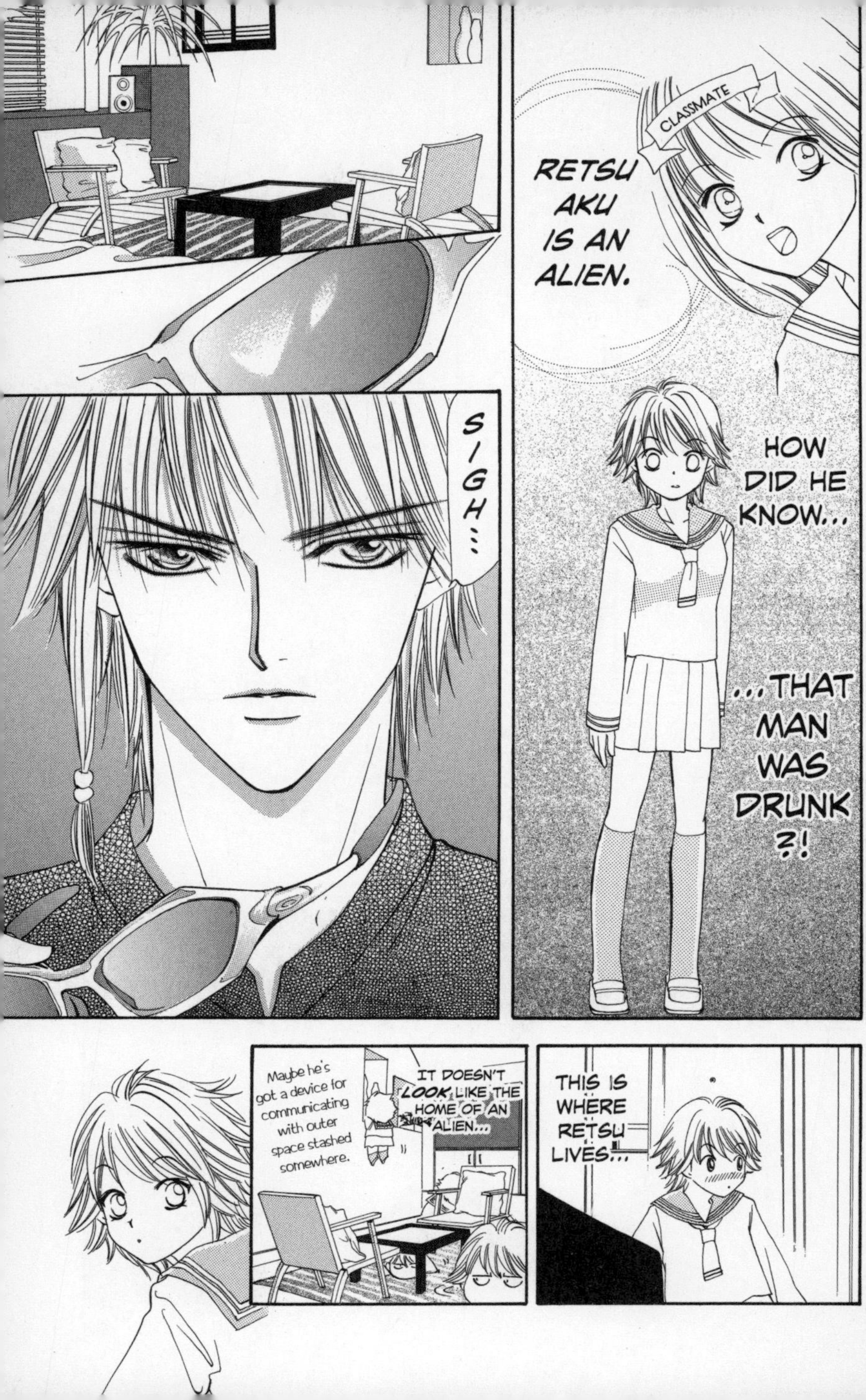
CLASSMATE
RETSU AKU IS AN ALIEN.
HOW DID HE KNOW...
...THAT MAN WAS DRUNK?!
SIGH...
THIS IS WHERE RETSU LIVES...
IT DOESN'T *LOOK* LIKE THE HOME OF AN ALIEN...
Maybe he's got a device for communicating with outer space stashed somewhere.

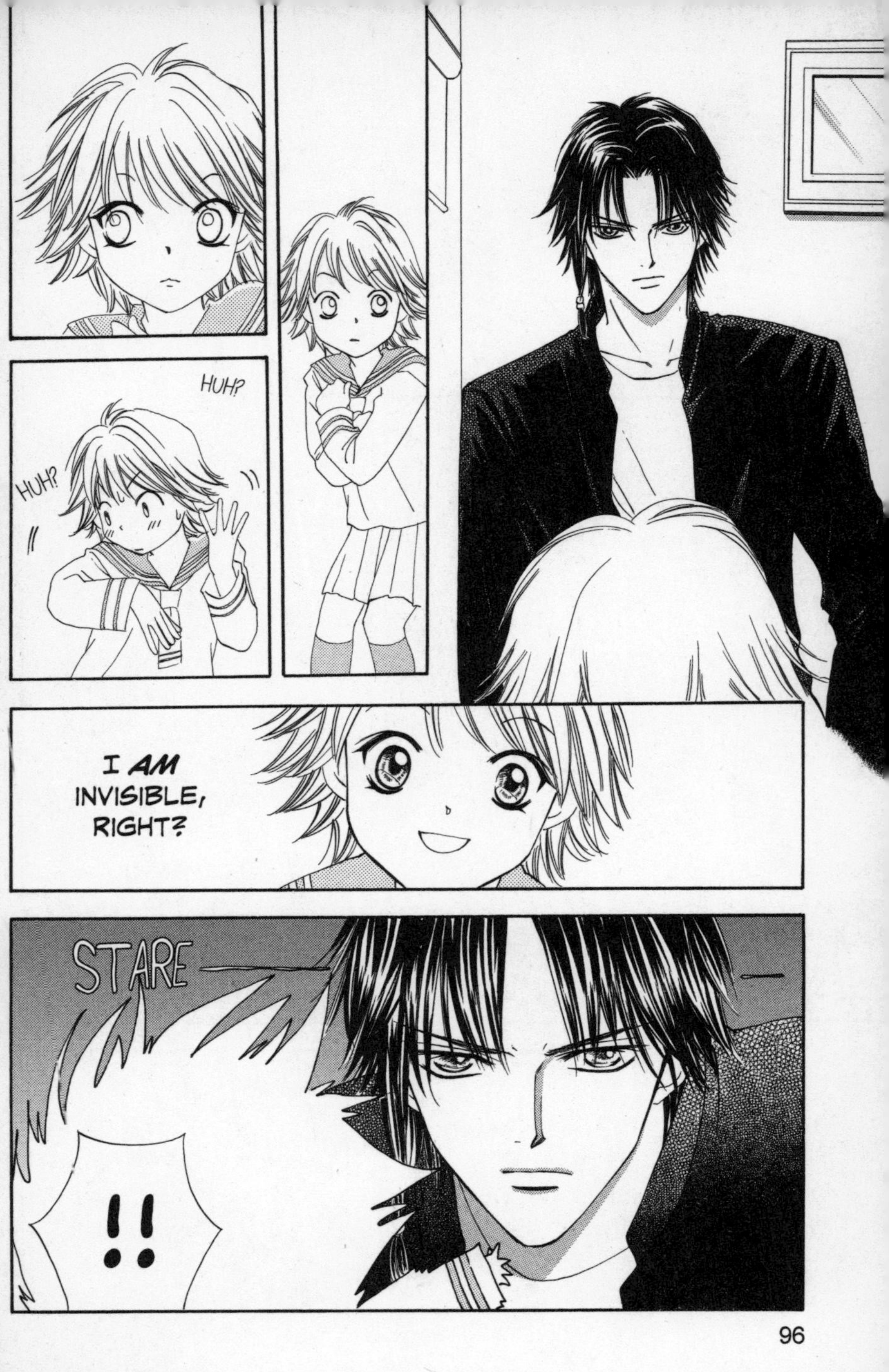
HUH?
HUH?
I *AM* INVISIBLE, RIGHT?
STARE
!!

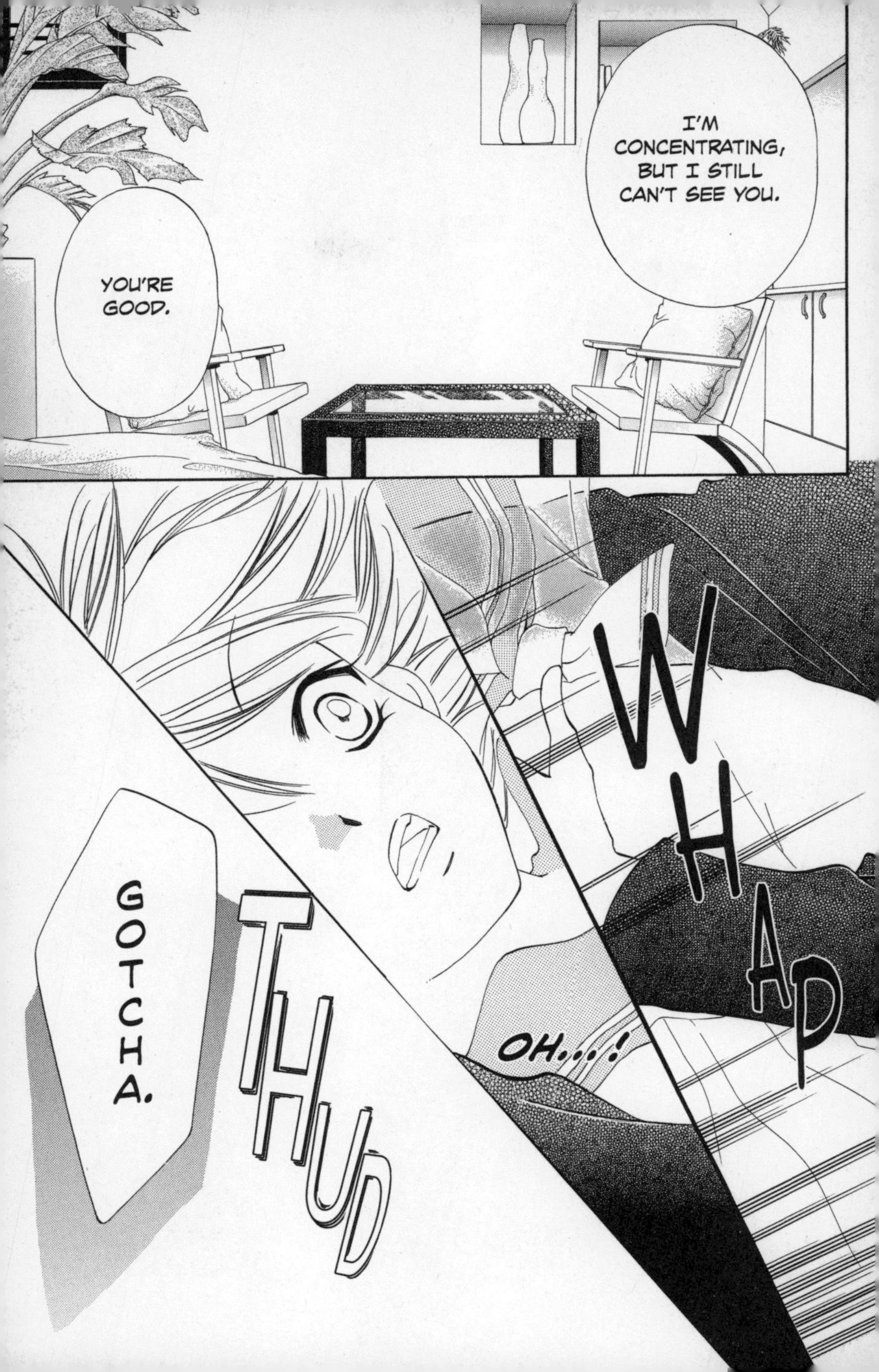
I'M CONCENTRATING, BUT I STILL CAN'T SEE YOU.
YOU'RE GOOD.
WHAP
OH...!
GOTCHA.
THUD

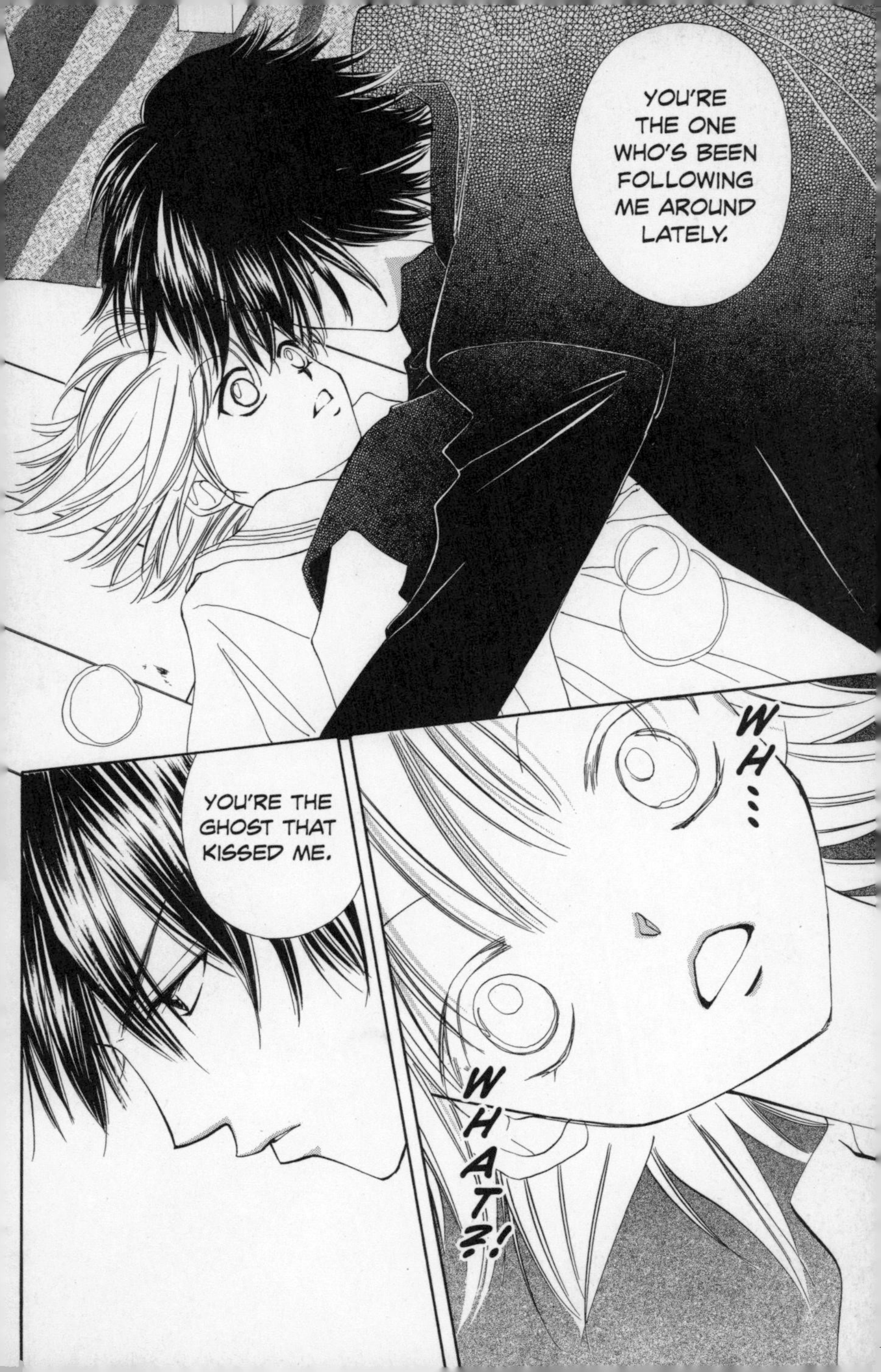
YOU'RE THE ONE WHO'S BEEN FOLLOWING ME AROUND LATELY.
WH...
YOU'RE THE GHOST THAT KISSED ME.
WHAT?!

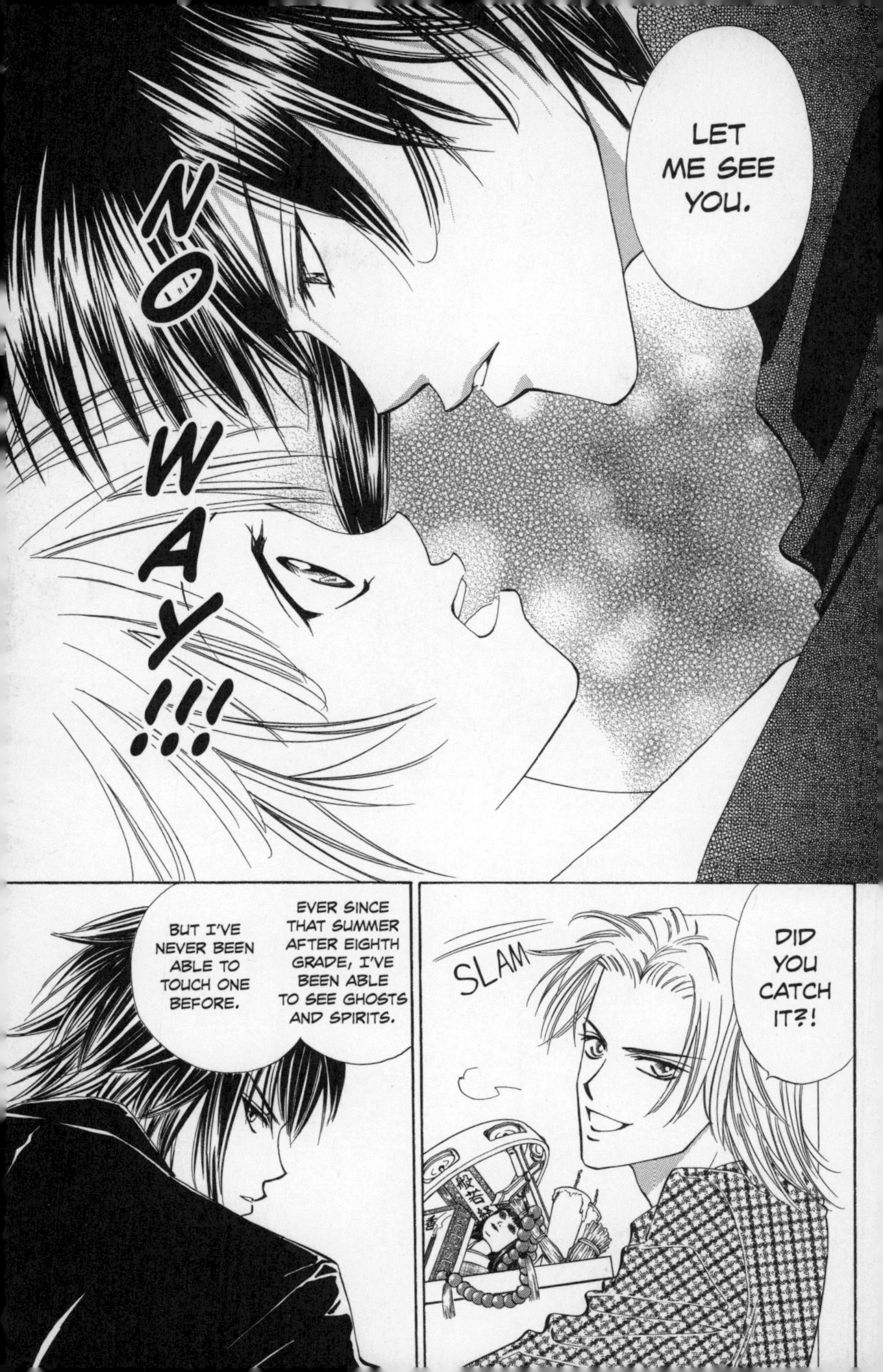
LET ME SEE YOU.
NO WAY!!!
DID YOU CATCH IT?!
SLAM
EVER SINCE THAT SUMMER AFTER EIGHTH GRADE, I'VE BEEN ABLE TO SEE GHOSTS AND SPIRITS.
BUT I'VE NEVER BEEN ABLE TO TOUCH ONE BEFORE.

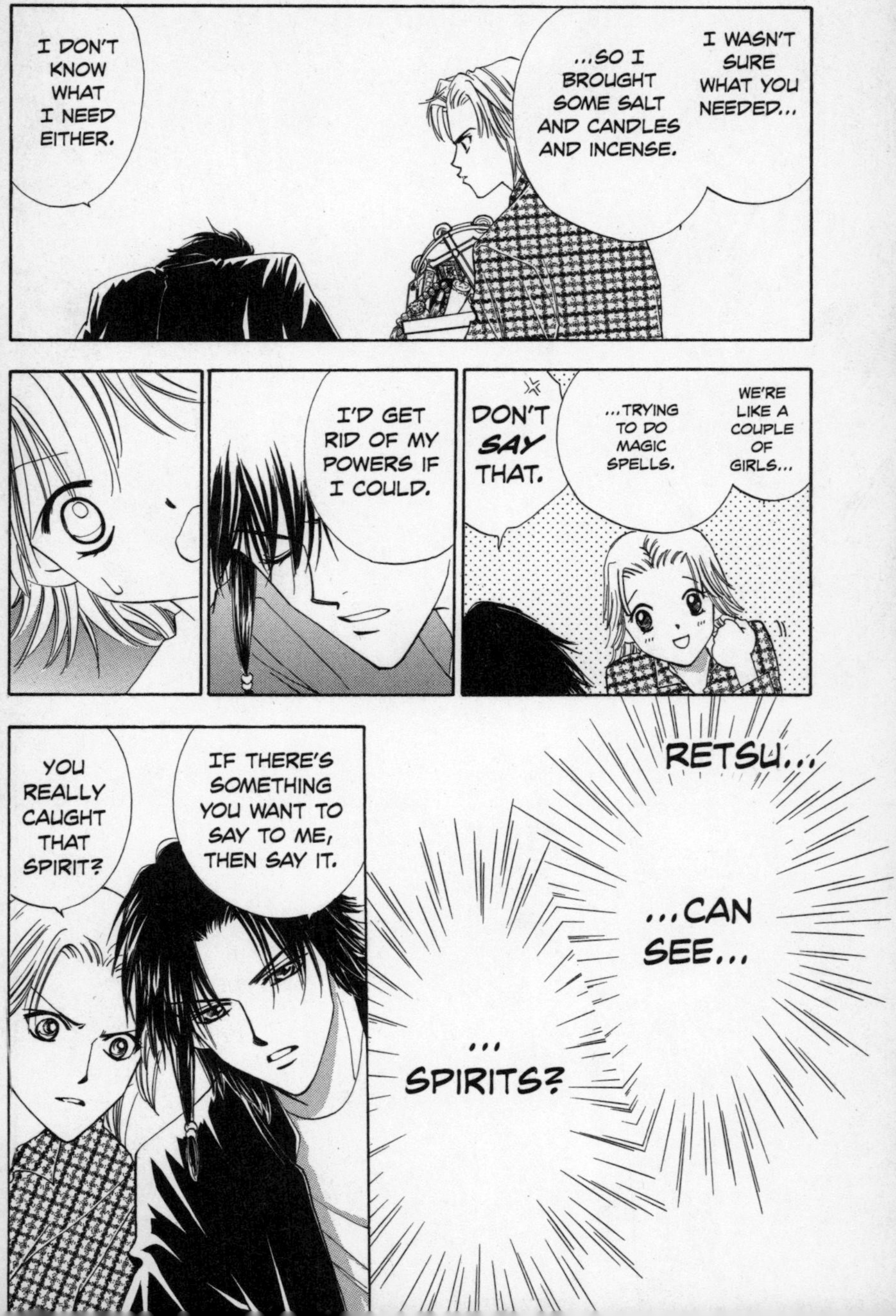
I WASN'T SURE WHAT YOU NEEDED...
...SO I BROUGHT SOME SALT AND CANDLES AND INCENSE.
I DON'T KNOW WHAT I NEED EITHER.
WE'RE LIKE A COUPLE OF GIRLS...
...TRYING TO DO MAGIC SPELLS.
DON'T *SAY* THAT.
I'D GET RID OF MY POWERS IF I COULD.
RETSU...
...CAN SEE...
...SPIRITS?
IF THERE'S SOMETHING YOU WANT TO SAY TO ME, THEN SAY IT.
YOU REALLY CAUGHT THAT SPIRIT?

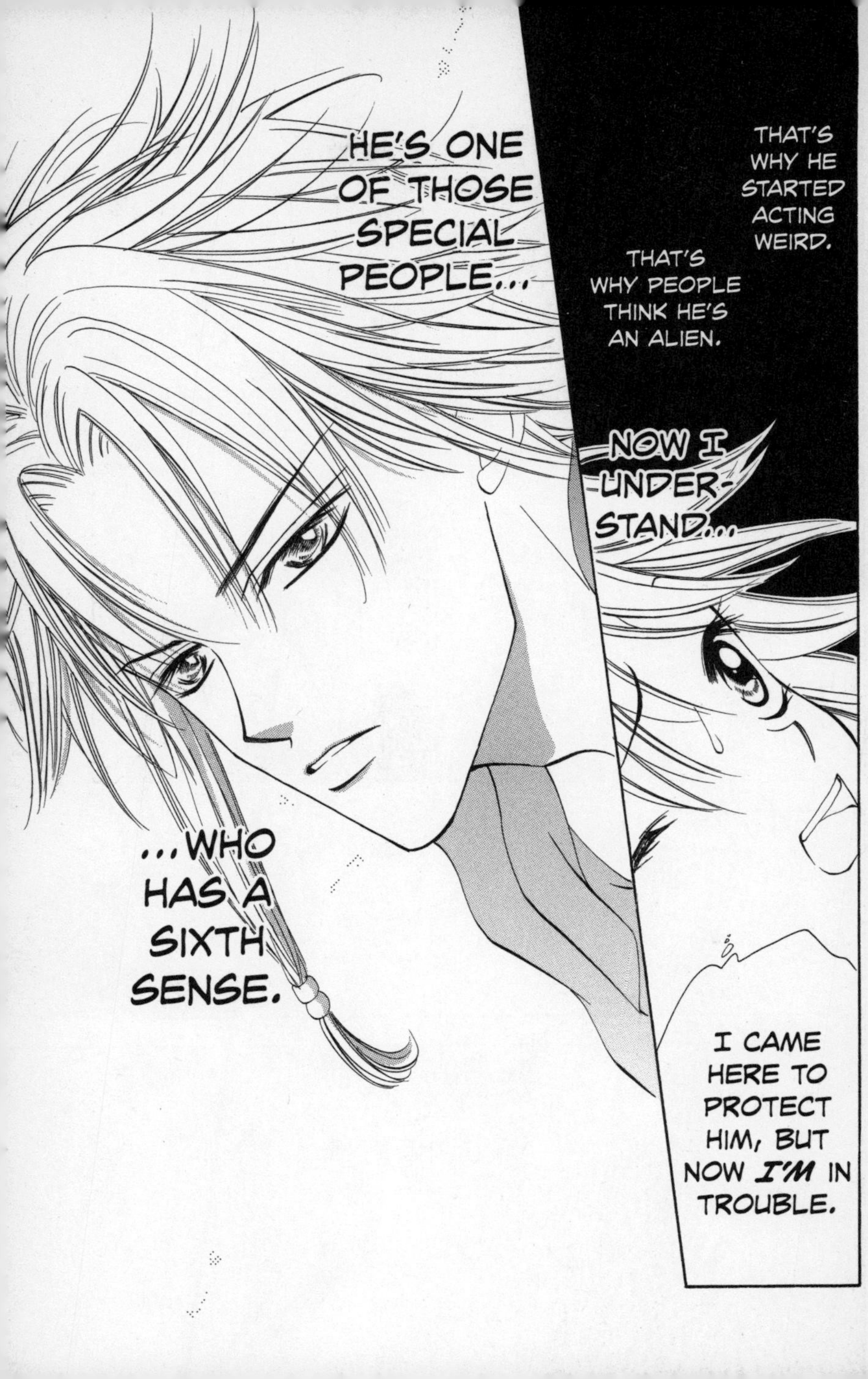
THAT'S WHY HE STARTED ACTING WEIRD.
THAT'S WHY PEOPLE THINK HE'S AN ALIEN.
NOW I UNDER-STAND...
I CAME HERE TO PROTECT HIM, BUT NOW *I'M* IN TROUBLE.
HE'S ONE OF THOSE SPECIAL PEOPLE...
...WHO HAS A SIXTH SENSE.

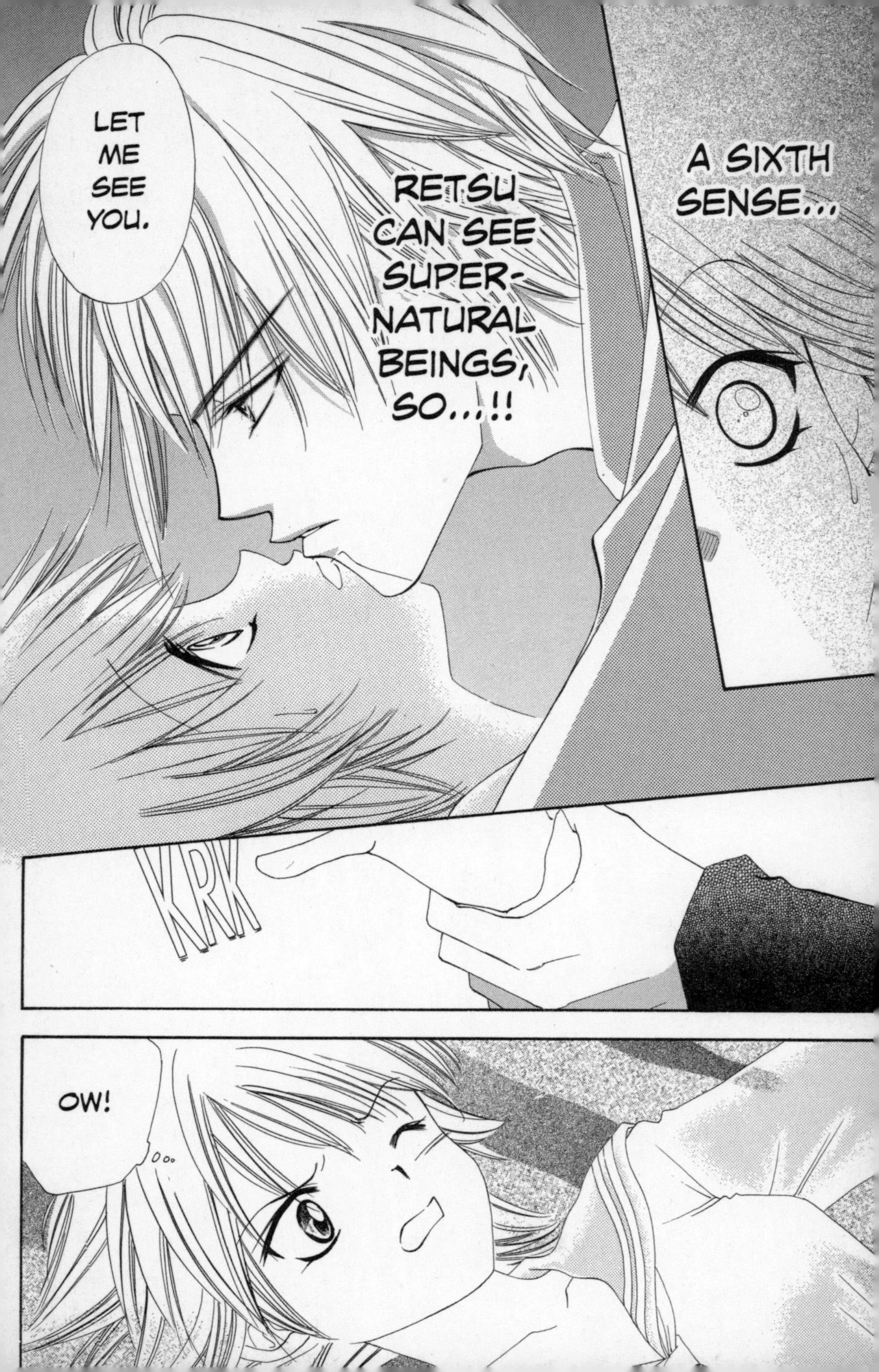
A SIXTH SENSE...
RETSU CAN SEE SUPER-NATURAL BEINGS, SO...!!
LET ME SEE YOU.
KRK
OW!

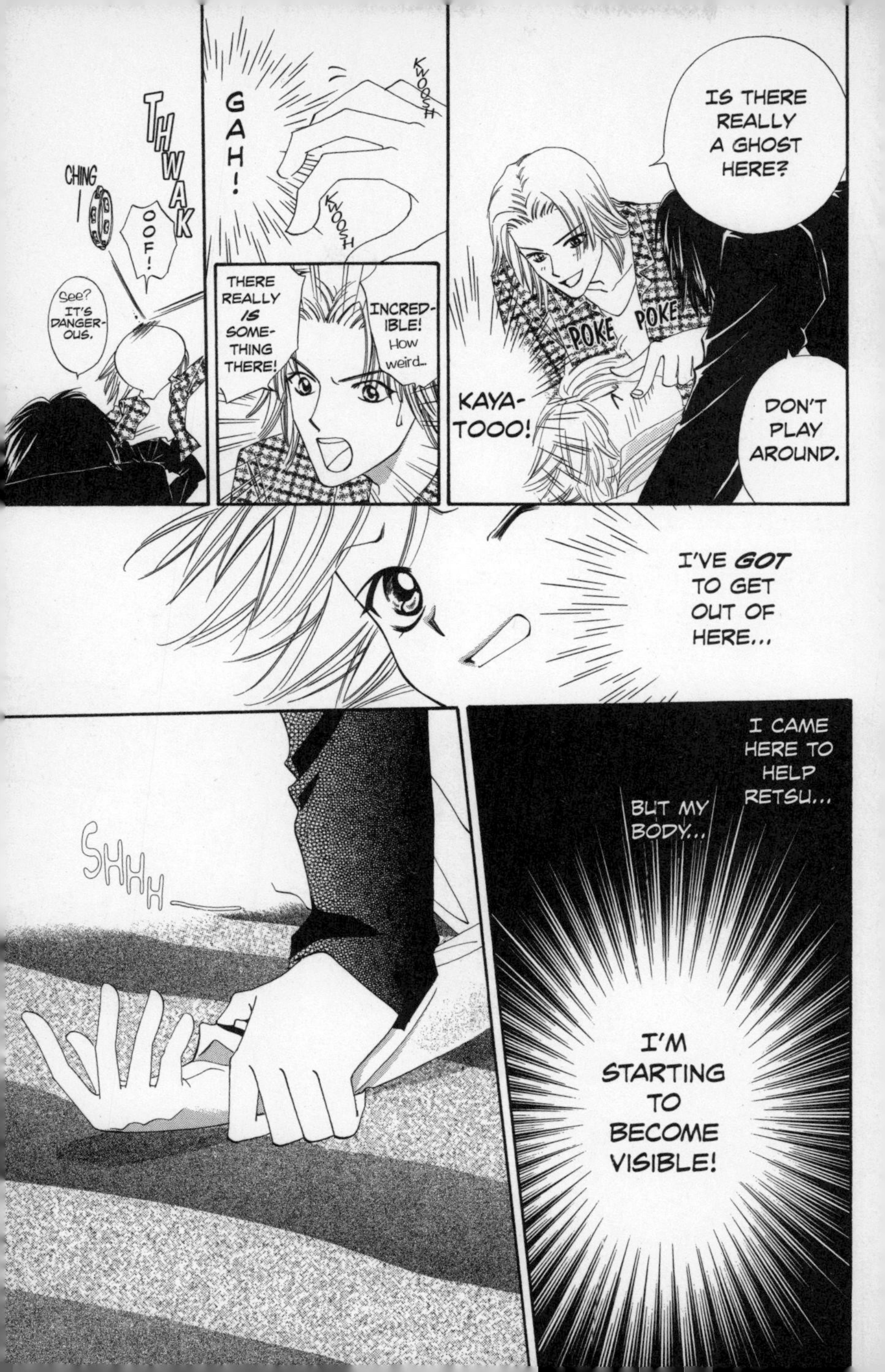
IS THERE REALLY A GHOST HERE?
POKE POKE
KAYA-TOOO!
DON'T PLAY AROUND.
GAH!
KWOOSH
KWOOSH
INCREDIBLE! How weird...
THERE REALLY IS SOMETHING THERE!
THWAK
OOF!
CHING
See? IT'S DANGEROUS.
I'VE GOT TO GET OUT OF HERE...
I CAME HERE TO HELP RETSU...
BUT MY BODY...
I'M STARTING TO BECOME VISIBLE!
SHHH

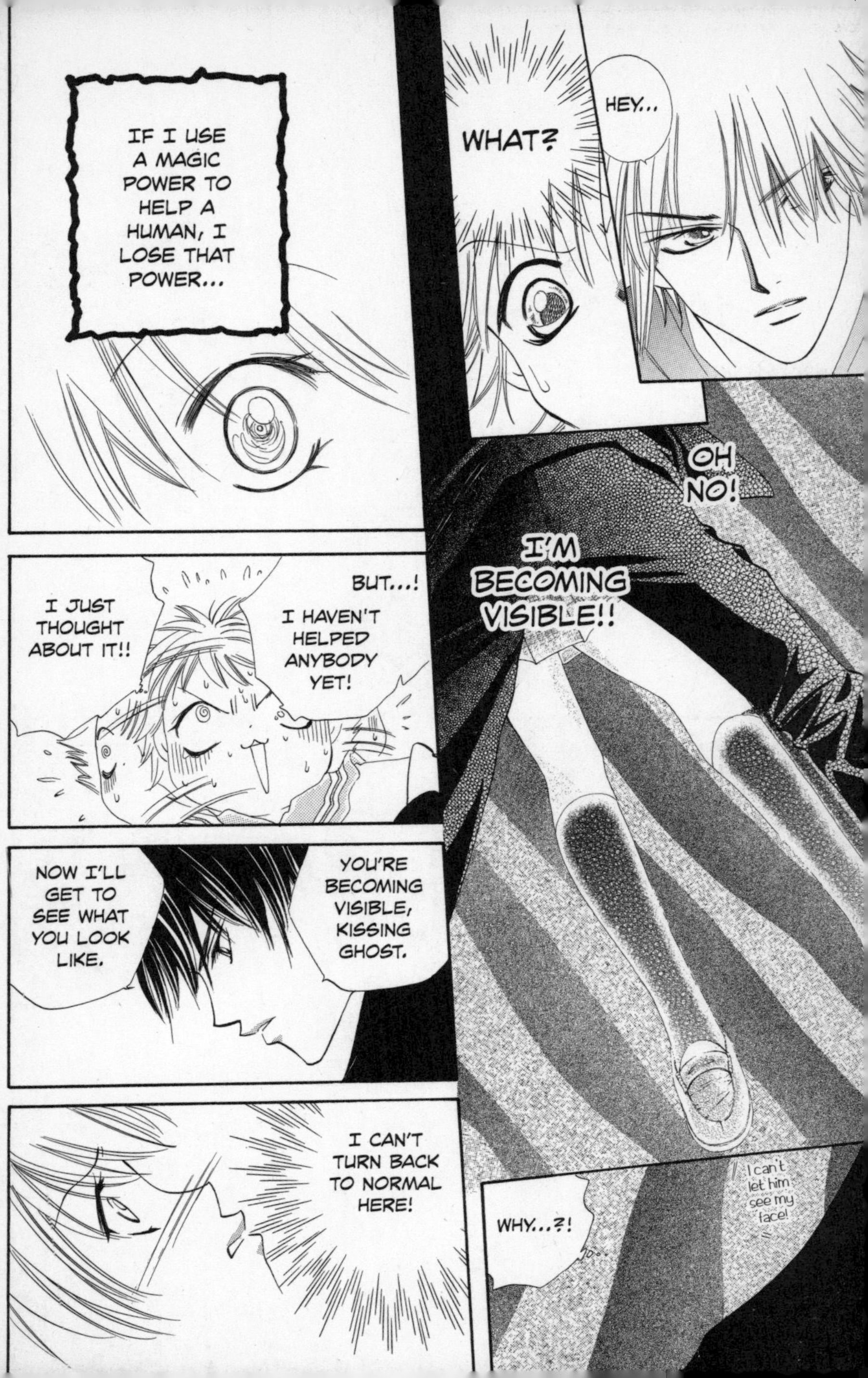
HEY...
WHAT?
OH NO!
I'M BECOMING VISIBLE!!
WHY...?!
I can't let him see my face!
IF I USE A MAGIC POWER TO HELP A HUMAN, I LOSE THAT POWER...
BUT...!
I HAVEN'T HELPED ANYBODY YET!
I JUST THOUGHT ABOUT IT!!
YOU'RE BECOMING VISIBLE, KISSING GHOST.
NOW I'LL GET TO SEE WHAT YOU LOOK LIKE.
I CAN'T TURN BACK TO NORMAL HERE!

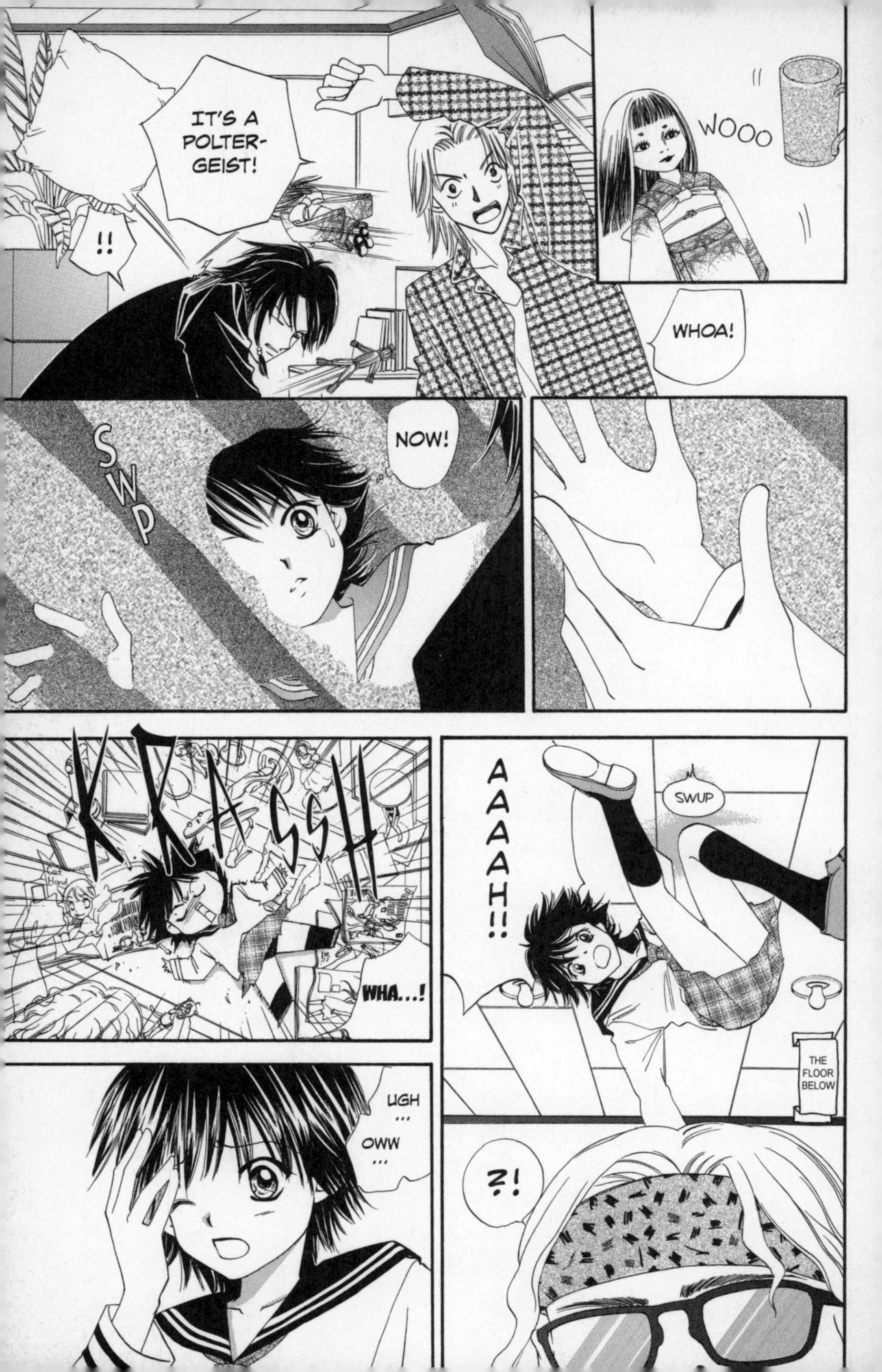
WOOO
IT'S A POLTER-GEIST!
!!
WHOA!
NOW!
SWP
AAAAH!!
SWUP
THE FLOOR BELOW
KRASSH
Cat Hand
WHA...!
UGH ...
OWW ...
?!

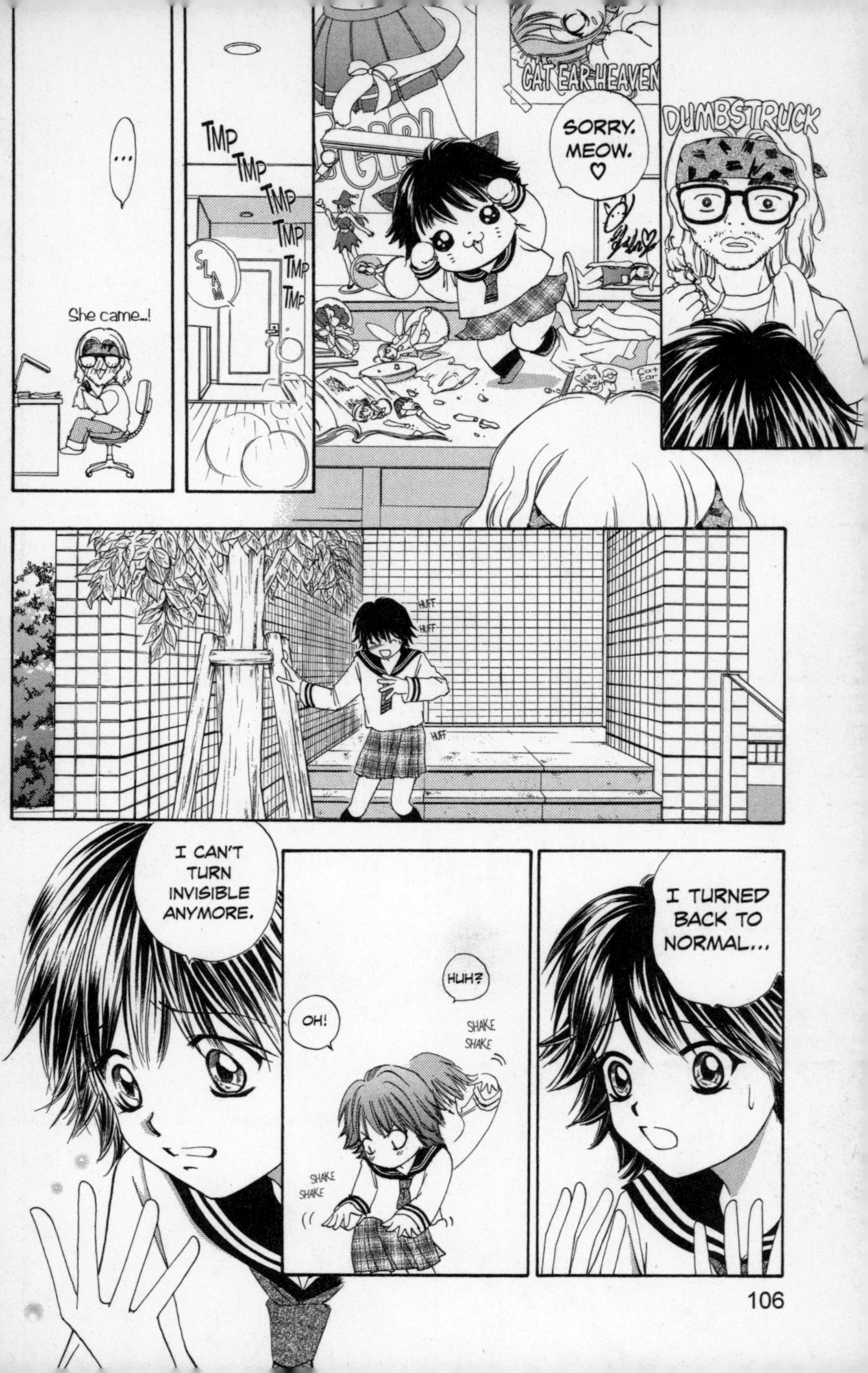
DUMBSTRUCK
CAT EAR HEAVEN
SORRY. MEOW. ♡
TMP TMP TMP TMP TMP TMP
SLAM
...
She came...!
HUFF
HUFF
HUFF
I TURNED BACK TO NORMAL...
HUH?
SHAKE SHAKE
OH!
SHAKE SHAKE
I CAN'T TURN INVISIBLE ANYMORE.

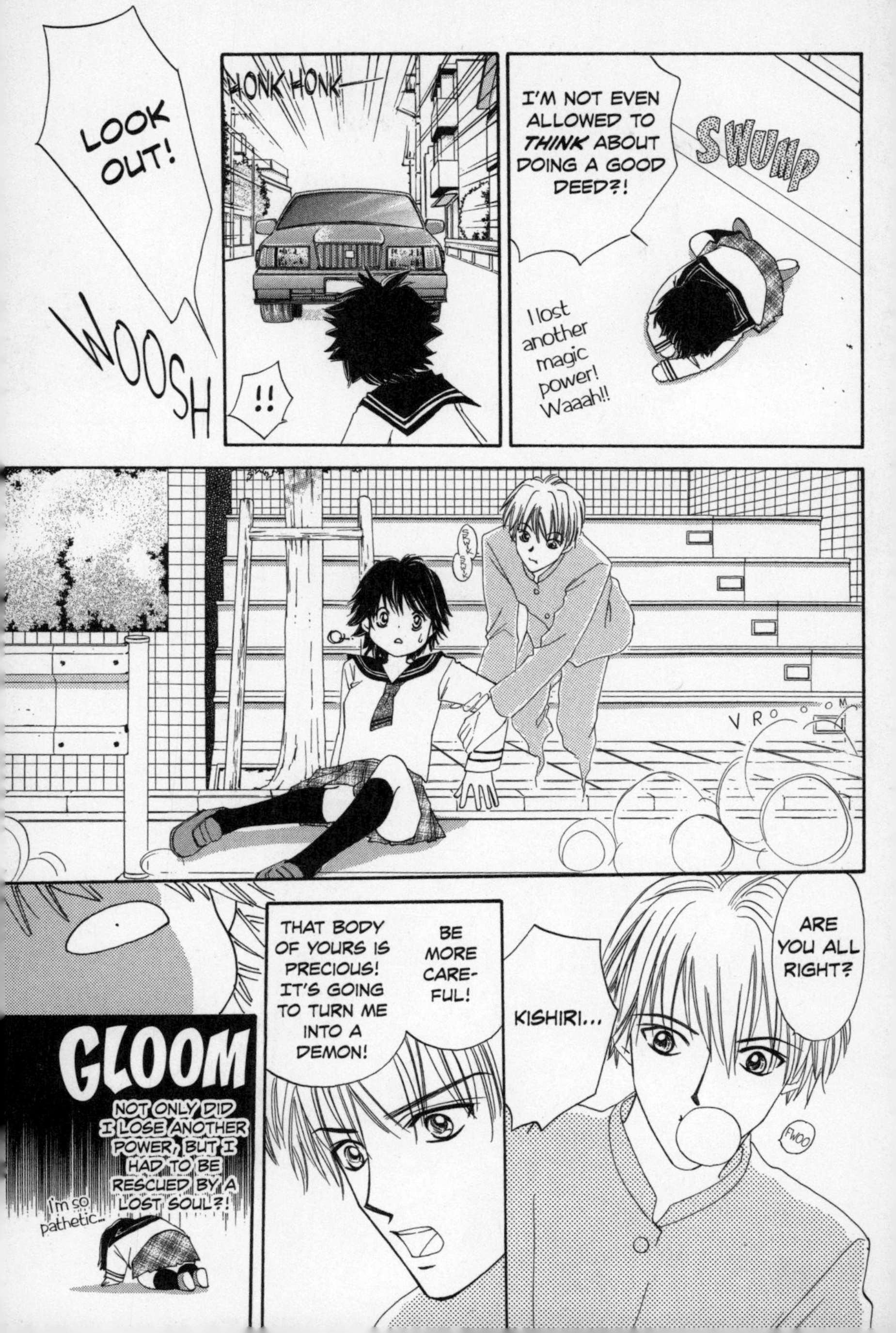
I'M NOT EVEN ALLOWED TO *THINK* ABOUT DOING A GOOD DEED?!
SWUMP
I lost another magic power! Waaah!!
HONK HONK
LOOK OUT!
WOOSH
!!
VROOOM
ARE YOU ALL RIGHT?
FWOO
KISHIRI...
BE MORE CARE-FUL!
THAT BODY OF YOURS IS PRECIOUS! IT'S GOING TO TURN ME INTO A DEMON!
GLOOM
NOT ONLY DID I LOSE ANOTHER POWER, BUT I HAD TO BE RESCUED BY A LOST SOUL?!
I'm so pathetic...

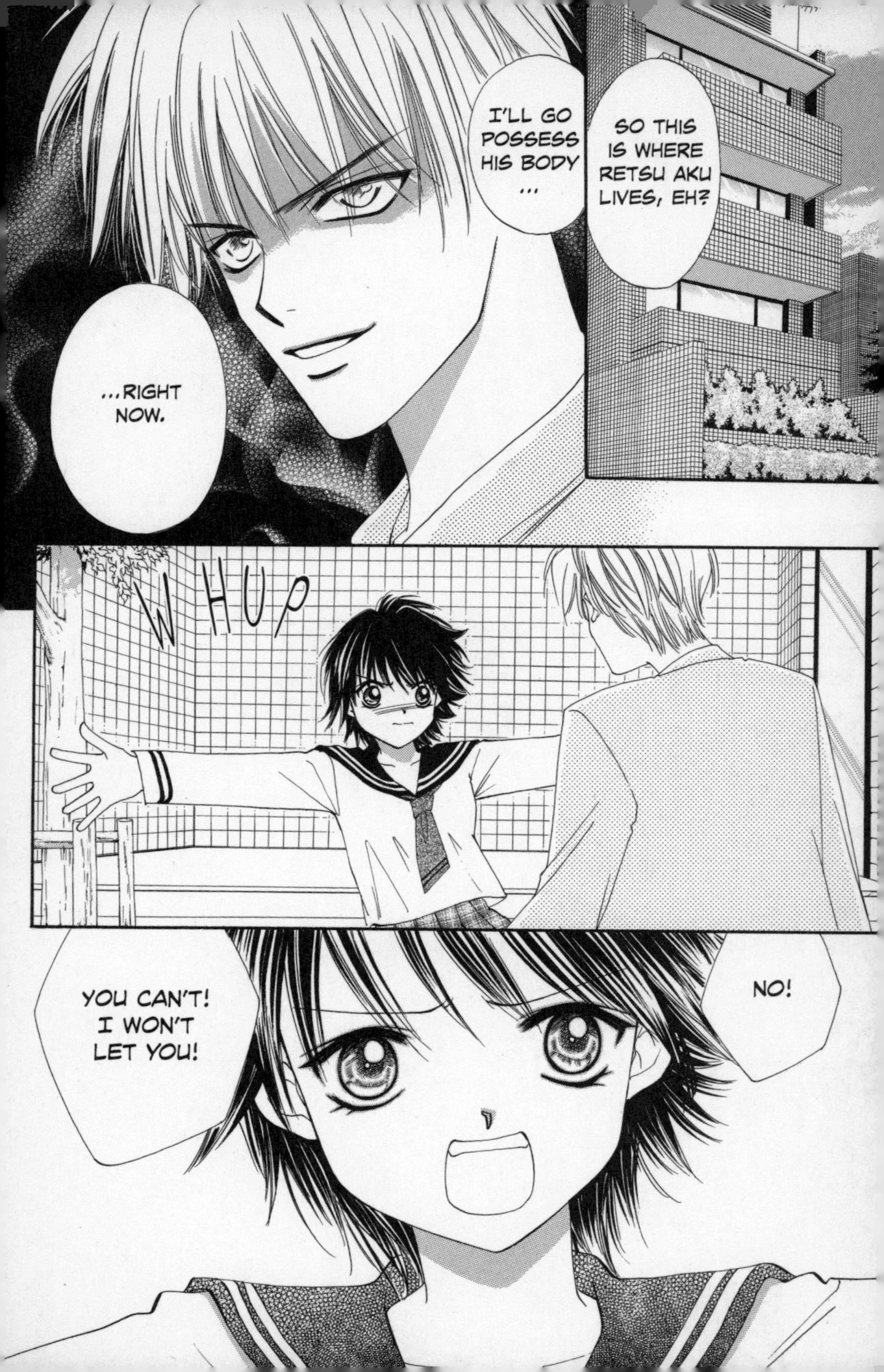
SO THIS IS WHERE RETSU AKU LIVES, EH?
I'LL GO POSSESS HIS BODY ...
...RIGHT NOW.
WHUP
NO!
YOU CAN'T! I WON'T LET YOU!

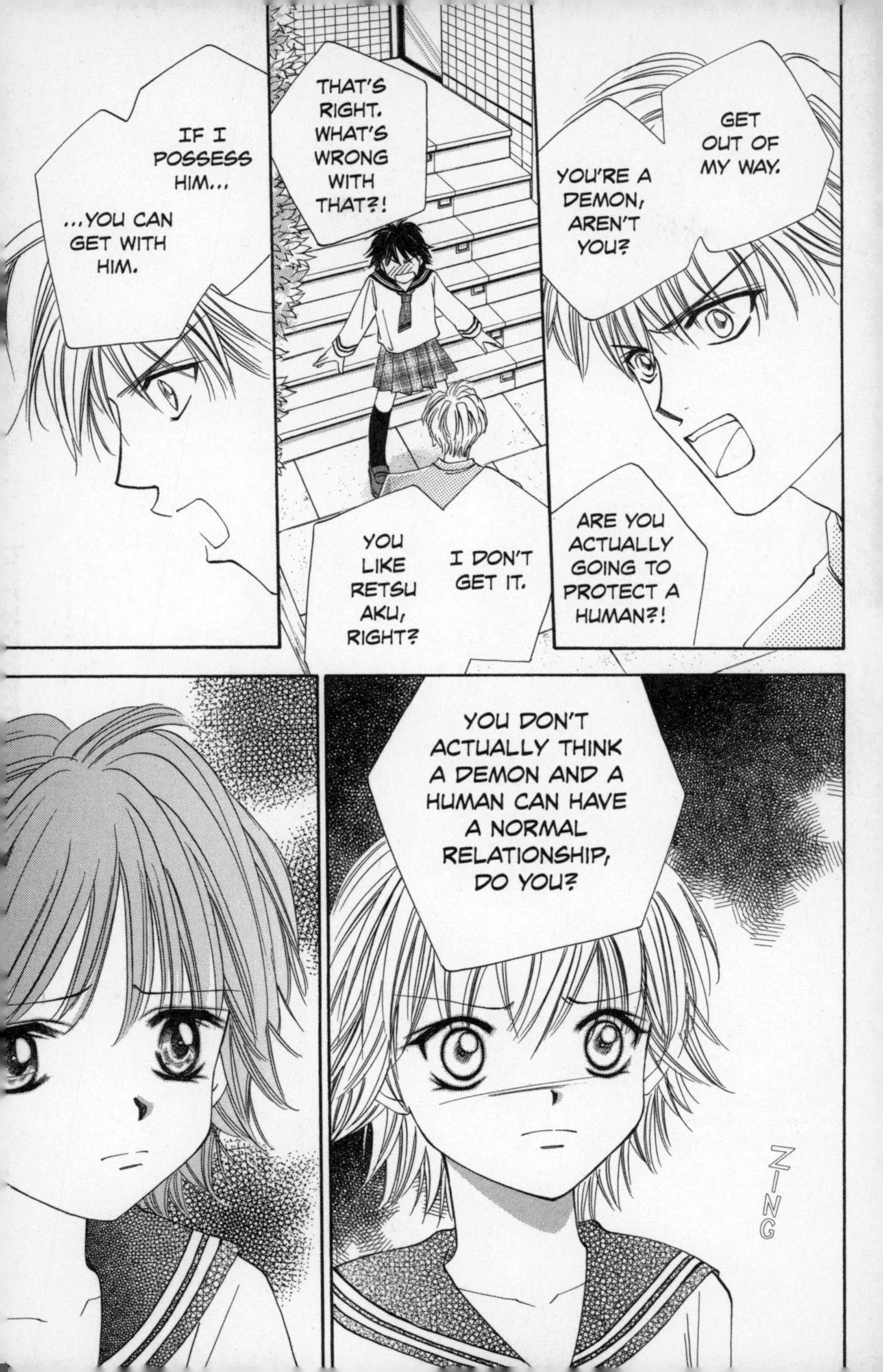
GET OUT OF MY WAY.
YOU'RE A DEMON, AREN'T YOU?
ARE YOU ACTUALLY GOING TO PROTECT A HUMAN?!
THAT'S RIGHT. WHAT'S WRONG WITH THAT?!
I DON'T GET IT.
YOU LIKE RETSU AKU, RIGHT?
IF I POSSESS HIM...
...YOU CAN GET WITH HIM.
YOU DON'T ACTUALLY THINK A DEMON AND A HUMAN CAN HAVE A NORMAL RELATIONSHIP, DO YOU?
ZING

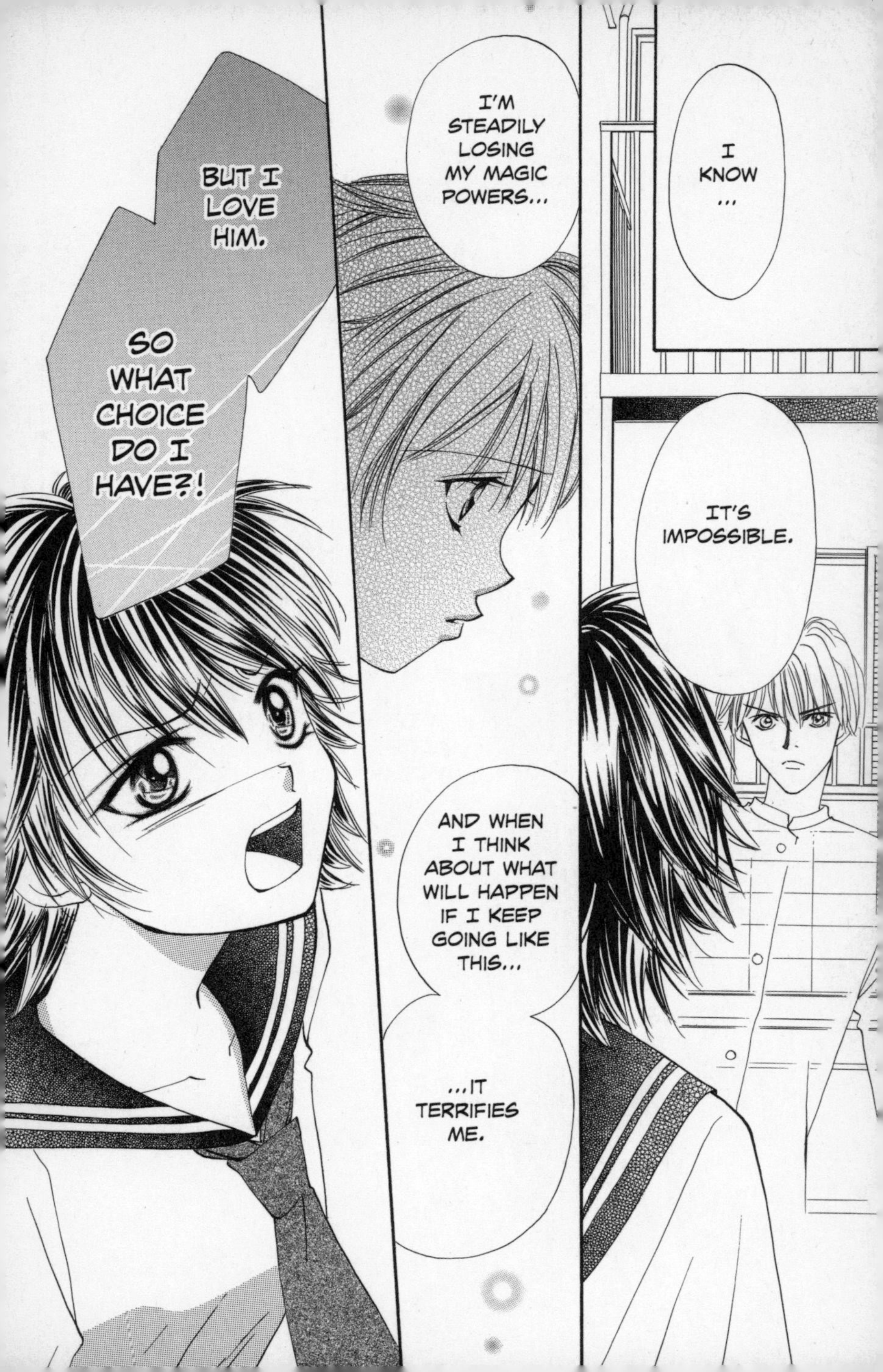
I KNOW ...
IT'S IMPOSSIBLE.
I'M STEADILY LOSING MY MAGIC POWERS...
AND WHEN I THINK ABOUT WHAT WILL HAPPEN IF I KEEP GOING LIKE THIS...
...IT TERRIFIES ME.
BUT I LOVE HIM.
SO WHAT CHOICE DO I HAVE?!

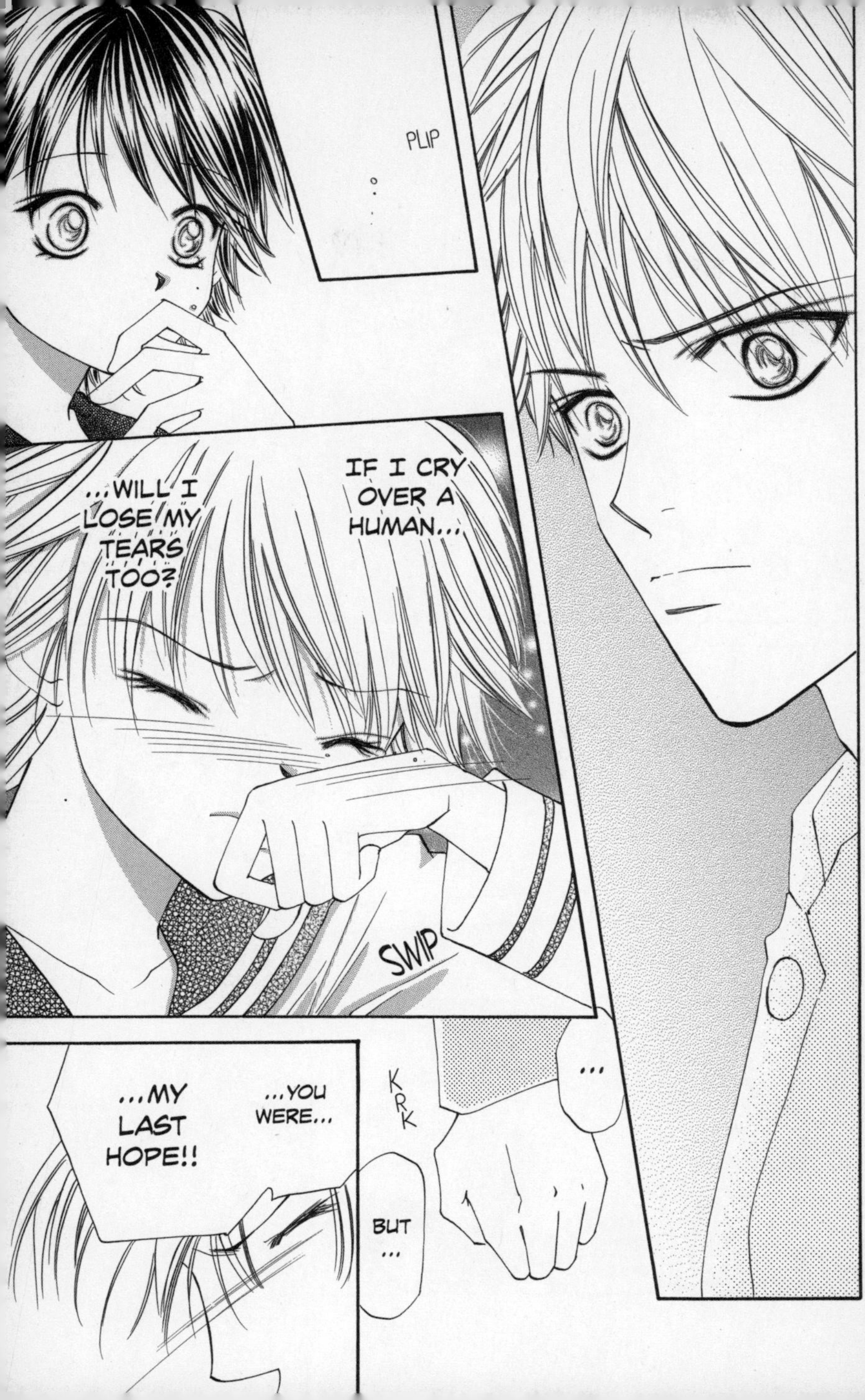
PLIP
IF I CRY OVER A HUMAN...
...WILL I LOSE MY TEARS TOO?
SWIP
...
KRK
...YOU WERE...
...MY LAST HOPE!!
BUT ...

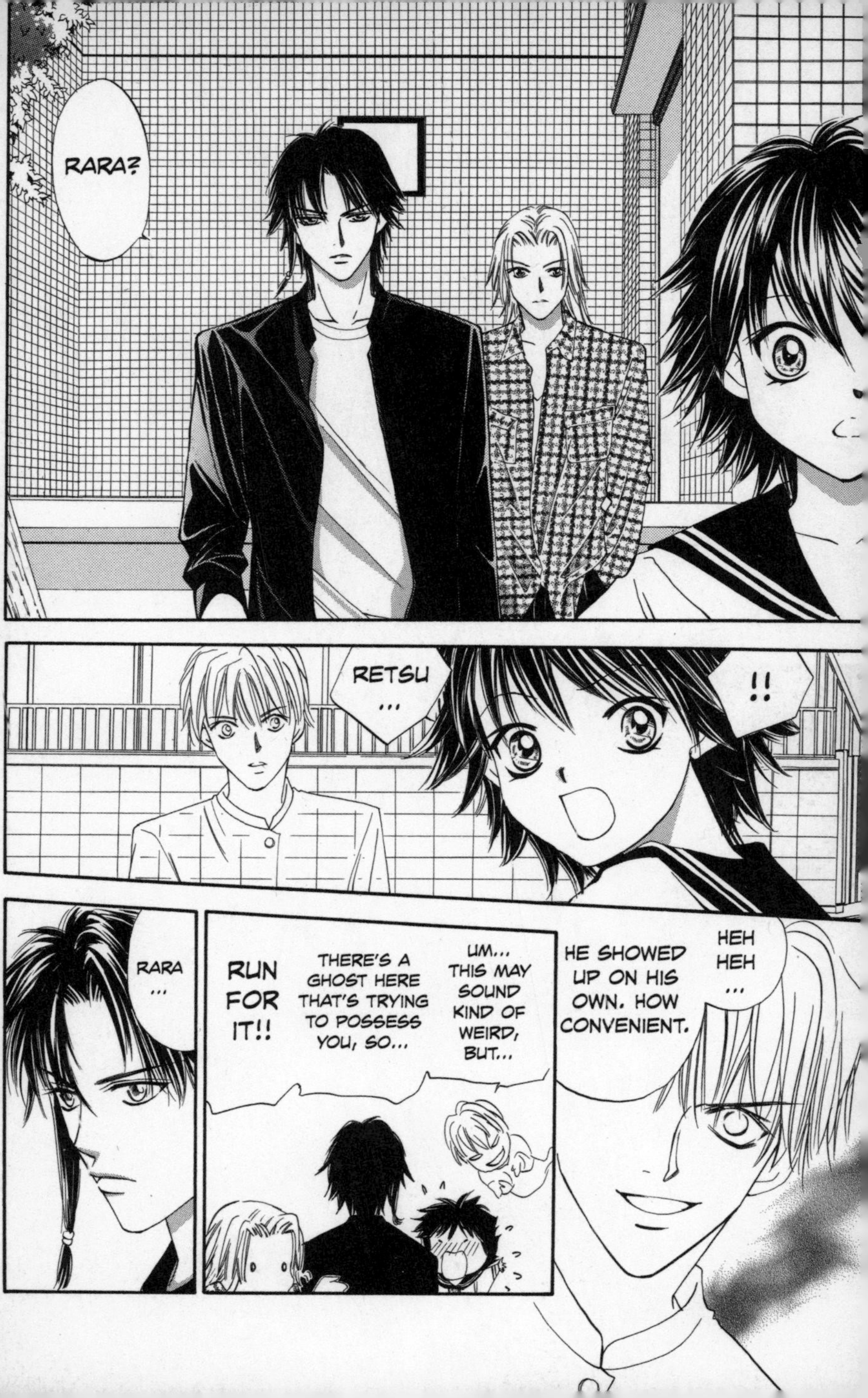
RARA?
!!
RETSU ...
HEH HEH ...
HE SHOWED UP ON HIS OWN. HOW CONVENIENT.
UM... THIS MAY SOUND KIND OF WEIRD, BUT...
THERE'S A GHOST HERE THAT'S TRYING TO POSSESS YOU, SO...
RUN FOR IT!!
RARA ...

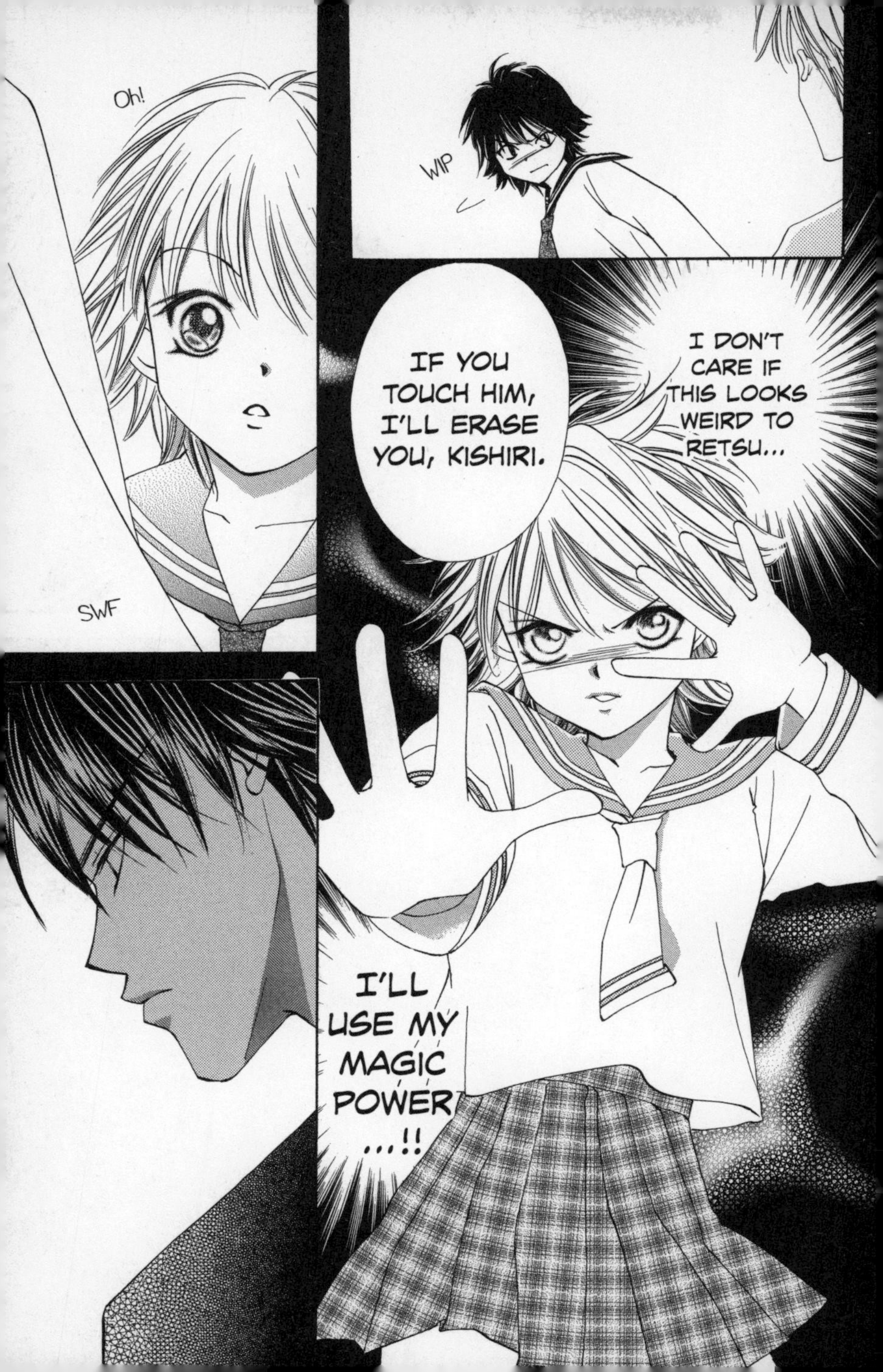
WIP
Oh!
SWF
I DON'T CARE IF THIS LOOKS WEIRD TO RETSU...
IF YOU TOUCH HIM, I'LL ERASE YOU, KISHIRI.
I'LL USE MY MAGIC POWER ...!!

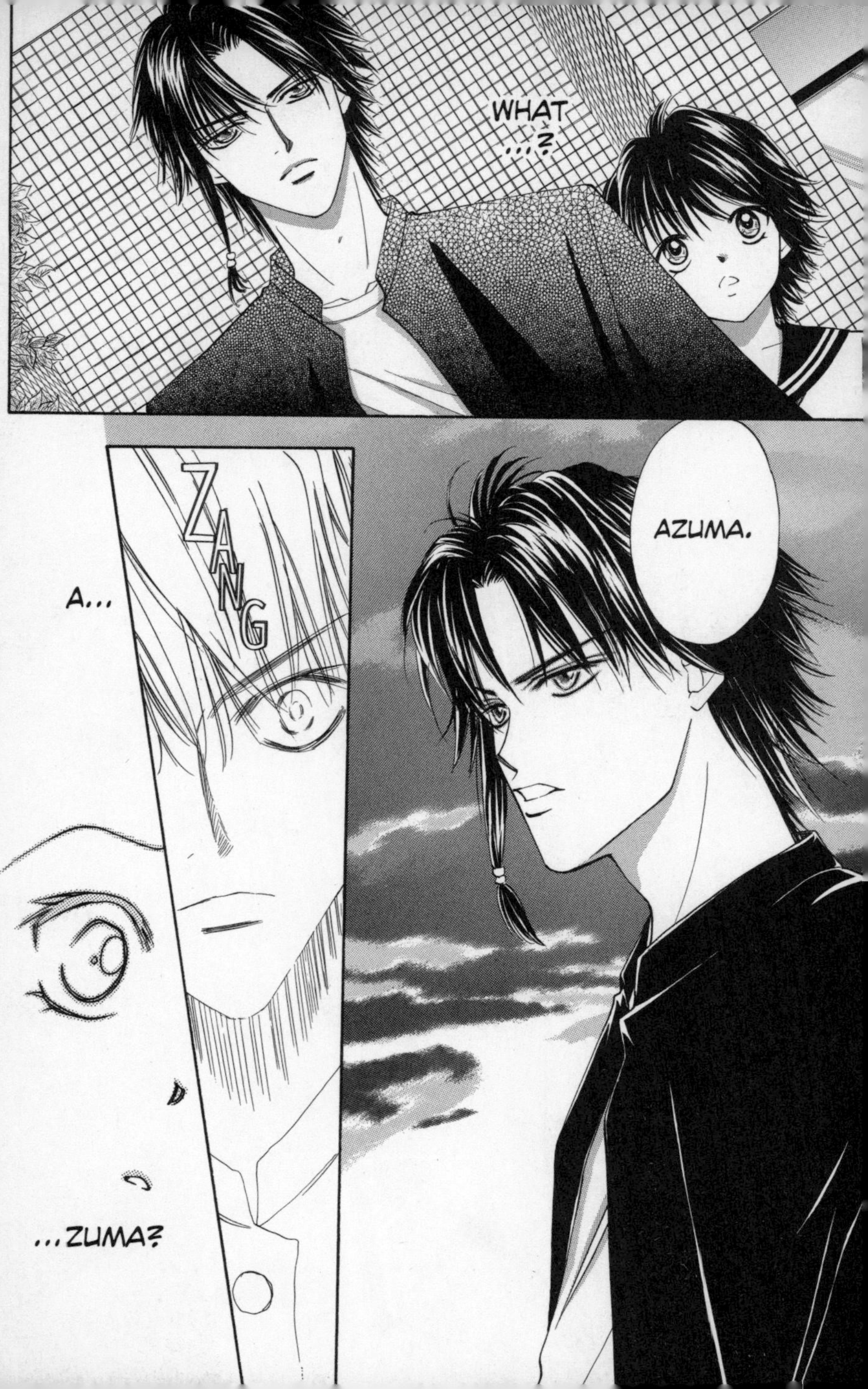
WHAT ...?
AZUMA.
ZANG
A...
...ZUMA?

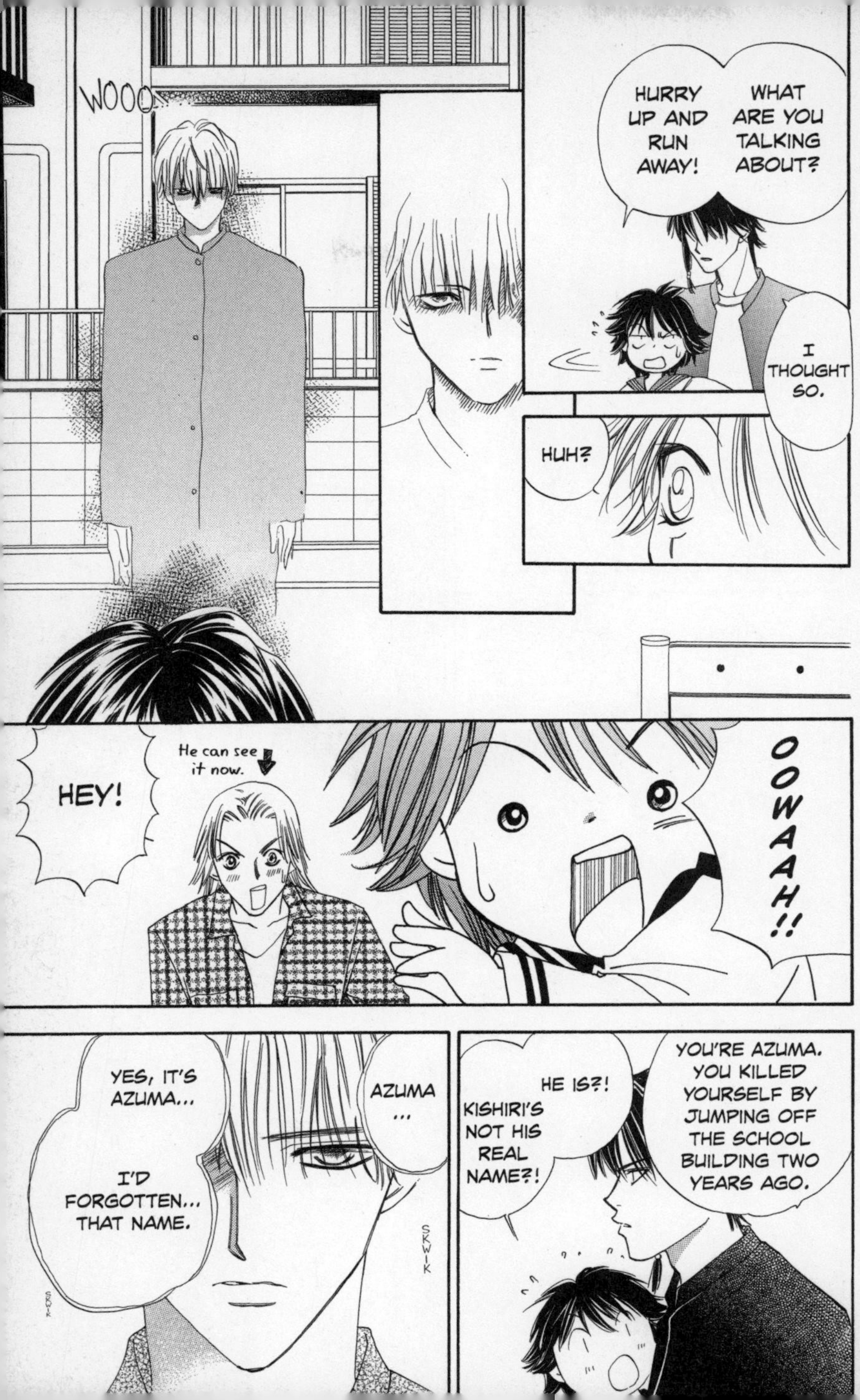
WHAT ARE YOU TALKING ABOUT?
HURRY UP AND RUN AWAY!
I THOUGHT SO.
HUH?
WOOO...
OOWAAAH!!
He can see it now.
HEY!
YOU'RE AZUMA. YOU KILLED YOURSELF BY JUMPING OFF THE SCHOOL BUILDING TWO YEARS AGO.
HE IS?!
KISHIRI'S NOT HIS REAL NAME?!
SKWIK
AZUMA...
YES, IT'S AZUMA...
I'D FORGOTTEN... THAT NAME.
SKWIK

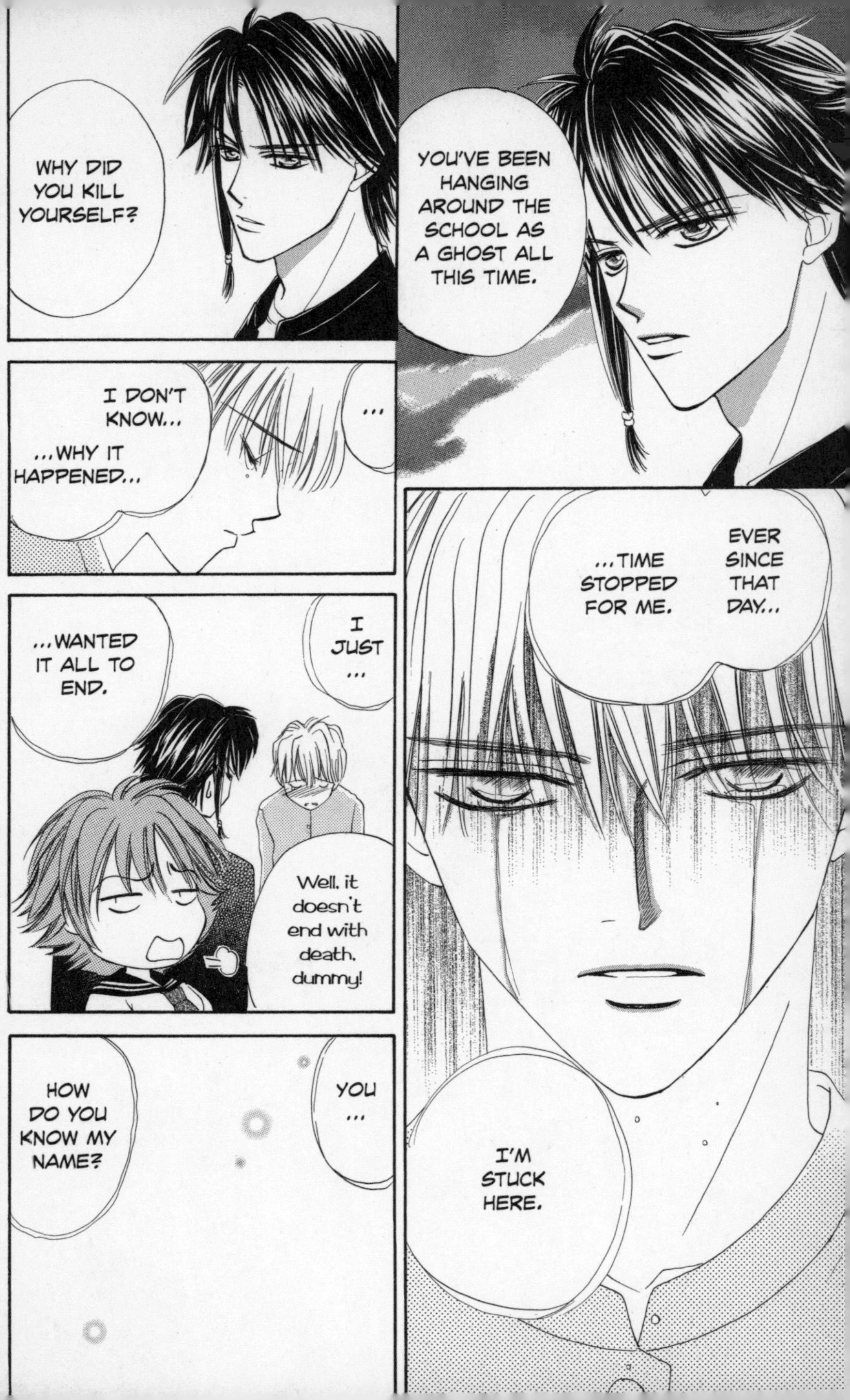
YOU'VE BEEN HANGING AROUND THE SCHOOL AS A GHOST ALL THIS TIME.
WHY DID YOU KILL YOURSELF?
...
I DON'T KNOW...
...WHY IT HAPPENED...
EVER SINCE THAT DAY...
...TIME STOPPED FOR ME.
I'M STUCK HERE.
I JUST ...
...WANTED IT ALL TO END.
Well, it doesn't end with death, dummy!
YOU ...
HOW DO YOU KNOW MY NAME?

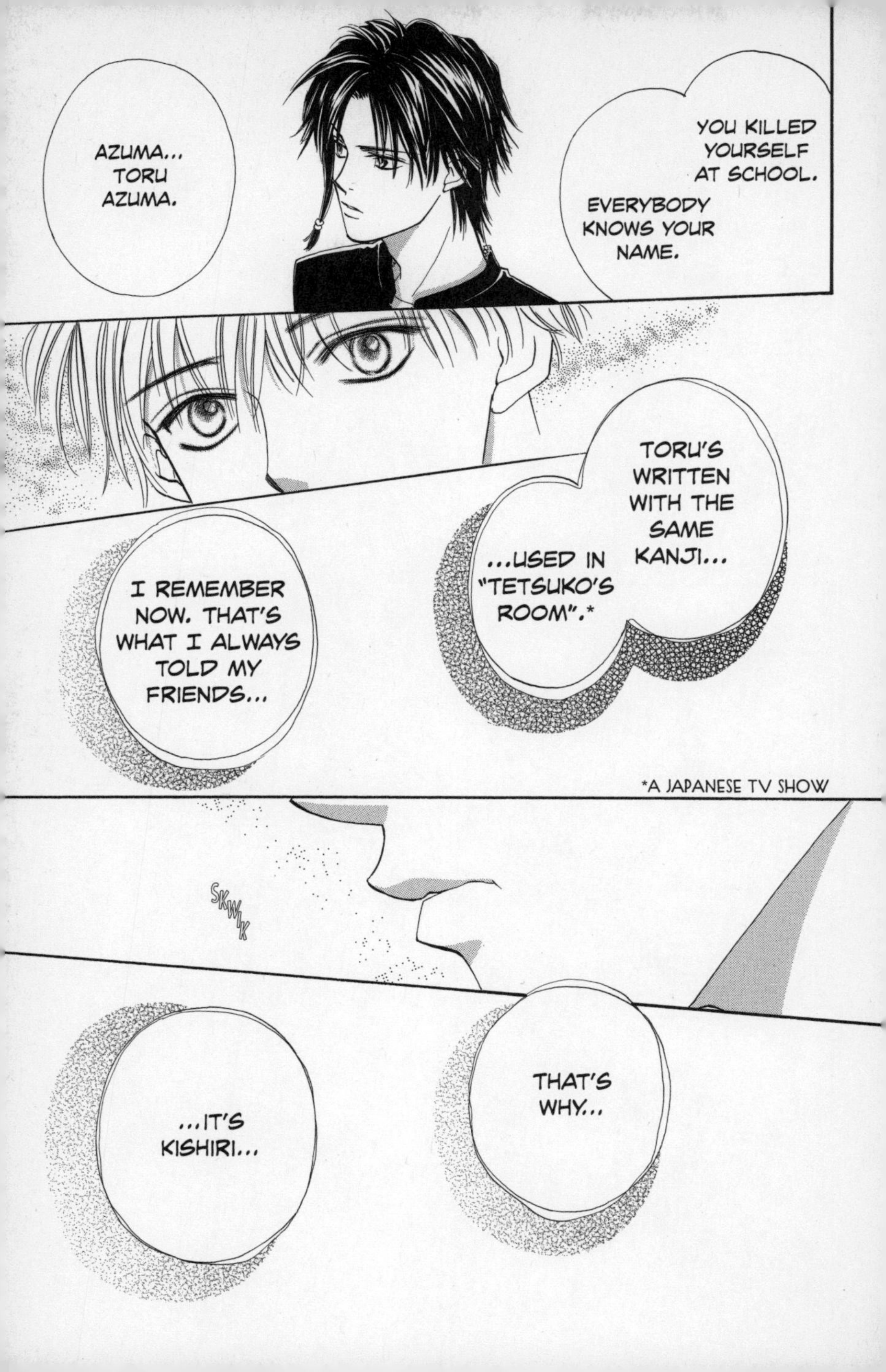
YOU KILLED YOURSELF AT SCHOOL.
EVERYBODY KNOWS YOUR NAME.
AZUMA... TORU AZUMA.
TORU'S WRITTEN WITH THE SAME KANJI...
...USED IN "TETSUKO'S ROOM".*
I REMEMBER NOW. THAT'S WHAT I ALWAYS TOLD MY FRIENDS...
SKWIK
THAT'S WHY...
...IT'S KISHIRI...
*A JAPANESE TV SHOW

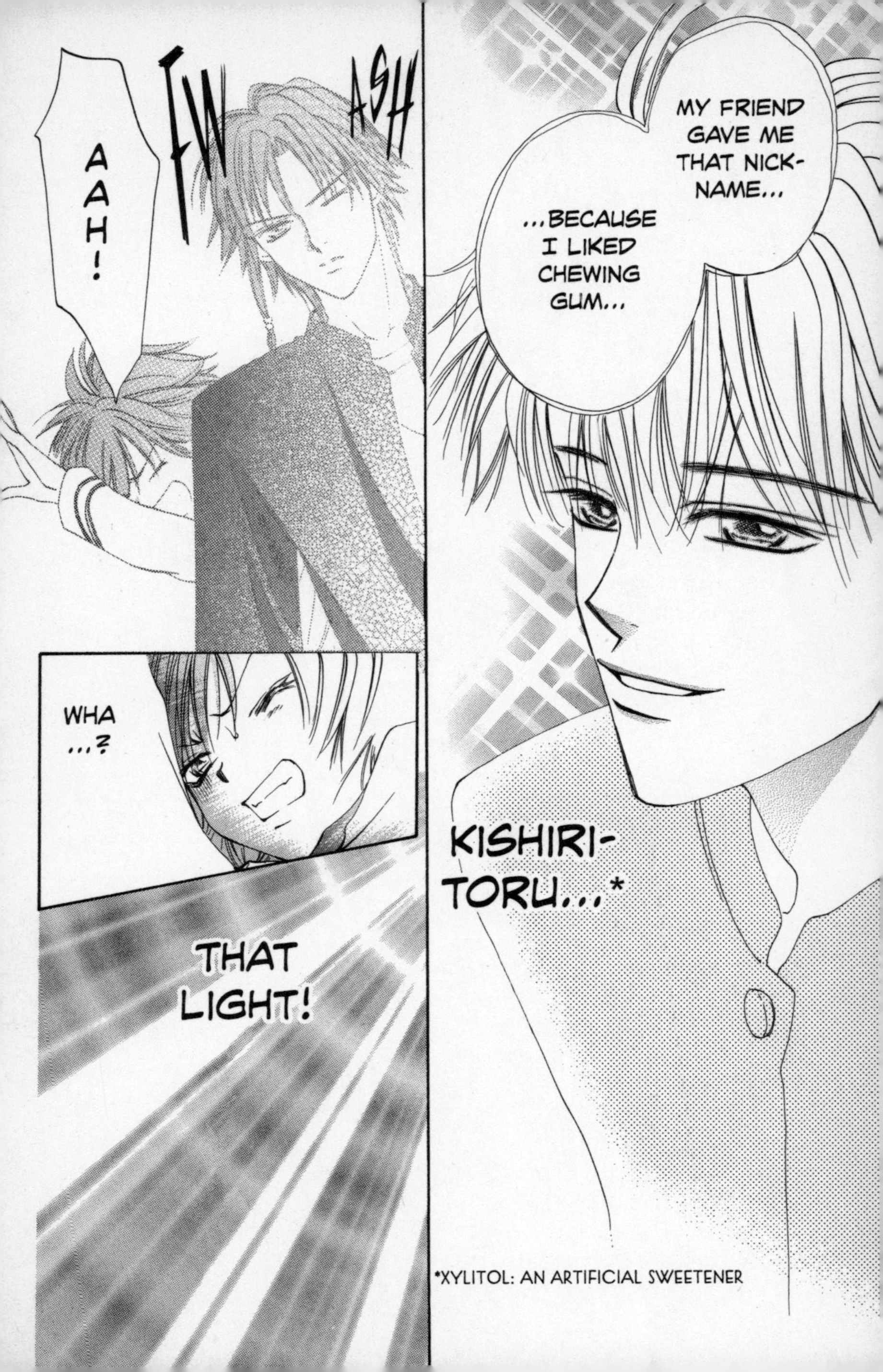
MY FRIEND GAVE ME THAT NICK-NAME...
...BECAUSE I LIKED CHEWING GUM...
KISHIRI-TORU...*
*XYLITOL: AN ARTIFICIAL SWEETENER
FWASH
AAH!
WHA...?
THAT LIGHT!

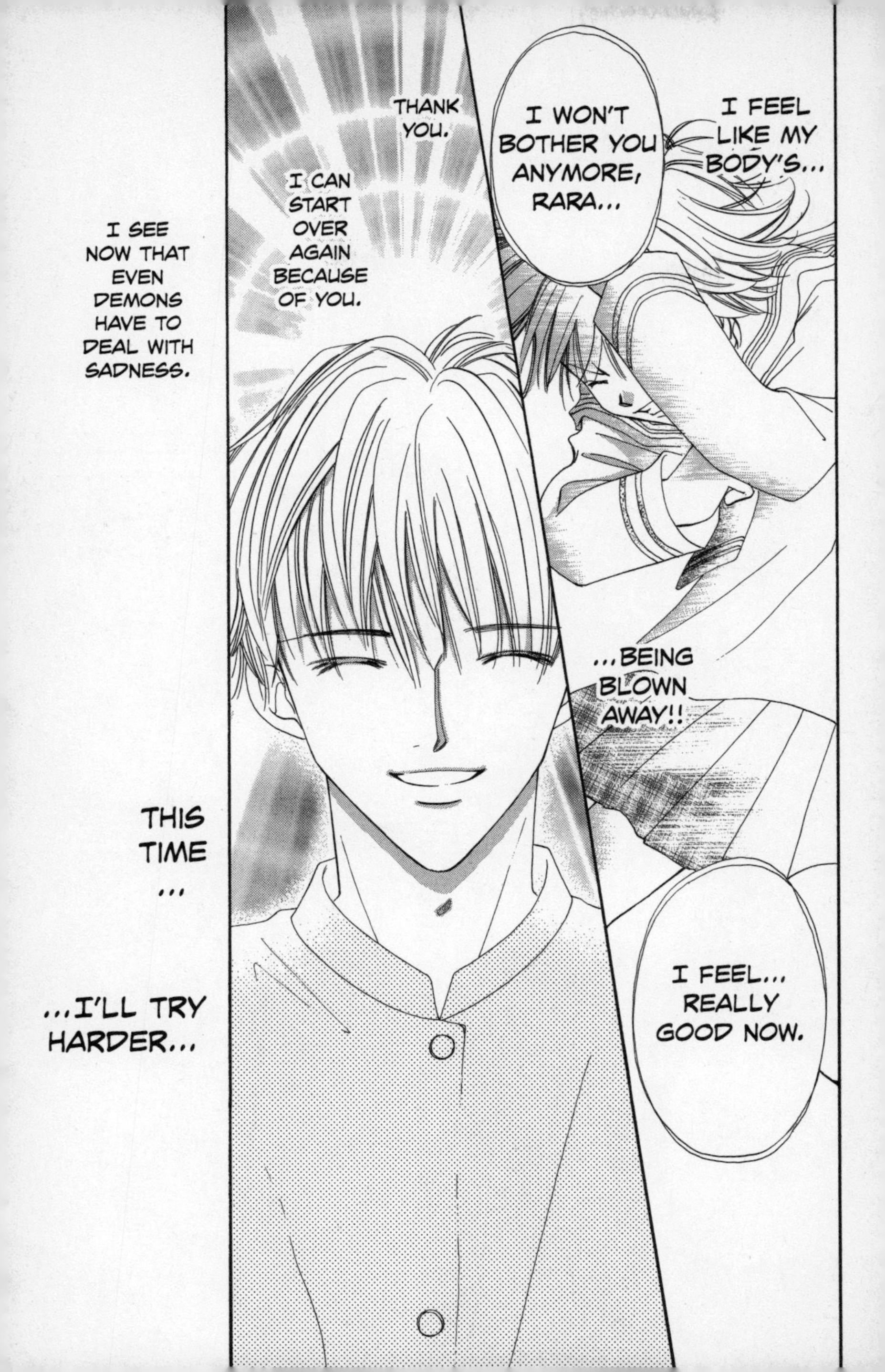
I FEEL LIKE MY BODY'S...
I WON'T BOTHER YOU ANYMORE, RARA...
...BEING BLOWN AWAY!!
I FEEL... REALLY GOOD NOW.
THANK YOU.
I CAN START OVER AGAIN BECAUSE OF YOU.
I SEE NOW THAT EVEN DEMONS HAVE TO DEAL WITH SADNESS.
THIS TIME ...
...I'LL TRY HARDER...

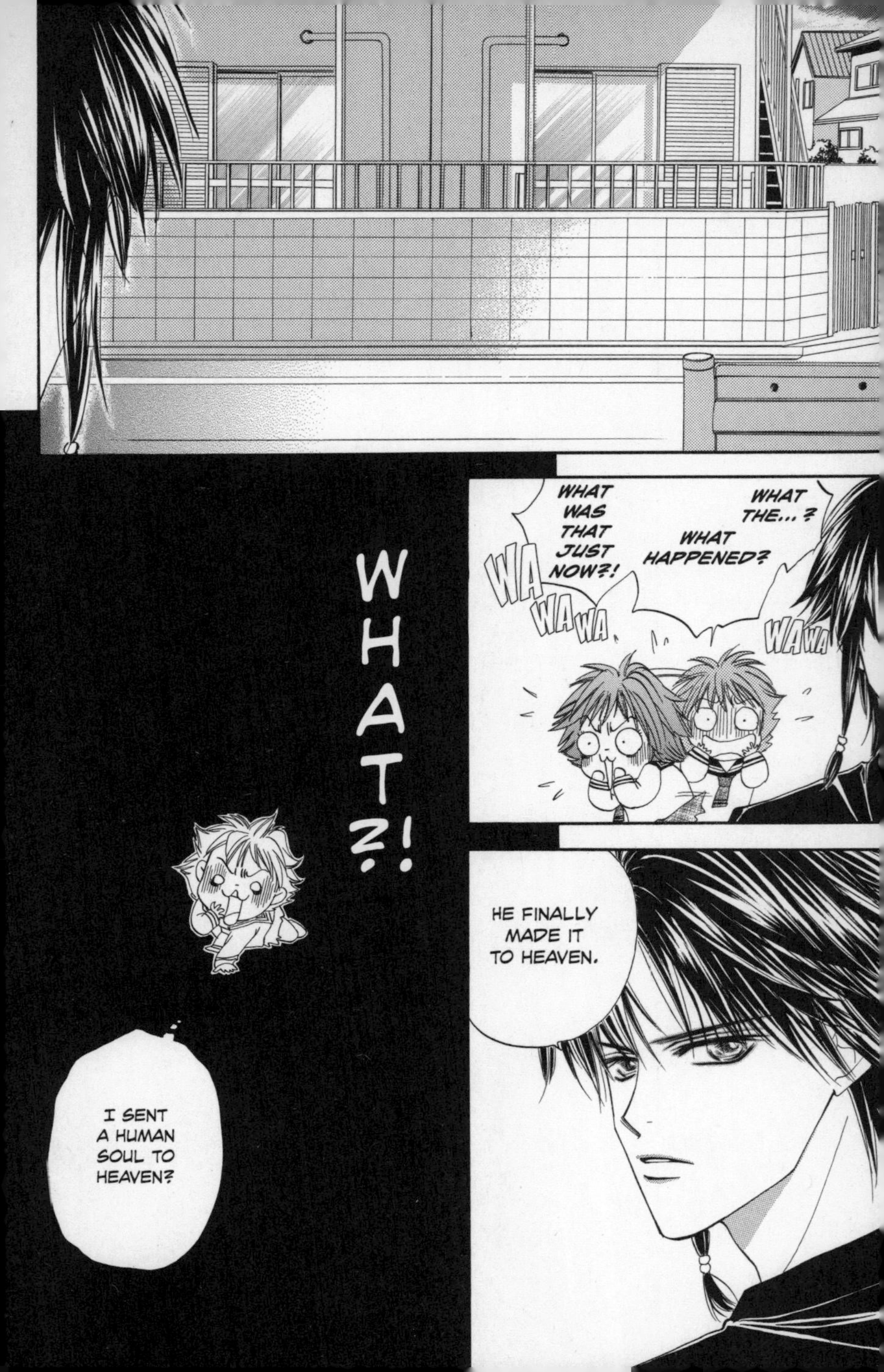
WHAT THE...?
WHAT HAPPENED?
WHAT WAS THAT JUST NOW?!
WAWA
WA WAWA
HE FINALLY MADE IT TO HEAVEN.
WHAT?!
I SENT A HUMAN SOUL TO HEAVEN?

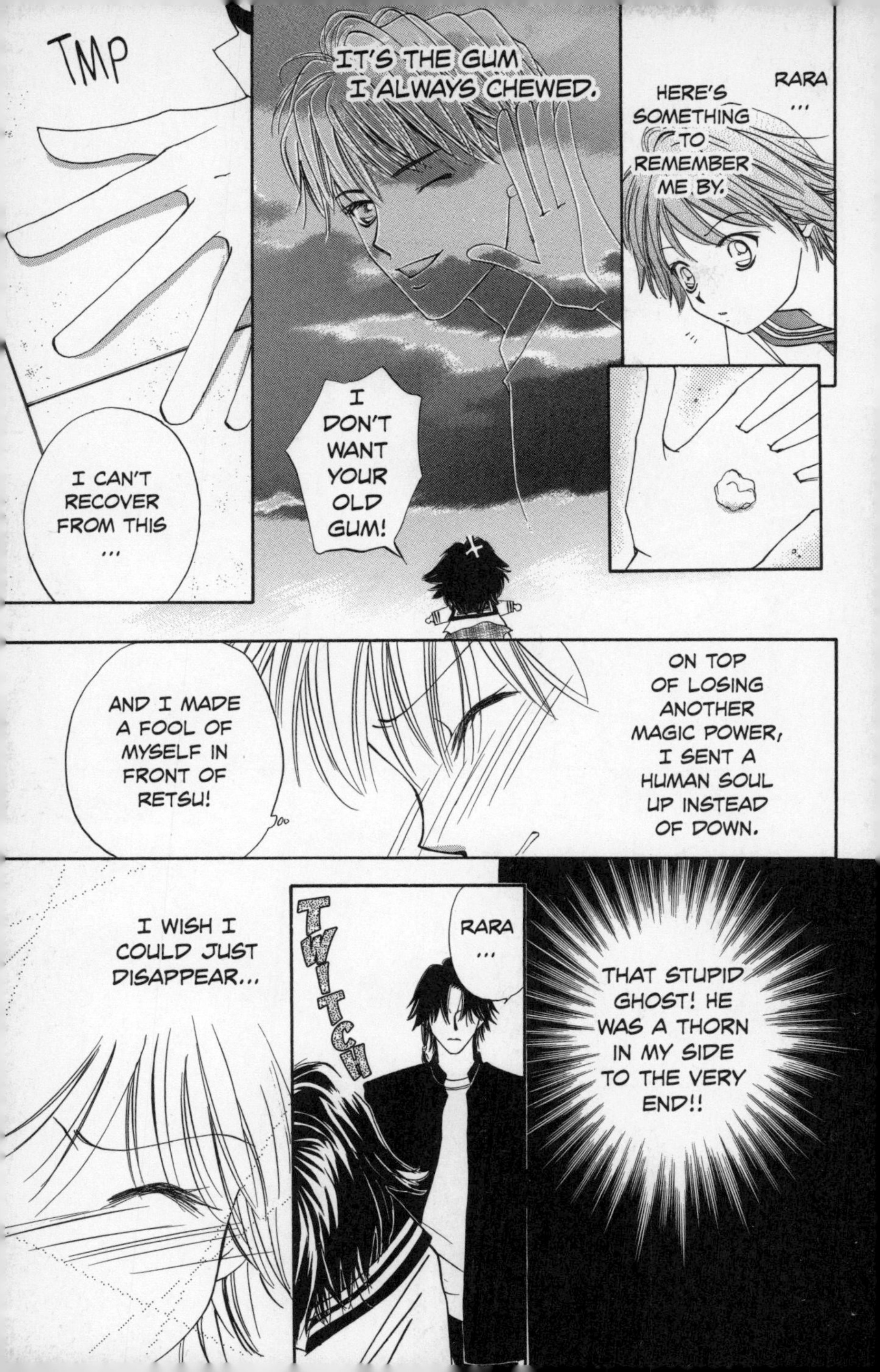
RARA ...
HERE'S SOMETHING TO REMEMBER ME BY.
IT'S THE GUM I ALWAYS CHEWED.
I DON'T WANT YOUR OLD GUM!
TMP
I CAN'T RECOVER FROM THIS ...
ON TOP OF LOSING ANOTHER MAGIC POWER, I SENT A HUMAN SOUL UP INSTEAD OF DOWN.
AND I MADE A FOOL OF MYSELF IN FRONT OF RETSU!
THAT STUPID GHOST! HE WAS A THORN IN MY SIDE TO THE VERY END!!
RARA ...
TWITCH
I WISH I COULD JUST DISAPPEAR...

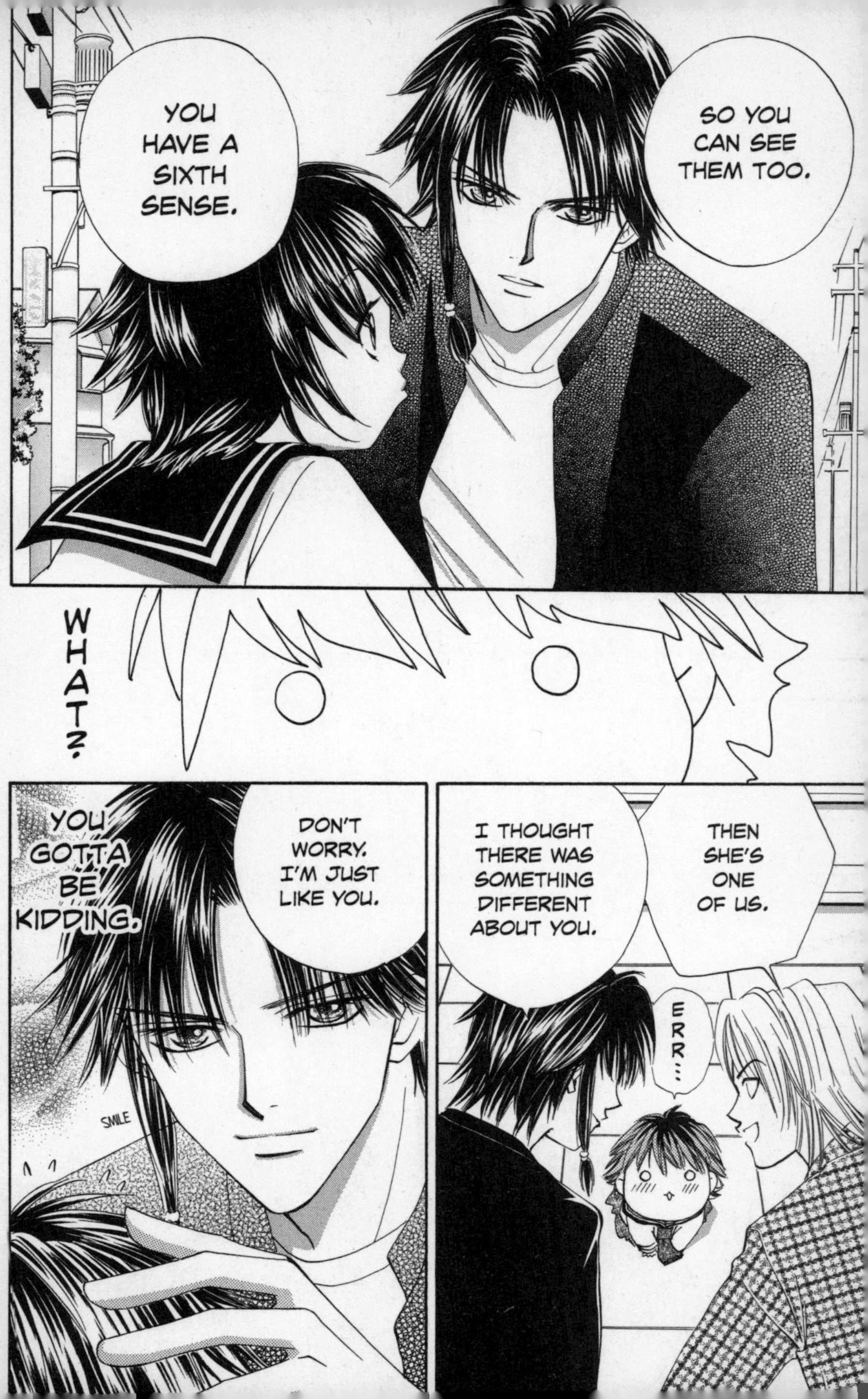
SO YOU CAN SEE THEM TOO.
YOU HAVE A SIXTH SENSE.
WHAT?
THEN SHE'S ONE OF US.
I THOUGHT THERE WAS SOMETHING DIFFERENT ABOUT YOU.
ERR...
DON'T WORRY. I'M JUST LIKE YOU.
YOU GOTTA BE KIDDING.
SMILE

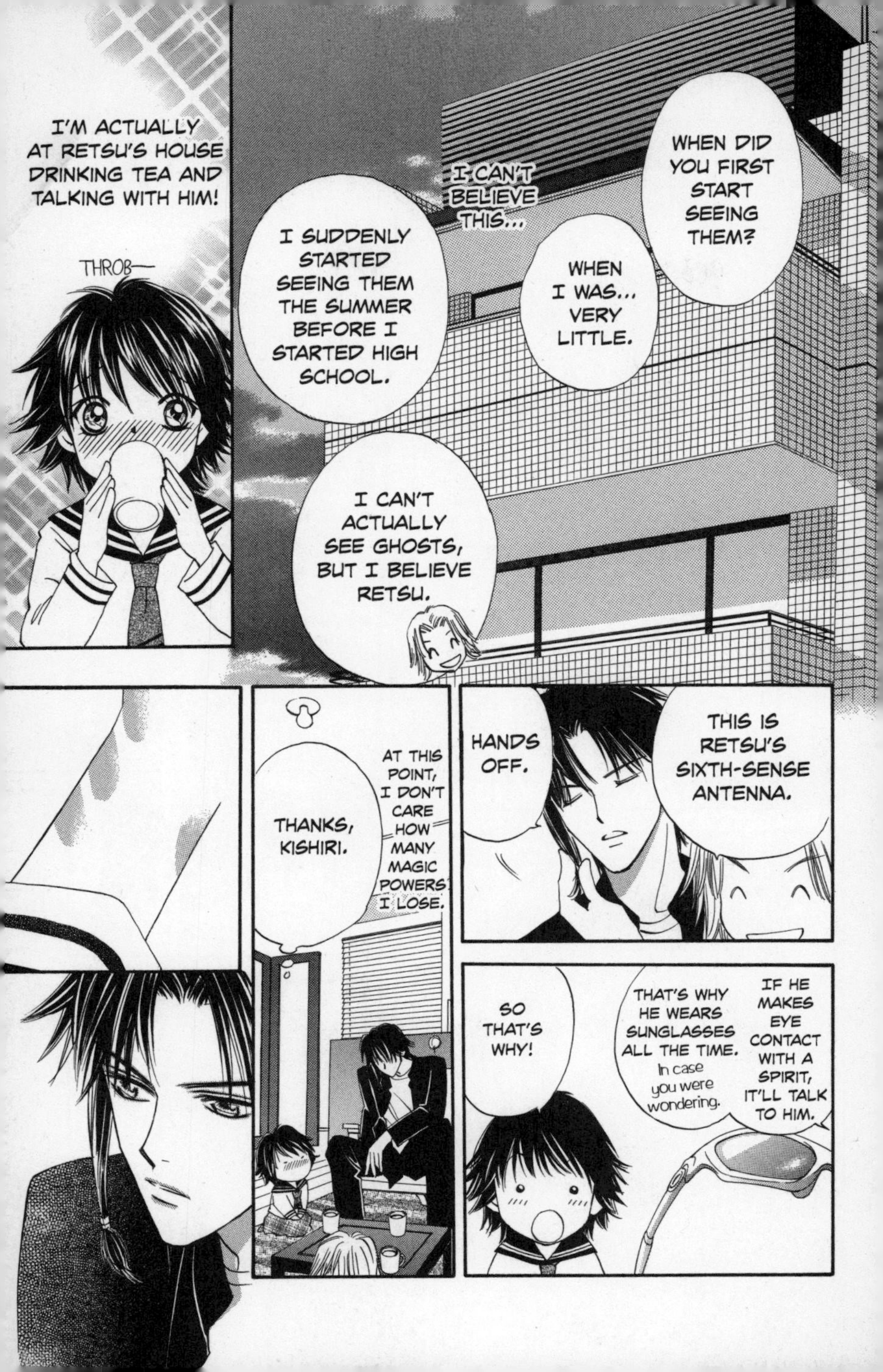
WHEN DID YOU FIRST START SEEING THEM?
WHEN I WAS... VERY LITTLE.
I CAN'T BELIEVE THIS...
I SUDDENLY STARTED SEEING THEM THE SUMMER BEFORE I STARTED HIGH SCHOOL.
I CAN'T ACTUALLY SEE GHOSTS, BUT I BELIEVE RETSU.
I'M ACTUALLY AT RETSU'S HOUSE DRINKING TEA AND TALKING WITH HIM!
THROB—
THIS IS RETSU'S SIXTH-SENSE ANTENNA.
HANDS OFF.
IF HE MAKES EYE CONTACT WITH A SPIRIT, IT'LL TALK TO HIM.
THAT'S WHY HE WEARS SUNGLASSES ALL THE TIME.
In case you were wondering.
SO THAT'S WHY!
AT THIS POINT, I DON'T CARE HOW MANY MAGIC POWERS I LOSE.
THANKS, KISHIRI.

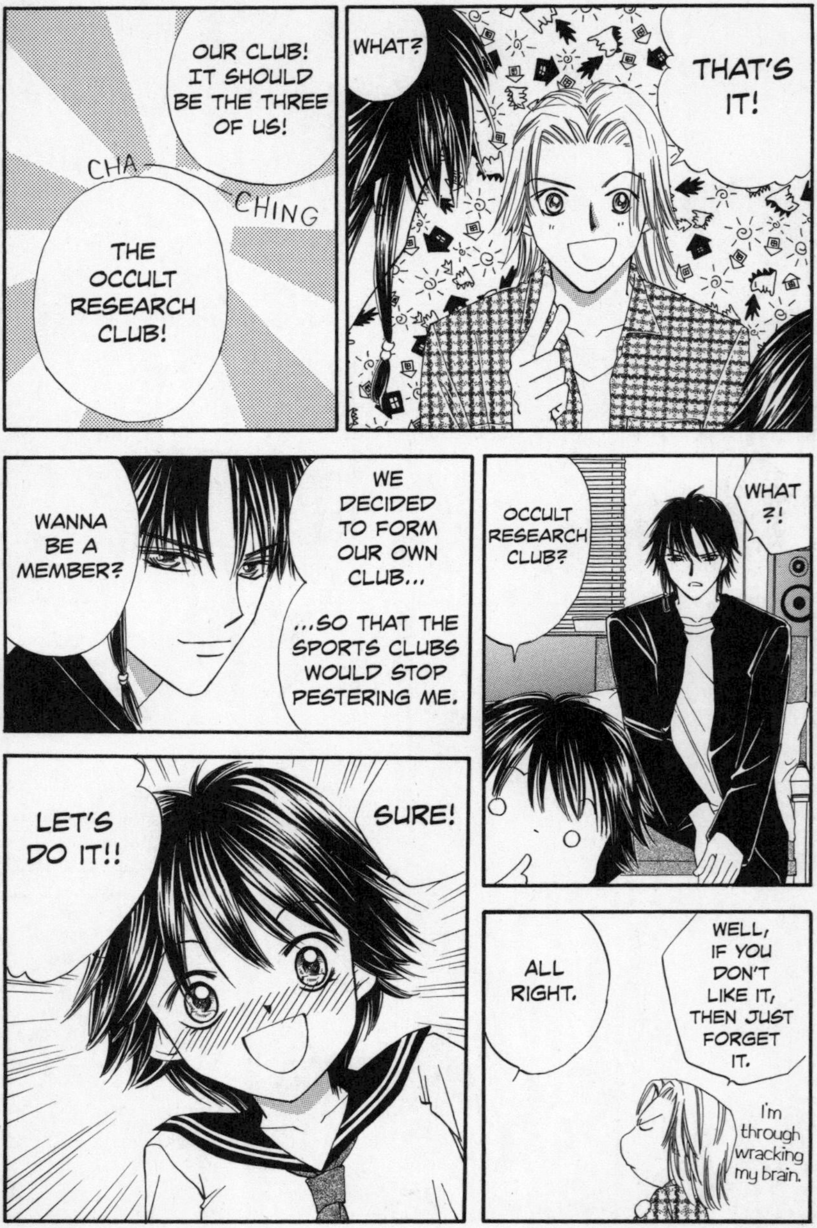
THAT'S IT!
WHAT?
OUR CLUB! IT SHOULD BE THE THREE OF US!
CHA-CHING
THE OCCULT RESEARCH CLUB!
WHAT?!
OCCULT RESEARCH CLUB?
WE DECIDED TO FORM OUR OWN CLUB...
...SO THAT THE SPORTS CLUBS WOULD STOP PESTERING ME.
WANNA BE A MEMBER?
WELL, IF YOU DON'T LIKE IT, THEN JUST FORGET IT.
ALL RIGHT.
I'm through wracking my brain.
SURE!
LET'S DO IT!!

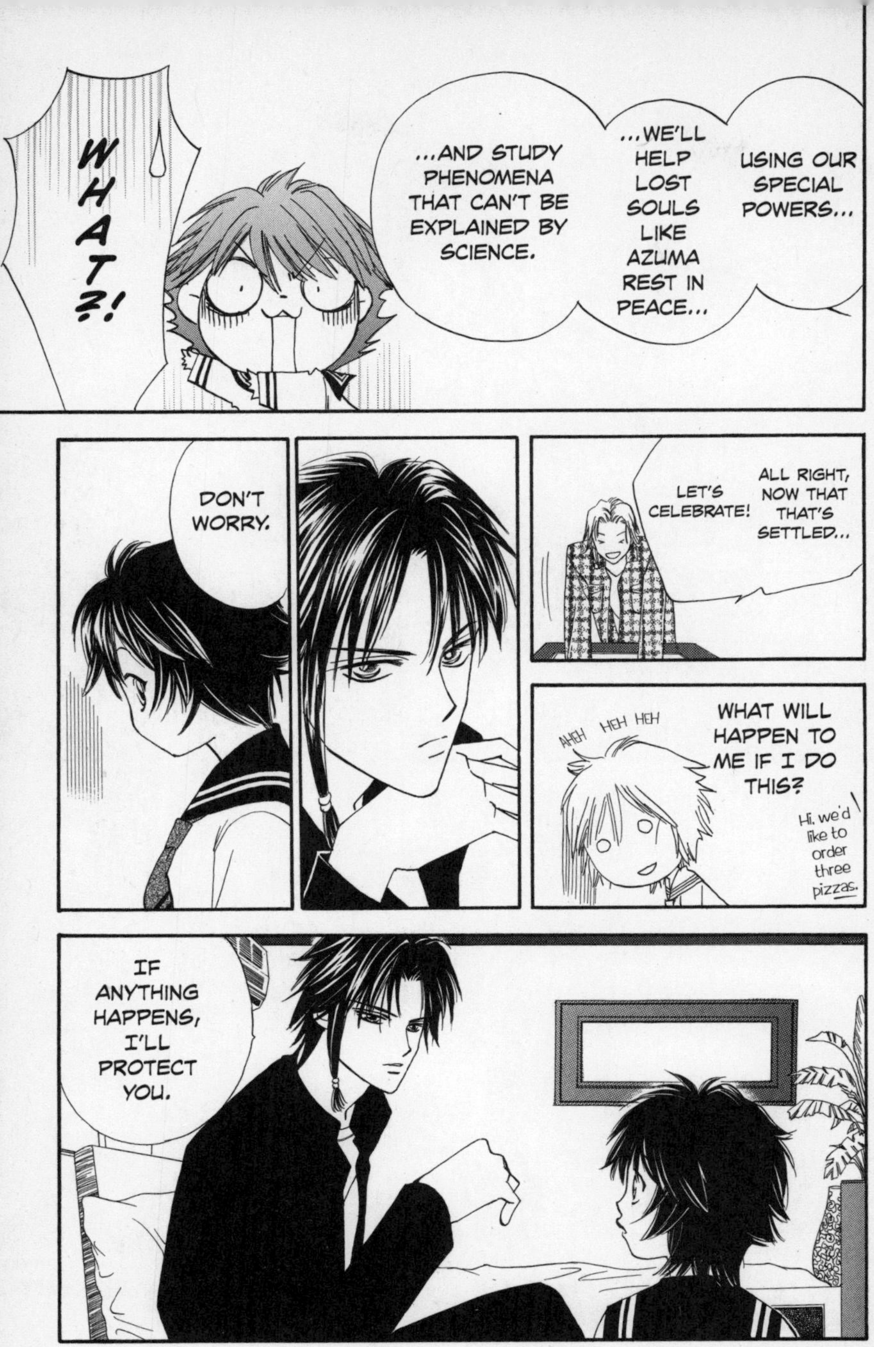
USING OUR SPECIAL POWERS...
...WE'LL HELP LOST SOULS LIKE AZUMA REST IN PEACE...
...AND STUDY PHENOMENA THAT CAN'T BE EXPLAINED BY SCIENCE.
WHAT?!
ALL RIGHT, NOW THAT THAT'S SETTLED...
LET'S CELEBRATE!
WHAT WILL HAPPEN TO ME IF I DO THIS?
AHEH HEH HEH
Hi, we'd like to order three pizzas.
DON'T WORRY.
IF ANYTHING HAPPENS, I'LL PROTECT YOU.

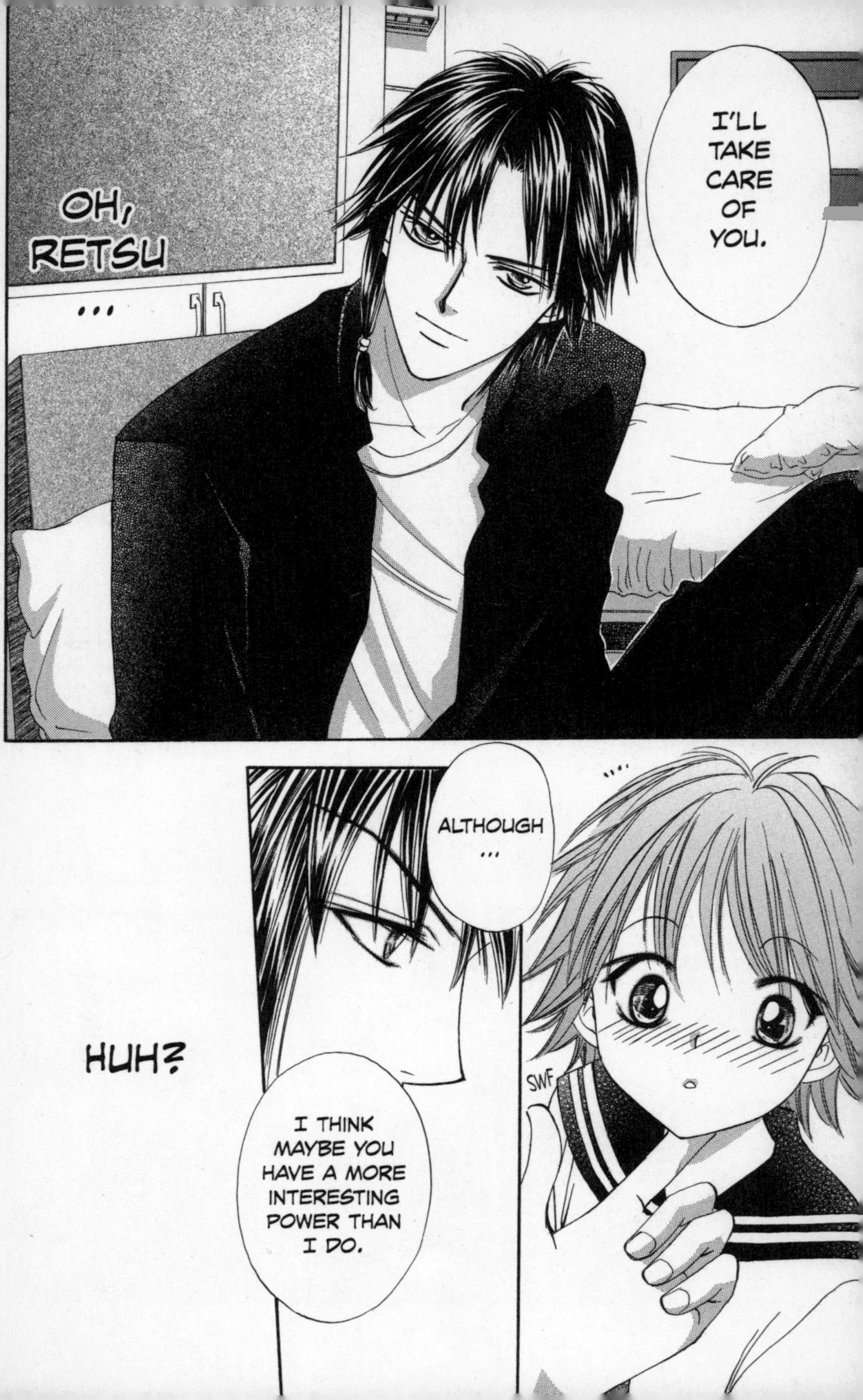
I'LL TAKE CARE OF YOU.
OH, RETSU ...
ALTHOUGH ...
I THINK MAYBE YOU HAVE A MORE INTERESTING POWER THAN I DO.
SWF
HUH?

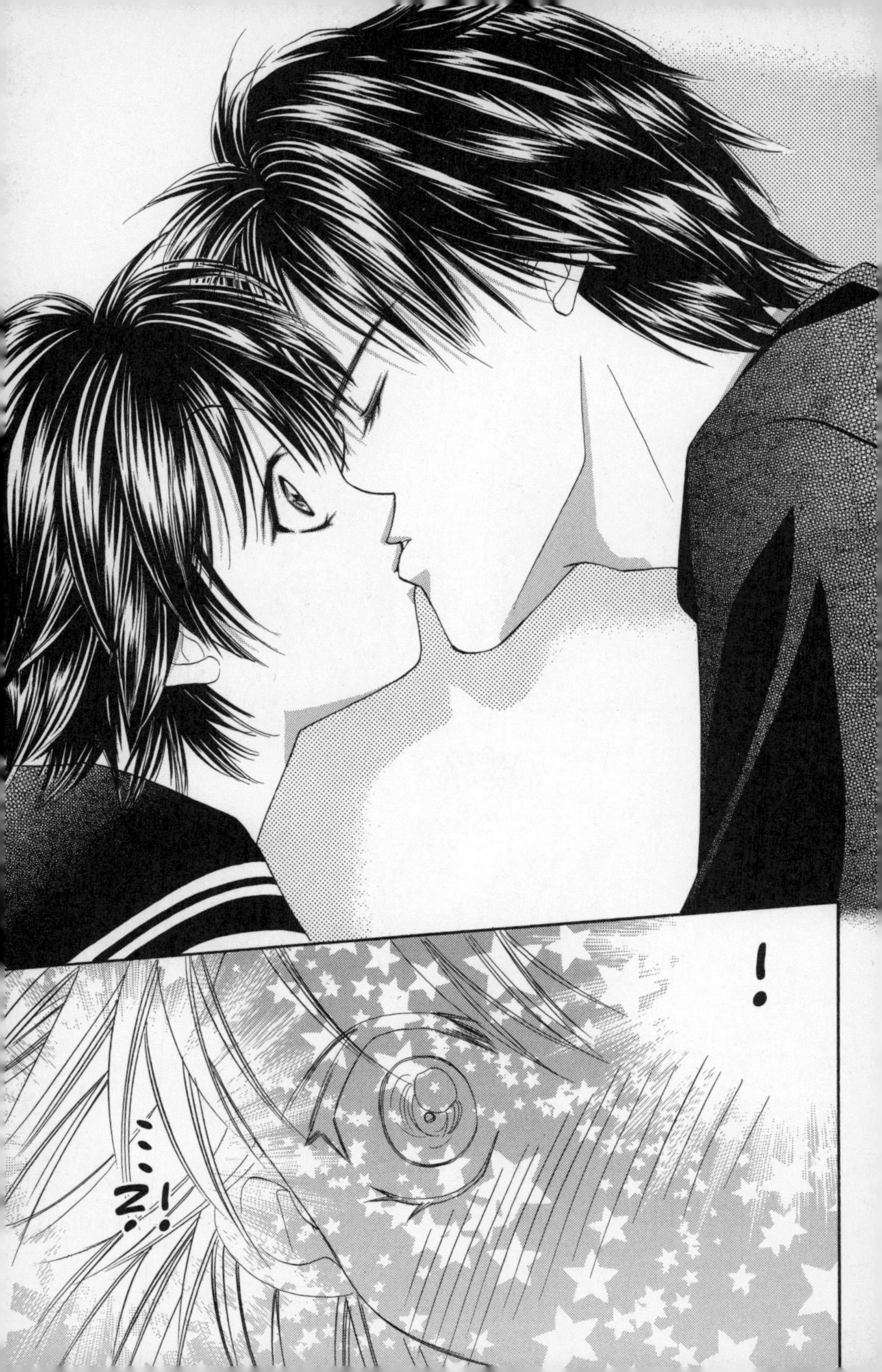
!
...?!

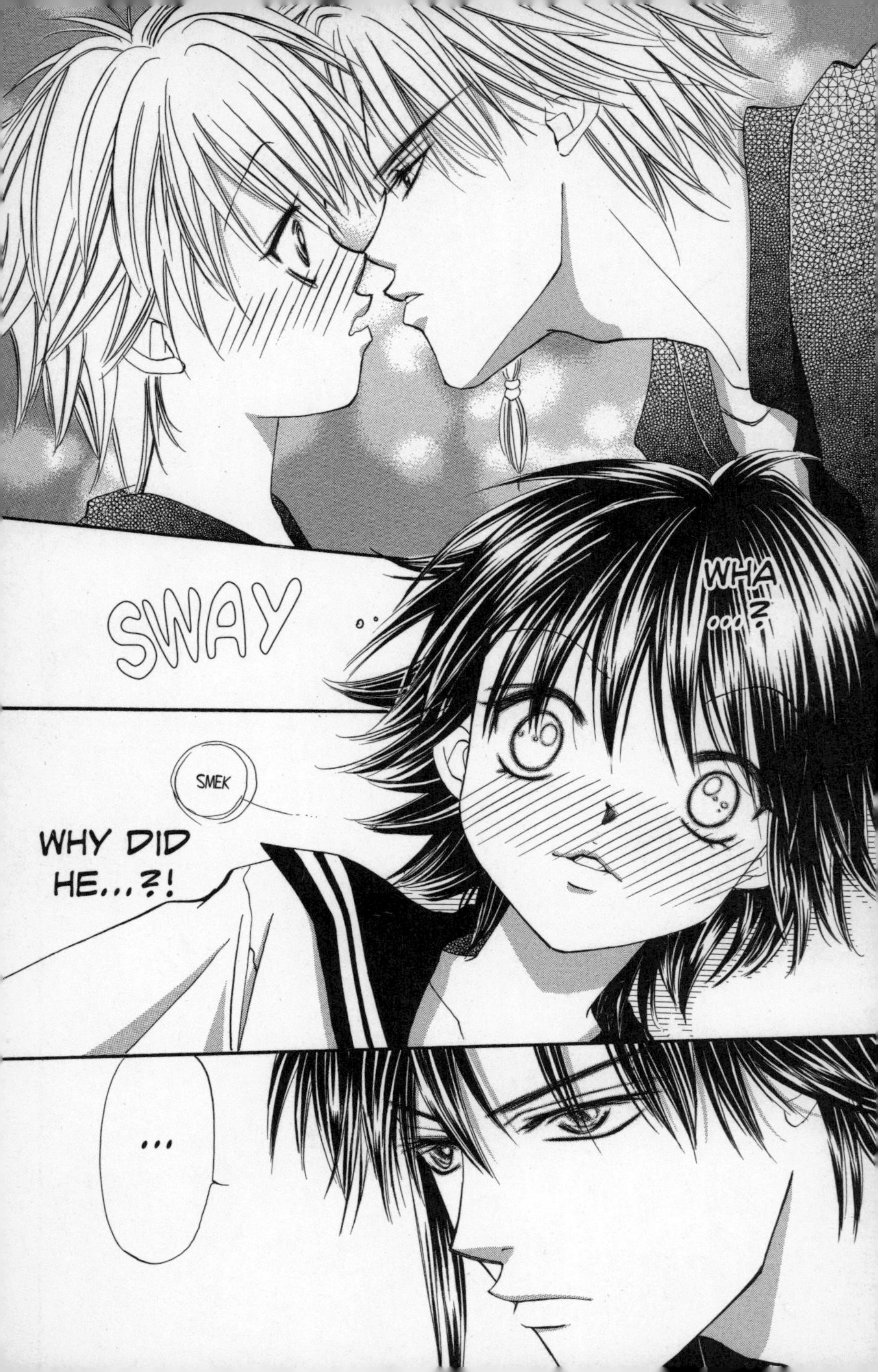
WHA...?
SWAY
SMEK
WHY DID HE...?!
...

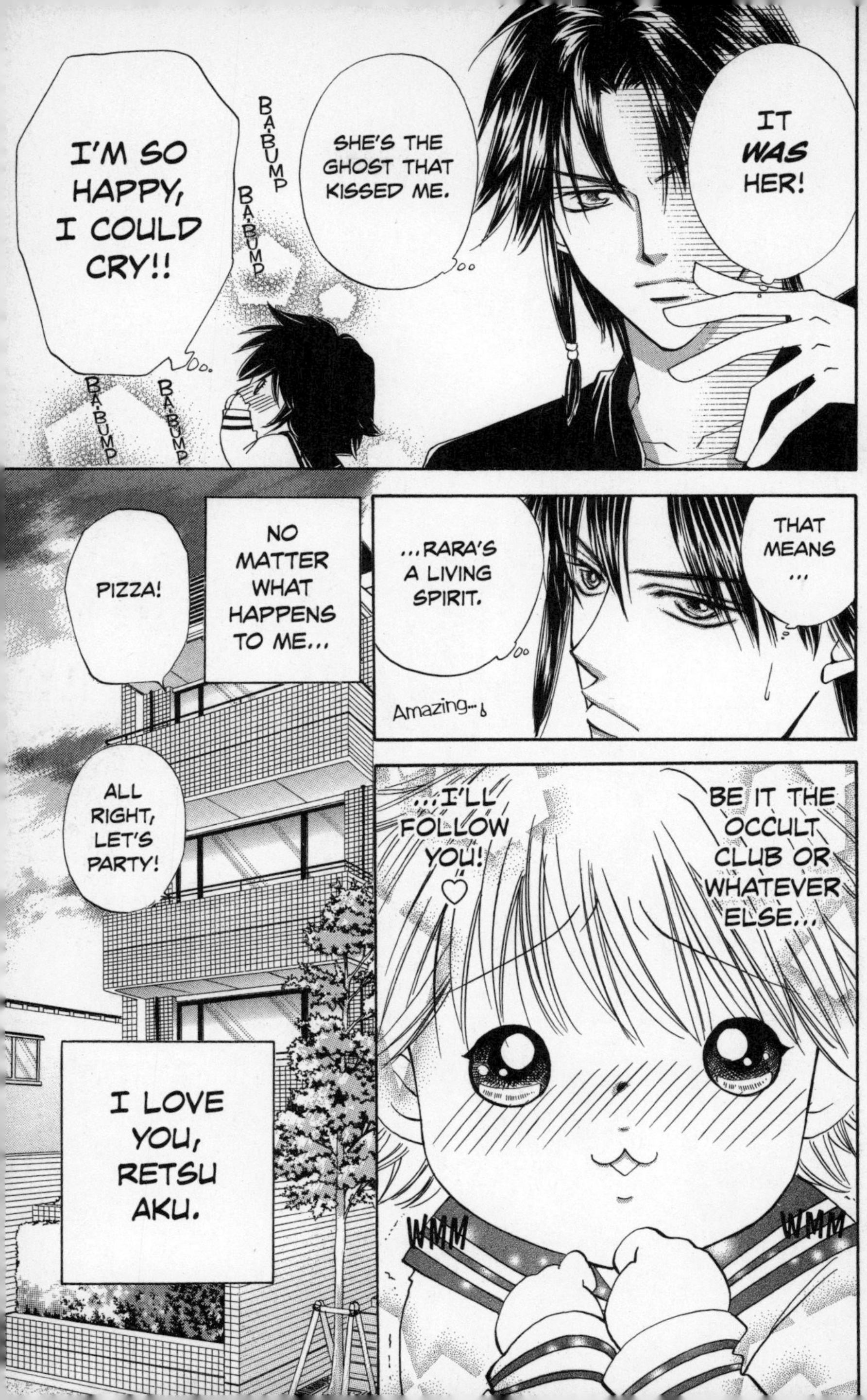
IT WAS HER!
SHE'S THE GHOST THAT KISSED ME.
BA-BUMP
BA-BUMP
I'M SO HAPPY, I COULD CRY!!
BA-BUMP
BA-BUMP
THAT MEANS ...
...RARA'S A LIVING SPIRIT.
Amazing...
BE IT THE OCCULT CLUB OR WHATEVER ELSE...
...I'LL FOLLOW YOU! ♡
WMM
WMM
NO MATTER WHAT HAPPENS TO ME...
PIZZA!
ALL RIGHT, LET'S PARTY!
I LOVE YOU, RETSU AKU.

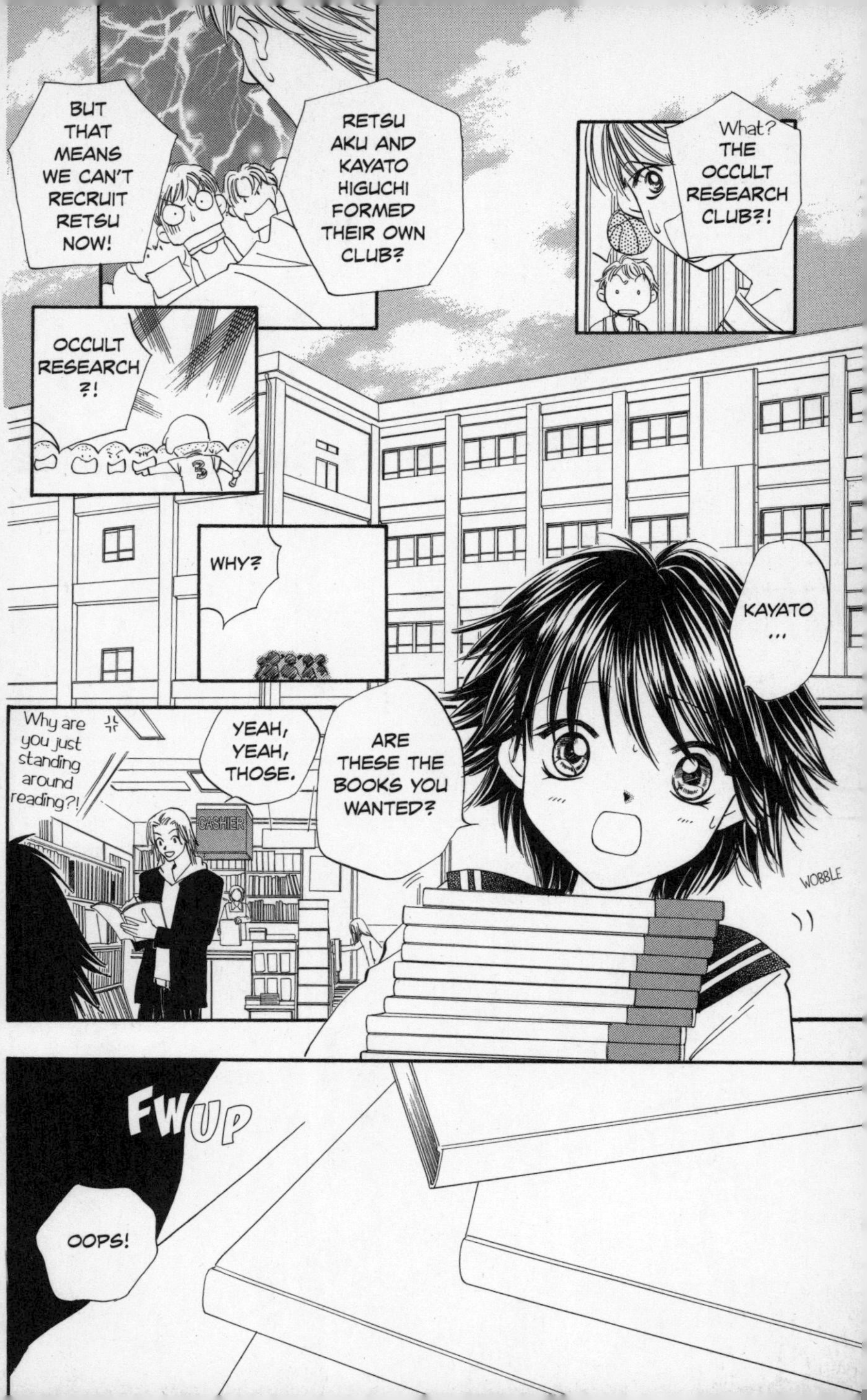
What? THE OCCULT RESEARCH CLUB?!
RETSU AKU AND KAYATO HIGUCHI FORMED THEIR OWN CLUB?
BUT THAT MEANS WE CAN'T RECRUIT RETSU NOW!
OCCULT RESEARCH?!
WHY?
KAYATO...
ARE THESE THE BOOKS YOU WANTED?
WOBBLE
YEAH, YEAH, THOSE.
Why are you just standing around reading?!
CASHIER
FWUP
OOPS!

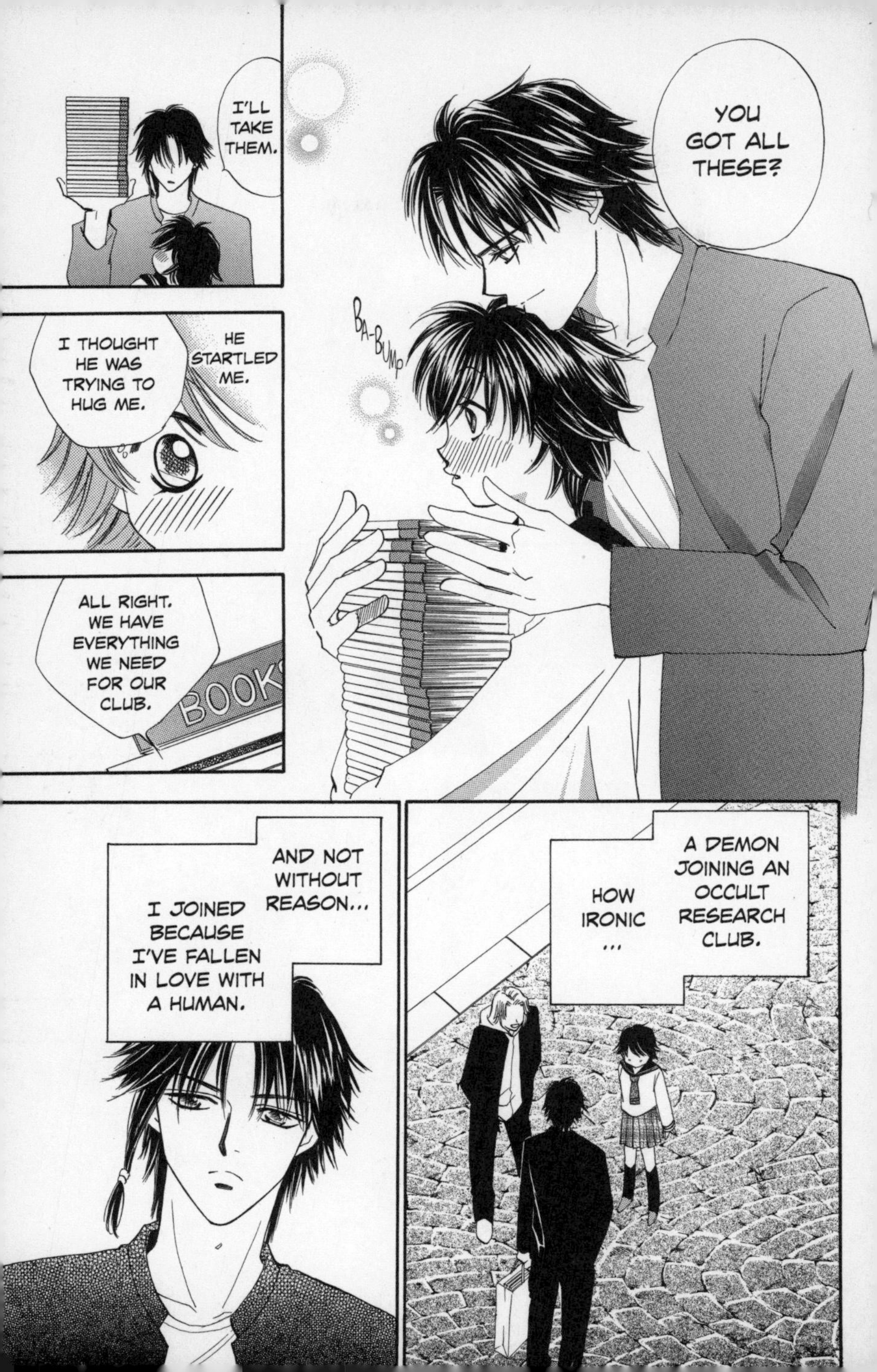
YOU GOT ALL THESE?
BA-BUMP
I'LL TAKE THEM.
HE STARTLED ME.
I THOUGHT HE WAS TRYING TO HUG ME.
ALL RIGHT. WE HAVE EVERYTHING WE NEED FOR OUR CLUB.
BOOKS
A DEMON JOINING AN OCCULT RESEARCH CLUB.
HOW IRONIC...
AND NOT WITHOUT REASON...
I JOINED BECAUSE I'VE FALLEN IN LOVE WITH A HUMAN.

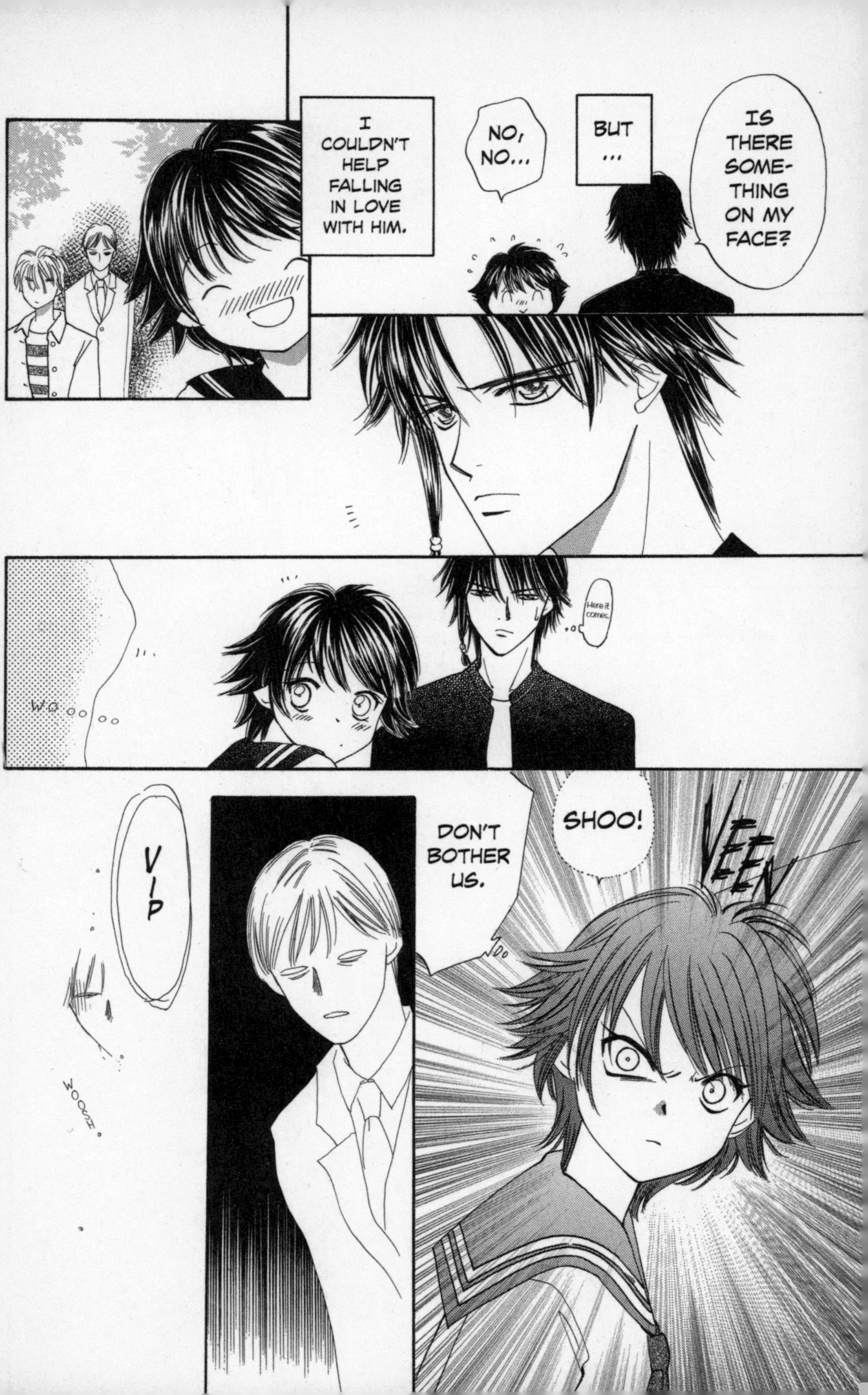
IS THERE SOMETHING ON MY FACE?
BUT ...
NO, NO...
I COULDN'T HELP FALLING IN LOVE WITH HIM.
Here it comes.
WOOOOOO
VEEN
SHOO!
DON'T BOTHER US.
VIP
WOOSH

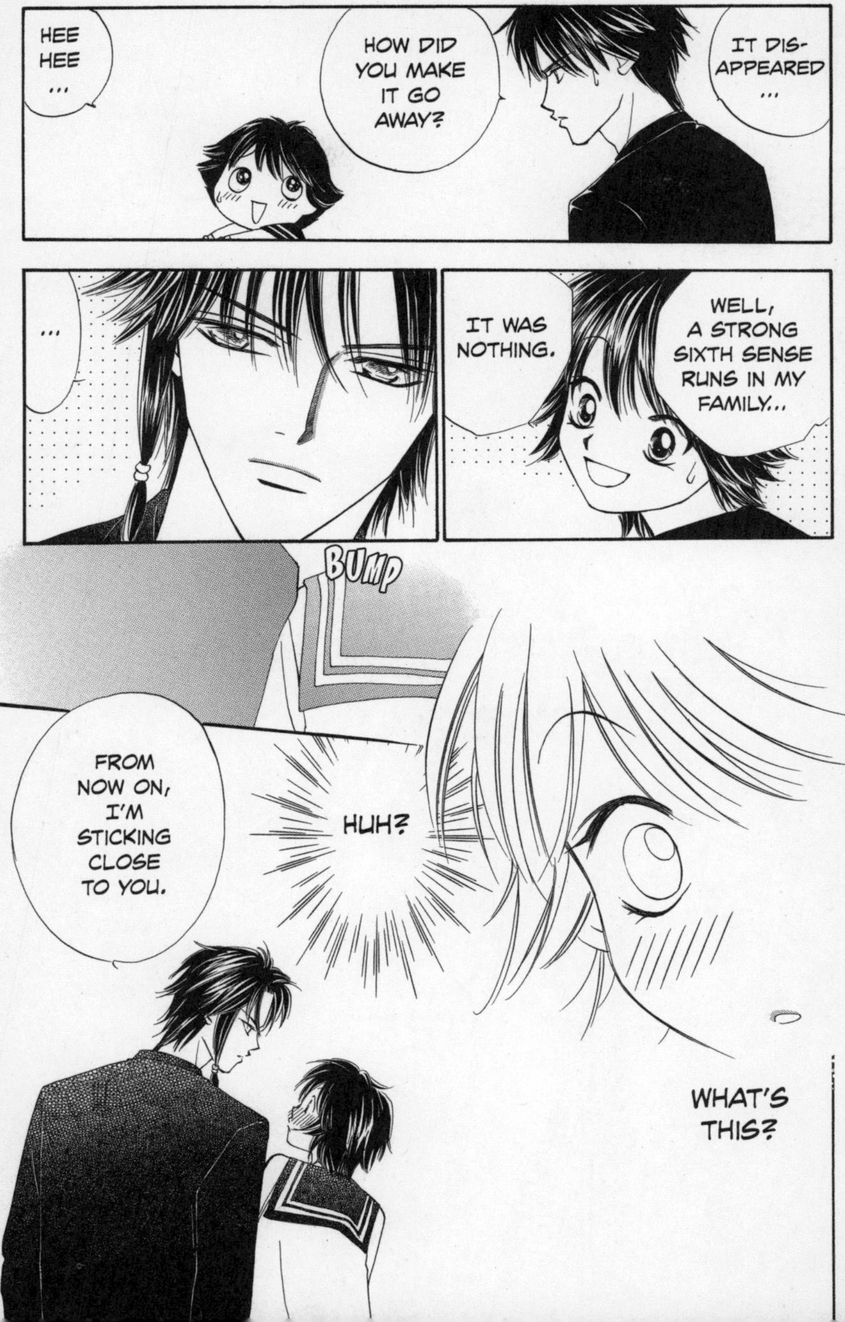

IT DIS-APPEARED...
HOW DID YOU MAKE IT GO AWAY?
HEE HEE...
WELL, A STRONG SIXTH SENSE RUNS IN MY FAMILY...
IT WAS NOTHING.
...
BUMP
FROM NOW ON, I'M STICKING CLOSE TO YOU.
HUH?
WHAT'S THIS?

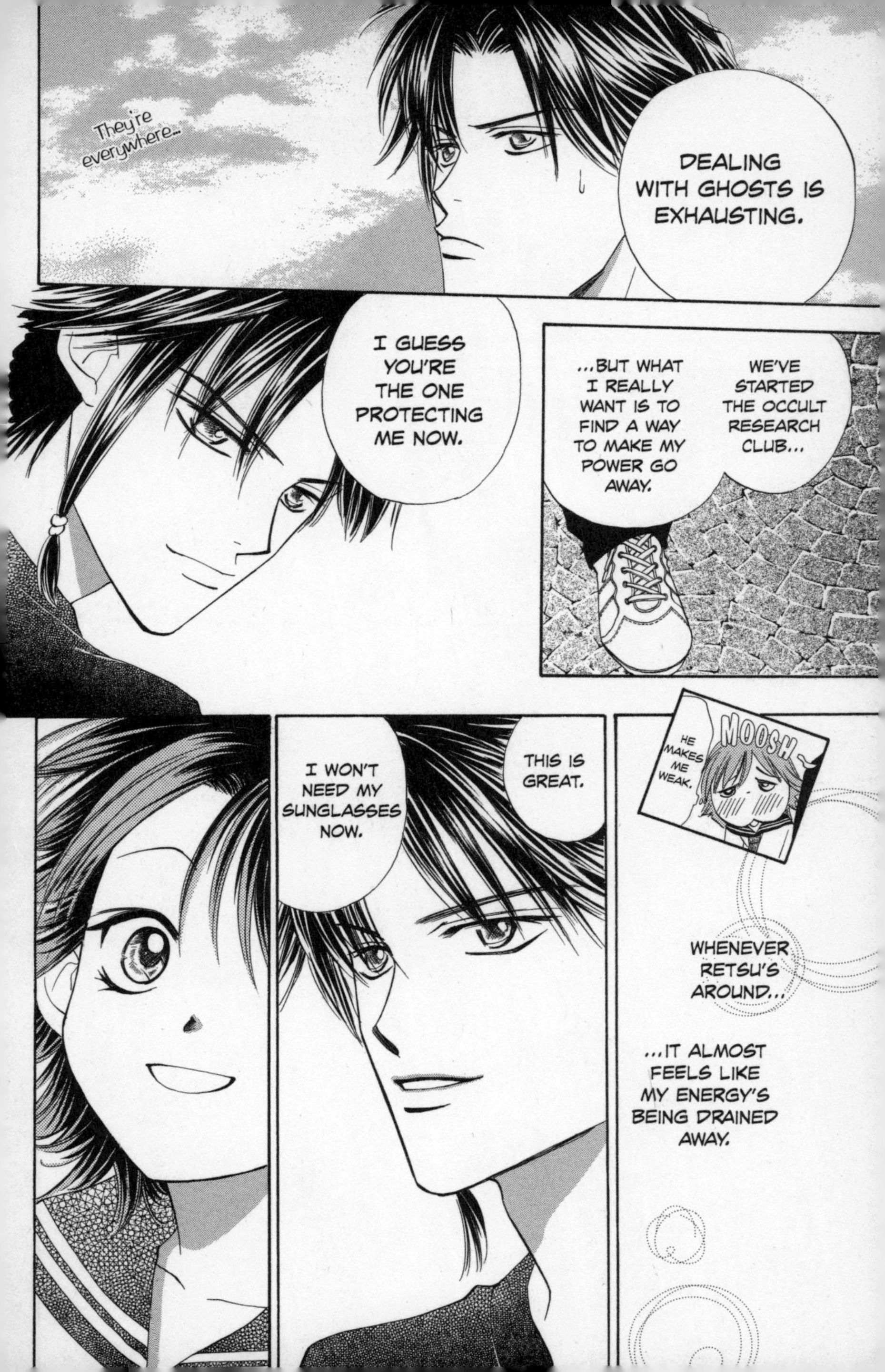
DEALING WITH GHOSTS IS EXHAUSTING.
They're everywhere...
WE'VE STARTED THE OCCULT RESEARCH CLUB...
...BUT WHAT I REALLY WANT IS TO FIND A WAY TO MAKE MY POWER GO AWAY.
I GUESS YOU'RE THE ONE PROTECTING ME NOW.
MOOSH
HE MAKES ME WEAK.
WHENEVER RETSU'S AROUND...
...IT ALMOST FEELS LIKE MY ENERGY'S BEING DRAINED AWAY.
THIS IS GREAT.
I WON'T NEED MY SUNGLASSES NOW.

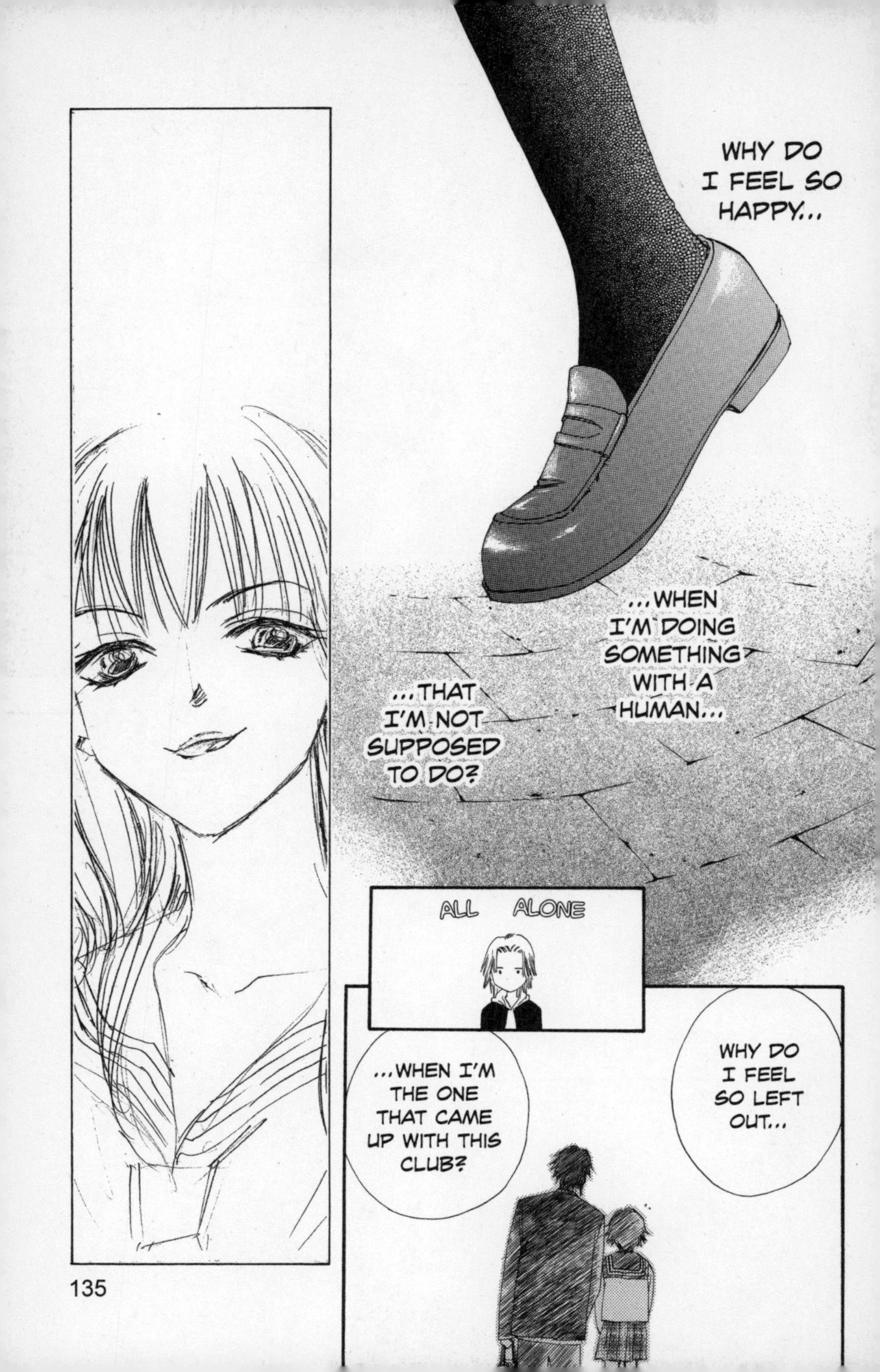
WHY DO I FEEL SO HAPPY...
...WHEN I'M DOING SOMETHING WITH A HUMAN...
...THAT I'M NOT SUPPOSED TO DO?
ALL ALONE
WHY DO I FEEL SO LEFT OUT...
...WHEN I'M THE ONE THAT CAME UP WITH THIS CLUB?

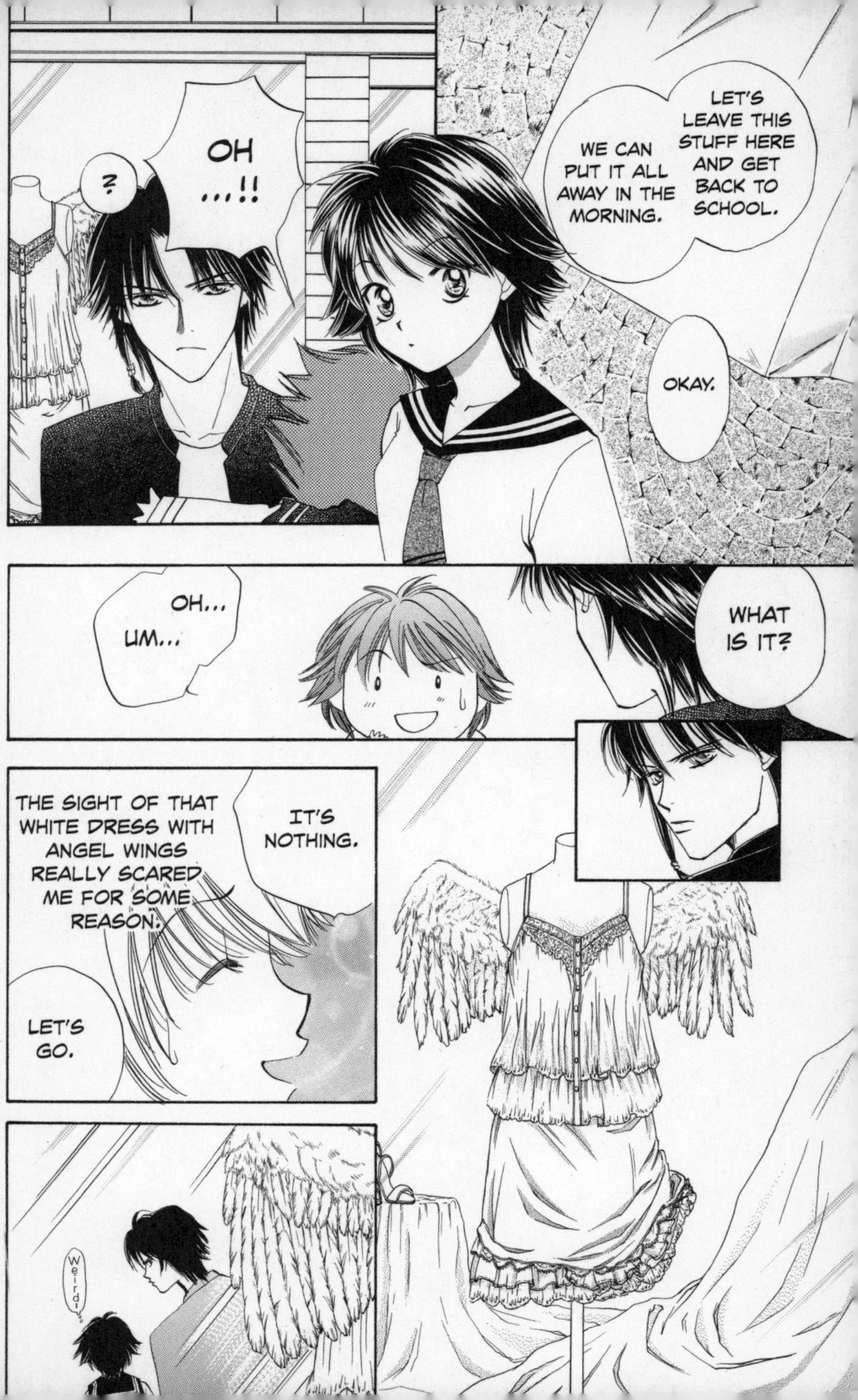
LET'S LEAVE THIS STUFF HERE AND GET BACK TO SCHOOL.
WE CAN PUT IT ALL AWAY IN THE MORNING.
OKAY.
OH ...!!
?
WHAT IS IT?
OH... UM...
IT'S NOTHING.
THE SIGHT OF THAT WHITE DRESS WITH ANGEL WINGS REALLY SCARED ME FOR SOME REASON.
LET'S GO.
Weird...

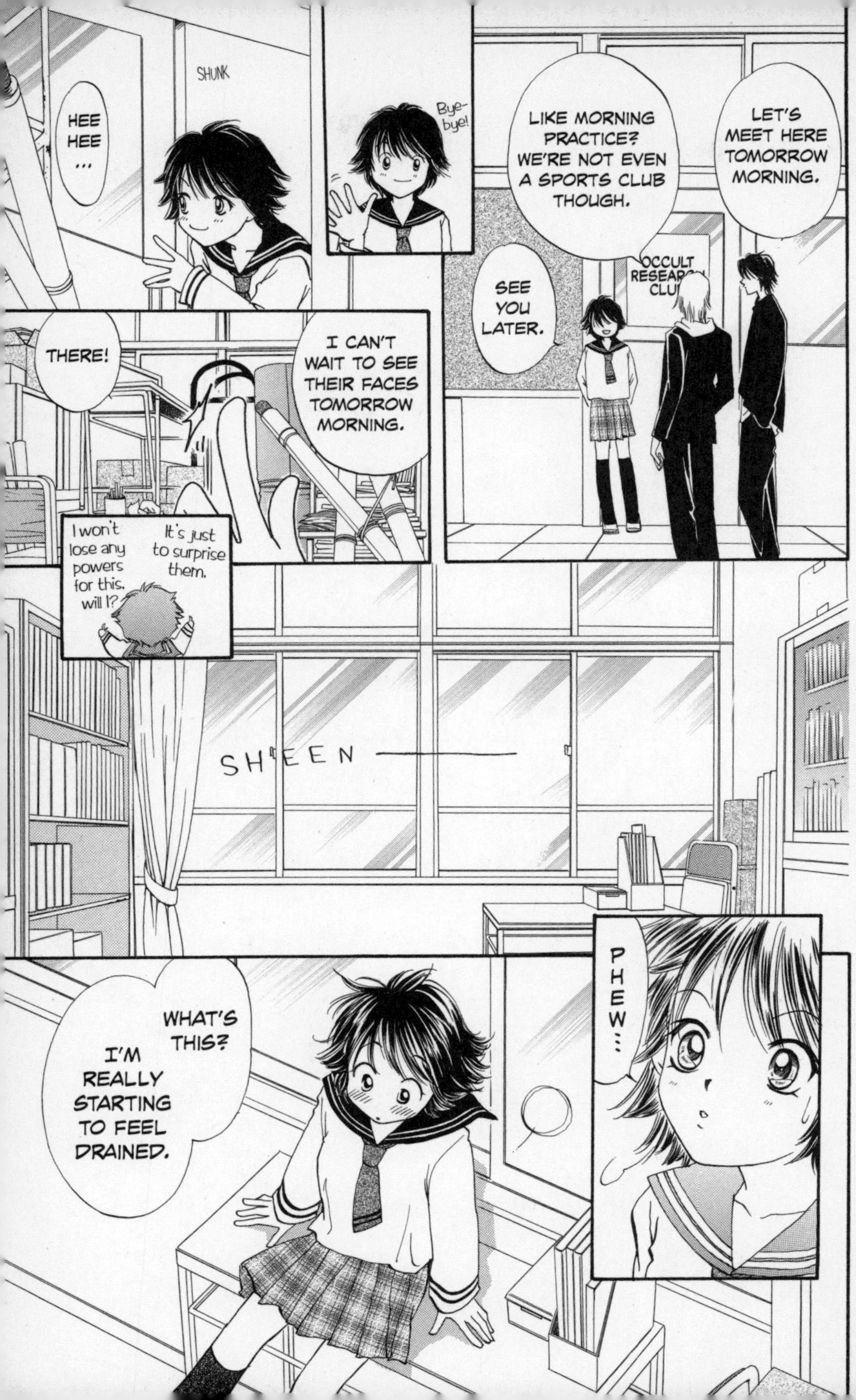
LET'S MEET HERE TOMORROW MORNING.
LIKE MORNING PRACTICE? WE'RE NOT EVEN A SPORTS CLUB THOUGH.
SEE YOU LATER.
OCCULT
Bye-bye!
SHUNK
HEE HEE ...
I CAN'T WAIT TO SEE THEIR FACES TOMORROW MORNING.
THERE!
It's just to surprise them.
I won't lose any powers for this, will I?
SHEEN
PHEW...
WHAT'S THIS?
I'M REALLY STARTING TO FEEL DRAINED.

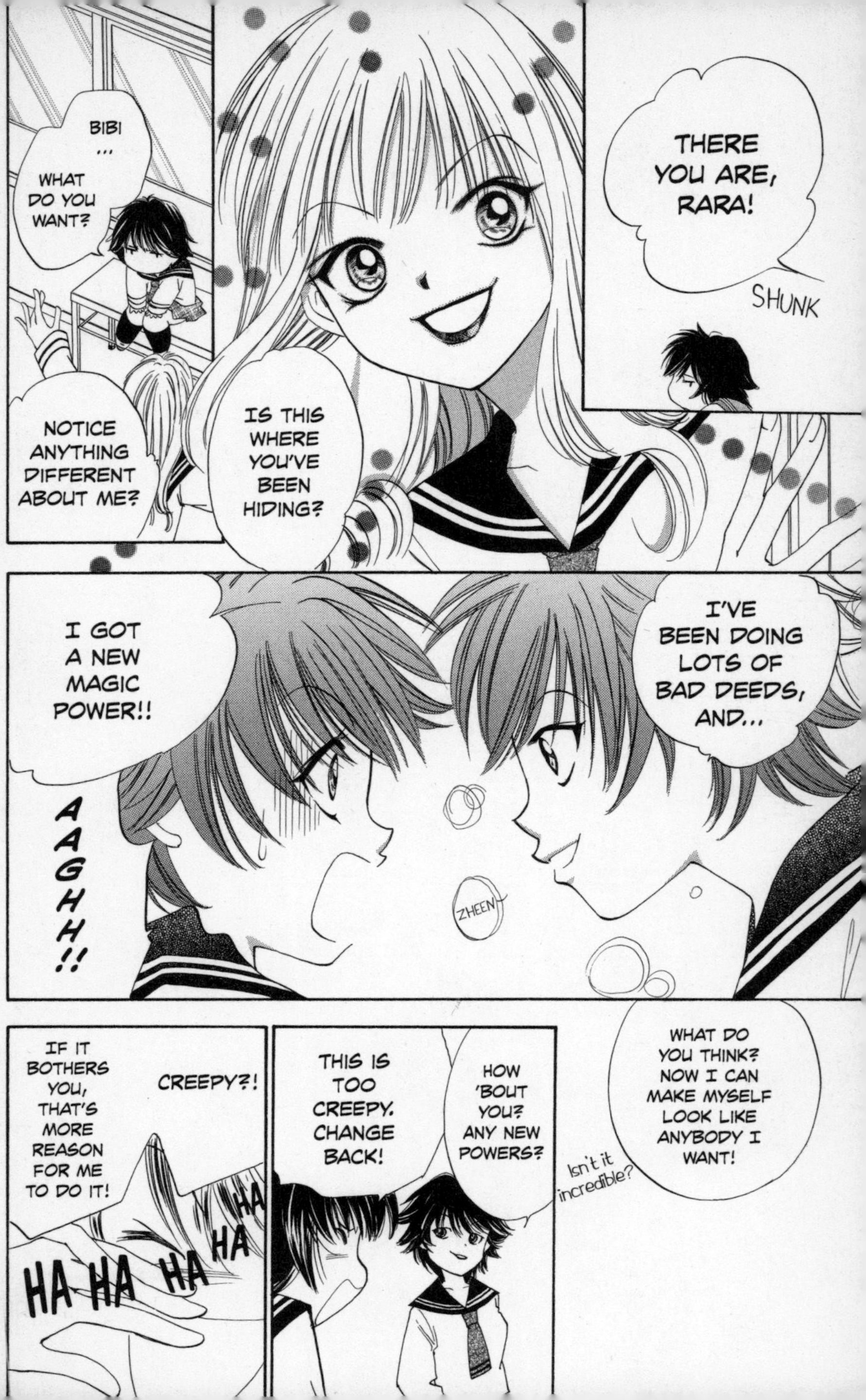
THERE YOU ARE, RARA!
SHUNK
IS THIS WHERE YOU'VE BEEN HIDING?
BIBI ... WHAT DO YOU WANT?
NOTICE ANYTHING DIFFERENT ABOUT ME?
I'VE BEEN DOING LOTS OF BAD DEEDS, AND...
I GOT A NEW MAGIC POWER!!
ZHEEN
AAGHH!!
WHAT DO YOU THINK? NOW I CAN MAKE MYSELF LOOK LIKE ANYBODY I WANT!
Isn't it incredible?
HOW 'BOUT YOU? ANY NEW POWERS?
THIS IS TOO CREEPY. CHANGE BACK!
CREEPY?!
IF IT BOTHERS YOU, THAT'S MORE REASON FOR ME TO DO IT!
HA HA HA HA HA

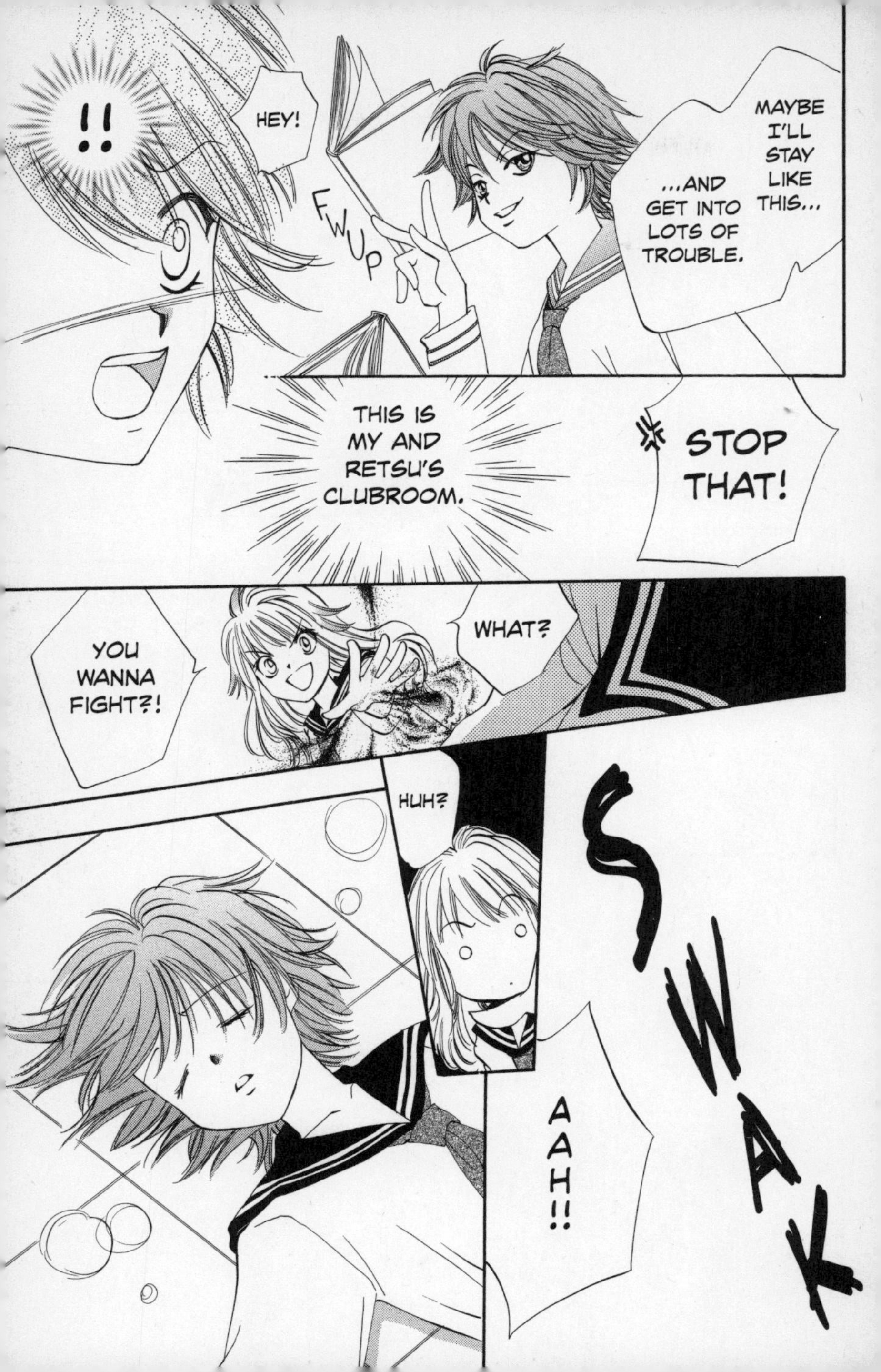
MAYBE I'LL STAY LIKE THIS...
...AND GET INTO LOTS OF TROUBLE.
FWUP
HEY!
!!
STOP THAT!
THIS IS MY AND RETSU'S CLUBROOM.
WHAT?
YOU WANNA FIGHT?!
SWAK
AAH!!
HUH?

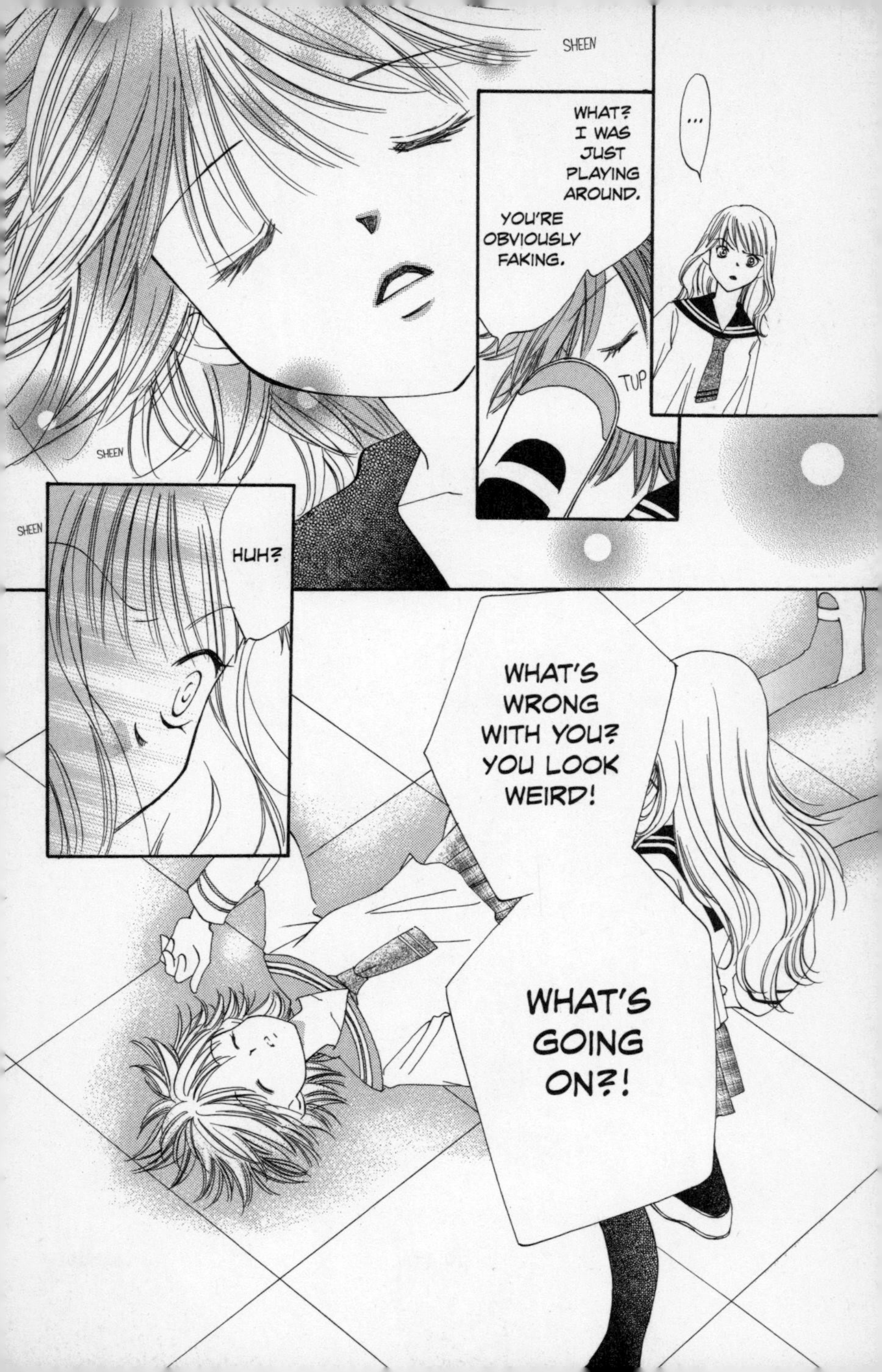

...
WHAT? I WAS JUST PLAYING AROUND.
YOU'RE OBVIOUSLY FAKING.
TUP
SHEEN
SHEEN
SHEEN
HUH?
WHAT'S WRONG WITH YOU? YOU LOOK WEIRD!
WHAT'S GOING ON?!

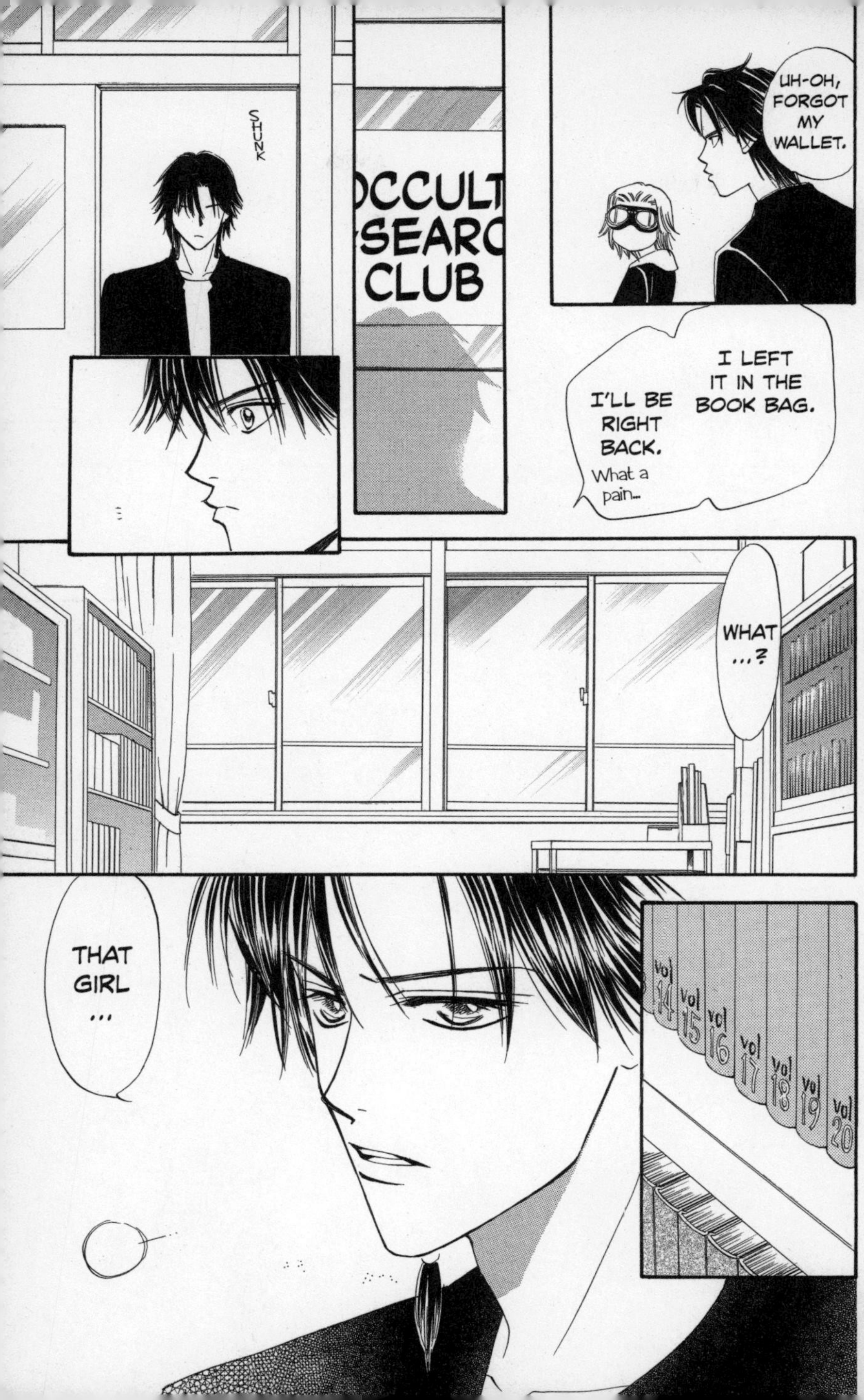
UH-OH, FORGOT MY WALLET.
I LEFT IT IN THE BOOK BAG.
I'LL BE RIGHT BACK.
What a pain...
OCCULT -SEARC CLUB
SHUNK
WHAT ...?
vol 14
vol 15
vol 16
vol 17
vol 18
vol 19
vol 20
THAT GIRL ...

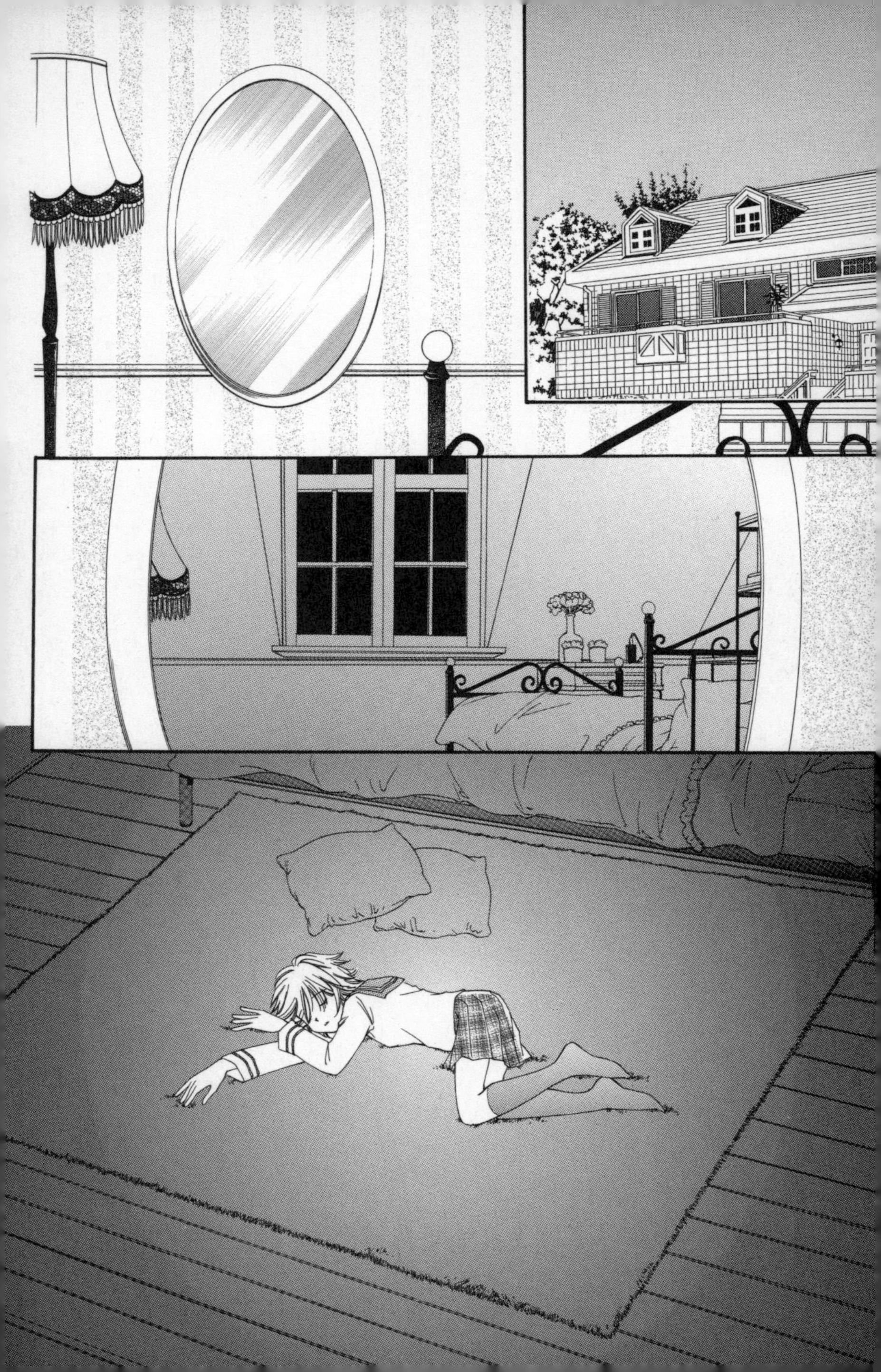

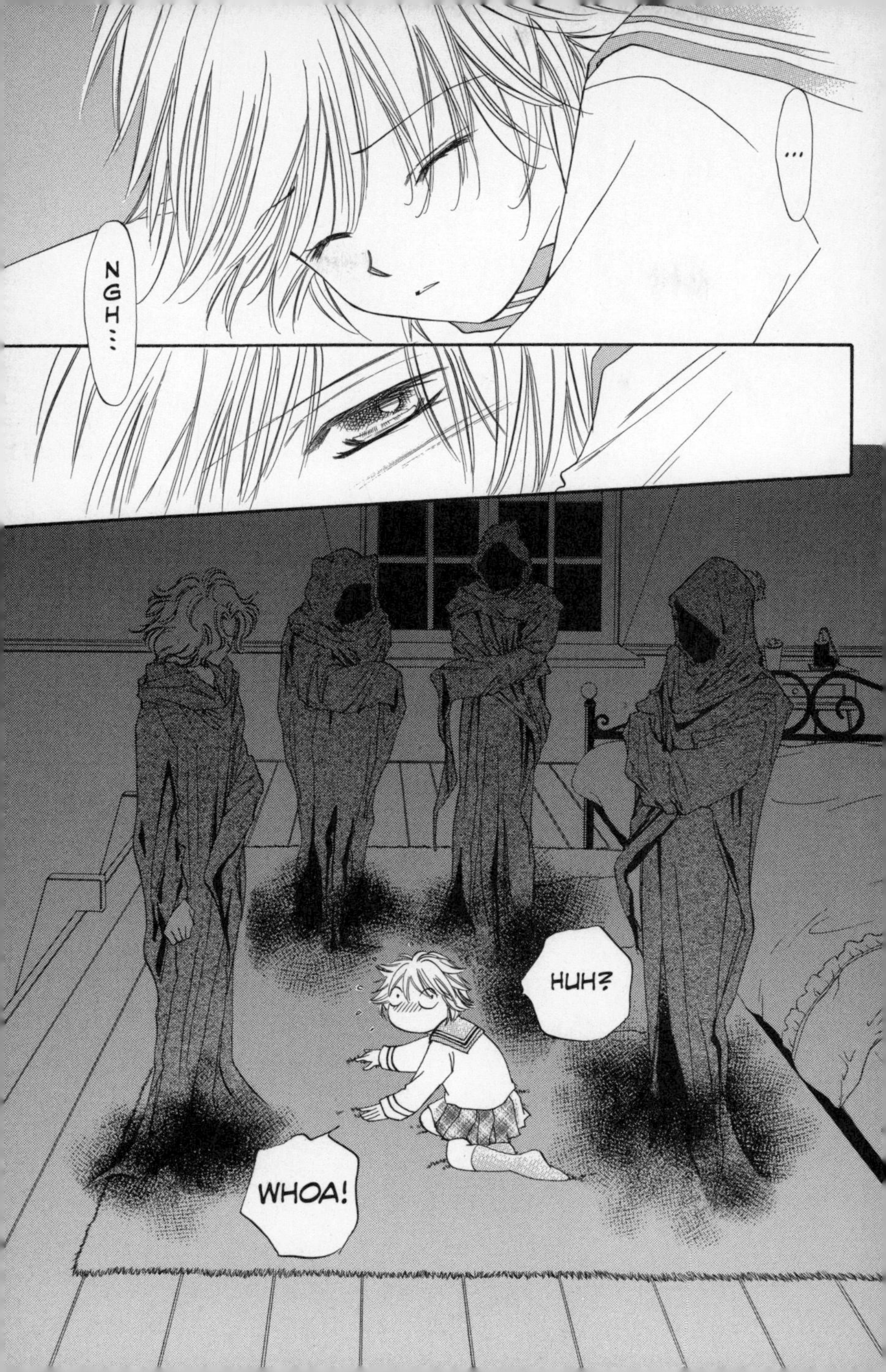
...
NGH...
HUH?
WHOA!

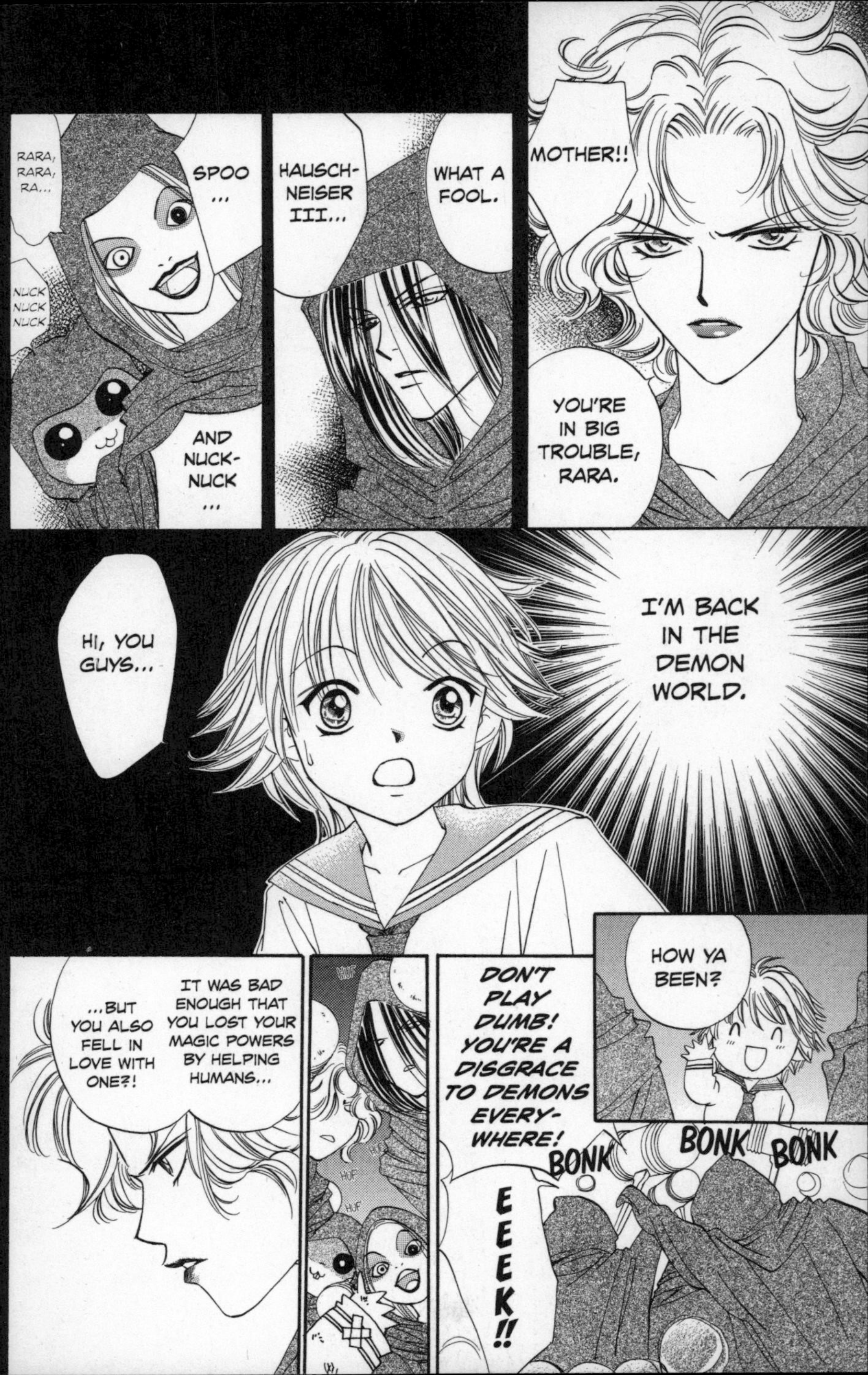
MOTHER!!
YOU'RE IN BIG TROUBLE, RARA.
WHAT A FOOL.
HAUSCHNEISER III...
SPOO...
RARA, RARA, RA...
NUCK NUCK NUCK
AND NUCK-NUCK...
I'M BACK IN THE DEMON WORLD.
HI, YOU GUYS...
HOW YA BEEN?
DON'T PLAY DUMB! YOU'RE A DISGRACE TO DEMONS EVERYWHERE!
BONK
BONK
BONK
EEEK!!
HUF
HUF
HUF
IT WAS BAD ENOUGH THAT YOU LOST YOUR MAGIC POWERS BY HELPING HUMANS...
...BUT YOU ALSO FELL IN LOVE WITH ONE?!

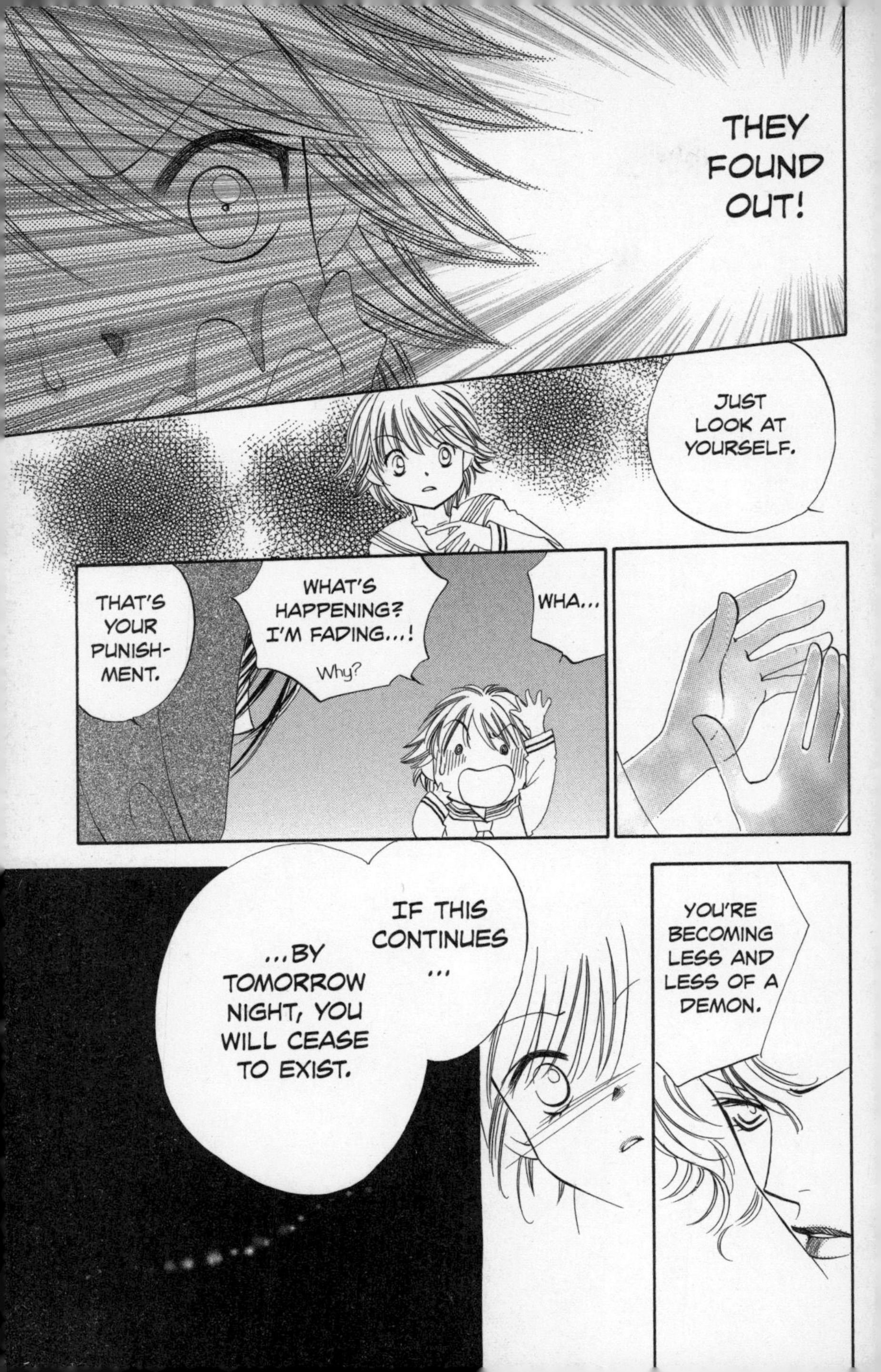
THEY FOUND OUT!
JUST LOOK AT YOURSELF.
WHA...
WHAT'S HAPPENING? I'M FADING...!
Why?
THAT'S YOUR PUNISHMENT.
YOU'RE BECOMING LESS AND LESS OF A DEMON.
IF THIS CONTINUES ...
...BY TOMORROW NIGHT, YOU WILL CEASE TO EXIST.

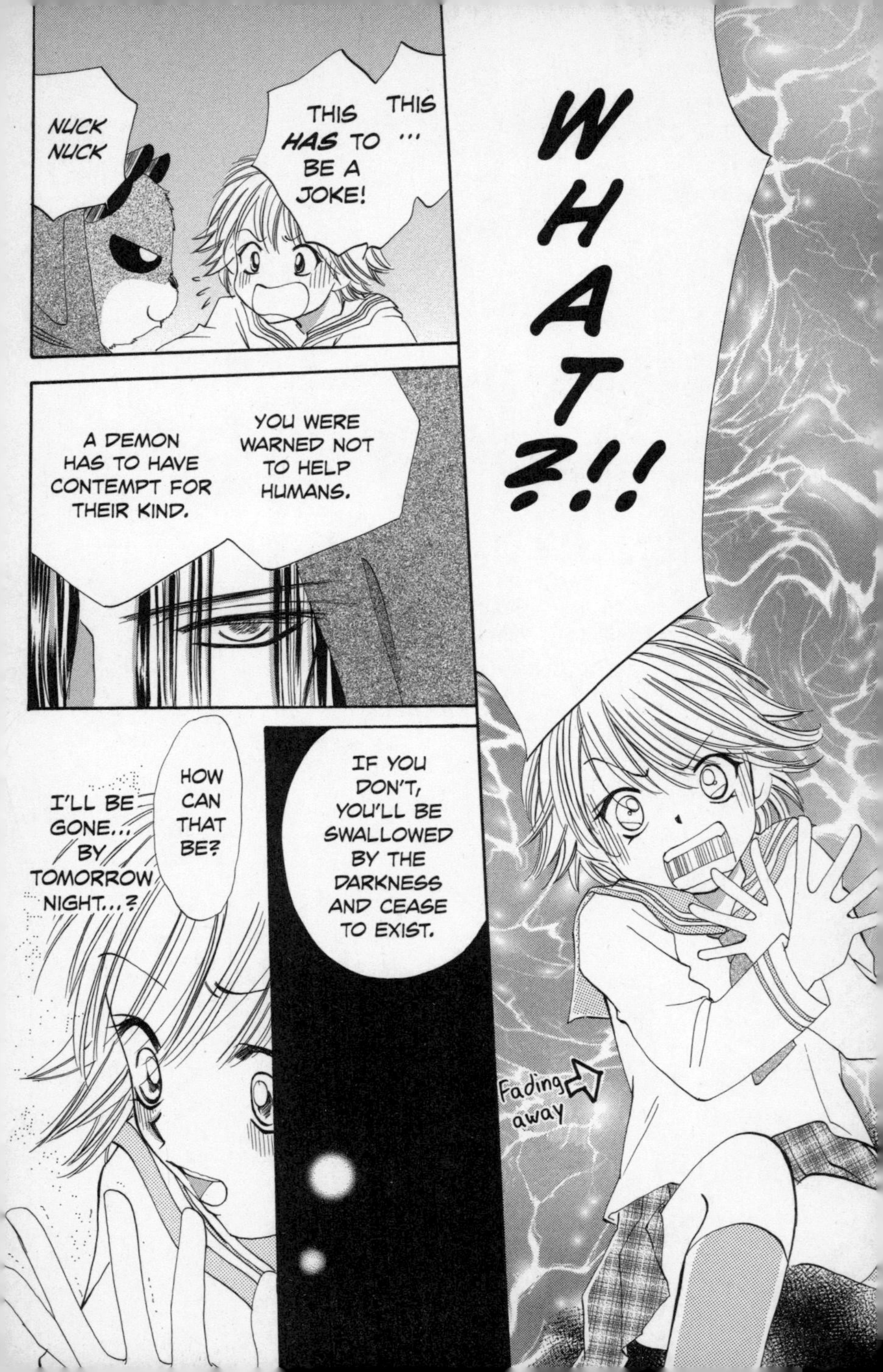
WHAT?!!
Fading away
THIS ...
THIS HAS TO BE A JOKE!
NUCK NUCK
YOU WERE WARNED NOT TO HELP HUMANS.
A DEMON HAS TO HAVE CONTEMPT FOR THEIR KIND.
IF YOU DON'T, YOU'LL BE SWALLOWED BY THE DARKNESS AND CEASE TO EXIST.
HOW CAN THAT BE?
I'LL BE GONE... BY TOMORROW NIGHT...?

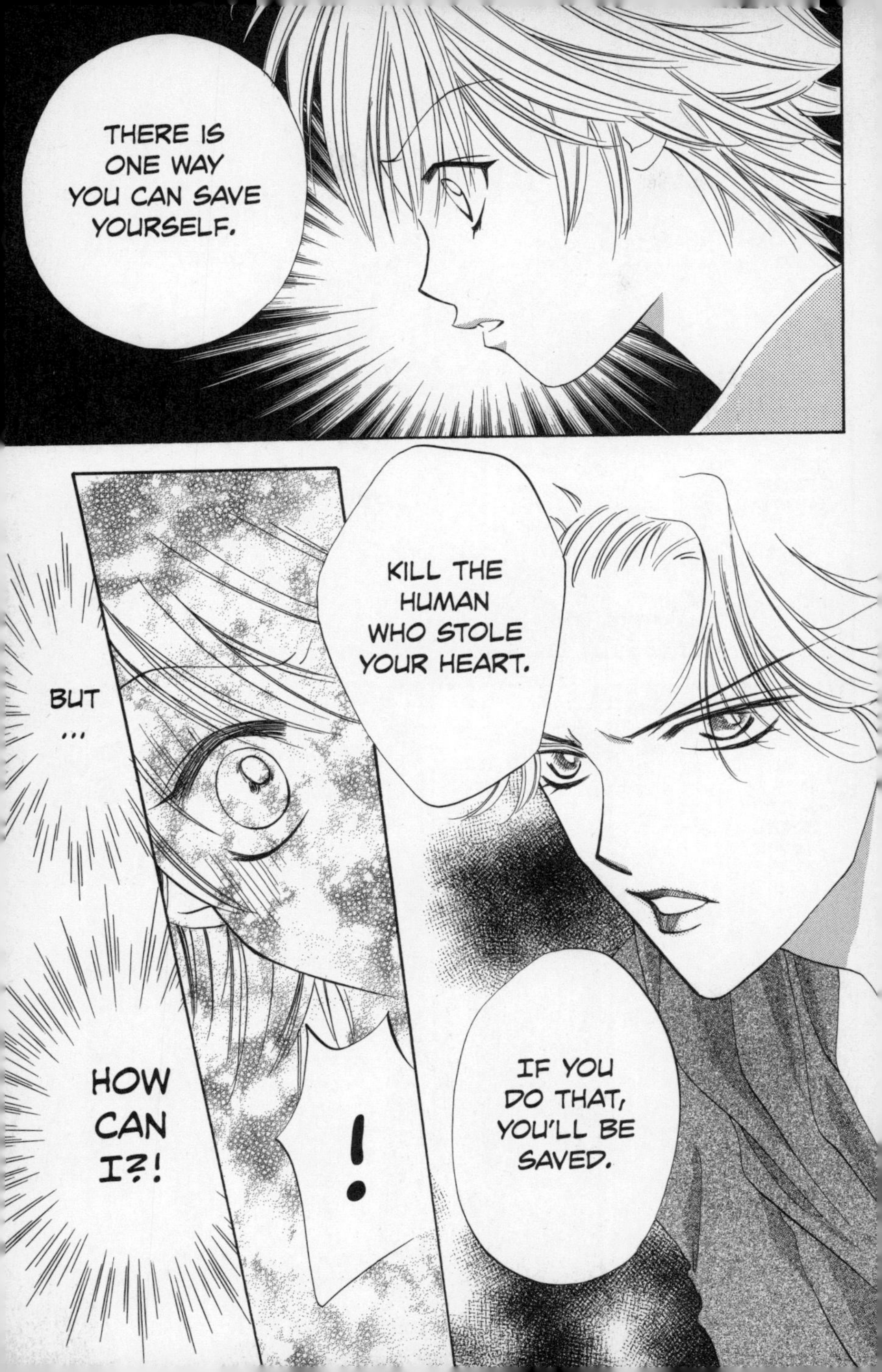
THERE IS ONE WAY YOU CAN SAVE YOURSELF.
KILL THE HUMAN WHO STOLE YOUR HEART.
IF YOU DO THAT, YOU'LL BE SAVED.
!
BUT ...
HOW CAN I?!

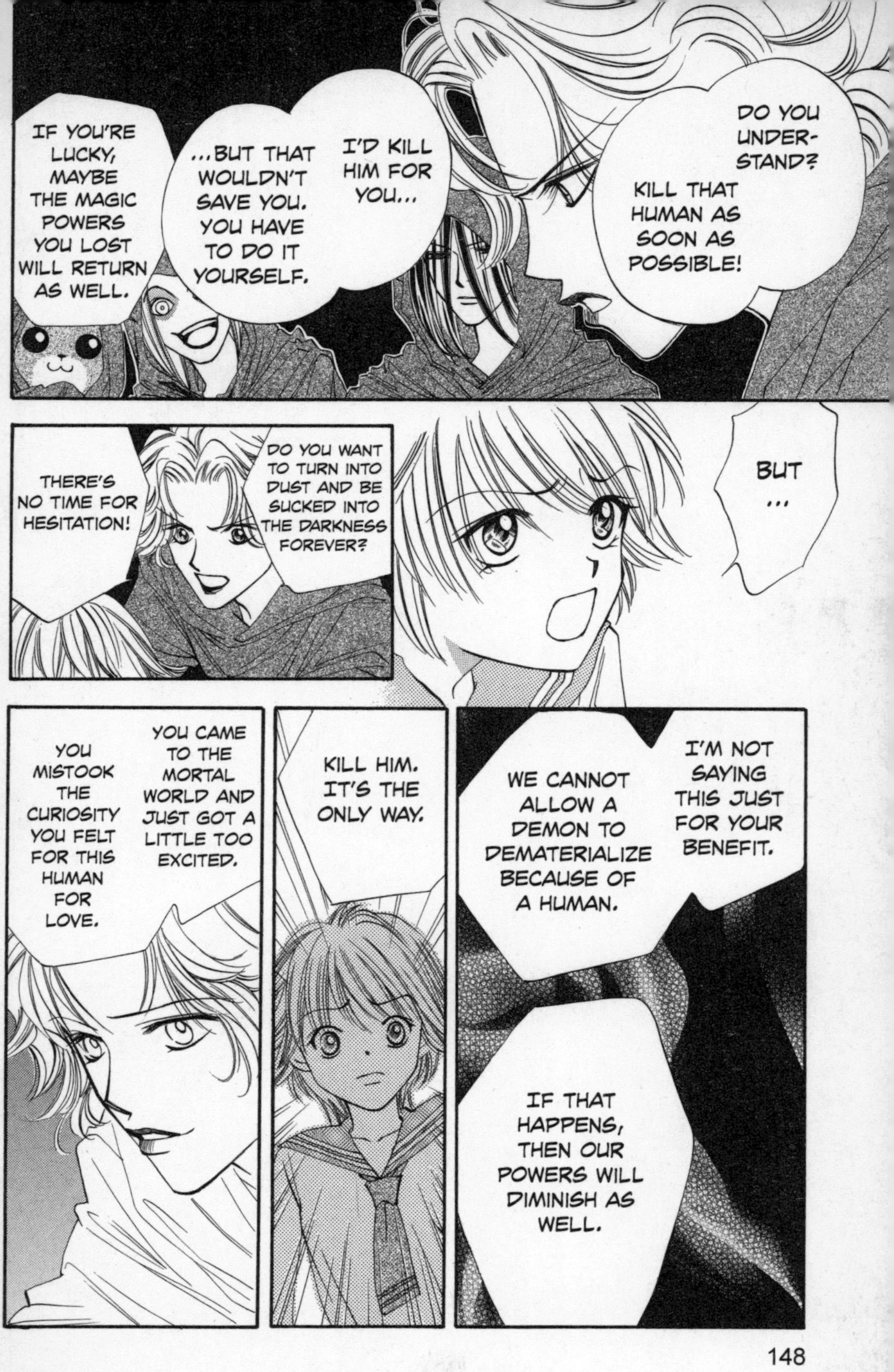
DO YOU UNDER-STAND? KILL THAT HUMAN AS SOON AS POSSIBLE!
I'D KILL HIM FOR YOU...
...BUT THAT WOULDN'T SAVE YOU. YOU HAVE TO DO IT YOURSELF.
IF YOU'RE LUCKY, MAYBE THE MAGIC POWERS YOU LOST WILL RETURN AS WELL.
BUT ...
DO YOU WANT TO TURN INTO DUST AND BE SUCKED INTO THE DARKNESS FOREVER?
THERE'S NO TIME FOR HESITATION!
I'M NOT SAYING THIS JUST FOR YOUR BENEFIT.
WE CANNOT ALLOW A DEMON TO DEMATERIALIZE BECAUSE OF A HUMAN.
IF THAT HAPPENS, THEN OUR POWERS WILL DIMINISH AS WELL.
KILL HIM. IT'S THE ONLY WAY.
YOU CAME TO THE MORTAL WORLD AND JUST GOT A LITTLE TOO EXCITED.
YOU MISTOOK THE CURIOSITY YOU FELT FOR THIS HUMAN FOR LOVE.

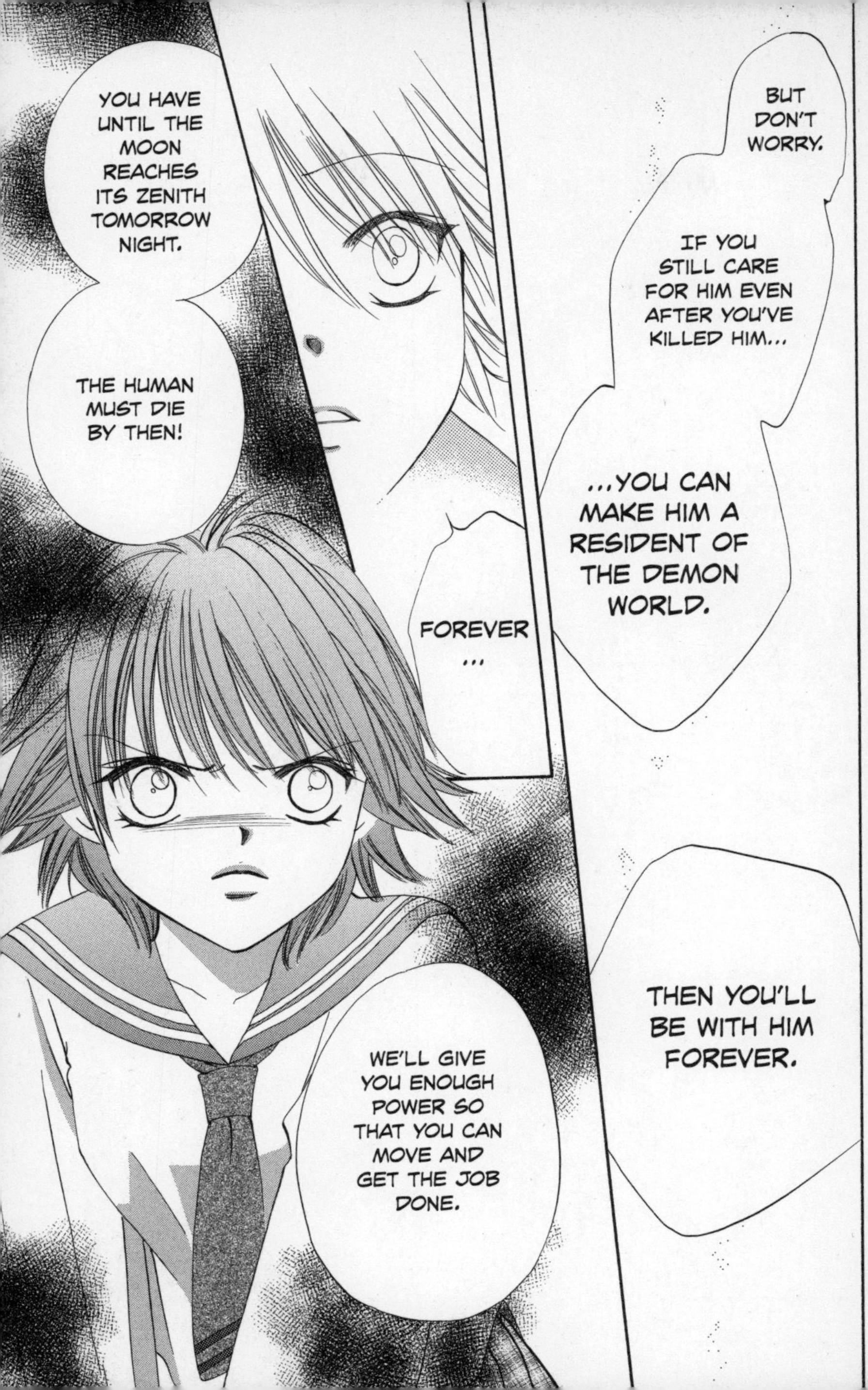
BUT DON'T WORRY.
IF YOU STILL CARE FOR HIM EVEN AFTER YOU'VE KILLED HIM...
...YOU CAN MAKE HIM A RESIDENT OF THE DEMON WORLD.
THEN YOU'LL BE WITH HIM FOREVER.
FOREVER ...
YOU HAVE UNTIL THE MOON REACHES ITS ZENITH TOMORROW NIGHT.
THE HUMAN MUST DIE BY THEN!
WE'LL GIVE YOU ENOUGH POWER SO THAT YOU CAN MOVE AND GET THE JOB DONE.

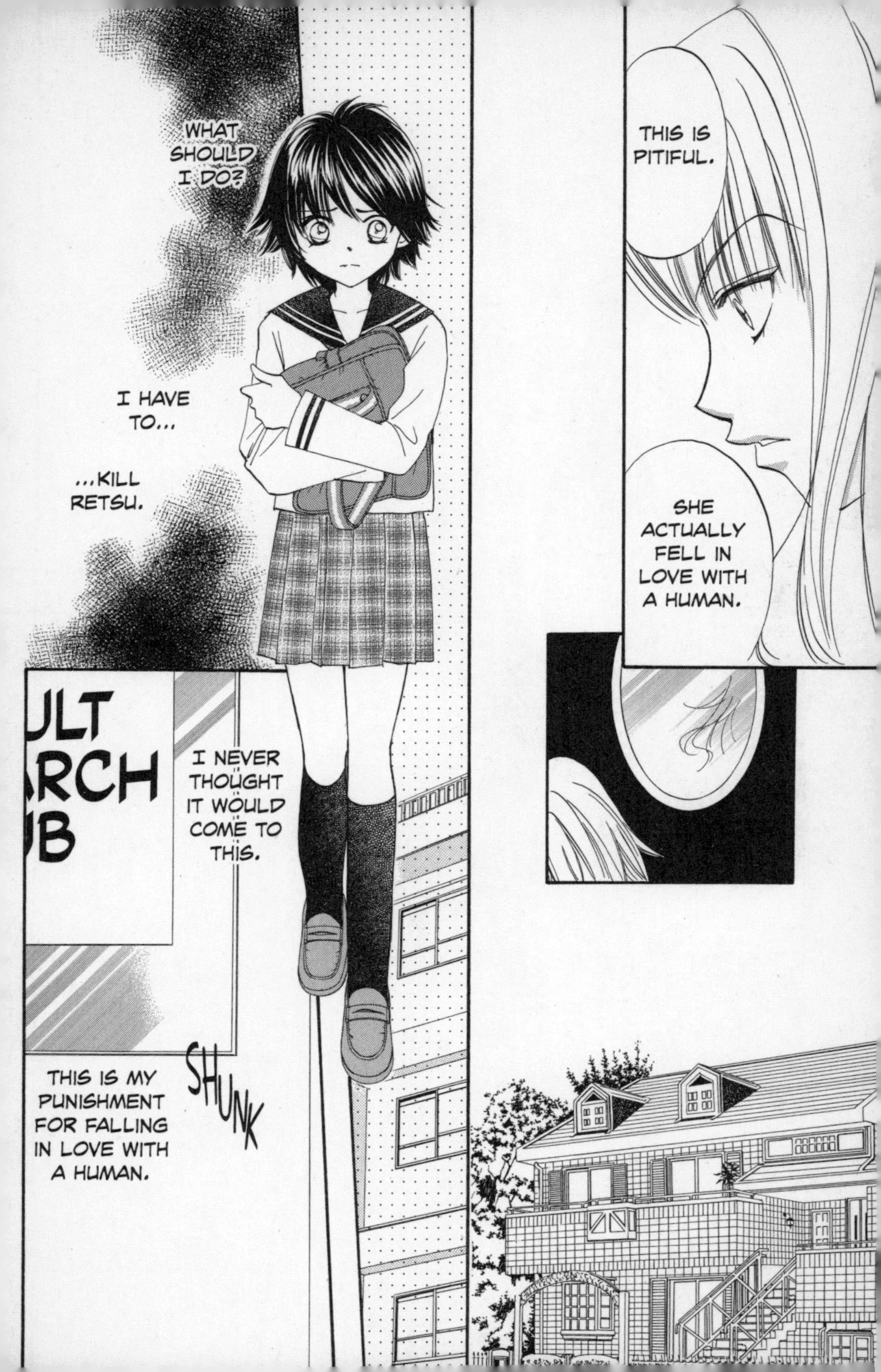
THIS IS PITIFUL.
SHE ACTUALLY FELL IN LOVE WITH A HUMAN.
WHAT SHOULD I DO?
I HAVE TO...
...KILL RETSU.
I NEVER THOUGHT IT WOULD COME TO THIS.
SHUNK
THIS IS MY PUNISHMENT FOR FALLING IN LOVE WITH A HUMAN.

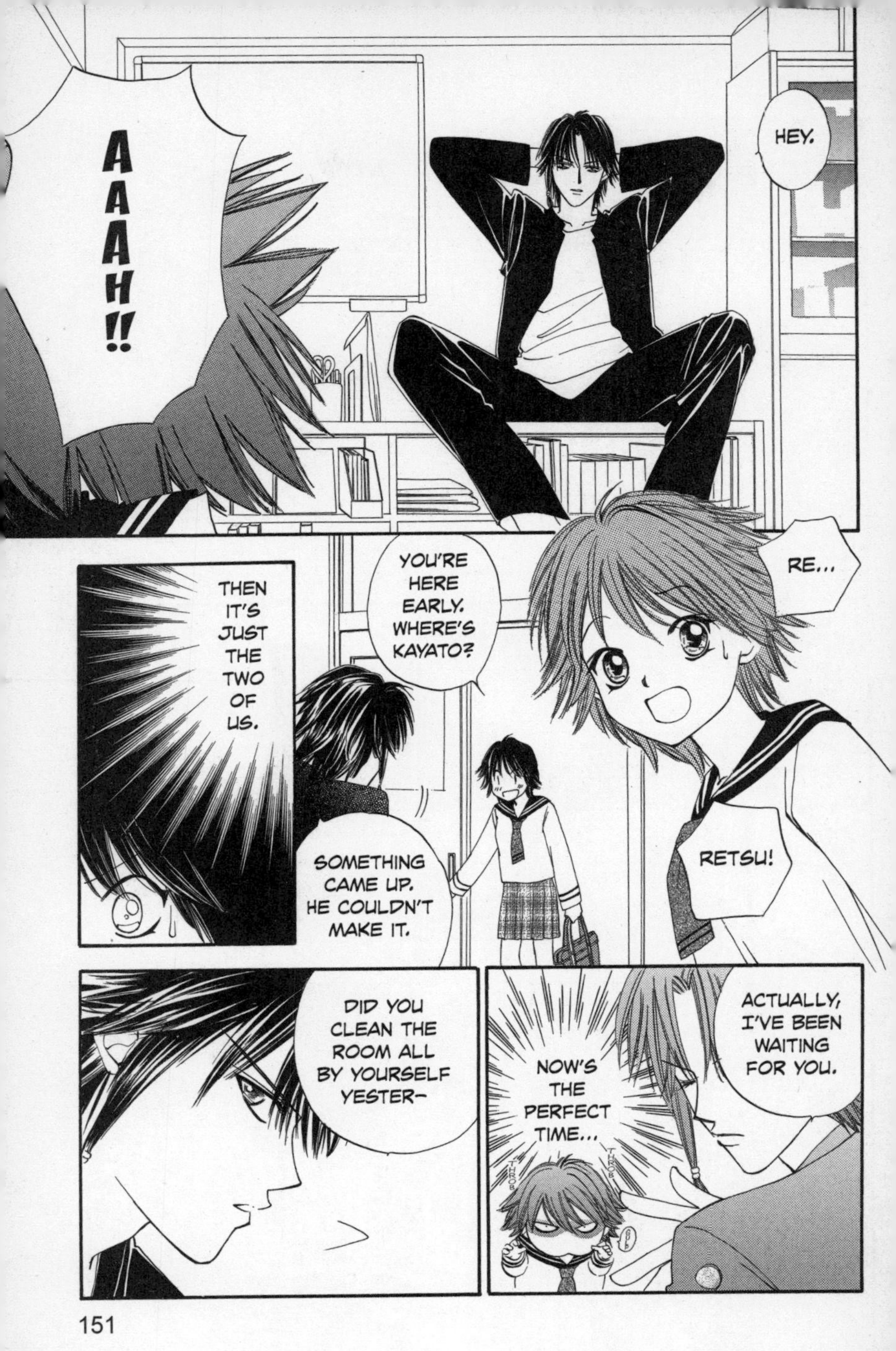
HEY.
AAAH!!
RE...
RETSU!
YOU'RE HERE EARLY. WHERE'S KAYATO?
SOMETHING CAME UP. HE COULDN'T MAKE IT.
THEN IT'S JUST THE TWO OF US.
ACTUALLY, I'VE BEEN WAITING FOR YOU.
NOW'S THE PERFECT TIME...
THROB
THROB
DID YOU CLEAN THE ROOM ALL BY YOURSELF YESTER-

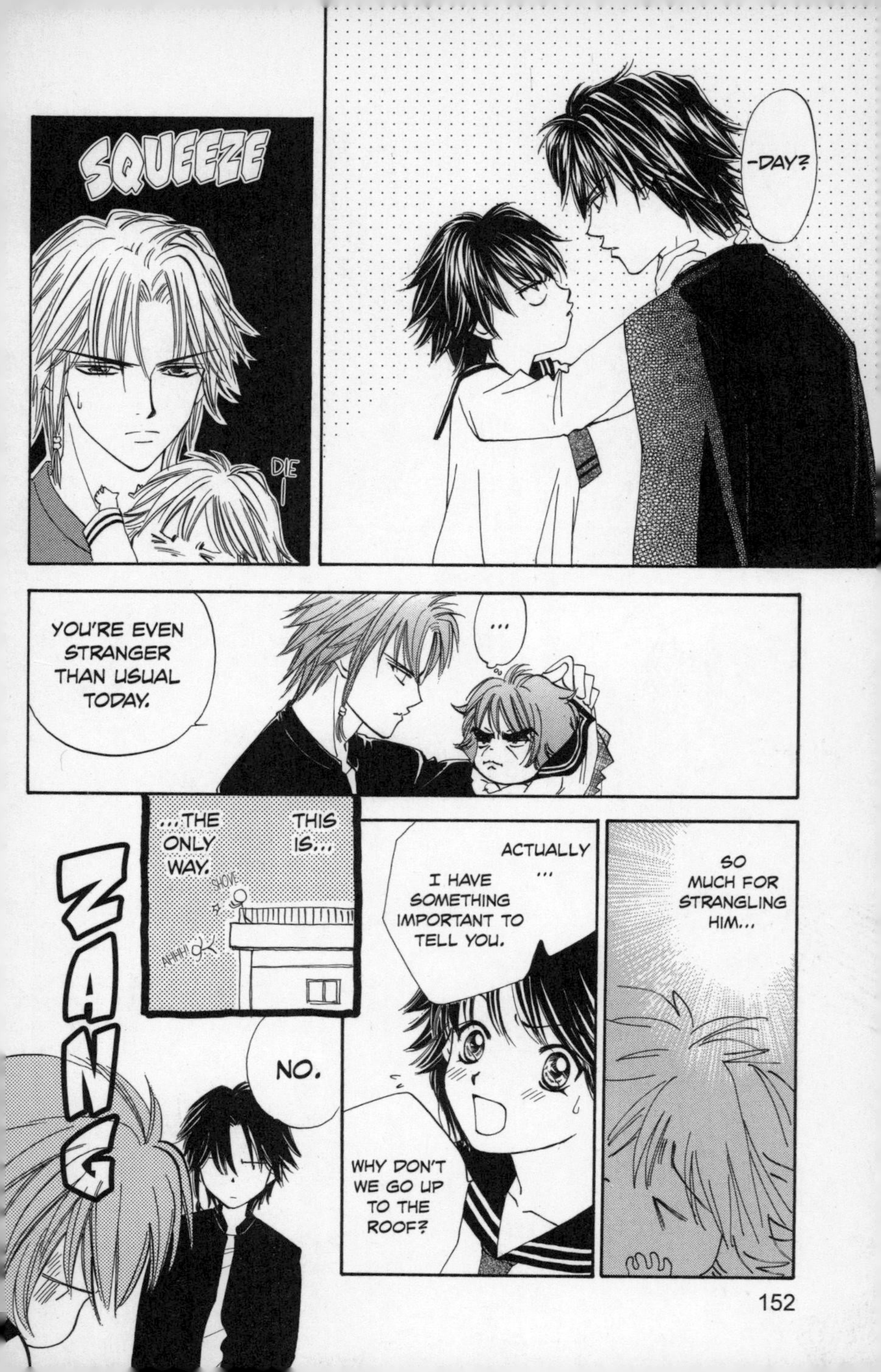
-DAY?
SQUEEZE
DIE
YOU'RE EVEN STRANGER THAN USUAL TODAY.
...
SO MUCH FOR STRANGLING HIM...
ACTUALLY...
I HAVE SOMETHING IMPORTANT TO TELL YOU.
WHY DON'T WE GO UP TO THE ROOF?
THIS IS...
...THE ONLY WAY.
SHOVE
AHHH!
ZANG
NO.

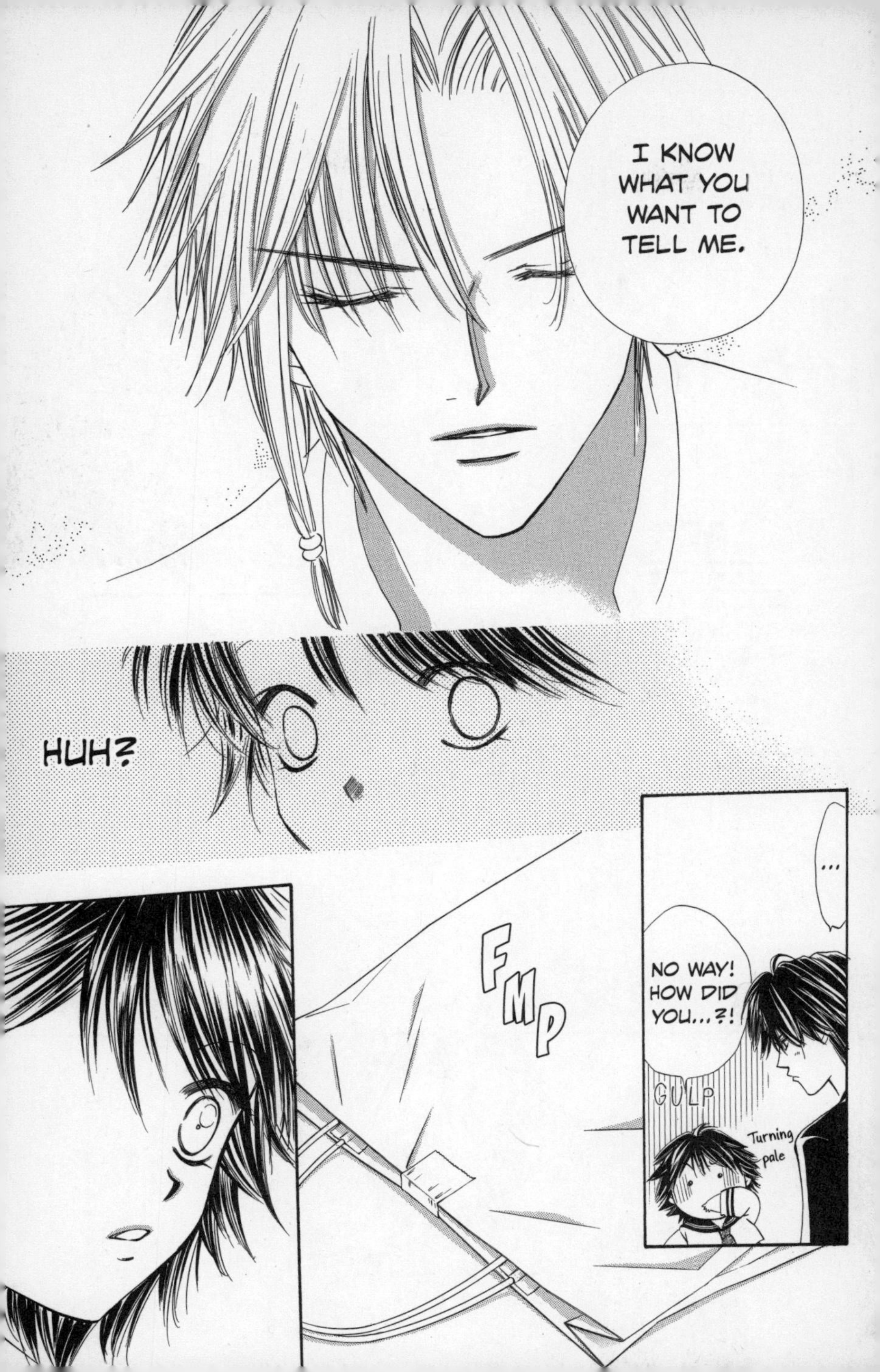
I KNOW WHAT YOU WANT TO TELL ME.
HUH?
...
NO WAY! HOW DID YOU...?!
GULP
Turning pale
FMP

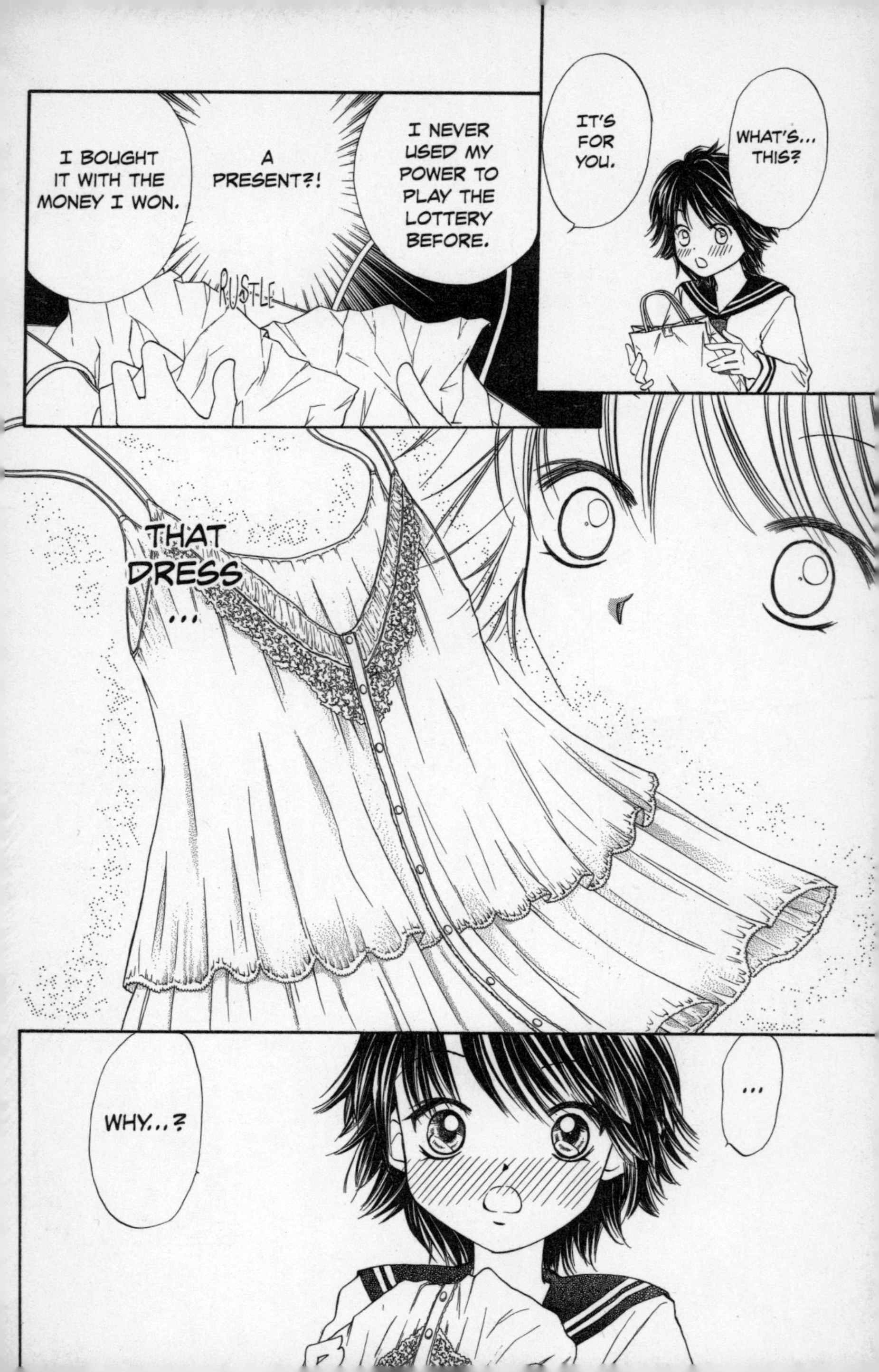
WHAT'S... THIS?
IT'S FOR YOU.
I NEVER USED MY POWER TO PLAY THE LOTTERY BEFORE.
A PRESENT?!
I BOUGHT IT WITH THE MONEY I WON.
RUSTLE
THAT DRESS ...
...
WHY...?

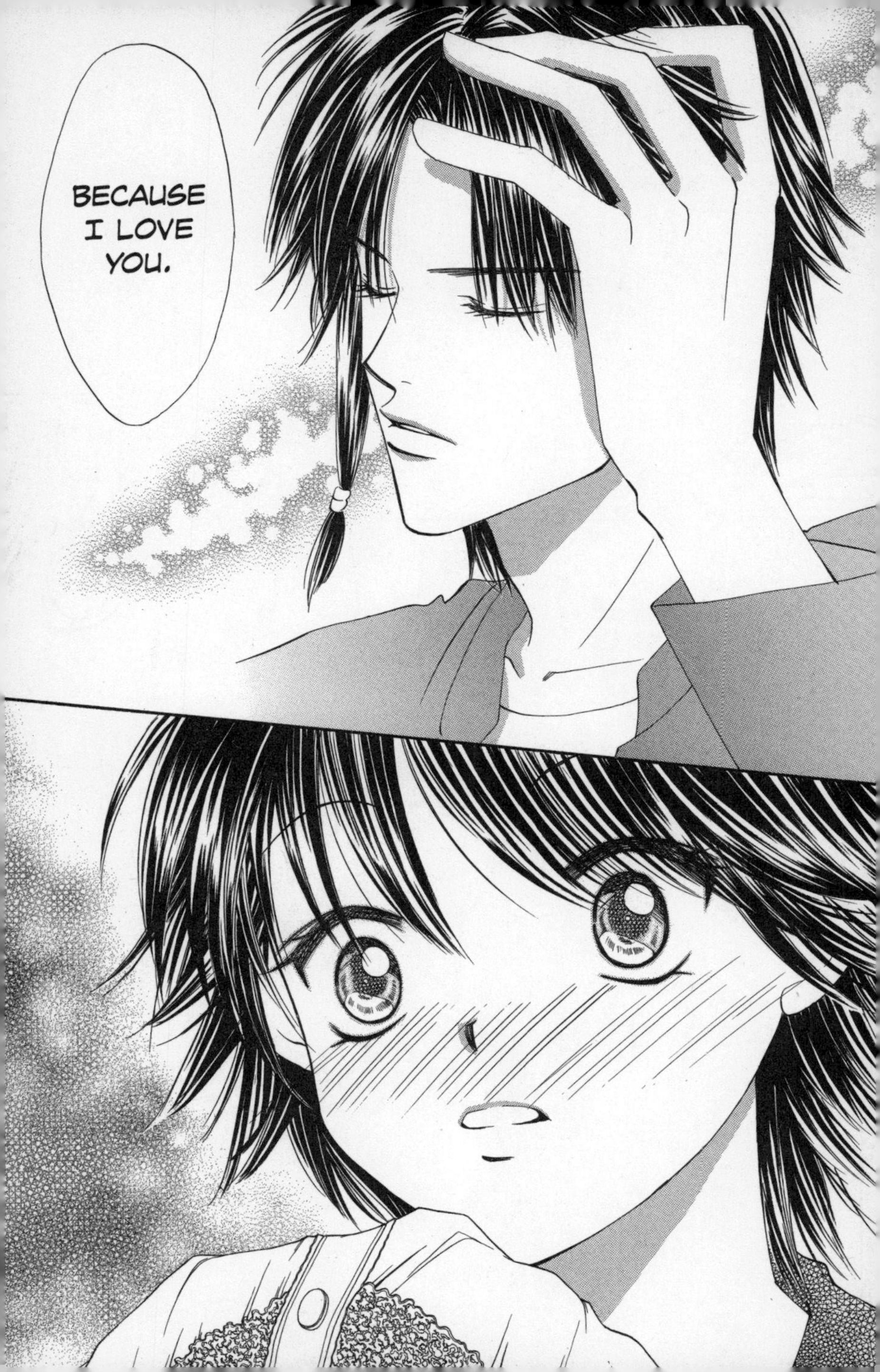
BECAUSE I LOVE YOU.

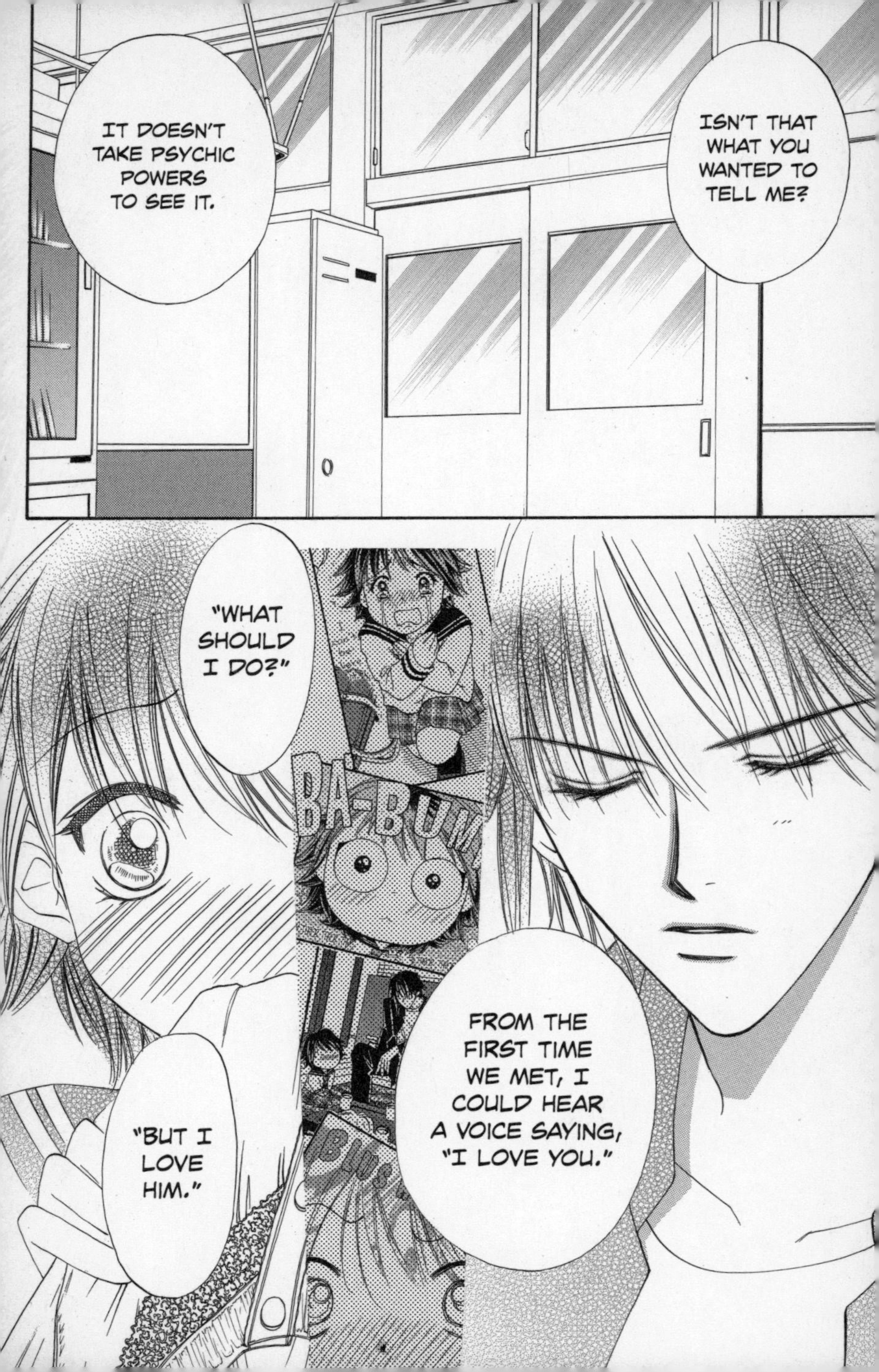
ISN'T THAT WHAT YOU WANTED TO TELL ME?
IT DOESN'T TAKE PSYCHIC POWERS TO SEE IT.
FROM THE FIRST TIME WE MET, I COULD HEAR A VOICE SAYING, "I LOVE YOU."
"WHAT SHOULD I DO?"
BA-BUM
"BUT I LOVE HIM."

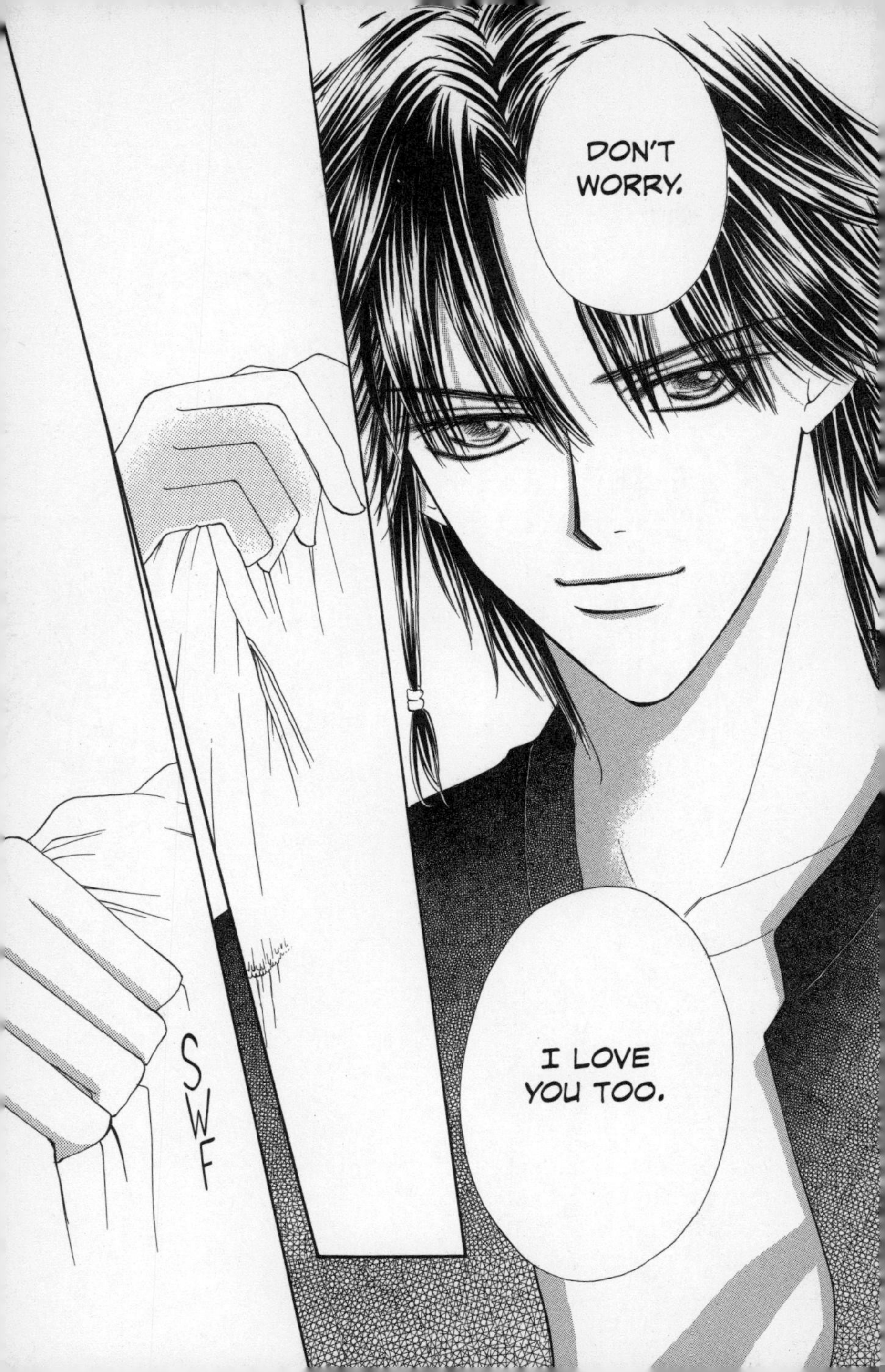
DON'T WORRY.
I LOVE YOU TOO.
SWF

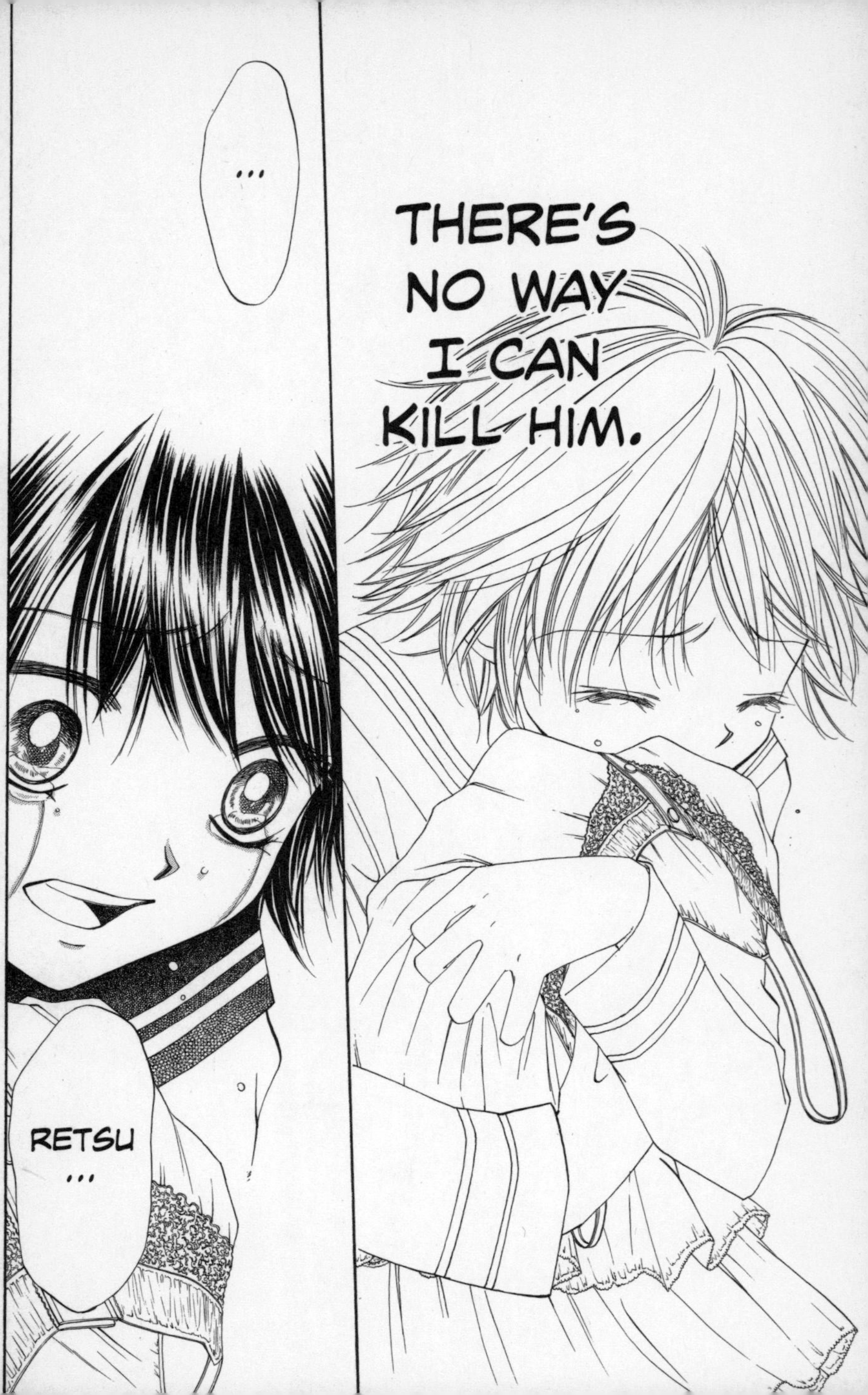
THERE'S NO WAY I CAN KILL HIM.
...
RETSU ...

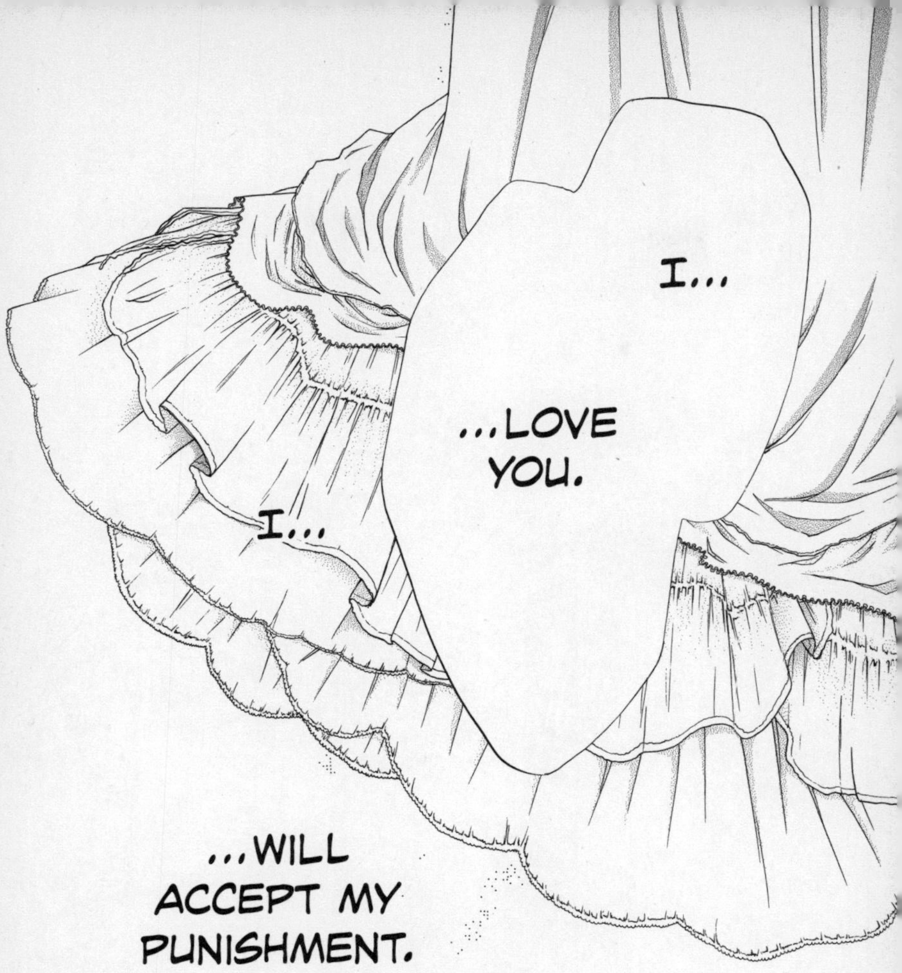
I...
...LOVE YOU.
I...
...WILL ACCEPT MY PUNISHMENT.

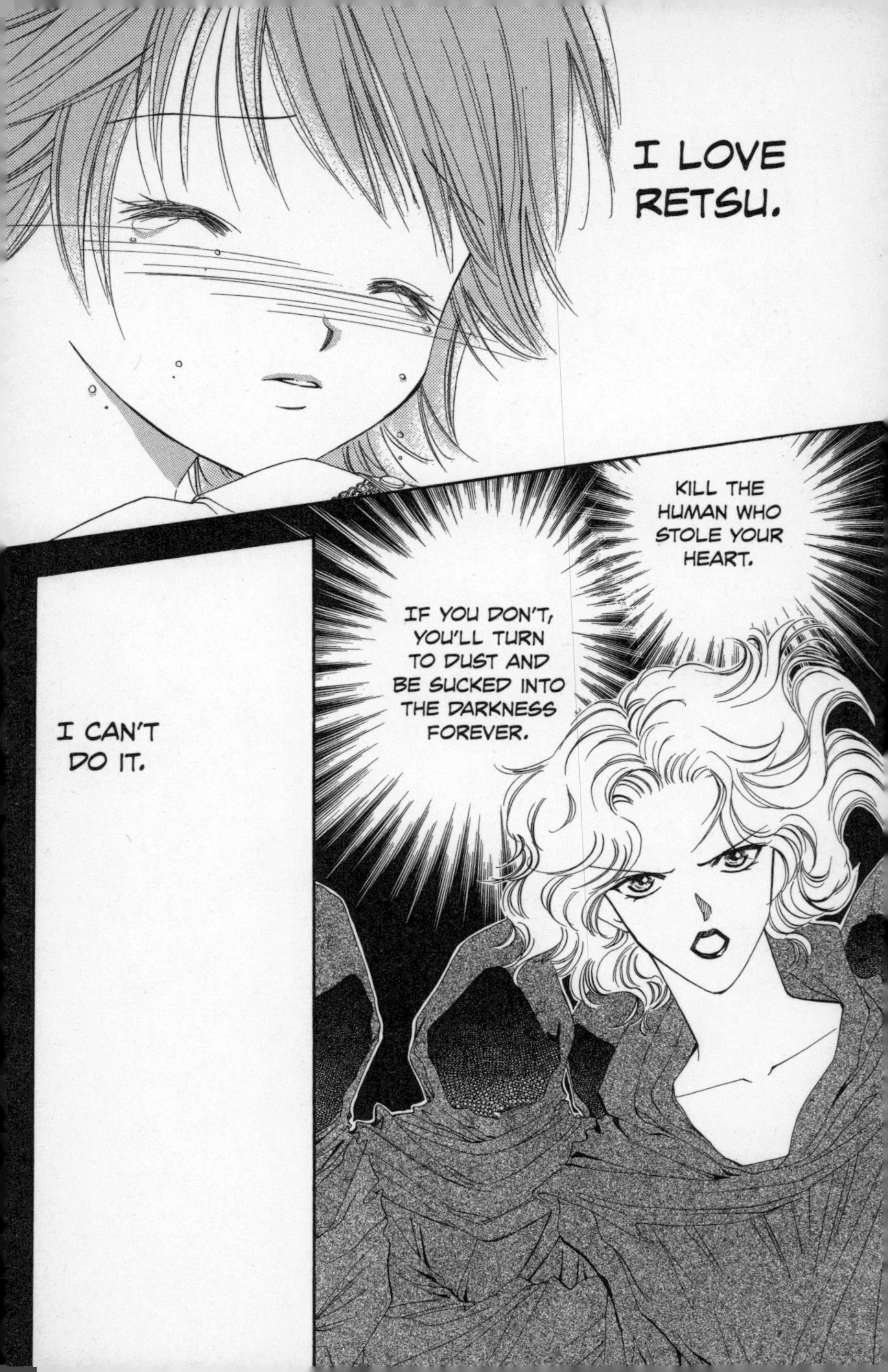
I LOVE RETSU.
KILL THE HUMAN WHO STOLE YOUR HEART.
IF YOU DON'T, YOU'LL TURN TO DUST AND BE SUCKED INTO THE DARKNESS FOREVER.
I CAN'T DO IT.

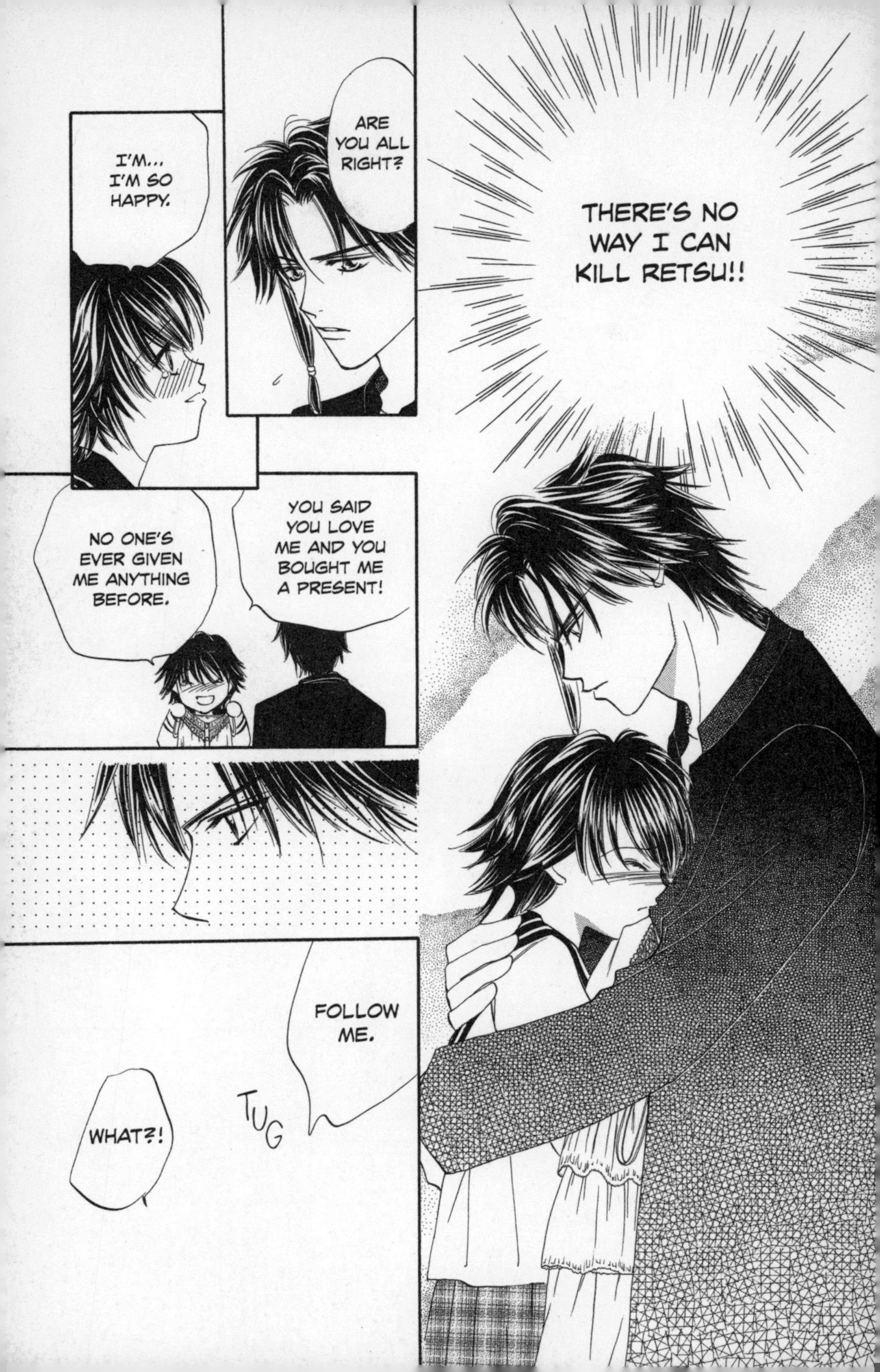
THERE'S NO WAY I CAN KILL RETSU!!
ARE YOU ALL RIGHT?
I'M... I'M SO HAPPY.
YOU SAID YOU LOVE ME AND YOU BOUGHT ME A PRESENT!
NO ONE'S EVER GIVEN ME ANYTHING BEFORE.
FOLLOW ME.
TUG
WHAT?!

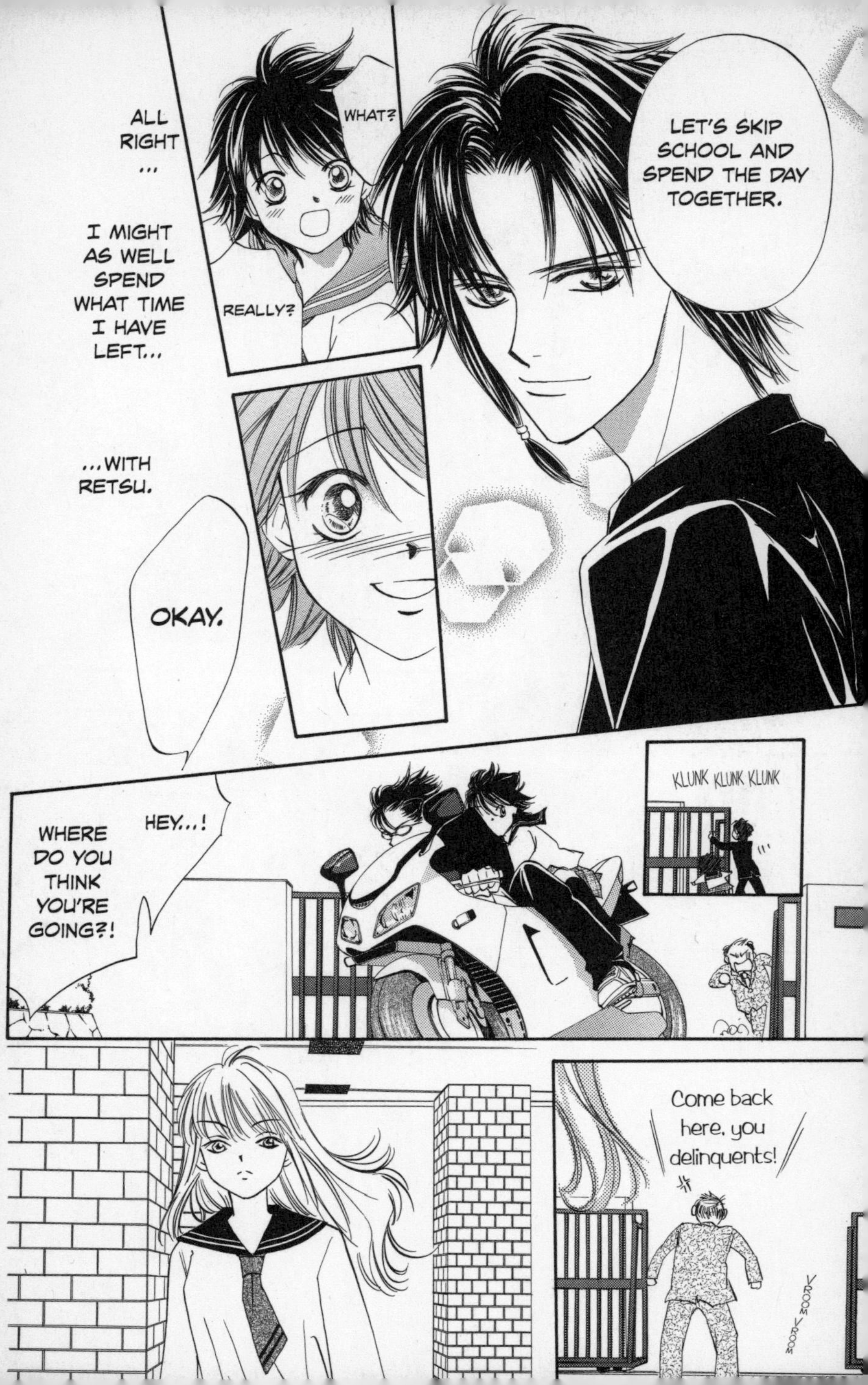
LET'S SKIP SCHOOL AND SPEND THE DAY TOGETHER.
WHAT?
REALLY?
ALL RIGHT ...
I MIGHT AS WELL SPEND WHAT TIME I HAVE LEFT...
...WITH RETSU.
OKAY.
KLUNK KLUNK KLUNK
HEY...!
WHERE DO YOU THINK YOU'RE GOING?!
Come back here, you delinquents!
VROOM VROOM

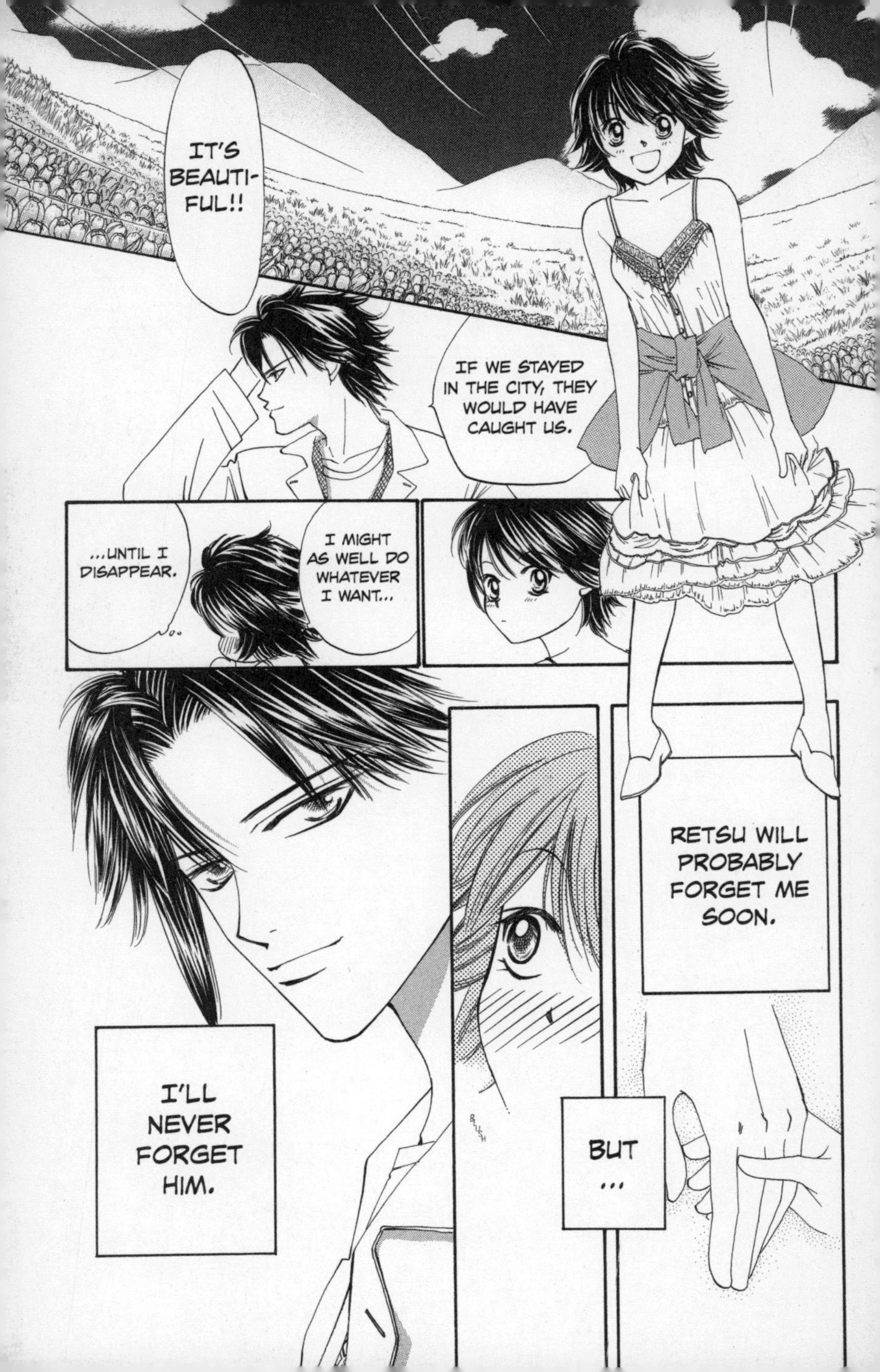
IT'S BEAUTI-FUL!!
IF WE STAYED IN THE CITY, THEY WOULD HAVE CAUGHT US.
I MIGHT AS WELL DO WHATEVER I WANT...
...UNTIL I DISAPPEAR.
RETSU WILL PROBABLY FORGET ME SOON.
BUT ...
BLUSH
I'LL NEVER FORGET HIM.

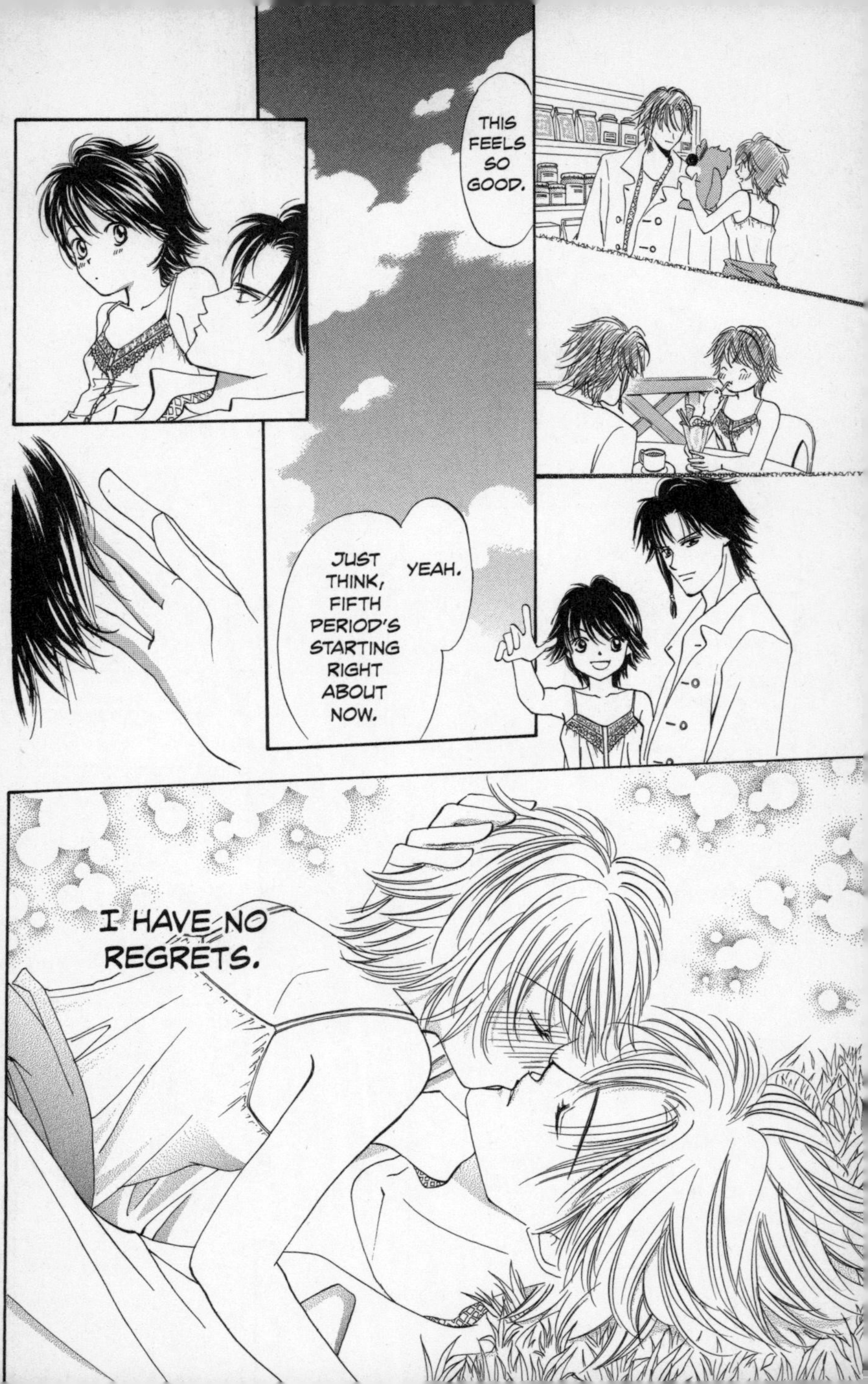
THIS FEELS SO GOOD.
JUST THINK, FIFTH PERIOD'S STARTING RIGHT ABOUT NOW.
YEAH.
I HAVE NO REGRETS.

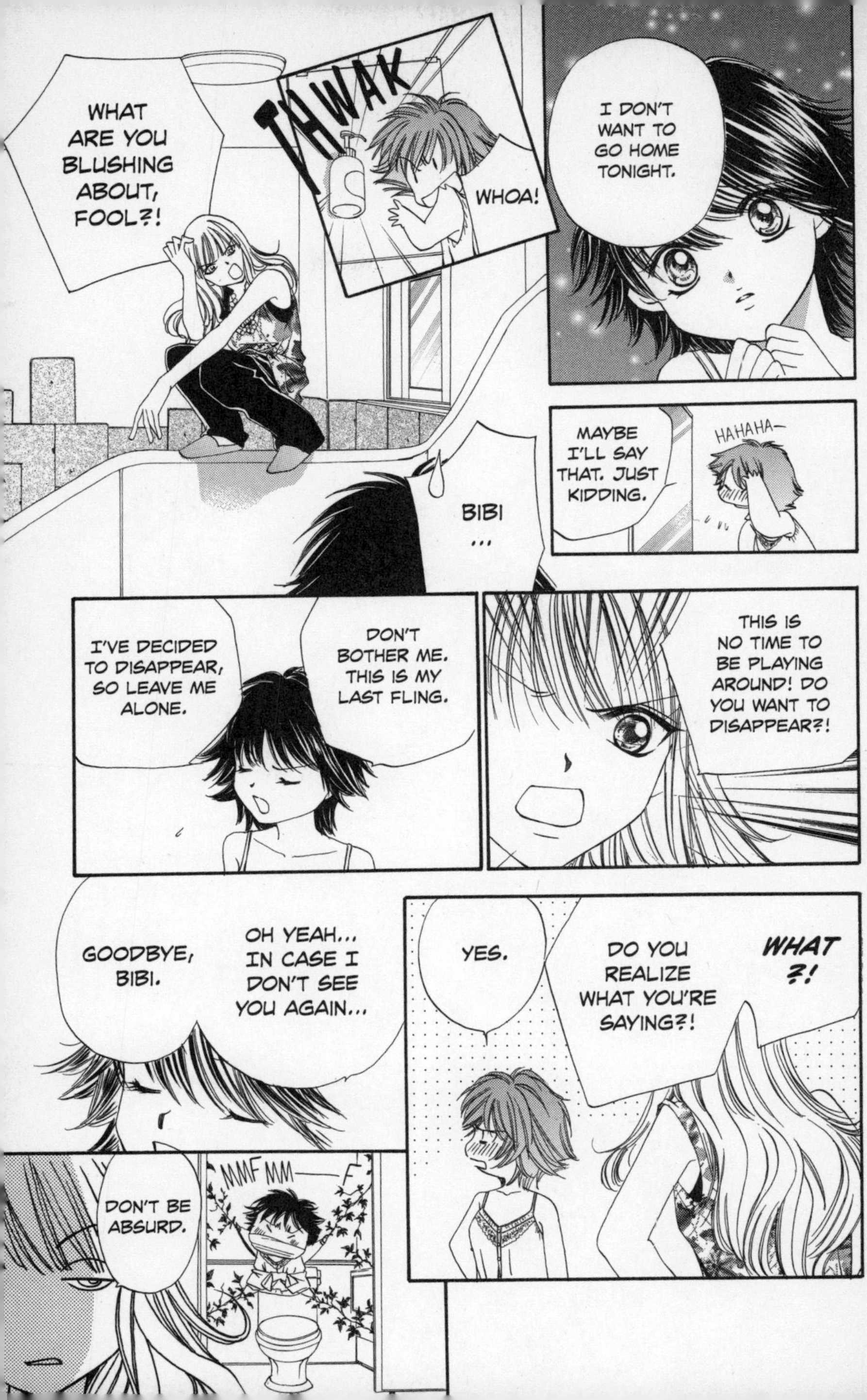
I DON'T WANT TO GO HOME TONIGHT.
MAYBE I'LL SAY THAT. JUST KIDDING.
HAHAHA—
THWAK
WHOA!
WHAT ARE YOU BLUSHING ABOUT, FOOL?!
BIBI ...
THIS IS NO TIME TO BE PLAYING AROUND! DO YOU WANT TO DISAPPEAR?!
DON'T BOTHER ME. THIS IS MY LAST FLING.
I'VE DECIDED TO DISAPPEAR, SO LEAVE ME ALONE.
WHAT ?!
DO YOU REALIZE WHAT YOU'RE SAYING?!
YES.
OH YEAH... IN CASE I DON'T SEE YOU AGAIN...
GOODBYE, BIBI.
MMF MM—
DON'T BE ABSURD.

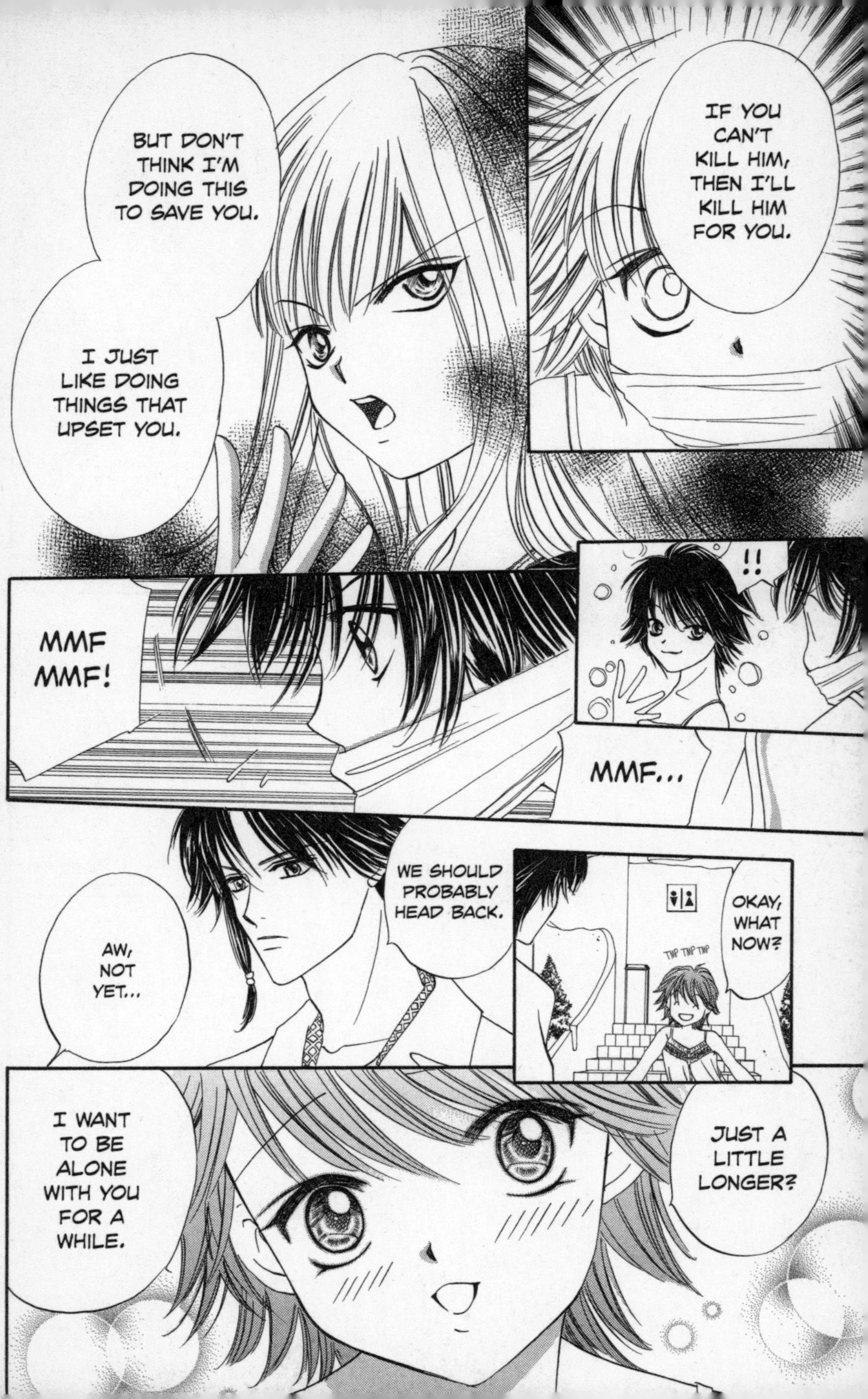
IF YOU CAN'T KILL HIM, THEN I'LL KILL HIM FOR YOU.
BUT DON'T THINK I'M DOING THIS TO SAVE YOU.
I JUST LIKE DOING THINGS THAT UPSET YOU.
!!
MMF MMF!
MMF...
OKAY, WHAT NOW?
TMP TMP TMP
WE SHOULD PROBABLY HEAD BACK.
AW, NOT YET...
JUST A LITTLE LONGER?
I WANT TO BE ALONE WITH YOU FOR A WHILE.

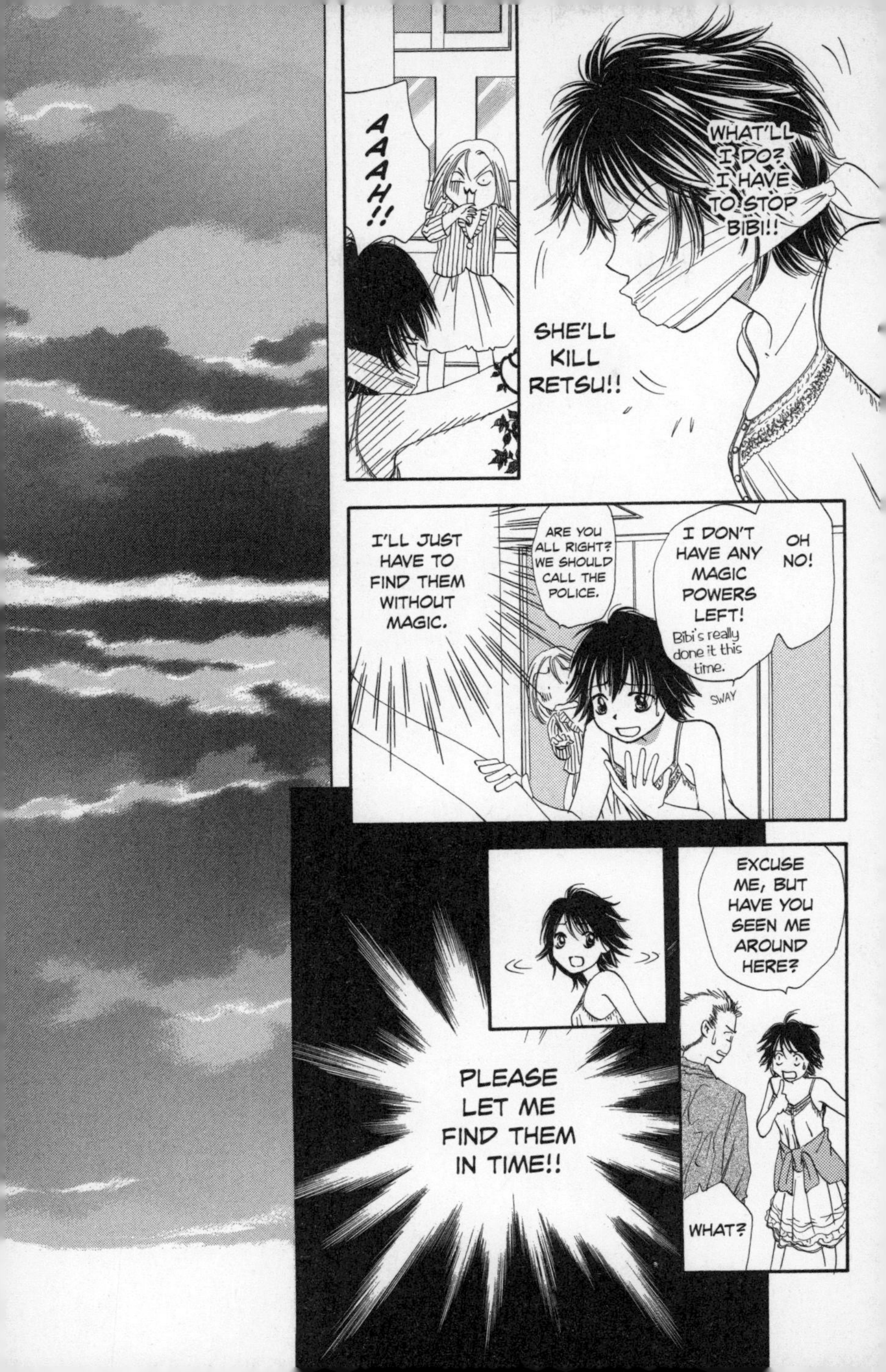
WHAT'LL I DO? I HAVE TO STOP BIBI!!
SHE'LL KILL RETSU!!
AAAAH!!
OH NO!
I DON'T HAVE ANY MAGIC POWERS LEFT!
Bibi's really done it this time.
SWAY
ARE YOU ALL RIGHT? WE SHOULD CALL THE POLICE.
I'LL JUST HAVE TO FIND THEM WITHOUT MAGIC.
EXCUSE ME, BUT HAVE YOU SEEN ME AROUND HERE?
WHAT?
PLEASE LET ME FIND THEM IN TIME!!

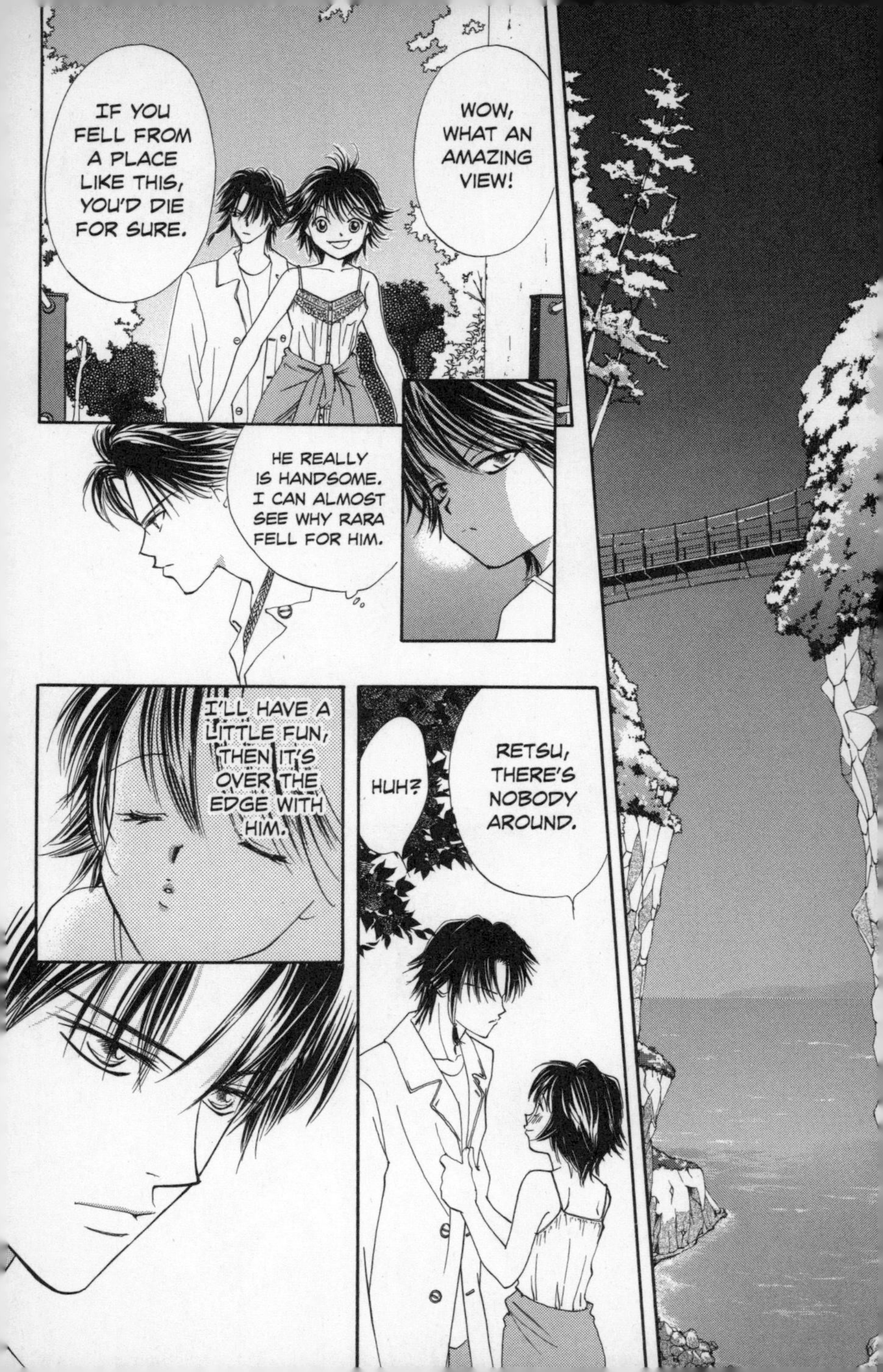
WOW, WHAT AN AMAZING VIEW!
IF YOU FELL FROM A PLACE LIKE THIS, YOU'D DIE FOR SURE.
HE REALLY IS HANDSOME. I CAN ALMOST SEE WHY RARA FELL FOR HIM.
RETSU, THERE'S NOBODY AROUND.
HUH?
I'LL HAVE A LITTLE FUN, THEN IT'S OVER THE EDGE WITH HIM.

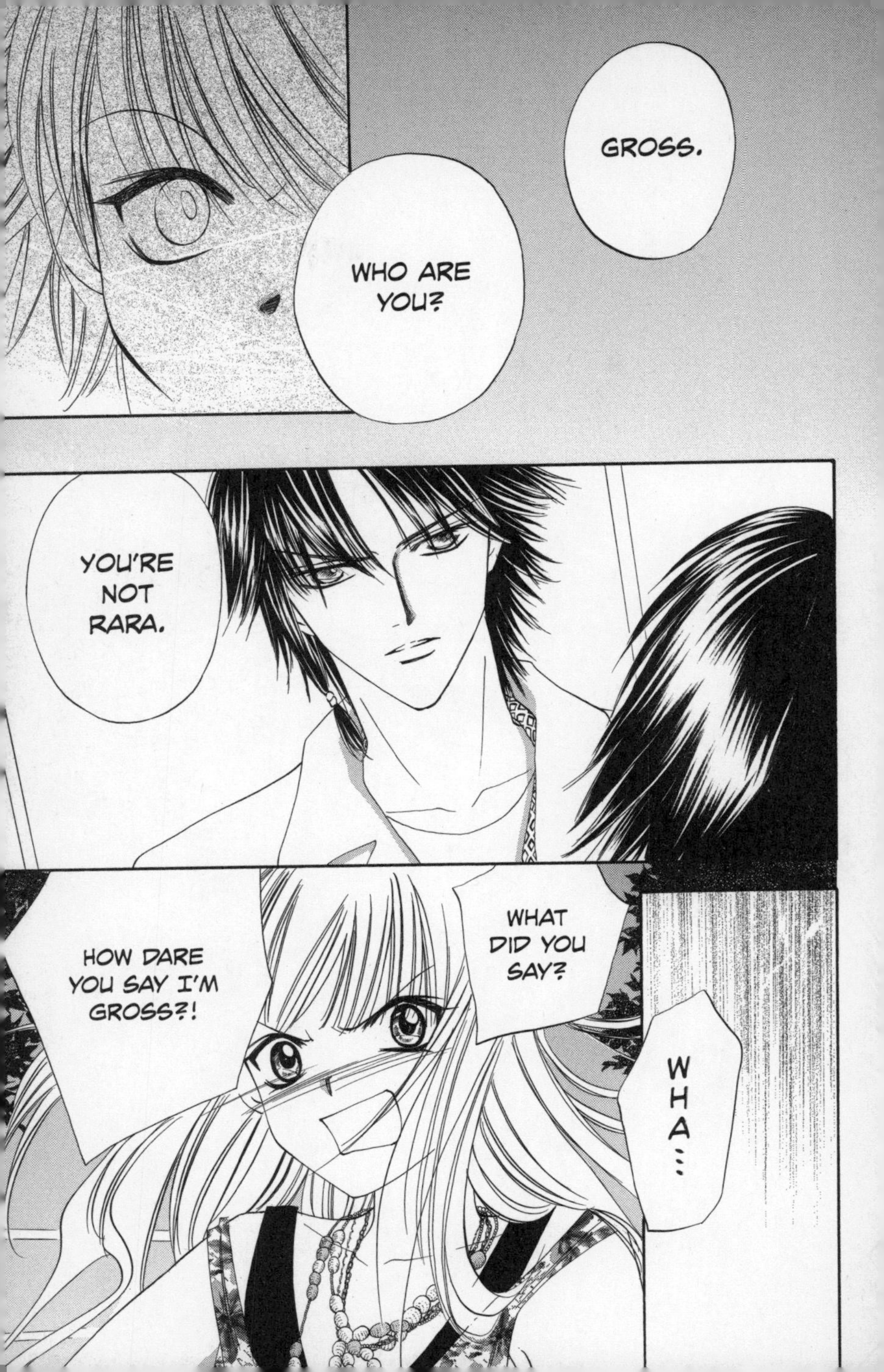
GROSS.
WHO ARE YOU?
YOU'RE NOT RARA.
WHA...
WHAT DID YOU SAY?
HOW DARE YOU SAY I'M GROSS?!

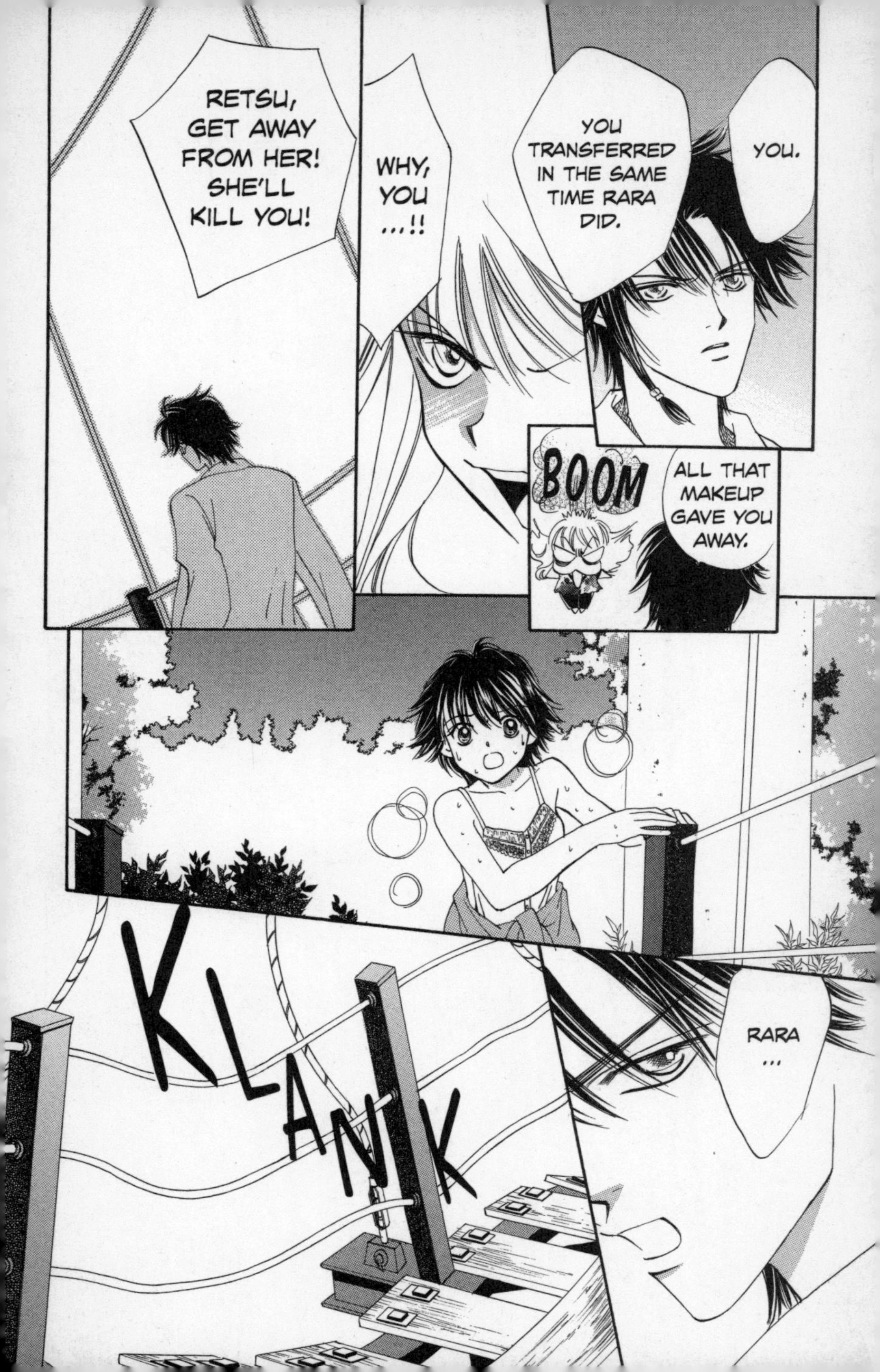
YOU.
YOU TRANSFERRED IN THE SAME TIME RARA DID.
ALL THAT MAKEUP GAVE YOU AWAY.
BOOM
WHY, YOU ...!!
RETSU, GET AWAY FROM HER! SHE'LL KILL YOU!
RARA ...
KLANK

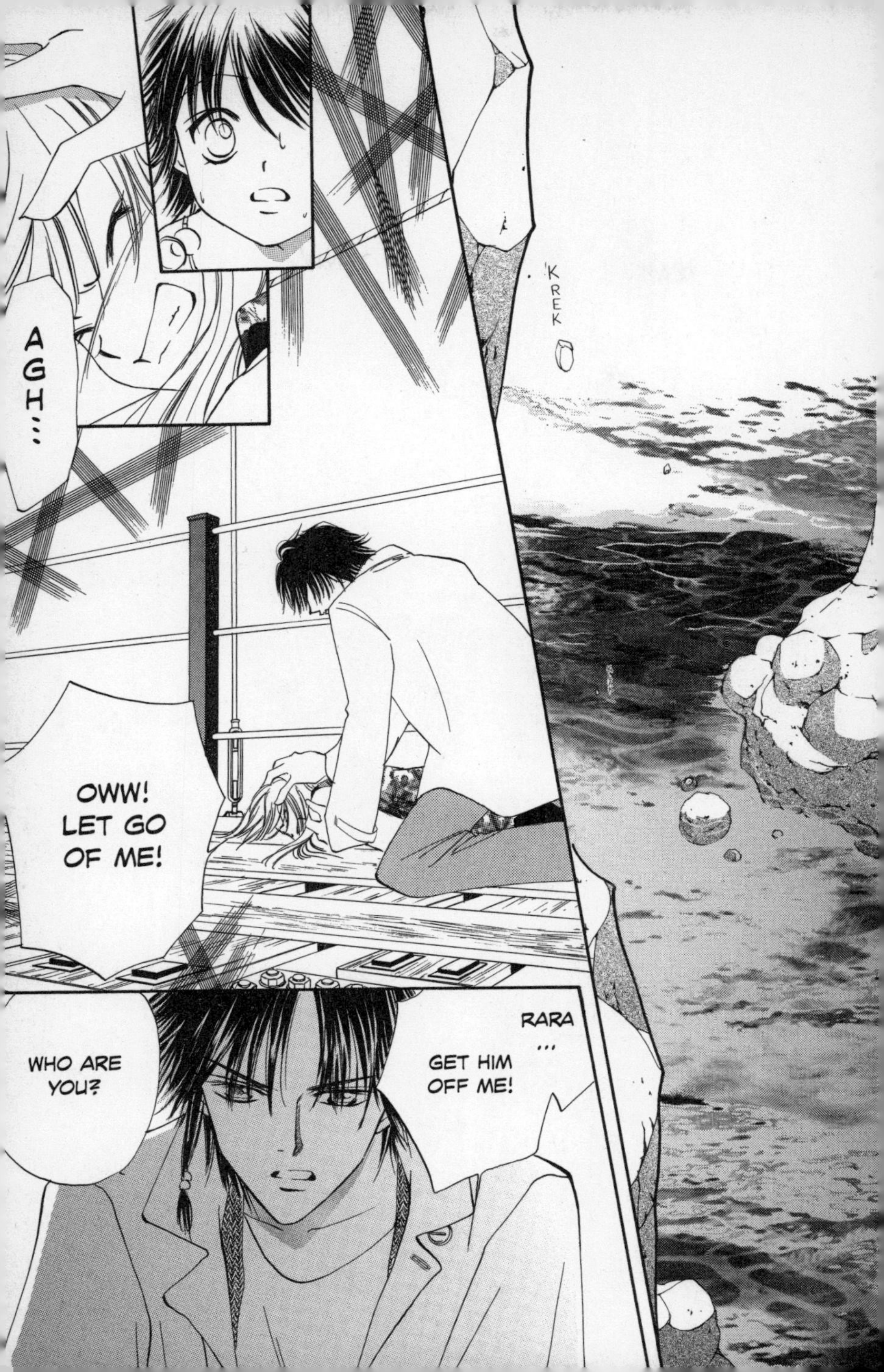
KREK
AGH...
OWW! LET GO OF ME!
RARA...
GET HIM OFF ME!
WHO ARE YOU?

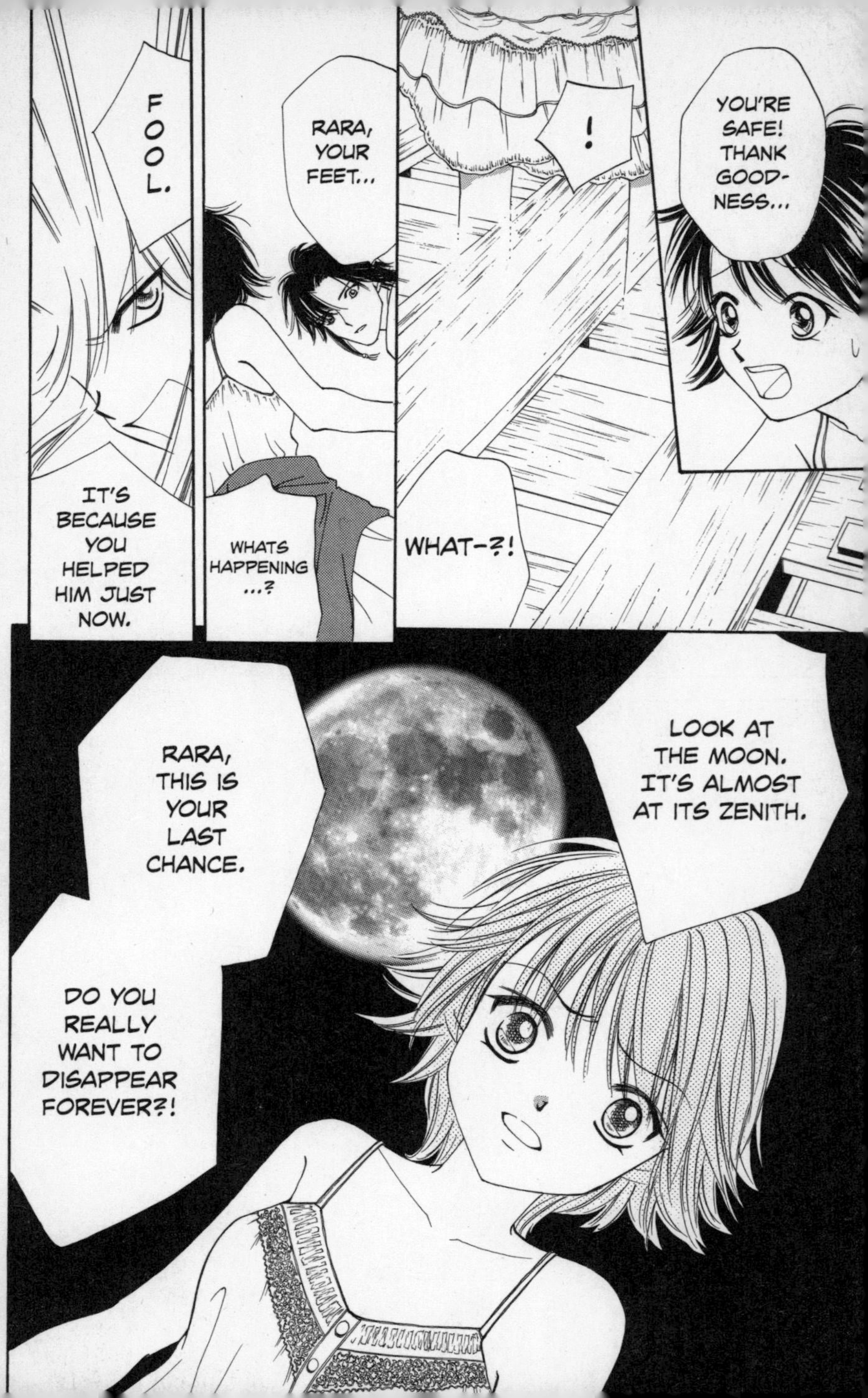
YOU'RE SAFE! THANK GOODNESS...
!
WHAT-?!
RARA, YOUR FEET...
WHATS HAPPENING ...?
FOOL.
IT'S BECAUSE YOU HELPED HIM JUST NOW.
LOOK AT THE MOON. IT'S ALMOST AT ITS ZENITH.
RARA, THIS IS YOUR LAST CHANCE.
DO YOU REALLY WANT TO DISAPPEAR FOREVER?!

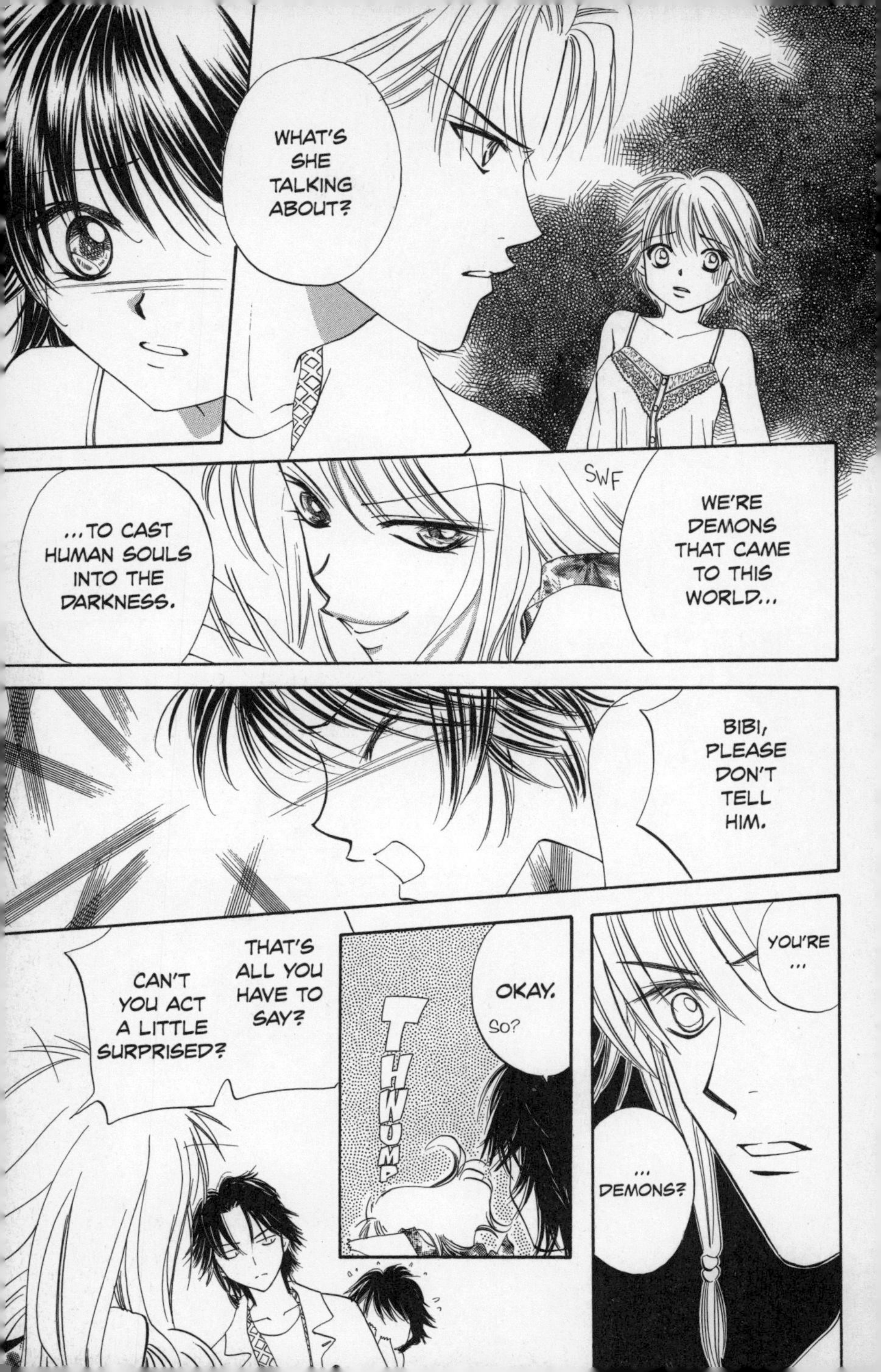
WHAT'S SHE TALKING ABOUT?
SWF
WE'RE DEMONS THAT CAME TO THIS WORLD...
...TO CAST HUMAN SOULS INTO THE DARKNESS.
BIBI, PLEASE DON'T TELL HIM.
YOU'RE ...
... DEMONS?
OKAY.
SO?
THWUMP
THAT'S ALL YOU HAVE TO SAY?
CAN'T YOU ACT A LITTLE SURPRISED?

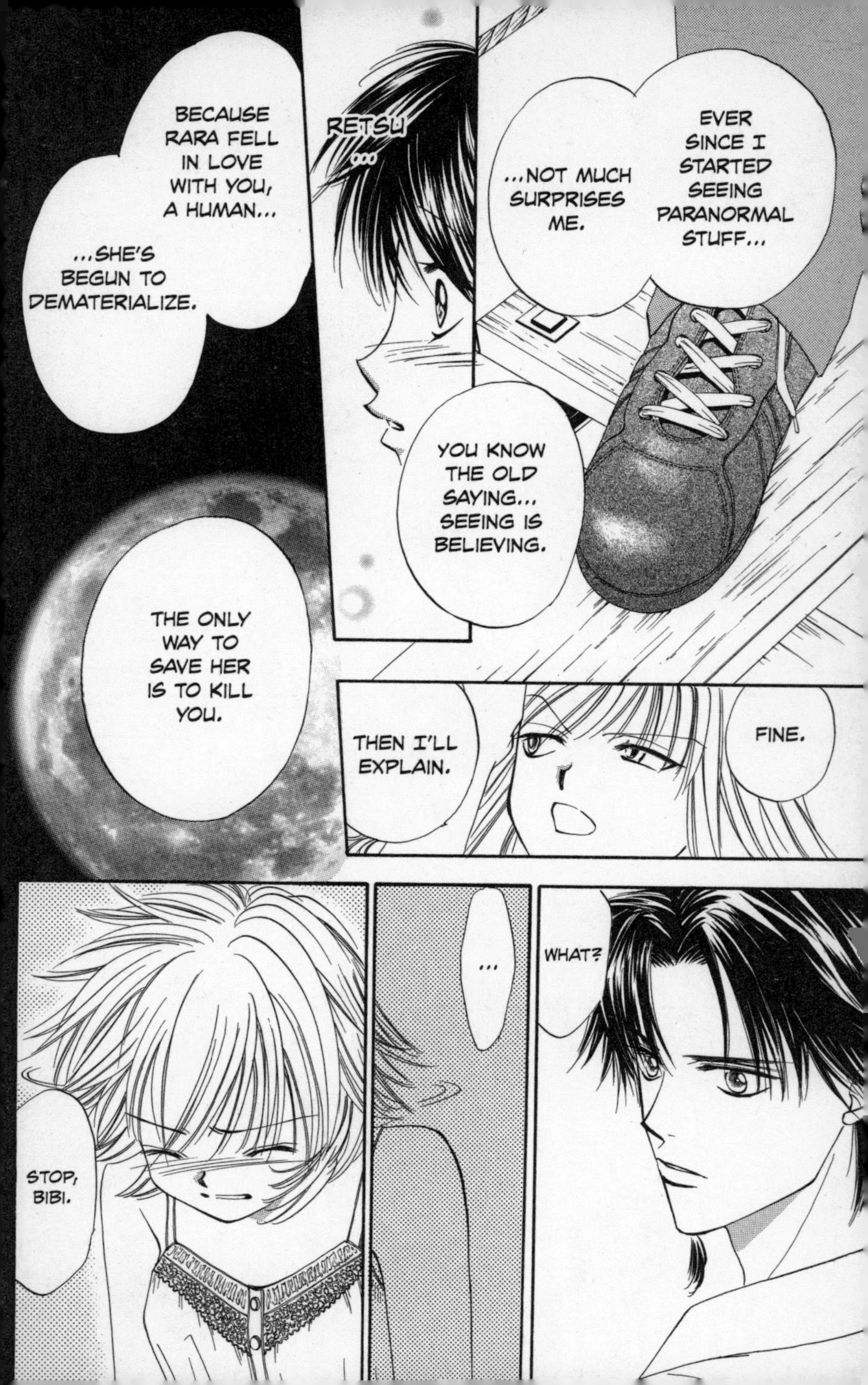
EVER SINCE I STARTED SEEING PARANORMAL STUFF...
...NOT MUCH SURPRISES ME.
YOU KNOW THE OLD SAYING... SEEING IS BELIEVING.
RETSU...
FINE.
THEN I'LL EXPLAIN.
BECAUSE RARA FELL IN LOVE WITH YOU, A HUMAN...
...SHE'S BEGUN TO DEMATERIALIZE.
THE ONLY WAY TO SAVE HER IS TO KILL YOU.
WHAT?
...
STOP, BIBI.

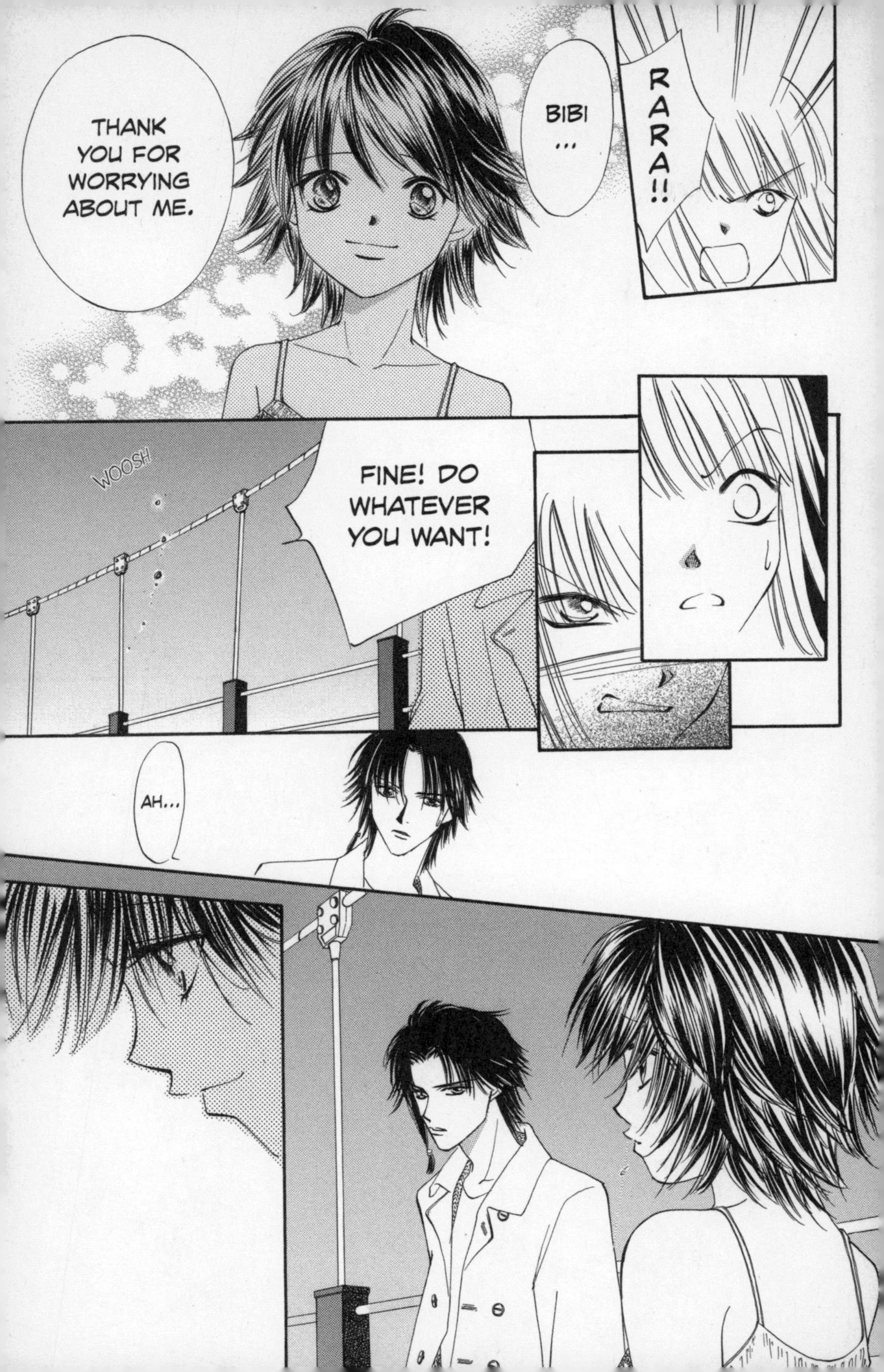
RARA!!
BIBI ...
THANK YOU FOR WORRYING ABOUT ME.
FINE! DO WHATEVER YOU WANT!
WOOSH
AH...

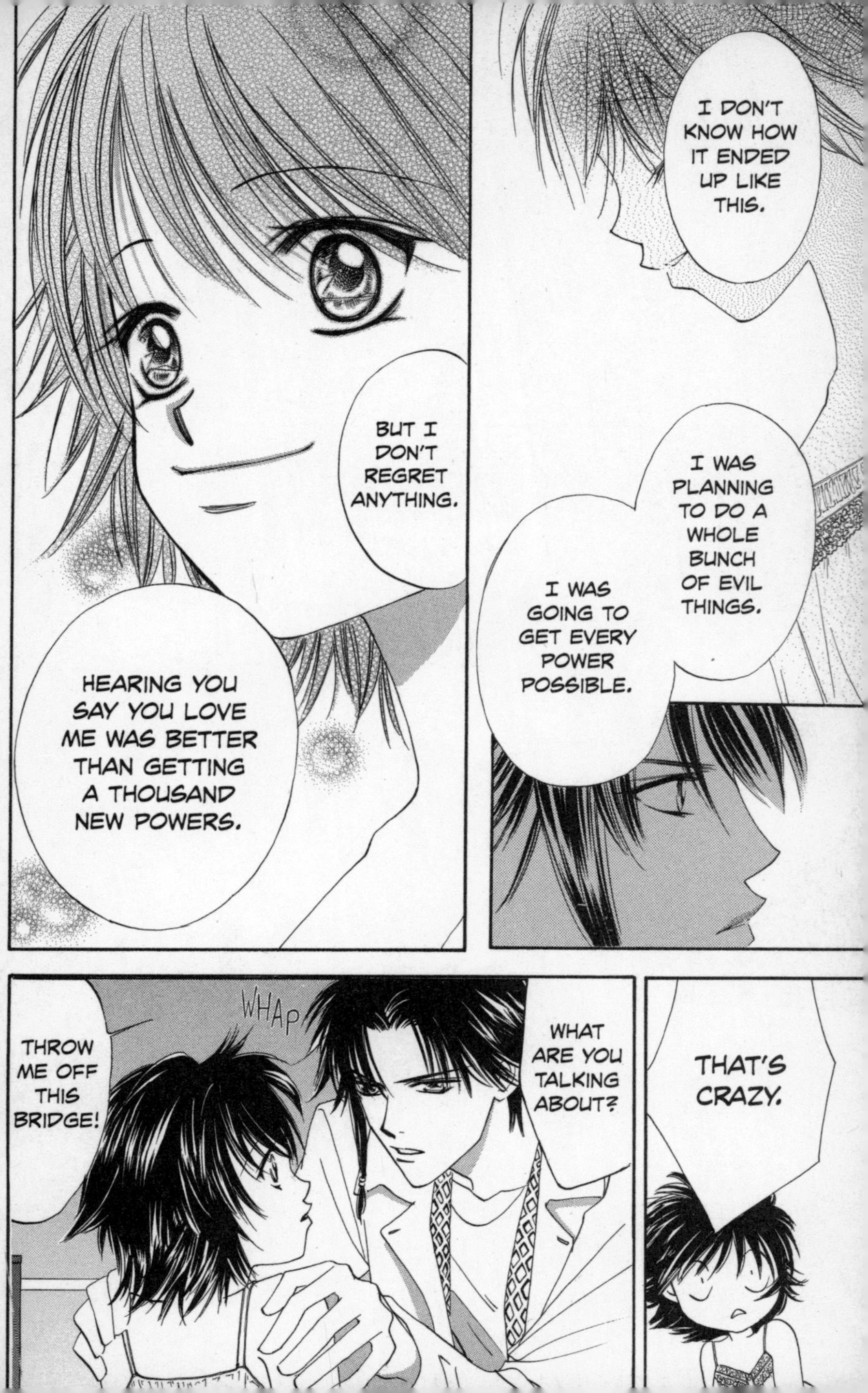
I DON'T KNOW HOW IT ENDED UP LIKE THIS.
I WAS PLANNING TO DO A WHOLE BUNCH OF EVIL THINGS.
I WAS GOING TO GET EVERY POWER POSSIBLE.
BUT I DON'T REGRET ANYTHING.
HEARING YOU SAY YOU LOVE ME WAS BETTER THAN GETTING A THOUSAND NEW POWERS.
THAT'S CRAZY.
WHAT ARE YOU TALKING ABOUT?
WHAP
THROW ME OFF THIS BRIDGE!

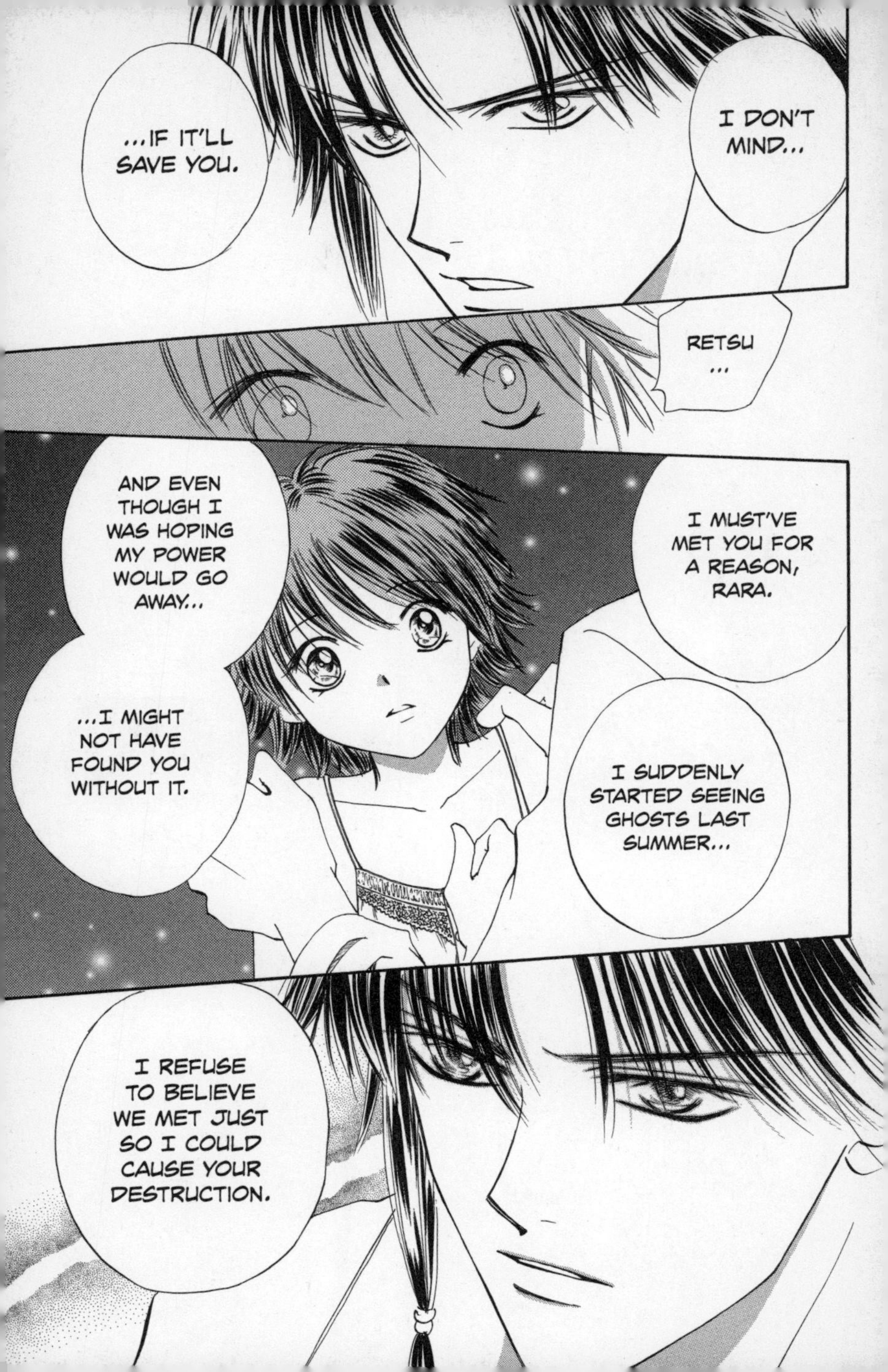
I DON'T MIND...
...IF IT'LL SAVE YOU.
RETSU ...
I MUST'VE MET YOU FOR A REASON, RARA.
I SUDDENLY STARTED SEEING GHOSTS LAST SUMMER...
AND EVEN THOUGH I WAS HOPING MY POWER WOULD GO AWAY...
...I MIGHT NOT HAVE FOUND YOU WITHOUT IT.
I REFUSE TO BELIEVE WE MET JUST SO I COULD CAUSE YOUR DESTRUCTION.

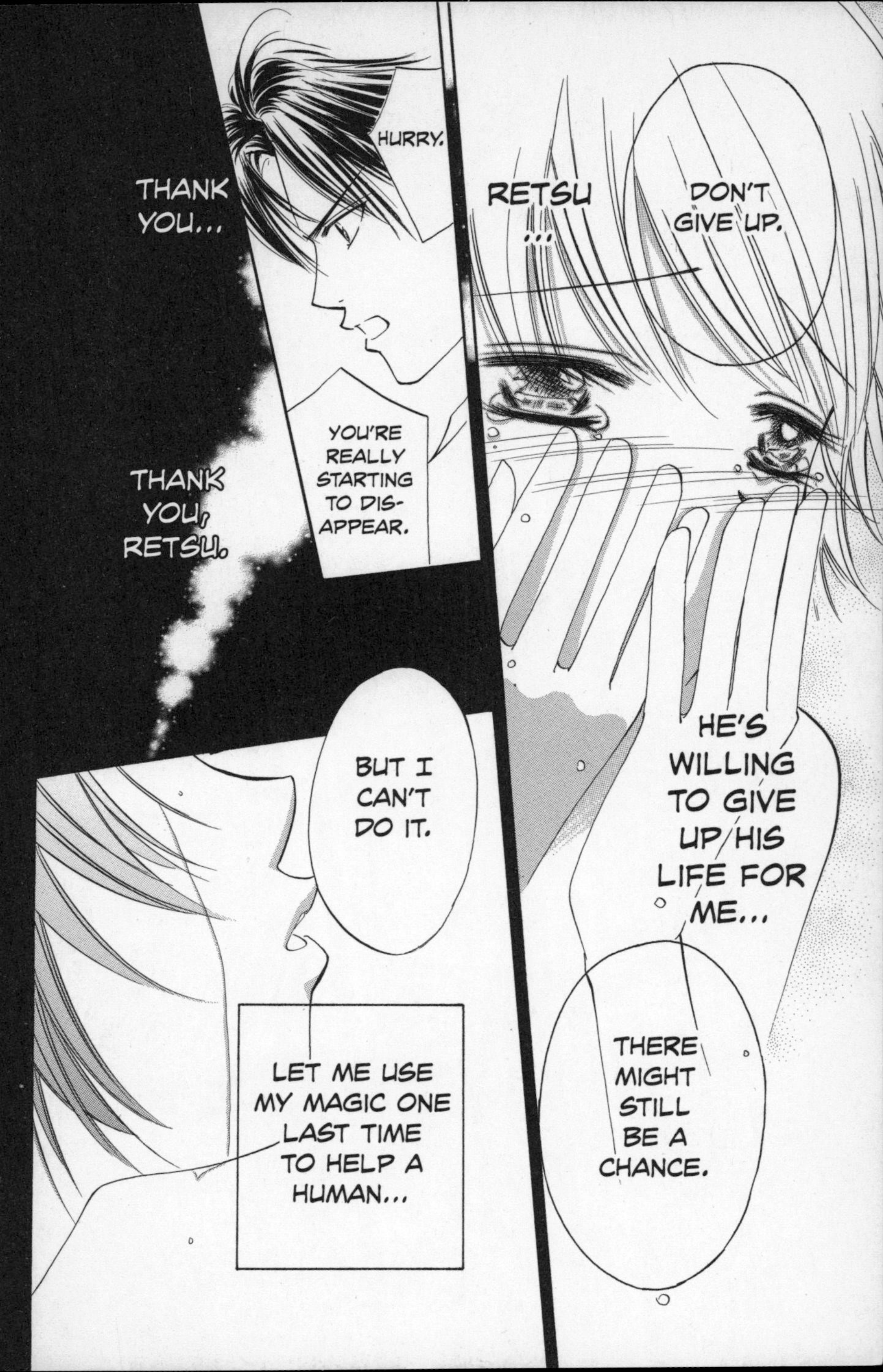
DON'T GIVE UP.
RETSU...
HE'S WILLING TO GIVE UP HIS LIFE FOR ME...
THERE MIGHT STILL BE A CHANCE.
HURRY.
YOU'RE REALLY STARTING TO DIS-APPEAR.
THANK YOU...
THANK YOU, RETSU.
BUT I CAN'T DO IT.
LET ME USE MY MAGIC ONE LAST TIME TO HELP A HUMAN...

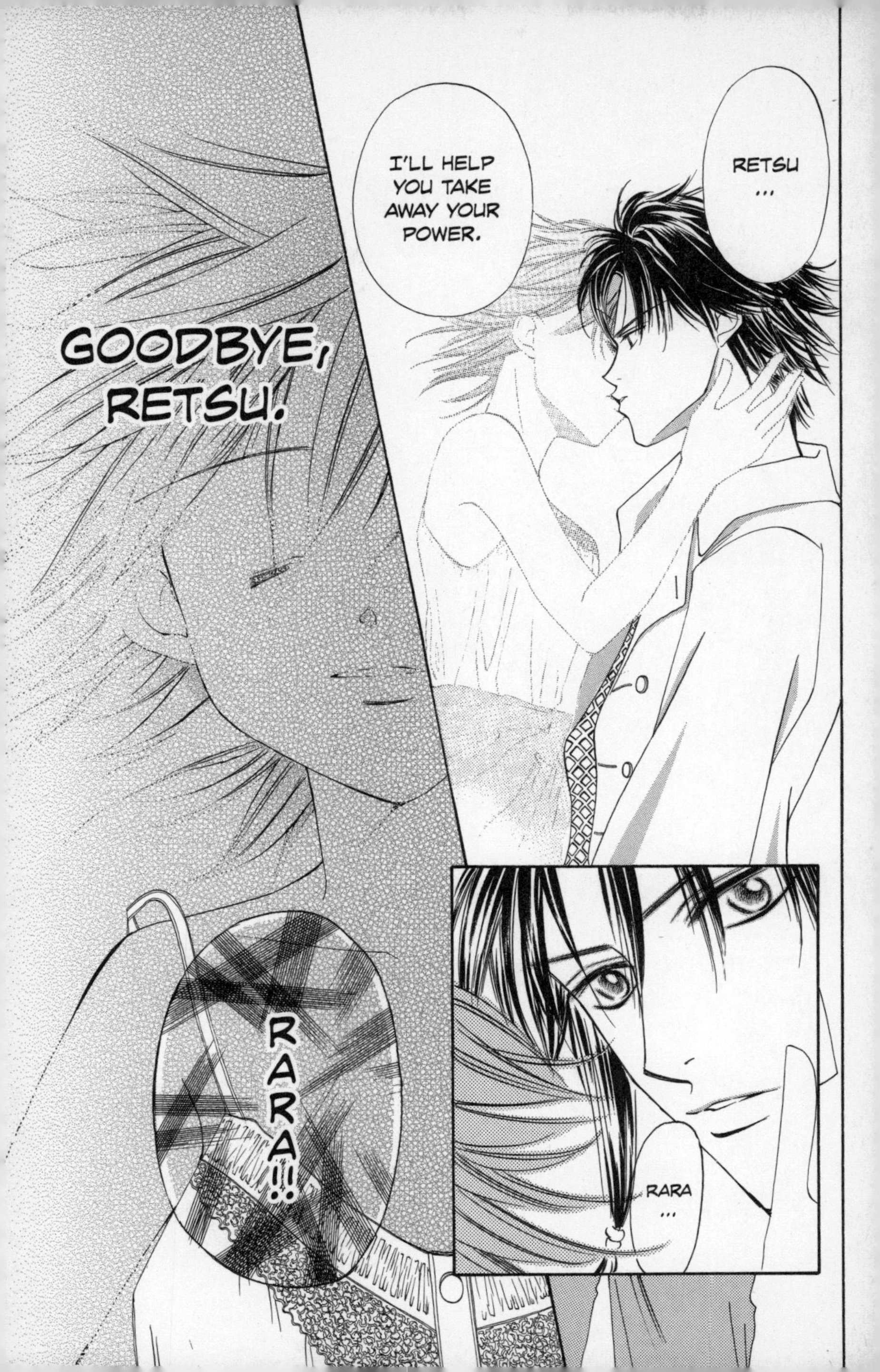
RETSU ...
I'LL HELP YOU TAKE AWAY YOUR POWER.
RARA ...
GOODBYE, RETSU.
RARA!!

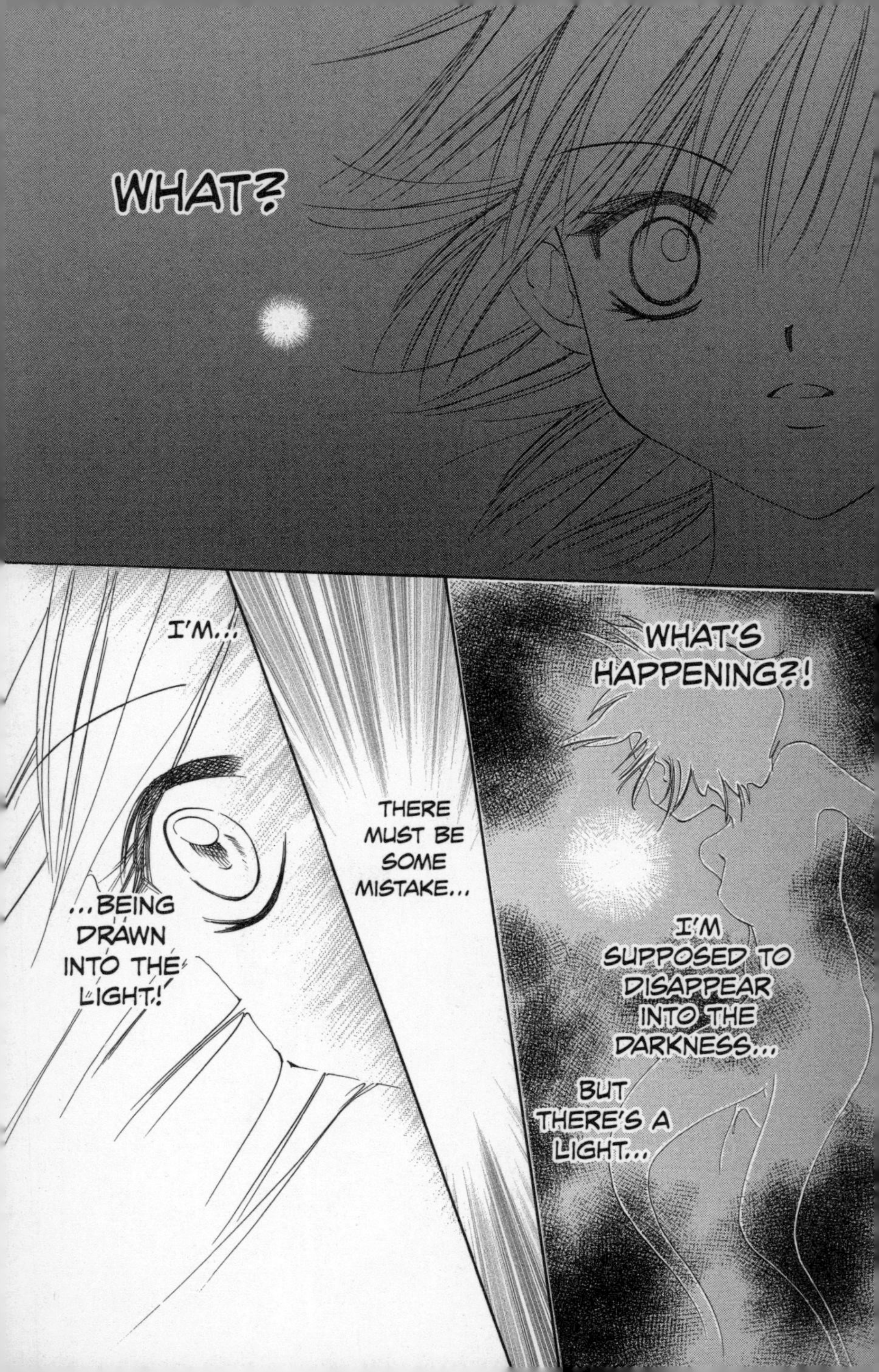
WHAT?
WHAT'S HAPPENING?!
I'M SUPPOSED TO DISAPPEAR INTO THE DARKNESS...
BUT THERE'S A LIGHT...
THERE MUST BE SOME MISTAKE...
I'M...
...BEING DRAWN INTO THE LIGHT!

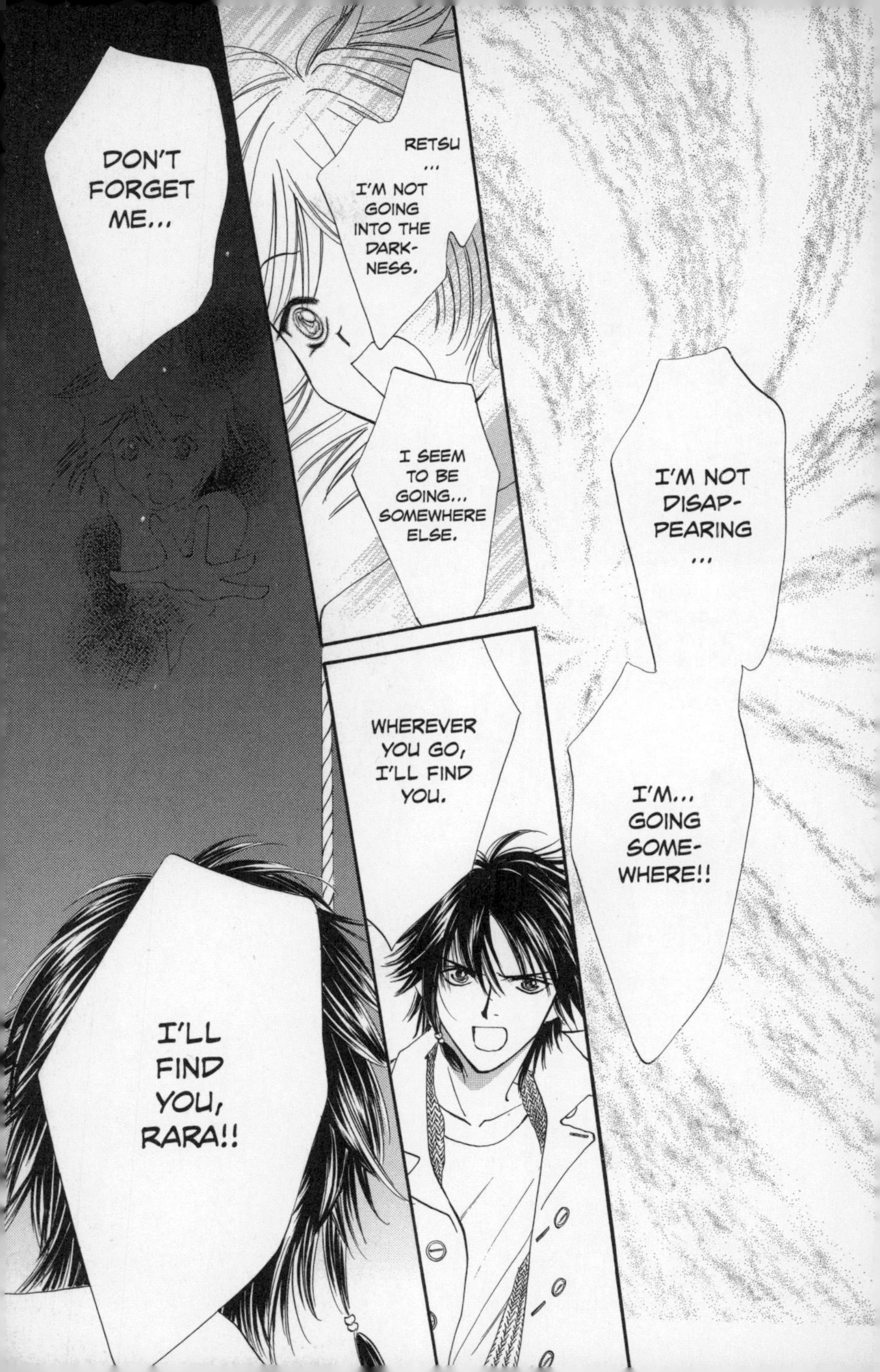
RETSU ... I'M NOT GOING INTO THE DARKNESS.
I SEEM TO BE GOING... SOMEWHERE ELSE.
I'M NOT DISAPPEARING ...
I'M... GOING SOMEWHERE!!
DON'T FORGET ME...
WHEREVER YOU GO, I'LL FIND YOU.
I'LL FIND YOU, RARA!!

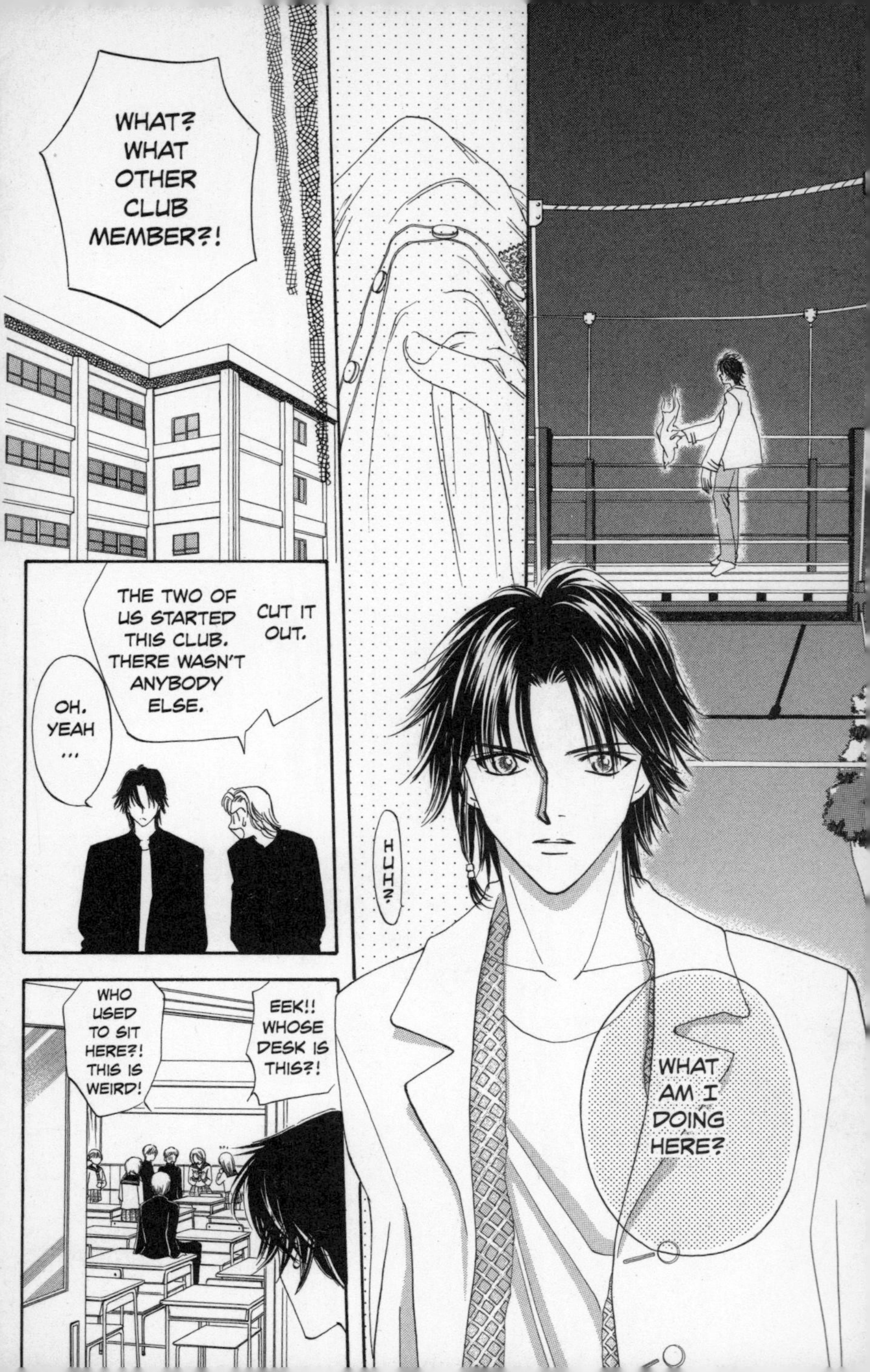
HUH?
WHAT AM I DOING HERE?
WHAT? WHAT OTHER CLUB MEMBER?!
THE TWO OF US STARTED THIS CLUB. THERE WASN'T ANYBODY ELSE.
CUT IT OUT.
OH. YEAH ...
EEK!! WHOSE DESK IS THIS?!
WHO USED TO SIT HERE?! THIS IS WEIRD!

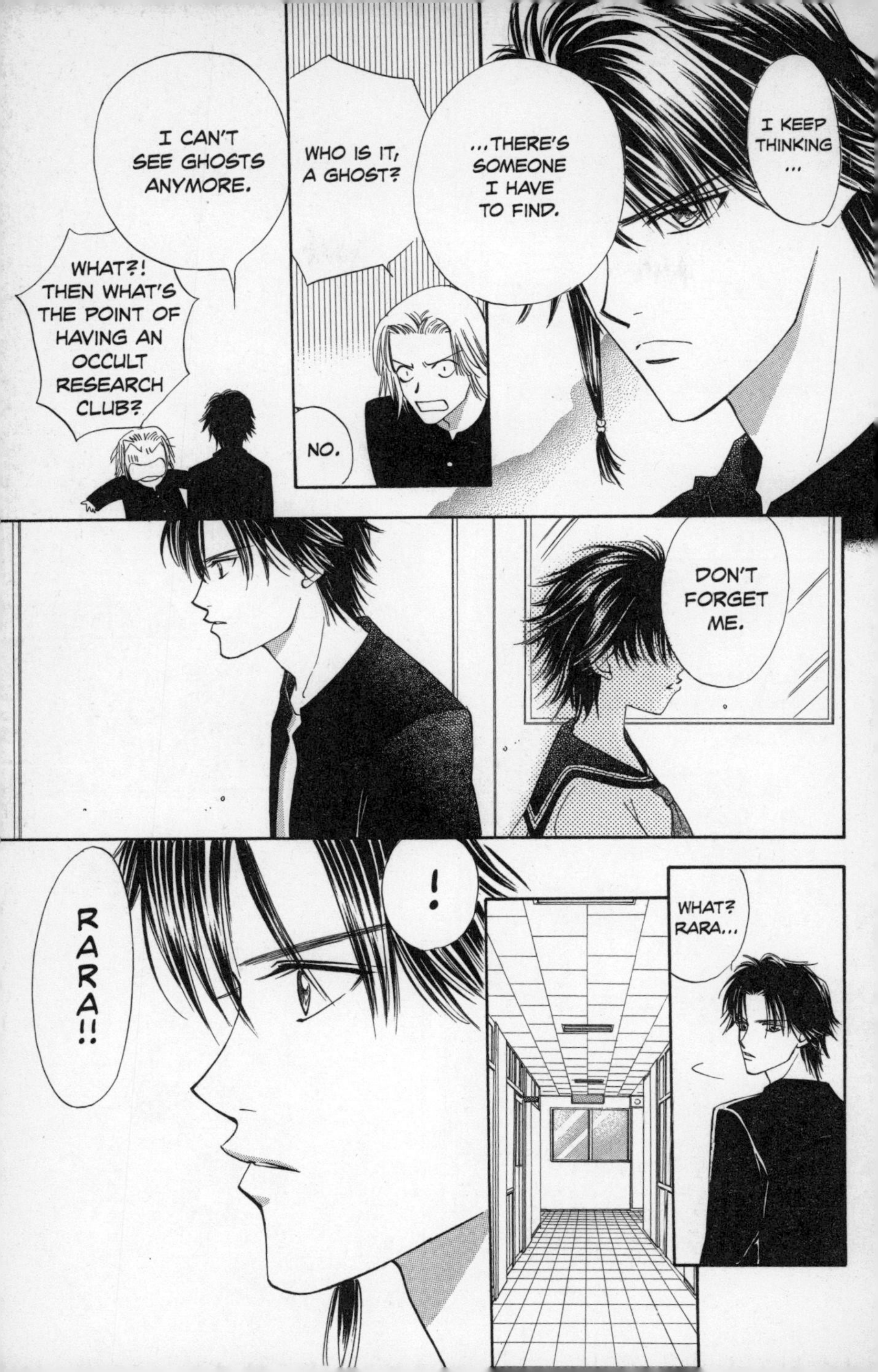
I KEEP THINKING...
...THERE'S SOMEONE I HAVE TO FIND.
WHO IS IT, A GHOST?
NO.
I CAN'T SEE GHOSTS ANYMORE.
WHAT?! THEN WHAT'S THE POINT OF HAVING AN OCCULT RESEARCH CLUB?
DON'T FORGET ME.
WHAT? RARA...
!
RARA!!

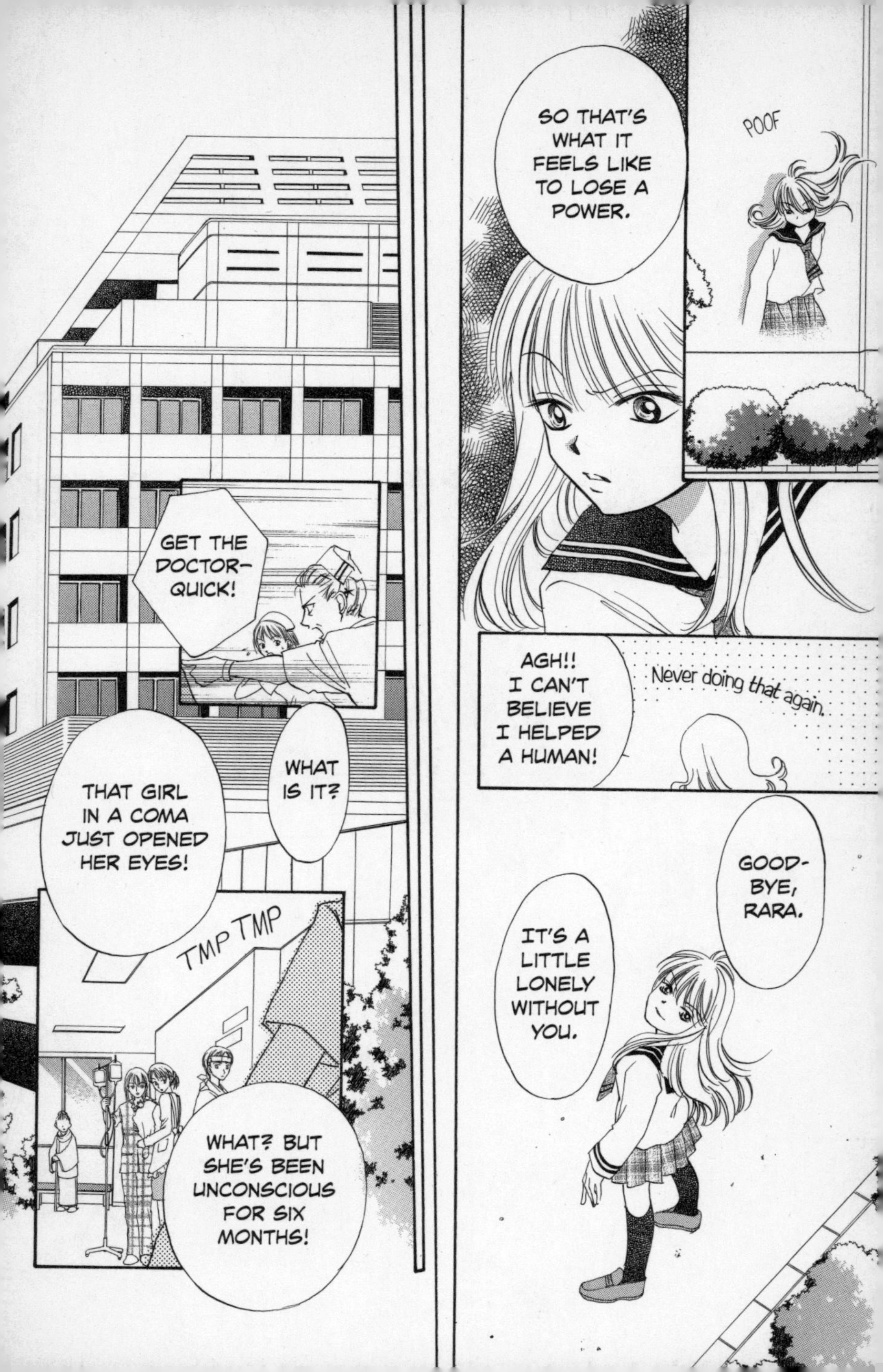
POOF
SO THAT'S WHAT IT FEELS LIKE TO LOSE A POWER.
Never doing that again.
AGH!! I CAN'T BELIEVE I HELPED A HUMAN!
GOOD-BYE, RARA.
IT'S A LITTLE LONELY WITHOUT YOU.
GET THE DOCTOR–QUICK!
WHAT IS IT?
THAT GIRL IN A COMA JUST OPENED HER EYES!
TMP TMP
WHAT? BUT SHE'S BEEN UNCONSCIOUS FOR SIX MONTHS!

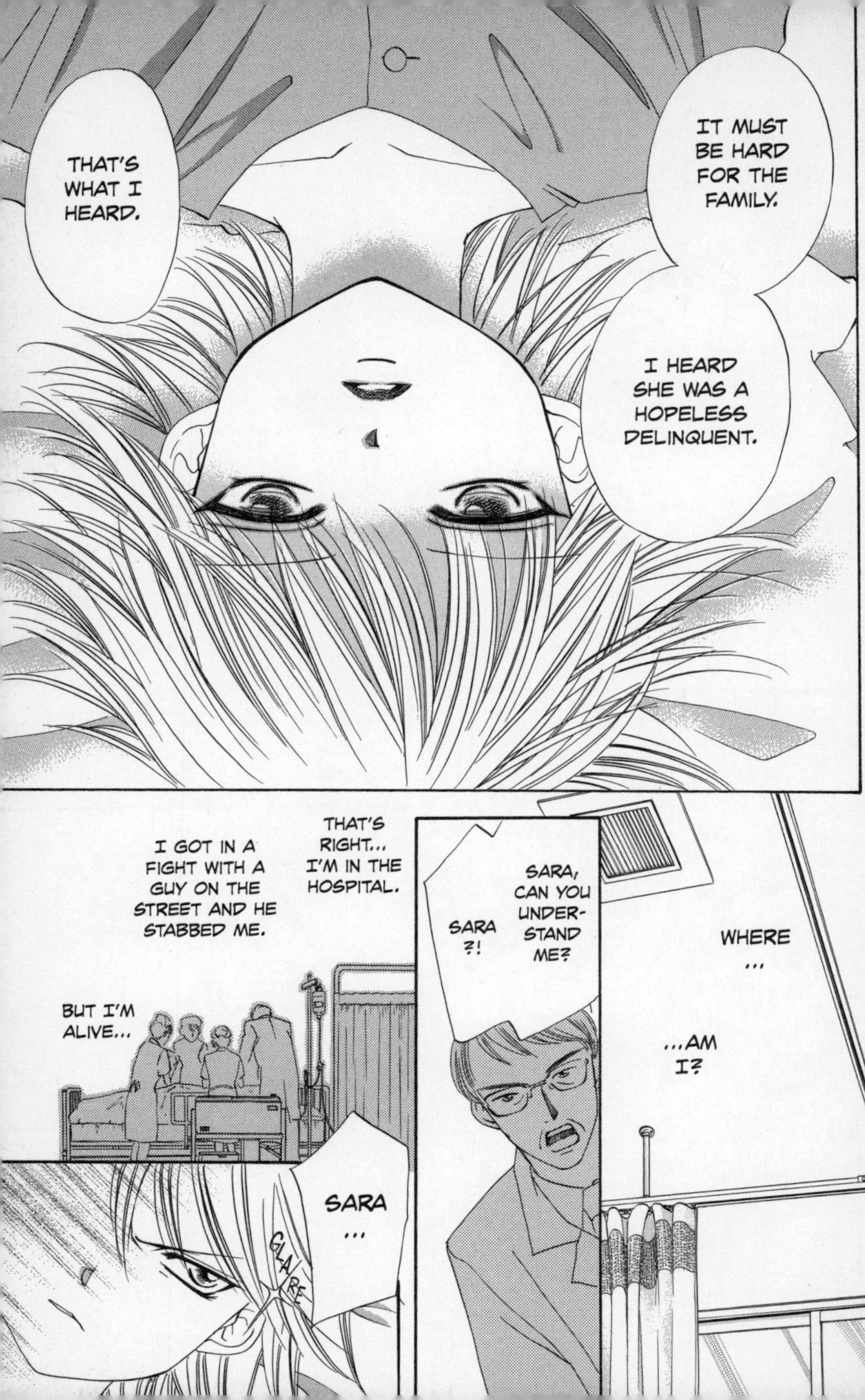
IT MUST BE HARD FOR THE FAMILY.
I HEARD SHE WAS A HOPELESS DELINQUENT.
THAT'S WHAT I HEARD.
WHERE ...
...AM I?
SARA, CAN YOU UNDERSTAND ME?
SARA ?!
THAT'S RIGHT... I'M IN THE HOSPITAL.
I GOT IN A FIGHT WITH A GUY ON THE STREET AND HE STABBED ME.
BUT I'M ALIVE...
SARA ...
GLARE

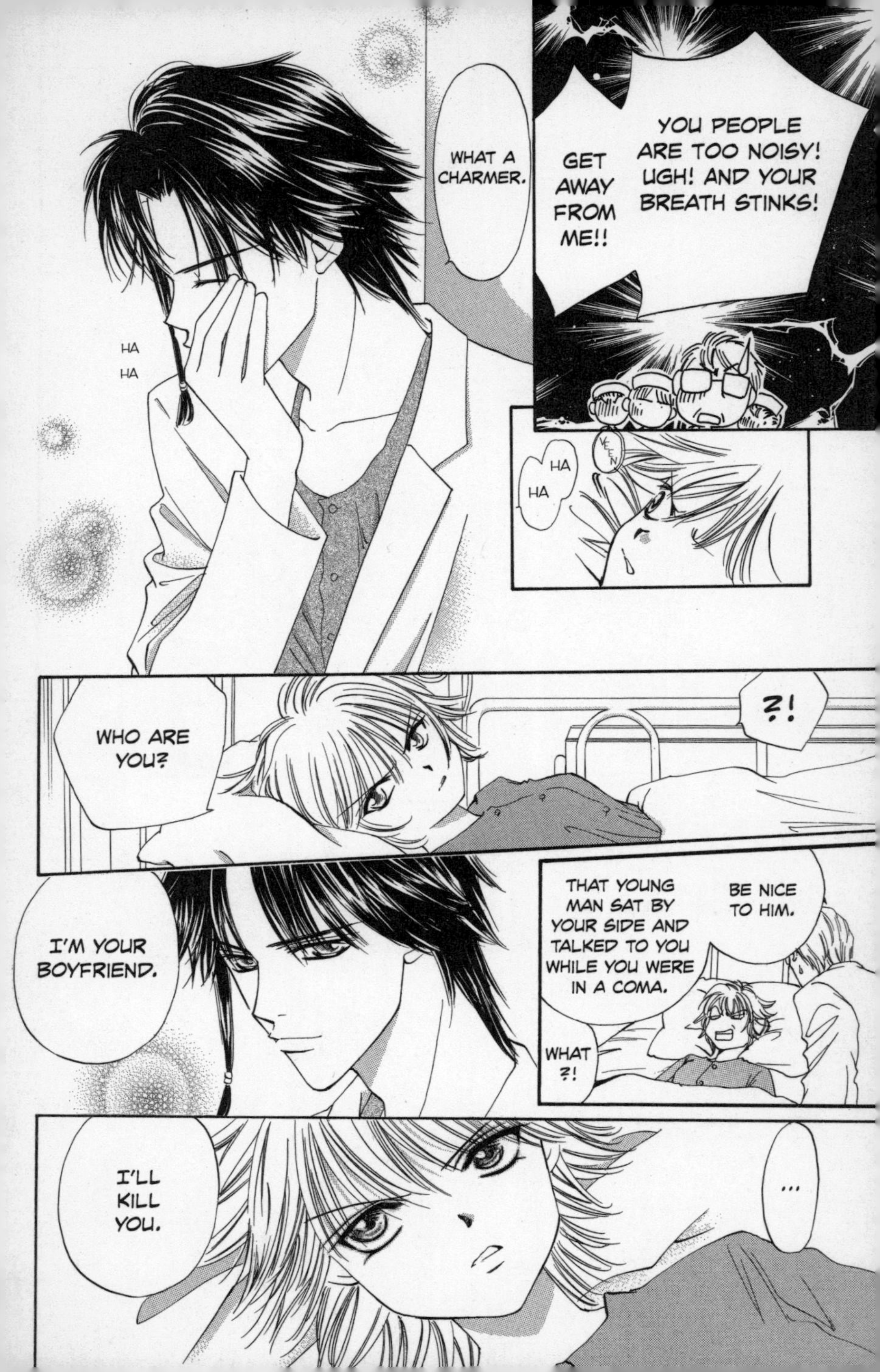
YOU PEOPLE ARE TOO NOISY! UGH! AND YOUR BREATH STINKS!
GET AWAY FROM ME!!
VEEN
HA HA
WHAT A CHARMER.
HA HA
?!
WHO ARE YOU?
BE NICE TO HIM.
THAT YOUNG MAN SAT BY YOUR SIDE AND TALKED TO YOU WHILE YOU WERE IN A COMA.
WHAT?!
I'M YOUR BOYFRIEND.
...
I'LL KILL YOU.

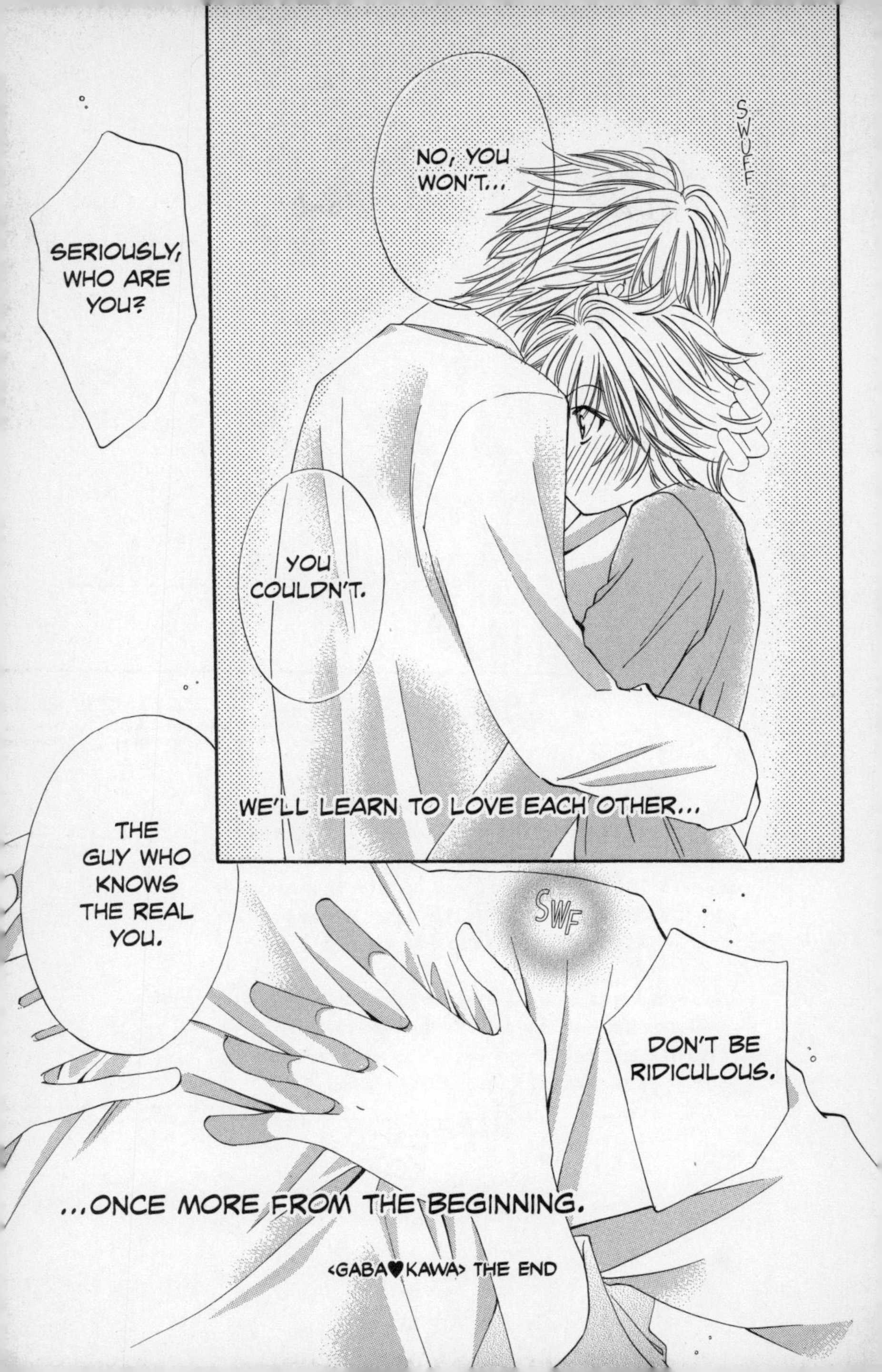
SWUFF
NO, YOU WON'T...
YOU COULDN'T.
WE'LL LEARN TO LOVE EACH OTHER...
SERIOUSLY, WHO ARE YOU?
SWF
DON'T BE RIDICULOUS.
THE GUY WHO KNOWS THE REAL YOU.
...ONCE MORE FROM THE BEGINNING.
‹GABA♥KAWA› THE END

**Born on August 10th in Hokkaido, Rie Takada
debuted in 1990 with *SP Girl* in Japan's *Sho-Comi*
Issue 17. She is also the author of *Punch!*, a romantic
comedy about martial arts. Her other works include
WILD ACT and *Happy Hustle High*.**

**Takada loves watching movies, but she doesn't
like horror (all the sounds they use are really
scary!). And yet, she was able to write a "scary"
supernatural title like *Gaba Kawa*...**

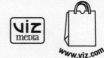

GABA KAWA

The Shojo Beat Manga Edition

This manga volume contains material that was originally published in English in *Shojo Beat* magazine, April–August 2008 issues. Artwork in the magazine may have been slightly altered from that presented here.

STORY AND ART BY
RIE TAKADA

English Adaptation/Lance Caselman
Translation/Noritaka Minami
Touch-up Art & Lettering/James Gaubatz
Design/Yukiko Whitley
Editor/Amy Yu

Editor in Chief, Books/Alvin Lu
Editor in Chief, Magazines/Marc Weidenbaum
VP, Publishing Licensing/Rika Inouye
VP, Sales and Product Marketing/Gonzalo Ferreyra
VP, Creative/Linda Espinosa
Publisher/Hyoe Narita

Printed in Canada

Published by VIZ Media, LLC
P.O. Box 77010
San Francisco, CA 94107

www.viz.com

Shojo Beat Manga Edition
10 9 8 7 6 5 4 3 2 1
First printing, December 2008

RATED T FOR TEEN

PARENTAL ADVISORY
GABA KAWA is rated T for Teen and is recommended for ages 13 and up. This volume contains suggestive themes.
ratings.viz.com